CW01657910

How Nations Learn

Praise for the Book

'The chapters examine how industrial latecomers have crafted strategic and pragmatic policy frameworks to unleash the universal passion for learning into business organizational practices that drive production capability development and foster innovation dynamics. The transformational experiences described in the book offer a multitude of ways in which learning is organized and applied to advance a nation's productive structures and build competitive advantage in the global economy.'

Michael H Best, Professor Emeritus, Author of *How Growth Really Happens: The Making of Economic Miracles through Production, Governance and Skills*, Winner of the 2018 Schumpeter Prize

'The analysis of development and catching-up has finally shifted away from surreal problems of 'optimal' market-driven allocation of resources, toward the processes of learning and capability accumulation. This is an important contribution in this perspective: And yet another nail into the coffin of the "Washington Consensus".'

Giovanni Dosi, Professor of Economics, Scuola Superiore Sant' Anna, Pisa, Italy

'Industrialisation has always been fundamental to sustained economic growth. It separates the world into high and low-income economies. To create inclusive prosperity, we urgently need to understand *How Nations Learn*. State-supported innovation is not only cardinal for catch-up, but also to abate climate breakdown (through crowding in new businesses, nurturing experimentation, and ensuring public benefits). By studying the economic history of technological advancement in Africa, Asia, and Latin America, this book makes a powerful case for industrial policy.'

Dr Alice Evans, Lecturer in International Development, King's College London

'*How Nations Learn* is a book based on big ideas. Why do some nations grow faster than others? How does the process of economic catch-up work? What does the technological learning of firms have in common with the policy lessons of governments? How do the answers to these questions vary across countries and regions of the world? The book provides answers to these queries from a distinguished interdisciplinary and international set of scholars, who draw on an impressive reservoir of both contemporary and historical experiences. *How Nations Learn* is an essential guide to how to navigate the key dilemmas of 21st century development, which should be particularly useful to latecomer countries and those grappling with the pitfalls of uneven development.'

Gary Gereffi, Professor of Sociology and Director of the Global Value Chains Center at Duke University

'Arkebe Oqubay and Kenichi Ohno's important edited book is basically about learning to "catch up". It focuses on firm level technology learning and policymakers' learning, including learning by doing, emulation and experimentation, involving innovation and leapfrogging. The volume draws on historical, firm, industry and country experiences to identify factors crucial to successful learning for catching-up, including latecomer advantages. The chapters suggest that the intensity, pace, "direction" and context of learning matter, besides stressing the significance of robust industrial policies and long-term strategic vision.'

Jomo Kwame Sundaram, retired Professor, UN Assistant Secretary General, 2008 Leontief Prize

'The limited capacity of developing countries to catch up the income level of developed countries has continued to be a major feature of international development over the past decades. Professors Oqubay and Ohno have been able to collect a fantastic set of papers on the crucial question of success and failure in achieving convergence: how technological learning takes place at the firm, sectorial and national level, allowing countries to catch up, but also how failure to do so leads to divergence. It considers both the success stories of Meiji Japan, Taiwan, Korea, Singapore and most recently of China, but also the strong challenges faced in other regions, and notably in Latin America and Africa. A must read for academic and policymakers alike.'

José Antonio Ocampo, Member of the Board of Banco de la República (Colombia), Chair of the United Nations Committee for Development Policy, and Professor, Columbia University

'While debates on the best strategies for development have been protracted and contentious, there is widespread agreement on the salience of industrial policy and technological progress, but a paucity of studies on how this has been accomplished. The few books published have often been regionally or country based, limited in their scope of explanation, and analytically narrowed by their fealty to a single theoretical tradition. In contrast, this timely collection brings new critical insights into the dynamics of learning with a comparative analysis that is richly diverse in its geographic and theoretical focus, multidimensional in its level of analysis, and probing in its evaluation of how countries developed key capacities and transcended exigent historical barriers. A welcome addition to the literature that is highly recommended.'

Howard Stein, Professor, Departments of Afroamerican and African Studies and Epidemiology, University of Michigan

'"Catch-up" economic development requires technological and policy learning. It increasingly requires unlearning as well. And will and discipline. The editors of *How Nations Learn* have assembled a stellar group of contributors to share what they have learnt about learning, across time periods and continents, spanning technological learning by companies and policy learning and capability building by states. A most valuable resource for anyone interested in historical lessons applied sensitively to contemporary development challenges.'

D. Hugh Whittaker, Professor of the Japanese Economy and Business, University of Oxford

How Nations Learn

Technological Learning, Industrial Policy, and Catch-up

Edited by
ARKEBE OQUBAY AND KENICHI OHNO

OXFORD
UNIVERSITY PRESS

OXFORD
UNIVERSITY PRESS

Great Clarendon Street, Oxford, OX2 6DP,
United Kingdom

Oxford University Press is a department of the University of Oxford.
It furthers the University's objective of excellence in research, scholarship,
and education by publishing worldwide. Oxford is a registered trade mark of
Oxford University Press in the UK and in certain other countries

© Oxford University Press 2019

The moral rights of the authors have been asserted

First Edition published in 2019
Impression: 1

All rights reserved. No part of this publication may be reproduced, stored in a retrieval system, or transmitted, in any form or by any means, without the prior permission in writing of Oxford University Press, or as expressly permitted by law, by licence or under terms agreed with the appropriate reprographics rights organization. Enquiries concerning reproduction outside the scope of the above should be sent to the Rights Department, Oxford University Press, at the address above

You must not circulate this work in any other form
and you must impose this same condition on any acquirer

Published in the United States of America by Oxford University Press
198 Madison Avenue, New York, NY 10016, United States of America

British Library Cataloguing in Publication Data
Data available

Library of Congress Control Number: 2019937836

ISBN 978–0–19–884176–0

Printed and bound by
CPI Group (UK) Ltd, Croydon, CR0 4YY

Links to third party websites are provided by Oxford in good faith and for information only. Oxford disclaims any responsibility for the materials contained in any third party website referenced in this work.

Foreword

The process of learning by nations must be situated in historical perspective, for there is the past in our present, and there is much that we can learn from history.

Until around 1750, Asia, Africa, and Latin America, now described as developing countries, accounted for three-quarters of world population and more than two-thirds of world income. Of this, Asia alone accounted for almost three-fifths of world population and world income, while China and India together accounted for about one-half of world population and world income. These two Asian giants also contributed 57 per cent of manufacturing production and an even larger proportion of manufactured exports in the world. The next two centuries witnessed dramatic changes in the world economy. Between 1820 and 1950, in terms of Maddison PPP statistics, the share of Asia, Africa, and Latin America in world income fell from two-thirds to one quarter, while the share of Europe, North America, and Japan in world income rose from one-third to three-quarters. The rise of 'The West' was concentrated in Western Europe and North America, followed by Japan later, whereas the decline and fall of 'The Rest' was concentrated in Asia, much of it attributable to China and India, although Latin America was the clear exception.

This evolution of the international economic order led to a profound change in the balance of economic and political power in the world. It was attributable to three developments. The first was the Industrial Revolution in Britain in the late eighteenth century which spread to Western Europe, even if slowly, during the first half of the nineteenth century. The second was the emergence of a newer, somewhat different form of colonialism in the early nineteenth century which culminated in the advent of imperialism that gathered momentum through the century. The third was the revolution in transport and communication in the mid-nineteenth century, manifest in the railway, the steamship, and the telegraph, which dismantled geographical barriers in distance and time. These three developments, which overlapped and partly coincided in time, transformed the world economy by creating patterns of specialization in production, associated with a division of labour through trade and investment, reinforced by the politics of imperialism.

This led to the 'Great Divergence' in per capita incomes. Between 1820 and 1950, as a proportion of GDP per capita in Western Europe and North America, GDP per capita in Asia dropped from a half to a tenth, in Africa from a third to a seventh, but much less in Latin America from three-fifths to two-fifths. It was also associated with the 'Great Specialization' in which Western Europe, followed by the United States and somewhat later Japan, produced manufactured goods, while Asia, Africa, and Latin America produced primary commodities. Between 1830 and 1913, the share of Asia, Africa, and Latin America in world manufacturing production, attributable mostly to Asia, in particular China and India, collapsed from 60 per cent to 7.5 per cent, while the share of Western Europe, North America, and Japan rose from 40 per cent to 92.5 per cent.[1] It also led to the demise of traditional industries in Asia, largely in China and India, which reduced their skill levels and technological capabilities over time. The industrialization of Western Europe and de-industrialization of Asia during the nineteenth century were two sides of the same coin.

The last quarter of the twentieth century witnessed the beginnings of a swing of the pendulum in the opposite direction, which gathered momentum circa 1990, with a striking increase in the global economic significance of developing countries. Between 1990 and 2015, the share of developing countries in world GDP, in current prices at market exchange rates, has jumped from a sixth to two-fifths, and in world manufacturing value added from a sixth to almost a half, both entirely at the expense of industrialized countries.[2] Thus, it is plausible to suggest that, by 2030, these shares of developing countries in the world economy might return to their 1820 levels. This process of catch-up so far has been driven by rapid economic growth, industrialization, and engagement with the world economy. However, the impressive performance in the aggregate conceals as much as it reveals. Uneven development has led to unequal outcomes. The catch-up is characterized by a high degree of concentration in Asia among continents, in country groups such as BRICS across continents, and in a few Asian countries that are success stories. The divergence in per capita incomes has stopped. But the convergence, compared with industrialized countries, is at best modest and significant in just a few countries. Economic growth has brought about a significant reduction in absolute poverty in most parts of the developing world. Yet, poverty and deprivation persist on a large scale. Inequality within countries has risen rapidly. And there are emerging divergences between countries. Even so, the catch-up, albeit uneven and unequal, is real. And this could be a momentous ongoing shift in world economic history.

In economic history, this idea of countries that are followers catching up with leaders can be traced back to Veblen in his writing about Germany following in the footsteps of England.[3] For the latter, it was characterized as the 'penalty of taking the lead'. This notion was conceptualized further by Alexander Gerschenkron, as the 'advantages of relative economic backwardness', to consider the experience of

[1] The evidence cited in this paragraph and earlier is from Deepak Nayyar, *Catch Up: Developing Countries in the World Economy*, Oxford University Press, Oxford, 2013.

[2] Calculated from United Nations, National Accounts Statistics.

[3] Thorstein Veblen, *Imperial Germany and the Industrial Revolution*, Macmillan, London, 1915.

Russia as a latecomer that was subsequently extended to include France, Italy, and Austria.[4] The essential hypothesis is as follows. Economic backwardness, relative to others, creates a tension between the actual stagnation and the potential prosperity. The gap provides the economic incentive to catch up, while the political process drives institutional innovation. Wider gaps create stronger incentives to leap forward. State intervention, then, creates the missing initial conditions for growth, to compensate for the scarcities of capital, skilled labour, entrepreneurship and technological capabilities. Greater backwardness needs greater intervention. The mobilization of savings for investment is critical. In Russia, this was done by the state, whereas in Germany the same role was performed by the creation of a banking system that financed industrialization. There are benefits to be derived by learning from the mistakes of predecessors, so that economic growth for latecomers is characterized by spurts with periods of high, sometimes exceptional, growth rates. Obviously, the model has limitations, but its generalizations from history provide analytical insights into how a mix of ideology and institutions, or economics and politics, might foster success in countries that are latecomers to industrialization.

It would seem that learning from history is essential for an understanding of how nations learn. Theory, history, and experience, together, suggest that the foundations of success in learning to industrialize lie in a creative interaction between the state and the market, beyond the predominance of the market model, adapting to each other as times and circumstances change, to function as mutual checks and balances.

There are lessons that emerge from the experience of countries that have led the catch-up process for other latecomers to industrialization and development. First, there are alternative paths to development, rather than unique solutions, so that one-size-does-not-fit-all. There are strategic choices to be made between development models, each with its mix of the state and the market or openness and intervention. The emphases, in terms of the relative importance of domestic, as compared with, external markets, resources, or technologies, also depend on country-specific conjunctures and circumstances, which are inevitably shaped by a complex mix of economic, social, and political factors in the national context, where history matters. Second, development is about creating production capabilities in economies, which need industrial up-gradation and diversification together with some capacity for innovation, without which industrialization cannot be sustained. Third, inclusive societies alone can sustain rapid economic growth and transform it into meaningful development that improves the well-being of their people. The ongoing catch-up, driven by rapid growth, is necessary though not

[4] Alexander Gerschenkron, *Economic Backwardness in Historical Perspective*, Harvard University Press, Cambridge, MA, 1962.

sufficient for reducing inequality within and between countries. But this catch-up will not be sustainable unless it reduces economic inequality within countries.[5]

It is individuals, firms, institutions, and governments, people rather than nations, that learn in the process of development. Even so, the whole can be greater than the sum total of the parts. Such learning takes place at the micro, meso, and macro levels. At the micro-level, it is about imparting education, where school education provides the base and higher education the cutting edge, but learning outcomes are just as important as spread and access. At the meso-level, it about nurturing managerial capabilities in individuals and technological capabilities in firms. At the macro-level, it is national production and technological capabilities, which are the outcome of a complex interaction between incentives, capabilities, and institutions, in which intervention by governments performs an essential corrective and strategic role.

It need hardly be stressed that learning from experience is of critical importance. It is about correcting for mistakes. Everybody would agree. But it is just as important to unlearn from experience. It is about questioning long-held beliefs and thinking anew. Most have not thought about it. Yet, this distinction is important to understand the nature of the relationship between ideas and outcomes, or ideologies and policies, in the wider context of development. Dominant ideologies are always reluctant to question their belief systems. It means ceding intellectual or political space. Hence, attempts to unlearn from development, which require changes in priors or thinking, are few and far between. And it should come as no surprise that non-dominant doctrines are always more willing to learn and even unlearn. It means capturing intellectual or political space.[6] Thus, a study on how nations learn needs to recognize that unlearning is just as important as learning.

This is an unusual book on an unexplored domain, in its quest for understanding how nations learn.[7] It considers conceptual perspectives and empirical evidence from different countries and different eras, with a focus on the late twentieth and early twenty-first centuries. In doing so, it reviews the literature to discuss the critical issues: learning by countries that are latecomers; development of technological capabilities; experiences of catch-up at different levels (firms, sectors, or economies); importance of historical perspectives; policy-learning by governments; and fostering processes of learning, for firms as well as governments, in countries that are laggards or caught in the middle-income trap.

[5] This argument is developed, at some length, elsewhere by the author, 'Can Catch Up Reduce Inequality?' in Peter van Bergeijk and Rolph van der Hoeven (eds), *Sustainable Development Goals and Income Inequality*, Edward Elgar, Cheltenham, 2017.

[6] For a detailed discussion on this theme, see Deepak Nayyar, 'Learning to Unlearn from Development', *Oxford Development Studies*, 2008, 36(3): 259–80.

[7] The literature on this subject is indeed limited. For a perceptive analysis of learning, situated in its wider context, see Joseph Stiglitz and Bruce Greenwald, *Creating a Learning Society: A New Approach to Growth, Development, and Social Progress*, Columbia University Press, New York, 2014.

The contents of the book are new. And its approach is different. The first part, which provides broad perspectives on global economic development, the strategic role of the state, and drivers of technological learning, sets the stage. The second part, with chapters on Japan, Taiwan, South Korea, China, and Singapore, analyses the experience of success stories in learning and catch-up, to highlight the lessons that emerge. The third part, with chapters on Latin America and Vietnam, analyses the experience of countries in the middle-income trap and a latecomer, and on Ethiopia, a late latecomer, with case studies at the firm level and industry level, to derive lessons from outcomes in countries that have not succeeded, or are in transition, or provide examples of success at a micro level. The concluding chapter draws together the strands of the arguments developed in different chapters, to outline an understanding of the notions and processes of learning discussed in the existing literature, and to examine the implications, in the form of potential lessons, for countries that are late latecomers to development in the twenty-first century.

The themes that run through the book are the dynamics of technological learning at the level of firms and of policy learning at the level of governments. Industrial policy for the manufacturing sector is seen as the primary driver of learning, while degrees of freedom in the use of policy space is seen as critical, in the catch-up process. The essential conclusion to emerge is that there is no simple formula or magic wand in this learning process, by different actors at different levels, that countries can import or replicate. Different countries find different solutions at different times for similar problems. In fact, actual experiences show that learning has been achieved through a mixture of deliberate imitation, or adaptation, of foreign technologies or practices and local innovations and practices, sometimes deliberate and sometimes accidental. Even so, there is much that countries can learn, as late latecomers, from what went wrong and what turned out right elsewhere in the past. In this process, it is necessary to contextualize the learning in time and space rather than simply replicate.

This book provides a sensible blend of simple analytical constructs and down-to-earth empirical work to coax stylized facts and draw robust conclusions. It shows that, despite the complexities of such an intangible domain, it is possible to extract some general principles that enrich our understanding. By doing so, it injects some new ideas and fresh thinking on the subject. There is much that readers can learn from this study on how nations learn.

Deepak Nayyar

New Delhi
November, 2018

Acknowledgements

The volume editors are very grateful to all the contributors to this volume and sincerely thank them for the personal commitment, efforts, and distinctive contribution they have made to ensure the success of this book.

The editors convey their appreciation to Adam Swallow, the Commissioning Editor, for outstanding support and encouragement, and to his team and the entire production operation at Oxford University Press for their professionalism and diligent work. We also convey our appreciation to the anonymous reviewers for their constructive comments and delegates of OUP who approved the final version of the book proposal.

We extend our heartfelt thanks to Dr Taffere Tesfachew for his exceptional contribution and all-rounded support to our volume. We thank the panel of external reviewers who provided invaluable guidance on the structure and content of the book, and the participants at our August 2018 Addis Ababa workshop for their insightful presentations, discussion, feedback, and collaboration.

Our appreciation goes to Mr Haddis Tadesse (Bill and Melinda Gates Foundation) and Mr Tewolde Gebremariam (CEO of EAL) for their continued support, and Ethiopian Airlines for their ongoing logistical support to this project.

Special thanks are due to Keith Povey Editorial Services Ltd (especially Nancy Richardson), for the pre-publication copy-editing of the volume, and 251 Communications for the cover design. And finally, our appreciation and gratitude goes to our project coordinator, Deborah M. Kefale, and the research team of Meron Tilahun, Yohannes Ghebru, Sergut Abate, Tsion Kifle, Edom Haile, and Binyam Arkebe for their support in the preparation of the manuscript and assistance throughout the project.

Contents

PART III: PATHWAYS TO LATE-LATE DEVELOPMENT

List of Figures

List of Tables

List of Contributors

Wan-wen Chu is adjunct research fellow at the Research Center for Humanities and Social Sciences (RCHSS), Academia Sinica in Taiwan, and adjunct professor of economics at the National Taiwan University. She has a PhD in economics from Stanford University. She has published studies on East Asian economic development, especially regarding industrial policy, and is the co-author of *Beyond Late Development: Taiwan's Upgrading Policies* (MIT, 2003, with Alice Amsden). Other books include *Engine of Economic Growth* (Taishe, 2002), *Globalization and the Taiwan Economy* (Taishe, 2003), and *The Causes of Taiwan's Postwar Economic Growth: The Why and How of Late Development* (Academia Sinica and Linking, 2017).

Tan Khee Giap is co-director of the Asia Competitiveness Institute and associate professor at Lee Kuan Yew School of Public Policy, National University of Singapore. He is also chairman of the Singapore National Committee for Pacific Economic Cooperation. Dr Tan graduated with a PhD from the University of East Anglia in 1987. He has consulted extensively with government ministries and statutory boards of Singapore. Dr Tan is the lead author of more than twenty books and has published extensively in international refereed journals. His current research interests include the competitiveness of sub-national economies of Asia, global liveable cities and ease of doing business index.

Kris Hartley is an assistant professor in the Department of Asian and Policy Studies at the Education University of Hong Kong. He conducts research on intergovernmental relations and cross-sector collaboration for addressing regional policy issues in Asia's urban mega regions. His research covers issues related to technology, economic development, and urbanization. He holds a PhD in Public Policy from the National University of Singapore and a Master of City Planning from the University of California, Berkeley.

Richard Kozul-Wright is director of the Globalisation and Development Strategies Division in UNCTAD. He has worked at the United Nations in both New York and Geneva. He holds a PhD in economics from the University of Cambridge and has published widely on a range of economic issues, inter alia, in *The Economic Journal*, the *Cambridge Journal of Economics*, *The Journal of Development Studies*, and the *Oxford Review of Economic Policy*.

Keun Lee is a professor of economics at Seoul National University, and winner of the 2014 Schumpeter Prize for his monograph *Schumpeterian Analysis of Economic Catch-up* (CUP, 2013). He is an editor of *Research Policy*, an associate editor of *Industrial and Corporate Change*, and a council member of the World Economic Forum since 2016. He served as the president of the International Schumpeter Society (2016–18), a member of the Committee for Development Policy of the UN (2014–18). He obtained his PhD in economics from the University of California, Berkeley. One of his most cited articles is a paper on Korea's technological catch-up published in *Research Policy*, with 1,081 citations (Google Scholar).

His h-index is now 37, with ninety-four papers with more than ten citations. He has a new book entitled *The Art of Economic Catch-up: Barriers, Detours and Leapfrogging in Innovation Systems*, which will be published by Cambridge University Press, March 2019.

Justin Yifu Lin is dean of the Institute of New Structural Economics and the Institute of South-South Cooperation and Development and honorary dean of the National School of Development at Peking University. He was the senior vice president and chief economist of the World Bank, 2008–12. Prior to this, Professor Lin served for fifteen years as founding director of the China Centre for Economic Research (CCER) at Peking University. He is the author of more than twenty books including *Beating the Odds: Jump-starting Developing Countries* (with Célestin Monga; Princeton University Press, 2017) and *Demystifying the Chinese Economy* (CUP, 2011). He is a corresponding fellow of the British Academy and a fellow of the Academy of Sciences for the Developing World.

Mariana Mazzucato PhD is professor in the economics of innovation and public value at University College London (UCL), where she is the founder and director of the Institute for Innovation & Public Purpose (IIPP). She is author of *The Entrepreneurial State: Debunking Public vs. Private Sector Myths* (Anthem 2013; Public Affairs, 2015) and *The Value of Everything: Making and Taking in the Global Economy* (Penguin and Public Affairs, 2018).

Kenichi Ohno is professor at the National Graduate Institute for Policy Studies, Tokyo. He holds a PhD in economics from Stanford University, California. He worked at the International Monetary Fund and taught at the University of Tsukuba and Saitama University before assuming his current position. He works closely with the Japanese government in designing international cooperation strategy. He has advised the Vietnamese government since 1995 and conducted industrial policy dialogue with the Ethiopian government since 2008. Besides this, he has done policy research in over twenty countries in Asia and Africa. His research interest includes industrialization, policy learning for catch-up, the development experiences of Japan and other successful latecomers, and international comparison of industrial policy quality. His books include *The History of Japanese Economic Development: Origins of Private Dynamism and Policy Competence* (Routledge, 2018), *Learning to Industrialize: From Given Growth to Policy-aided Value Creation* (Routledge, 2013), *Eastern and Western Ideas for African Growth* (Routledge, 2013, co-edited), *The Economic Development of Japan: The Path Traveled by Japan as a Developing Country* (2006), and *Japanese Views on Economic Development* (Routledge, 1998, co-edited). He received the Presidential Medal for Friendship from the Vietnamese government and the Japanese Foreign Minister Award for contributing to Japan–Vietnam economic relationship.

Arkebe Oqubay PhD is a Senior Minister and Special Advisor to the Ethiopian Prime Minister and has been at the centre of policymaking for over twenty-five years. He is a former mayor of Addis Ababa and winner of the Best African Mayor of 2005 by ABN, and finalist for the World Mayor Award 2005 for transforming the city. He is a recipient of the Order of the Rising Sun, Gold and Silver Star presented by the Emperor of Japan. He currently serves as board chair of several leading public organizations and international advisory boards. He is a research associate at the Centre of African Studies in the University of London, and holds a PhD in development studies from SOAS, University of London. His recent work includes the path-breaking *Made in Africa: Industrial Policy in Ethiopia* (OUP,

2015); *The Oxford Handbook of the Ethiopian Economy* (OUP, 2019); *China–Africa and an Economic Transformation* (OUP, 2019); *African Economic Development: Evidence, Theory, and Policy* (OUP, forthcoming); and *The Oxford Handbook of Industrial Hubs and Economic Development* (OUP, forthcoming). He was recognized as one of the *100 most influential Africans* of 2016, and a 'leading thinker on Africa's strategic development' by the *New African,* for his work, both theoretical and practical, on industrial policies. His research focus includes structural transformation, catch-up, industrial policy, and policymaking, with a special emphasis on Africa.

Wilson Peres, is a senior economic affairs officer at the Division of Production, Productivity and Management of the UN Economic Commission for Latin America and the Caribbean (ECLAC), Chile. He was previously the chief of ECLAC's Industrial and Technological Development Unit, Investment and Corporate Strategies Unit, and Innovation and ICT Unit. He has been a consultant to the OECD Development Centre, as well as a visiting research fellow and lecturer at the University of California, San Diego (UCSD) and Universidad de Chile in Santiago. His publications include *The New Digital Revolution: From the Consumer Internet to theIindustrial Interne,* (ECLAC, 2015), 'Industrial Policies in Latin America' in A. Szirmai, W. Naudé, and L. Alcorta (eds) *Pathways to Industrialization in the Twenty-First Century* (OUP, 2013).

Daniel Poon is an economist at United Nations Conference on Trade and Development (UNCTAD). He holds a master's degree from Carleton University's School of Public Policy and Administration with a specialization in Chinese and Asian development strategies. He has published various articles and commentaries on issues of development finance, industrial policy, and South-South cooperation, most recently co-author of chapter 'Asian Development after the Asian Drama' in a UNU-WIDER edited volume.

Annalisa Primi PhD is a senior economist and head of the Structural Policies and Innovation Unit of the Development Centre of the OECD. Prior to that she worked at the OECD Directorate of Science, Technology and Industry and Directorate of Public Governance and Territorial Development. Previously, Dr Primi worked in the Productive and Business Development Division of ECLAC between 2003 and 2009. Her research focuses on the relationship between innovation, productive development, and intellectual property and the role of the state in the formation of development trajectories.

Taffere Tesfachew PhD is an independent consultant with more than thirty-five years of experience in conducting research and analysis on trade, investment, industrial policy, and technology-related issues. Until April 2016, he was the director of the Division on Africa and Least Developed Countries (LDCs) at UNCTAD. He holds an MA in economics from the University of Lancaster, an MPhil and a PhD from IDS, University of Sussex. He has published on a range of topics, including: "Technological Learning and Industrialization in Ethiopia" (*The Oxford Handbook of the Ethiopian Economy*, OUP, 2019); "The Role of Policy in Promoting Enterprise Learning during Early Industrialization"; "The Unfinished Agenda in International Technology Transfer"; "Government Policies and the Urban Informal Sector", among others.

Khuong Vu is an associate professor at the Lee Kuan Yew School of Public Policy (National University of Singapore). His research and teaching concentrate on economic development strategy and policy analysis, with a special focus on Asian economies and their transformation in the fourth industrial revolution. Before started his academic career, Dr. Vu spent more than twenty years working for the Vietnamese government. Dr. Vu received a BA in mathematics from Hanoi University (with highest honours) and an MBA and PhD from Harvard University.

Robert H. Wade is a New Zealander, worked as an economist at World Bank and taught at the Institute of Development Studies (Sussex University), Princeton, MIT, Brown, and LSE. Professor Wade conducted fieldwork in Pitcairn Island, central Italy, India, South Korea, Taiwan, and from inside the World Bank. He was awarded the Leontief Prize for Advancing the Frontiers of Economic Thought in 2008. His book *Governing the Market* (Princeton University Press, 1990) was awarded Best Book or Article in Political Economy by the American Political Science Association.

Tan Kong Yam is professor of economics at the Nanyang Technological University (NTU) in Singapore. He was the assistant director in charge of exchange rate policy at the Monetary Authority of Singapore (1984–7). From 1985–8, he was also the chief assistant to Dr Goh Keng Swee, the former deputy prime minister of Singapore invited by Mr Deng Xiaoping to advise China on economic development strategy. From June 2002 to June 2005, he was a senior economist at the World Bank office in Beijing. Prior to that, he was the chief economist of the Singapore government (1999–2002). He is a graduate of Princeton University and Stanford University. His research interests are in economic and business trends in Asia Pacific and economic reforms in China. He has published over ten books and articles in major journals.

George Yeo is chairman of Kerry Logistics Network. From 1988 to 2011, he served in the Singapore government, as Minister for Information and the Arts, Health, Trade and Industry, and Foreign Affairs. Before resigning to enter politics, he was an officer in the Singapore Armed Forces and attained the rank of brigadier general. Mr Yeo has a BA in engineering from Cambridge University and an MBA from Harvard University.

Jun Zhang is a professor of economics and dean of the School of Economics at Fudan University, Shanghai, China. He is also the founding director of the China Center for Economic Studies, a Shanghai-based think tank for the Chinese economy. His recent contributions have been to *The World Economy*, *China Economic Review*, *Economic Systems*, *Comparative Economic Studies*, *Journal of Asian Economics*, *Journal of the Asia Pacific Economy*, et al. He has authored and edited numerous books including *Economic Transition with Chinese Characteristics: Thirty Years of Reform and Opening Up* (McGill-Queen University Press, 2008), *Transformation of the Chinese Enterprises* (Cengage Learning, 2009), *Unfinished Reforms of the Chinese Economy* (World Scientific Publishing, 2013), and *End of Hyper Growth in China* (Palgrave Macmillan, 2016).

1

Technological Learning, Industrial Policy, and Catch-up

Introduction

Arkebe Oqubay and Kenichi Ohno

1.1 Background to *How Nations Learn*

Why do some nations catch up while others lag behind or remain stuck in the 'middle-income trap'? More importantly, how do nations learn and what are the key determinants of successful learning and catch-up? *How Nations Learn* attempts to provide answers to these questions with contributions from eminent scholars in the field of technological learning, innovation, industrial policies, and catch-up. The main focus of the book is on how technological learning and policy learning occur at the firm and government level respectively. The varied perspectives put forward by a diverse group of authors not only attempt to deepen the understanding of how learning and catch-up occur, but also aim to stimulate further discussion and debate around learning. The volume seeks to clarify key notions and concepts, and to examine empirical evidence of the processes of learning and catch-up.

The ever-changing global economic, social, and political landscape of the twenty-first century has made technological learning and catch-up increasingly complex, particularly for nations that are latecomers to industrialization and structural transformation. The economic slowdown after the 2008 global financial crisis, the hyper-globalization of the world economy, the increasing trend towards protectionism and trade conflict, the accelerated pace of technological advancement and innovation, constrained policy space, and the impact of climate change, which disproportionately affects emerging and developing economies, have all resulted in added complexities for countries trying to catch up in the twenty-first century.[1]

How Nations Learn was conceived as a result of two factors: first, an observation that only a limited number of countries had managed to successfully catch up, begging the question of why catch-up is a rare phenomenon. Second, while the

[1] See emerging issues of trade, see UNCTAD (2018).

literature on learning has addressed the 'what', particularly what firms need to learn to enhance their technological capabilities, less emphasis is given to 'how' technological and policy learning occurs and what influences it from the firm and national perspective.

Historically, industrial policy was a vehicle for structural transformation, and a core strategy behind the successful catch-up of countries in East Asia.[2] However, some nations such as Malaysia and Thailand have remained stuck in the 'middle-income trap', while many African countries have been left behind in a 'low-income trap'. Ensuring successful catch-up is neither automatic nor inevitable, depending as it does on how nations learn, within the broader thrust of technological learning and industrial policies.

This book examines how latecomer nations have been able to learn and catch up, and bring together abstract theories and empirical evidence from country and sectoral case studies to identify lessons for successful technological and policy learning in the twenty-first century.

1.2 Aims, Motivation, and Focus

The principal motivation for an edited volume on how nations learn is the need to revisit ongoing discourse on learning, how learning occurs, and latecomer advantages, and to seek lessons for nations embarking on industrialization in the twenty-first century. These 'late latecomers' to technological learning and structural transformation are at a very early stage of the catch-up process. In addition, many nations that started industrialization earlier face challenges and slowdown on reaching middle-income status. The volume explores past learning and catch-up experiences by different countries and from different starting positions and their relevance to late-latecomer countries. Special emphasis is given to the nexus between learning, in particular technological and policy learning, and the process of catching up; how the pace and direction of catch-up is influenced and shaped by learning; and why some countries manage to catch up fast, with relative ease, while others encounter difficulties. These are all important issues for policymakers in late-latecomer countries seeking inspiration and specific policy lessons.

Applying the lessons of one set of countries' development experiences to policies and strategies in another requires careful analysis and considerable caution, because every country has its own geographical, political, historical, demographic, and socio-economic characteristics. Starting economic conditions and changes in the international economic environment affect the appropriateness of policies at different points in time.

[2] On centrality of structural transformation and special feature of manufacturing as driver of growth, see List (1956), Kaldor (1967), and Passineti (1993).

This is not to deny the usefulness of identifying lessons from successful cases. History is full of examples of individuals and firms from different nations learning from each other, either independently or collectively. Often, the problem is not identifying lessons but ensuring that the circumstances that led to the success are also considered, including obstacles and failures encountered in the process (Arrow, 1962). Learning from past experience requires an understanding of the context (i.e. the history, political economy, economic geography, geopolitical and global economic developments) in which it occurred. It is important to recognize the diversity of approaches to learning and catching up, and that there is no 'best practice' that any country can adopt that will guarantee success. The main challenge is distinguishing how specific policy lessons can generate positive outcomes in different contexts.

How Nations Learn focuses on both conceptual perspectives and empirical evidence from different countries and different eras, with particular focus on the late twentieth and early twenty-first centuries. Clearly it is people and firms, rather than nations, that learn. The objective of the book, however, is to extend the analysis beyond individuals, firms, and institutions to understand the systemic aspect of learning—the role of the state as a learner (policy learning) and facilitator of learning by the private sector (technology learning), just as a National Innovation System (NIS) is used as a conceptual framework and systemic approach to local technological capability building (Fagerberg, Mowery, and Nelson, 2005).

A useful starting point is to ask why individuals and/or firms in some countries learn or learn faster and catch up while others do not. Although many firm- and industry-level studies have deepened our understanding of what firms and individuals learn, there has been less emphasis on how learning takes place and what influences learning nationally. The pace and direction of learning is, to a large extent, determined by policies, incentives, institutions, the role of the state, and the intensity of policy learning. It is this systemic, national aspect of learning that this book aspires to understand. From the editors' perspective, its practical utility lies in its ability to identify the broader mechanisms and apparatus of learning that play a key role in facilitating economic or industrial catch-up. Examining a large number of cases across different sectors, countries, and periods, the reader will observe that some basic aspects are common to all learning while others are unique to each society and not internationally transferable.

1.3 Themes and Analytical Perspectives

First, the book reviews the literature on learning, in particular technological learning and successful catch-up by latecomers through learning from forerunners (Amsden, 1989, 2001; Gerschenkron, 1962; Hirschman, 1958), learning by doing and by experimentation, and emulation to match or excel. A clear understanding of the factors shaping the intensity, pace, and direction of learning, and the effects of the changing international context on learning and catch-up in latecomers is critical. We review evidence from a diverse group of countries, in particular those from the Far East and South East Asia (Amsden, 1989, 2001; Chang, 2003; Lin, 2012; Nolan, 2014) that have shown mixed results in learning and catch-up. As continental European and East Asian economies have shown, late developers can catch up through learning by doing, pragmatic approach, imitation and emulation, with active industrial policies and a leading role for the state (Amsden, 1989, 2001; Amsden and Chu, 2003; Reinert, 2009; Wade, 1990).

There is also a stream of literature that links catch-up and economic development with the development of technological capabilities, learning, and innovation (Abramovitz, 1986; Lall, 1996; Nelson, 1996; Kim and Nelson, 2000). Catch-up and learning has been influenced by the broader institutions and varieties of capitalism (Hall and Soskice, 2001; Huo, 2016). An economic history of catch-up in Europe and its periphery can be found in *The Spread of Modern Industry to the Periphery since 1871* (O'Rourke and Williamson, 2017). This study provides in-depth analyses of the profound divergences characterizing this epoch while arguing that industrialization anchored in the manufacturing sector has been pivotal to modern-day economic growth.[3]

Second, the book reviews learning and catch-up experiences from the perspective of different levels—firm, industrial/sectoral, and national. Pioneering arguments by Gerschenkron (1962) and Hirschman (1958) on latecomer advantages and strategies for catch-up emphasized that latecomers can take advantage of their latecomer status to catch up despite their distance from technological frontiers. The earliest conceptual contribution on catch-up and late development can be traced to List (1856), while empirical perspectives have been enriched in recent years by development economists including Amsden (1989, 2001), Wade (1990), Chang (2003), and more recently Keun Lee (2013). New perspectives based on more recent experiences of learning, in particular policy learning by doing, are provided by Ohno (2013) and Oqubay (2015) among others.

Third, the book emphasizes the importance of historical perspectives in identifying lessons for late latecomers (Nayyar, 2013; Veblen, 1915). Not all nations with latecomer advantage have managed to translate technological learning into catch-up; deciphering the historical experiences will enable late-latecomer nations to gain a better understanding of the context in which successful learning and catch-up was achieved.

Fourth, the book enhances understanding of the link between catch-up (defined as a narrowing of a firm's or country's technological and economic gap vis-à-vis a

[3] See also Campos and Root(1996), and Komiya, Okuno, and Suzumura (1988).

leading country or firm) and learning efforts, including policy intensity. For late latecomers, a clear understanding of the pull and push factors in learning and catch-up, and the role of the state in this process, is critical. Learning also requires making strategic choices and keeping an eye on the future, going beyond learning by doing, and in some cases leapfrogging. Experience shows that the nexus between learning and catch-up is influenced by strategic choices, policy actions, and the broad economic environment, so the state is a key agent of learning and catch-up (Mazzucato, 2011, 2018). The roles of the state and of disruptive technologies in catch-up are exemplified by catch-up trends in South Korea, Taiwan, the United States, and China. It is in this context that understanding 'how nations learn' will be important for late-latecomer countries.

Finally, the analytical focus of the book is on how late-latecomer nations and those in the middle-income trap can accelerate learning, in particular technological learning at different levels, to upgrade their productive capacity, improve the quality of their goods and services, and create a robust and dynamic private sector. Despite the immense volume of work on policy approaches, there is a paucity of literature on how learning occurs and the lessons that can be learned and implemented effectively in diverse contexts. The latest addition by Andersson and Axelsson (2016), an edited volume containing many insightful contributions, employs empirical evidence and case studies to show that there is no 'one-size-fits-all' approach to catch-up and economic development. We believe there is room for another edited volume to fill the gap on the 'how' aspect of learning and catch-up. Technological learning (at firm level), industrial policy and policy learning (at government level), and catch-up are the building blocks of this volume.

1.4 Structure of the Book

Following this introduction are twelve chapters divided into three parts and a concluding chapter. Part I addresses the broader policy and institutional contexts in which successful technological learning and catch-up has occurred.

In Chapter 2, Robert Wade focuses on trends in global economic development, the ideological perspectives that have influenced economic thinking, and their impact on catch-up over the past seven decades. He highlights that contrary to the assumption of the 'old-style' development economists that starting late has advantages, only a handful of non-Western emerging and developing countries have succeeded in catching up with developed economies since the Second World War. The restrictive institutional structure of the international economic system and the gravitational forces operating at that level, including the emergence of global value chains (GVCs) dominated by large corporations, have made it increasingly difficult for latecomers to escape the periphery and catch up with developed economies.

In Chapter 3, Daniel Poon and Richard Kozul-Wright examine the political economy of technological learning and catch-up in East Asia and the lessons for other latecomers, in particular the role of the developmental state and its pragmatic approach to policy formulation and experimentation. Using evidence from the Chinese experience, Poon and Kozul-Wright illustrate how targeted industrial policies and controls over the domestic financial system have enabled some East Asian economies to promote export-oriented production capacity in strategic sectors and achieve the structural transformation and technological learning necessary to catch up. They argue that pragmatic experimentalism has been a common feature in the rapid catch-up growth economies in East Asia generally, and China in particular.

Chapter 4 by Mariana Mazzucato focuses on mission-oriented innovation, and the industrial policies and strategic role of the state. Governments are increasingly seeking economic catch-up that is innovation-led or smart, inclusive, and sustainable in the context of major social and environmental challenges. Tackling climate change, improving public health and well-being, and adjusting to demographic changes are expected to be overarching considerations. Mazzucato highlights that industrial policies and mission-oriented innovation policy should respond to these 'grand challenges' by identifying concrete issues across the various sectors encompassing production, distribution, and consumption patterns. This implies not only a rapid rate but also a pattern and direction for economic catch-up; and innovation requires investments and risk taking by both private and public actors, increasingly also involving the third sector. Moreover, the state has a role not only in fixing markets but also in co-creating and shaping them; 'mission-oriented policies' focused on solving societal problems can set directions while enabling bottom-up experimentation, exploration, and learning; and missions also require consensus building in civil society. The changes this requires in mindset, theoretical frameworks, institutional capacities, and policies are non-trivial, but mission-oriented innovation policy is not a step into the unknown. This chapter provides substantial theory, evidence, case studies, and experience accumulated over many decades of successful practice.

Part II reviews the evidence from successful learning and catch-up experiences in East Asia. In Chapter 5, Kenichi Ohno examines Japan's rapid technological learning and catch-up during the Meiji era in the second half of the nineteenth century. As a latecomer to industrialization, Japan embarked on technological learning by selectively acquiring frontline technology and know-how from the West and assimilating them locally through learning by doing, technology licensing, and joint-venture partnerships with foreign technology suppliers. Ohno underlines that private-sector dynamism supported by an activist state and a passion to learn were the main drivers of technological learning and catch-up in the Meiji era.

Chapter 6, by Wan-wen Chu, focuses on Taiwan's rapid post-war growth, technological learning, and catch-up, particularly the role of industrial policies in facilitating an environment conducive to learning. The chapter maps the pattern of learning and growth, starting with import substitution in the 1950s, the transition to export promotion in the 1960s and 1970s, and the entry into the high-tech sector in the 1980s. The chapter explores Taiwan's 'adaptive' industrial policies for successful industrial upgrading and catch-up. It also compares the development paths of Taiwan and South Korea, finding differences in national and international contexts, targeted sectors, interactions with multinational economies, and the role of national champions.

In Chapter 7, Keun Lee considers how firms develop the absorptive capacity required to promote learning and catch-up. Using a data set of more than 3,000 foreign technology acquisition contracts filed by Korean firms between 1970 and 1993, Lee conducts an econometric analysis to establish how firms develop absorptive capacity and what role foreign technology plays in building it. Absorptive capacity building is a dynamic process that becomes even more effective when combined with access to foreign knowledge, particularly the tacit knowledge essential for assimilation of foreign technologies and creation of local technological capability.[4]

Chapter 8, by Justin Lin and Jun Zhang, focuses on China, a recent catch-up story, and how the country has been able to broaden the technological complexity of its export sectors and turn its comparative advantage into competitive advantage through pragmatic and strategic industrial policies that combined technological learning with policy learning. Lin and Zhang present evidence-based analysis of China's dynamic learning and catch-up experience, and identify the role models that inspired the Chinese leadership to pursue their rapid catch-up growth agenda. They argue that New Structural Economics—which emphasizes the importance of dynamic comparative advantage, the structure of factor endowments, and building on initial conditions—provides a more fitting explanation for China's rapid growth and catch-up than mainstream industrialization 'dogma'.

The chapter by George Yeo, Tan Khee Giap, and Tan Kong Yam examines the learning and catch-up of Singapore since 1965, focusing on the state's role in determining the policies, incentives, and key institutions that drove the pace and direction of technological learning and catch-up. While Singapore is much smaller than other successful catch-up countries in East Asia, its unique learning and industrialization experience sheds light on how countries less well endowed with human and natural resources can promote technological and policy learning that triggers the process of catch-up. In recounting the Singapore experience, Yeo, Giap, and Yam also highlight the lessons of past policy failures.[5]

[4] See also Arrow (1962) and Cohen and Levinthal (1989) on absorptive capacity and learning by doing.

[5] See also Oqubay and Lin (forthcoming) on hubs development and industrial upgrading.

Part III examines the experiences of countries that have remained stuck in the middle-income trap after initial industrialization efforts, as well as late latecomers to industrialization that lag well behind in technological learning and catch-up. The latter includes many less developed economies in Africa and Latin America that have embarked on industrialization in the twenty-first century in a highly competitive global economic environment less conducive to policy experimentation and independence. Using firm- and industry-level evidence, Part III explores the potential as well as the challenges facing this group of countries in their efforts to promote technological learning and catch-up.

In Chapter 10, Wilson Peres and Annalisa Primi analyse the industrialization experiences of Latin American countries, particularly the reasons for their diverse patterns and degrees of technological learning and catch-up success. The chapter focuses on eight countries—Argentina, Brazil, Chile, Colombia, Costa Rica, Ecuador, Mexico, and Uruguay—and on the policy approaches and implementation challenges of the last decade. While recognizing the persistent structural weaknesses in these economies, including their poor record of production and export diversification, the chapter identifies three areas that offer hope for a positive future outcome: closing the skills gap in the digital economy; successful penetration of global value chains in highly sophisticated niche products; and recently introduced successful start-up programmes that indicate a new dynamism and potential for technological learning and catch-up in the region.

Chapter 11, by Arkebe Oqubay and Taffere Tesfachew, presents firm-level evidence of technological learning and catch-up in Africa, a continent that continues to lag behind in both technological learning and industrialization.[6] Oqubay and Tesfachew analyse the technological learning of one of the most successful and dynamic airlines in Africa, Ethiopian Airlines (EAL), and how it was able to catch up by successfully narrowing the gap between itself and leading global players in the industry. The chapter reviews EAL's journey to building an internationally competitive airline, and explores the challenges and complexities of learning, and how the airline was able to manage crises by developing a strong corporate culture and independence. Key to EAL's successful learning and catch-up have been its partnership with the leading global player TWA, limited government interference in its operations and management, and its strong commitment to an 'Ethiopianization' strategy which increased the intensity of learning.

Chapter 12, by Khuong Vu and Kris Hartley, explores the policies and strategies promoting technological learning and catch-up in one of the fast-growing latecomer economies of South East Asia—Vietnam. Khuong and Hartley analyse

[6] See Cramer, Oqubay, and Sender (forthcoming).

the role of state and industrial policies, from the post-conflict late 1970s reform years to the creation of macroeconomic conditions and an open economy conducive to technological learning and diversification into manufacturing-based export-led industrialization in the 1980s and beyond.[7] The chapter identifies five key actions necessary to initiate successful and productive learning and catch-up: making strategic choices; establishing institutional arrangements; building coordination capacity; carrying out development initiatives; and responding to emerging opportunities and challenges. While all these dimensions are important for learning, Khuong and Hartley argue that making sound strategic choices is particularly critical for initiating a productive learning process.

Finally, Chapter 13, by Arkebe Oqubay and Taffere Tesfachew, reviews two cases of successful industry-level learning and catch-up in one of the fastest-growing African countries—Ethiopia.[8] The floriculture and cement industries, representing export-oriented and import-substituting industries respectively, demonstrate that with strategic industrial policy, supported by an active state willing to engage in policy learning, including learning from role models and through policy experimentation, successful technological learning, and catch-up can be fostered at industry level even in low-income late-latecomer countries. The chapter also reviews Ethiopia's recent university reforms, and the strategic and dynamic learning approach to the development of industrial hubs, which together have been critical for enhancing the country's skills base, and developing and broadening domestic absorptive capacity. Oqubay and Tesfachew show that successful learning and catch-up by African countries is linked to the intensity, pace, and direction of learning, and that policy learning by government is essential if industrial policy is to serve as a vehicle for catch-up.

The final chapter is a contribution to the ongoing debate (and literature) on learning and catch-up, and the implications for late latecomers, with its focus on two important areas: (a) our understanding of the notions and processes of learning and catch-up as discussed in existing literature; and (b) implications (and potential lessons) for countries still to go through technological learning and catch-up (i.e. late latecomers).[9] The discussion focuses on the key dynamics of technological learning; industrial policy and manufacturing as prime drivers of learning and catch-up; and finally, catch-up and the scope for policy space in the twenty-first century.

[7] See also Thirlwall (2013) on the strategic role of exports.

[8] See Cheru, Cramer, and Oqubay (2019).

[9] The concepts and themes of this volume were developed further during an inception workshop held in Addis Ababa in August 2018 for authors and independent reviewers. The valuable comments and suggestions received during the workshop helped to tighten the arguments, themes, and analytical perspectives presented in the book. The editors hope that this book will meet the expectations of our esteemed readers and that it will help to fill the gap in the literature.

Acknowledgement

The authors are grateful to Taffere Tesfachew for his important inputs to this chapter and his exceptional and all-round support to this volume, James Mittleman for constructive suggestions, Deborah M. Kefale and Binyam Arkebe for their inputs to improve the draft and for their continued support.

References

Abramovitz, Moses (1986) 'Cathing Up, Forging Ahead and Falling Behind', *Journal of Economic History* XLVI (2): 385–406.

Amsden, Alice (1989) *Asia's Next Giant: South Korea and Late Industrialization*. Oxford: Oxford University Press.

Amsden, Alice (2001) *The 'Rise of the Rest': Challenges to the West from Late-industrializing Economies*. Oxford: Oxford University Press.

Amsden, Alice and Wan-wen Chu (2003) *Beyond Late Development: Taiwan's Upgrading Policies*. Cambridge, MA: MIT Press.

Andersson, Martin and Tobias Axelsson (eds) (2016) *Diverse Development Paths and Structural Transformation in the Escape from Poverty*. Oxford: Oxford University Press.

Arrow, Kenneth (1962) 'The Economic Implications of Learning by Doing', *Review of Economic Studies* 28: 155–73.

Campos, Jose Edgardo, and Hilton L. Root (1996) *The Key to the Asian Miracle: Making Shared Growth Credible*. Washington, DC: Brookings Institution.

Chang, Ha-Joon (2003) *Kicking away the Ladder: Development Strategy in Historical Perspective*. London: Anthem Press.

Cheru, Fantu, Christopher Cramer, and Arkebe Oqubay (2019) *The Oxford Handbook of the Ethiopian Economy*. Oxford: Oxford University Press.

Cohen, Wesley and Daniel Levinthal (1989) 'Innovation and Learning: The Two Faces of R&D', *The Economic Journal* 99(397): 569–96.

Cramer, Christopher, Arkebe Oqubay, and John Sender (forthcoming) *African Economic Development: Evidence, Theory, and Policy*. Oxford: Oxford University Press.

Fagerberg, Jan, David Mowery, and Richard Nelson (eds) (2005) *The Oxford Handbook of Innovation*. Oxford: Oxford University Press.

Gerschenkron, Alexander (1962) *Economic Backwardness in Historical Perspective*. Cambridge, MA: Harvard University Press.

Hall, Peter and David Soskice (2001) *Varieties of Capitalism: The Institutional Foundations of Comparative Advantage*. Oxford: Oxford University Press.

Hirschman, Albert (1958) *Strategy of Economic Development*. New Haven, CT: Yale University Press.

Huo, Jingjing (2016) *How Nations Innovate: The Political Economy of Technological Innovation in Affluent Capitalist Economies*. Oxford: Oxford University Press.

Kaldor, Nicholas (1967) *Causes of the Slow Rate of Economic Growth of the United Kingdom*. Cambridge: Cambridge University Press.

Kim, Linsu and Richard Nelson (eds) (2000) *Technology, Learning, and Innovation*. Cambridge: Cambridge University Press.

Komiya, Ryutaro, Masahiro Okuno, and Kotaro Suzumura (eds) (1988) *Industrial Policy of Japan*. Cambridge, MA: Academic Press.

Lall, Sanjaya (1996) *Learning from the Asian Tigers: Studies in Technology and Industrial Policy*. London: Macmillan.

Lee, Keun (2013) *Schumpeterian Analysis of Economic Catch Up: Knowledge, Path-Creation and the Middle Income*. Cambridge: Cambridge University Press.

Lin, Justin Yifu (2012) *The Quest for Prosperity: How Developing Countries Can Take Off*. Princeton, NJ. Princeton University Press.

List, Friedrich (1956) *National System of Political Economy*, Vols I–IV. Memphis, TN: Lippincott.

Mazzucato, Mariana (2011) *The Entrepreneurial State: Debunking Public vs. Private Sector Myths*. London: Anthem Press.

Mazzucato, Mariana (2018) *The Value of Everything: Making and Taking in the Global Economy*. London: Allen Lane.

Nayyar, Deepak (2013) *Catch Up: Developing Countries in the World Economy*. Oxford: Oxford University Press.

Nelson, Richard (1996) *The Sources of Economic Growth*. Cambridge, MA: Harvard University Press.

Nolan, Peter (2014) 'Globalization and Industrial Policy: The Case of China', *The World Economy* 37(6): 747–64.

Ohno, Kenichi (2013) *Learning to Industrialize: From Given Growth to Policy-aided Value Creation*. New York: Routledge-GRIPS Publications Development Forum Studies.

Oqubay, Arkebe (2015) *Made in Africa: Industrial Policy in Ethiopia*. Oxford: Oxford University Press.

Oqubay, Arkebe, and Justin Yifu Lin (forthcoming) *The Oxford Handbook of Industrial Hubs and Economic Development*. Oxford: Oxford University Press.

O'Rourke, H. Kevin and Jeffrey G. Williamson (eds) (2017) *The Spread of Modern Industry to the Periphery since 1871*. Oxford: Oxford University Press.

Passineti, Luigi (1993) *Structural Economic Dynamics: A Theory of the Economic Consequences of Human Learning*. Cambridge: Cambridge University Press.

Reinert, Erik (2009) *How Rich Countries Got Rich and Why Poor Countries Stay Poor*. London: Constable.

Thirlwall, Anthony (2013) *Economic Growth in an Open Developing Economy: The Role of Structure and Demand*. New York: Edward Elgar.

UNCTAD (2018) *Trade and Development Report 2018: Power, Platforms and the Free Trade Delusion*. Geneva: UNCTAD.

Veblen, Thorstein (1915) *Imperial Germany and the Industrial Revolution.*

Wade, Robert (1990) *Governing the Market: Economic Theory and the Role of Government in East Asian Industrialization*. Princeton, NJ: Princeton University Press.

PART I
CONTEXT AND PERSPECTIVES

2

Catch-up and Constraints in the Twentieth and Twenty-first Centuries

Robert H. Wade

2.1 Introduction

The old-style development economists—including Gerschenkron, Prebisch, Lewis, Myrdal, Chenery, Hirschman, Adelman, Seers, and many more—would surely be disappointed by the record of global economic development in the past half century, at least when looking at the slowness of catch-up as distinct from the dramatic falls in global poverty even while population increased at the fastest rate in human history. Gerschenkron's 'late development effect', or 'the advantages of backwardness', seems noticeable more by its absence than its presence, despite new technology being widely available to people around the world and despite no shortage of people with entrepreneurial talent.

But perhaps they would not be surprised. At the core of their understanding of the process of catch-up development were the following propositions:

(1) Development is a disruptive process of non-marginal changes over time, opposed by many in the society, generating inevitable conflict, and placing a premium on fragile conflict resolution institutions—a premium which calls for not exposing the economy to unmediated international competitive pressures.

(2) The price system in a developing country cannot play the role accorded it in developed countries as the major allocator of resources, because markets are too undeveloped and because relying on markets would tend to sustain the existing production specialization based on static comparative advantage with decreasing returns to scale—a point which also implies the desirability of less than full-scale integration into the international economy.

(3) Capital being extremely scarce (or was at the time the pioneers were writing and for decades after), the state has a large role in husbanding the mobilization and use of scarce capital, on a scale big enough to make centrally planned, non-marginal changes in the production structure *towards increasing return activities* which may well lie beyond the economy's static comparative advantage; but it must use mostly decentralized market allocation rather than centrally planned allocation (Reinert, 1994).

(4) The social returns to large, lumpy, and risky investment projects typically far exceed the private returns to private investors—which again implies a directive role for the state.

2.2 The Eclipse of Development Economics and the Rise of Neoliberalism

As we know, these propositions fell radically out of favour in the international (Western-dominated) development community starting in the 1970s and intensifying in the 1980s and later. This was the time of ascendancy of the development recipe that came to be known as the Washington Consensus, but which is more accurately called the Washington–London–Paris–Brussels–Berlin Consensus. Anyone questioning the universal applicability of the Washington Consensus was treated as religious sects treat heretics.

Today, many development economists have scarcely heard of Prebisch or Myrdal, or cumulative causation, or Kaldor's growth laws, and would agree, if pressed, that developing countries should mostly follow static comparative advantage and integrate deeply into global production networks with the state providing only macro stability and general supply-side support, including infrastructure, incentives for education (public or private), incentives for health care (public or private), and above all, law and order, protection of private property rights, including the rights of capital owners to move their capital freely around the world. They think of development policy as mostly about the supply side, leaving the demand side to be taken care of by exports—a presumption which conveniently occludes questions about whether income and wealth distribution should be made more equal.

Why this sharp shrinkage in the legitimate role of the state in the process of economic development? Perhaps for two linked reasons. First, in the West, led by the United States, the success of 'social democratic capitalism' during the post-war decades up to the late 1960s squeezed the rate of profit (success in terms of the ability of the labour movement to translate rising productivity into higher wages and of the ability of governments to keep recessions short). Business leaders and the already wealthy began to press for radical reforms intended to restore the rate of profit and reverse the erosion of their pre-eminence in the social structure, hankering back to the golden age of oligopolistic capitalism of the early twentieth century.

Fortunately for them a sect of professional economists had long been developing the paradigm which they proudly called neoliberalism, which aimed to secure the same kind of social order wanted by business leaders and the wealthy and banish the Keynesian 'pro-government-intervention' ideas prevailing during the post-war decades (Slobodian, 2018). This sect had the good fortune to include the governor of the central bank of Sweden, a passionate opponent of social democracy. He had the idea of commemorating the 300th anniversary of the central bank by creating a prize to be called the Nobel Prize in Economics (a name which both the Nobel Foundation and the Nobel family initially rejected, so that its official but not used title is The Sveriges Riksbank Prize in Economic Sciences in Memory of Alfred Nobel. The governor knew he could select the awarding committee members to ensure that the prize went disproportionately to clearly neoliberal economists in order to show the world that neoliberal economics was the best, most scientific economics, in contrast to social democratic economics.

The project to remake the world in line with neoliberal principles has been dramatically successful. A *New York Times* reporter summarized the prevailing belief at the World Economic Forum (of business leaders and politicians) meeting in Davos, Switzerland in 2002:

> [A] nation that opens its economy and keeps government's role to a minimum invariably experiences more rapid economic growth and rising incomes.
> (Uchitelle, 2002)

The prominent *Financial Times* economics editor Martin Wolf described his neoliberal vision of the desirable world order as follows:

> It cannot make sense to fragment the world economy more than it already is but rather to make the world economy work as if it were the United States, or at least the European Union [meaning that governments of nation states should have no more control over economic transactions across their borders than US states have across theirs, or at least no more than European Union states have across theirs] ... The potential for greater economic integration is barely tapped. We need more global markets, not fewer. (2004: 4, emphasis added)

In the same spirit, here is Alan Greenspan, former chair of the US Federal Reserve, shortly before Lehman Bros collapsed in 2008:

> [We] are fortunate that, thanks to globalization, policy decisions in the US have been largely replaced by global market forces. National security aside, it hardly makes any difference who will be the next president. The world is governed by market forces. (quoted in Tooze, 2008, emphasis added)

Notice the implied low value attached to national sovereignty and liberal democratic politics which runs through neoliberal ideology. This goes with passionate opposition to measures that curb income and wealth concentration at the top, where the captains of industry live. One of the pioneers of neoliberal economics, Ludwig von Mises, wrote in 1922: 'Our whole civilization rests on the fact that men have always succeeded in beating off the attack of the re-distributors' (Slobodian, 2018: 277).

Much later, Robert Lucas (2004), who was awarded the ersatz Nobel Prize, said:

> Of the tendencies that are harmful to sound economics, the most seductive, and in my opinion the most poisonous, is to focus on questions of distribution . . . The potential for improving the lives of poor people by finding different ways of distributing current production is nothing compared to the apparently limitless potential of increasing production.

Inside the World Bank the break with old-style development economics came with the appointment, by the right-wing Reagan administration, of the former president and CEO of Bank of America, Ted Clausen, as president in 1981; and the appointment, by the same government, of Anne Kreuger as chief economist, who in turn appointed Deepak Lal as her effective number two.

These two believed that the state is essentially predatory, because captured by coalitions of interest groups to extract rents from the private sector by suitable regulations, trade and fiscal policies, and, of course, by outright corruption. In this worldview, the process of economic development requires that the state should be active in providing the prerequisites of markets (private property rights, especially the rights of capital owners), but beyond that, should have a closely circumscribed role in the economy so as to minimize predation and let the private sector learn what it needs to learn in order to maximize profits for the owners. Kreuger and Lal set about eliminating economists in their part of the Bank who did not fully sign on, a process Lal described as 'cleaning the stables'.[1] Across the Bank, many people with industry expertise were fired, or else, to stay in Bank employment and retain US residency and gold-plated pension rights, they rebranded themselves as experts in environment or primary education or good governance.

Of course, economists on the intellectual frontiers write papers qualifying the broadly free-market consensus, and enjoy frisking the papers of others. But beyond the frontiers—among working economists, government officials, business people—the narrative favouring a global regime of 'free markets plus international law to protect the human rights of the owners of capital' has been dominant over the past four decades (dominant even after the East Asian/Latin American/Russian crash of 1997–8 and the North Atlantic crash and ensuing long slump starting in 2007, both of which you might have thought would prompt a leftward rethinking of a kind that did occur in the Hard Times after 1929). This narrative owes its power to the way it legitimizes the interests of Western international business by dressing them in the values of individualism, liberty, and universalism at the core of conservative thinking in Western culture, affirming them as values for all peoples.

Ayn Rand (a Russian who lived her adult life in the United States) was one of the philosophers of neoliberalism; her writings shaped the thinking of the early

[1] Lal was president of the Mont Pelerin Society in 2008–10.

neoliberal economists like Ludwig von Mises and Friedrich Hayek (co-founders of the Mont Pelerin Society in 1949, which ever since has functioned as a hub of the global neoliberal movement). She made explicit the class war subtext of neoliberal thinking, justifying the dominance of capital and capitalists. In a famous 1961 essay, 'America's Persecuted Minority: Big Business', she wrote:

> All the evils, abuses, and iniquities, popularly ascribed to businessmen and to capitalism, were not caused by an unregulated economy or by a free market, but by governmental intervention into the economy. (Frank, 2012: 206)

Ludwig von Mises was another who made explicit his championing of the dominance of capital and capitalists over the rest of the people. He wrote to congratulate Rand on her novel, *Atlas Shrugged*:

> You have the courage to tell the masses what no politician told them: you are inferior and all the improvements in your conditions which you simply take for granted you owe to the efforts of men who are better than you. (Frank, 2012: 147)

However, contrary to popular understanding, neoliberalism has not been a strictly laissez-faire ideology. It calls for strong state action to protect the rights of the owners of capital, not only within each nation but between nations—hence it calls for strong international law to protect the rights of internationally mobile capital. Leading lights in the movement—including the International Chamber of Commerce—have co-opted the language of human rights to their cause. They argue for a normative world order built on national and international institutions which protect the rights of individuals to trade and move capital wherever they wish: one rule for all in the world economy. So they have strongly supported organizations like the GATT and the WTO, or at least, idealized versions of these international organizations.

This mindset has deeply penetrated the mainstream of the economics profession. So it is no surprise that when some of these economists noticed—in the 1980s—the striking success of North-east Asian economies, they came up with explanations which largely overlooked the role of the state in identifying economic activities (including sectors) with increasing returns to scale and high potential for future growth, and giving those activities support not given to others (Wade, 2004).

The World Bank's book, *The East Asian Miracle*, published in 1993, is a relatively sophisticated case in point. It examined the causes of success in eight 'high-performing Asian economies': Japan, the three first-generation newly industrialized economies of South Korea, Taiwan, and Singapore, and three second-generation South-east Asian economies of Thailand, Malaysia, and Indonesia, plus Hong Kong.

The book argues that in these countries, the state made important contributions to their fast growth by ensuring the fundamentals: low inflation and competitive exchange rates; human capital; effective and secure financial systems; low price distortions; easy access to foreign technology; and low bias against agriculture. In other words, the states implemented effective 'horizontal' policies, applied across all sectors. But '*strategic interventions [policies to promote specific industries or even specific firms] generally did not work*' (World Bank 1993: 354, emphasis added; Wade 1996).

The book's take-away message:

> [O]penness to international trade, based on largely neutral incentives, was *the critical factor* in East Asia's rapid growth. (World Bank, 1993: 292, emphasis added)

This argument makes North-east Asia a powerful confirmation of the neoliberal answer to Adam Smith's question: how does market capitalism generate human welfare? The answer is market liberalization—and in a global context, the answer, as Martin Wolf said, is global integration, or moving towards 'the world as one economic country', having no more restrictions on economic flows or ownership claims across borders than US states have across theirs. It is an argument not just for free trade but also for free capital movement and perhaps even free labour mobility; conversely, it downplays the value of both national sovereignty and liberal democracy. The people may choose, but capital must decide. In short, the World Bank concluded that East Asia's rise was no mystery.

Mainstream economists not only missed the directive role of the state in East Asia; they also missed the key role of domestic demand—which would have led them to emphasize the relative equality of domestic income and wealth distribution and the state's role in bringing it about. Their blindness is the dark side of a major reason for the success of the neoclassical paradigm through the twentieth century. As Aba Lerner (1972) explained, 'An economic transaction [in this paradigm] is a *solved political problem*... Economics has gained the title Queen of the Social Sciences by choosing solved political problems as its domain' (emphasis added). He meant that the assumption of complete information and complete contracts embedded in the paradigm, meant that any dispute in a transaction (e.g. between employer and employee) can be adjudicated and enforced in courts, rather than by action by the parties themselves. There is no coercion, no opportunism, no overt power, no problem of income distribution. Hence the Queen of the Social Sciences can reign alone, ignoring insights from other disciplines such as political science, international relations, law, philosophy, sociology, psychology, history, or ecology (Bowles and Carlin, 2017).

2.3 Catch-Up?

I now discuss the 'big picture' of economic development performance over the past seven and more decades. There is important good news on the rise in life expectancy, fall in child mortality, and fall in frequency of extreme poverty (Deaton, 2013).

Here, however, I concentrate on the bad news about catch-up (Nayyar, 2013). A World Bank study (2013) found that of the 101 countries which in 1960 fell within its 'middle-income' range, only thirteen had become 'high income' by 2008, almost half a century later. Of these, four are peripheral Western Europe (Ireland, Portugal, Spain, and Greece). Four are miscellaneous (Equatorial Guinea, Israel, Mauritius, and Puerto Rico). Five are North-east Asia plus one (Japan, Taiwan, Hong Kong, South Korea, and Singapore). All have small populations, except Japan.

The point can be made even more starkly. How many non-Western countries have become developed in the past two centuries? If we stretch the categories of 'countries', 'non-Western', and 'developed' (developed to mean, a home-grown industrialization in capital- and technology-intensive sectors), we reach maybe seven: in rough chronological order, Japan and Russia in the late nineteenth century; Taiwan, South Korea, Hong Kong, Singapore, and Israel in the second half of the twentieth century. All but the first two have very small populations.

Of course, mainland China also looks on course to enter this group within a few decades, bringing what is now the biggest population in the world. In just three years, 2011–13, China used as much cement as the United States did in the whole of the twentieth century. China's Made in China 2025 programme calls for global leadership, or at least excellence, by 2025, in sectors including artificial intelligence, 5G telecoms, the internet of things, self-driving cars, and battery technology.

But note two qualifications. First, China's progress up the value-added ladder has relied heavily on foreign technologies and intellectual property, particularly American. The Trump government is trying, as of 2018, to wage a trade war on China with the aim of slowing its ability to compete with US companies in high-tech sectors. China is particularly vulnerable to cut-offs in US semiconductors, semiconductor equipment, and aerospace.

Second, China remains a poor country overall. While growing fast, its average income, around US$17,000 in PPP terms (2017), is still only around 28 per cent of the United States', which is about the same as the world average income. It comes in at 76 in the country rankings, compared to the United States at 11.[2] (But note that the margin of error or uncertainty about PPP exchange rate numbers is plus or minus 25 per cent, according to Angus Deaton and Alan Heston (2010), implying that China's per-capita income in international dollars is (2017) somewhere between 21 and 35 per cent of the US per capita income.) If we instead use lagged market exchange rates, China's average income is only around 15 per cent of the United States'. Comparing countries' incomes at market exchange rates gives a more accurate indication of one country's ability to purchase goods and services in others, and is thus (when combined with total GDP) a better indicator

[2] These are the World Bank rankings. The CIA puts (2017) China at 83, United States at 13, with more or less the same average income figures. Wikipedia, 'List of countries by GDP (PPP) per capita', accessed 30 September 2018.

of relative overall power. Militarily, too, China is far behind the United States, though expanding fast from a low base. The bottom line is that 'China as emerging super-power' is an exaggeration, but it may well join the current set of 'great powers' within the next two decades.

China is one big qualification to the 'lack of catch-up' story. Another qualification is that the global growth pattern apparently changed in the early 2000s. Emerging and developing countries (EDEs, to use IMF terminology) began to grow fast enough to converge upward towards the income levels of advanced countries. Led by the newly designated BRICS (Brazil, Russia, India, China, and South Africa), they were heralded as the locomotives of the world economy, the first time in over two centuries that locations outside Western Europe, North America, and Japan had led global growth. Buoyed by optimism and neoliberal conviction, EDEs went all out to integrate further into the world economy, helped by policies, aid, and urgings from advanced countries.

They liberalized their capital accounts, and facilitated foreign financial organizations' entry to their domestic market, and residents' borrowing and investing abroad. They scrambled to attract into their territories the production of 'tasks' or 'intermediate' goods and services (as distinct from production of final goods and services), to fit within the new international division of labour where global value chains (GVCs) have substantially replaced both arms-length market transactions and transfers within vertically integrated multinational corporations (MNCs) in cross-border trade.

EDE states were relaxed about protecting their economies against global boom–bust cycles—for Western experts declared it the era of the Great Moderation, with boom–bust cycles a thing of the past. Firms stopped hedging against foreign exchange risk when they borrowed abroad, and governments stopped making them do so. Why spend money on hedging when there's no risk?

Policymakers and policy analysts generally assumed that private governance by Western big firms in GVCs was substituting for public governance in the host developing countries. The best role for the state in these conditions was a 'light-touch regulatory state' regulating (but not much restricting) market competition. The state should regulate but not shape the exogenous forces of globalization and technology. The developmental state—the type that flourished earlier in capitalist East Asia (flourished according to some commentators, though, as noted, few proper economists)—is obsolete in these highly globalized and financialized conditions.

Then came the Great Crash of 2007–9 in North Atlantic countries, led by the United States, followed by the Long Recession. After a lag of several years, EDE growth converged downwards towards the very low growth rates of advanced countries.

Recovery from the Great Crash has been unusually slow. In the 100 worst financial crashes in advanced countries over the past century, it took an average of seven years to regain pre-crisis average income. This one took nine to ten years on average (to 2016–17) and will take considerably longer in some places, like the southern European Mediterranean (Akyüz, 2017).

By 2017, the United States had resolved the financial crisis but not the economic crisis, which continues to generate political upheavals (the lack of economic resolution, including the lack of restraint on surging income and wealth concentration at the top, helped to usher in the governance disaster known as Trump). The eurozone has not even resolved the financial crisis, let alone the economic crisis. We see the primitive spectacle of the European Central Bank, the EMU bail-out fund, and the International Monetary Fund—with cooperation from the Bank of Greece—lashing out at the Greek elected government that has refused to do all that it is told. The object is to ensure that:

(a) the interests of creditors (mostly North-western European and American) are protected at all costs;
(b) neither the Greek nor any other government—especially a Left one—can expect a debt write-down; and
(c) the wishes of multilateral organizations (reflecting the wishes of the major governments, like Germany, and their corporate backers) prevail over the agenda of the weaker semi-sovereign states.

The Crash and Long Recession should have shaken confidence in the long dominant neoliberal ideas about markets and states, as in the West after the 1929 crash and Great Depression. Instead, rethinking has occurred only at the margins, and the neoliberal ideal of (a) self-adjusting markets supported by a small, regulatory state, (b) maximum integration of national economies into the international economy, and (c) maximum legal protection of the human rights of the owners of capital, remains ascendant in the West, in the international governance organizations which advanced countries control (like the OECD, World Bank, and IMF), and even in much of the economic policy community in many middle-income countries (Wade, 2017).

I now describe the gravitational forces operating to reproduce the core–periphery structure of the world economy, or more specifically, to maintain the 'middle-income trap' or 'glass ceiling'. These forces help to sustain the long-term growth pattern of divergence or very slow convergence of middle-income countries, Eastern China being the obvious escapee (Fischer, 2015). Space limits mean that I concentrate not on long-run causes but only on those that have been particularly important in recent decades.

2.4 Global Value Chains (GVCs) Now Structure Production and Trade

It is clear that in today's world economy only a few really large economies have even the possibility of 'doing a Japan, Taiwan, or Korea'—building up a phalanx of mostly nationally owned modern industries with deep supply chains within the domestic economy, able to produce whole products or almost whole products competitively enough to sell in Western markets or as first-tier suppliers to Western or Japanese MNCs. High entry barriers in the face of existing MNC dominance, and neoclassically inspired trade and investment rules, make such a project unviable for most.

The world economy has, since the late 1980s, become dominated by hierarchical GVCs, in which lead firms fragment production of final products into parts and components, and outsource the various sub-sections or stages to geographically dispersed producers and sub-producers. Around 80 per cent of global trade now flows through GVCs led by multinational corporations (UNCTAD, 2013).

From the perspective of neoliberal economics, the rise of GVCs is a blessing for EDEs, because it permits their producers low-cost entry into international production and trade, as compared to producing whole products. Millberg and Winkler remark, critically, 'the goal of industrial upgrading within GVCs has become nearly synonymous with economic development itself' (2013: 238).

But participation in manufacturing GVCs may well provide limited opportunities to develop production capabilities, because of the forces making for specialization in repetitive tasks such as assembling components made elsewhere, which prevent movement into higher value-added segments like design, R&D, and supply-chain management. Participation also forces subordinate governments to have:

- free or almost free trade;
- secure property rights (including 'investor-against-state' laws which enable a foreign investor to take a host government to an international arbitration panel if the government introduces measures which may hurt the foreign investor's future profits, including actions to protect public health, such as restrictions on cigarette advertising); and
- tolerance for high concentrations of market power in the hands of lead companies located elsewhere (Mayer and Philips, 2017).

The key point is that the new phase of globalization characterized by GVCs (since the late 1980s) tips the balance of power in the world economy firmly in favour of MNCs, because if one host government does not agree to their conditions, or if labour costs in one country rise too high, the firm can readily shift production elsewhere. Thomas Palley (2018) describes the economic theory of this phase of globalization as 'barge economics', from the remark by Jack Welch, former CEO of General Electric, that business would like to put 'every plant you own on a barge', so that it could move its factories from place to place according to changes in cost conditions. Barge economics is what makes it so difficult for producers in low-wage countries and their governments to upgrade in GVCs, because in these circumstances power lies with the business owners—who can invite, or not invite, particular subordinate producers to rise in their value chains, and if the producers press for better conditions, the owners can always 'float the barge' elsewhere.

It is often said, wrongly, that the rise of GVCs has occurred autonomously from the state, due mainly to technological change cutting the cost of moving information and materials. This ignores the active role of Western states in promoting the rise of GVCs—especially Western states sailing under the neoliberal banner of self-adjusting markets and requiring host governments' policy compliance with this ideology as a condition of access to their high-income markets.

The US government had negotiated some twenty free-trade agreements (FTAs) by 2015; the EU is part of thirty FTAs; Japan of fourteen (Mayer and Phillips, 2017). But these are not 'free-trade' agreements. They contain rules of origin, such that a high proportion of the value added in products outsourced to lower-cost countries must come from the lead country—which makes for regional production chains. And they often contain tariff escalation clauses, such that if an EDE starts to produce higher value-added products within a chain, its exports face higher tariffs in the lead country—which keeps the high value-added activities in the lead country, protecting the basic core–periphery structure of the world economy.[3]

2.5 Rising Dependence on Capital-Goods Imports and on Highly Monopolized Patentable Knowledge

EDEs depend heavily, almost by definition, on imported capital goods, reflecting low domestic technological innovation capacity. This dependence has intensified since the 1980s with the ICT revolution. ICT and other leading technologies of the current era are more difficult to copy, to reverse engineer, than were the mechanical technologies of the post-Second-World-War decades. So the world technological frontier has moved further out of reach for most developing countries than it was in earlier decades. This is particularly so because modern capitalism is more knowledge intensive than earlier, and more of that knowledge is better protected by patents—especially since 1994 with the formation of the WTO and its Agreement on Trade-Related Aspects of Intellectual Property Rights (TRIPS), and many later so-called free-trade agreements.

Note the paradox (Pagano, 2014). Knowledge is a non-rivalrous good, in the sense that its use by one user does not reduce its availability to others, unlike a piece of physical capital. So the marginal cost of using knowledge in a developing

[3] Engel and Tagliari (2017) have a chapter in the 'Global Value Chain Development Report 2017' which paints a rosy picture of the development pay-offs from integration into GVCs, saying little about downsides.

country which is produced elsewhere, should be close to zero—because the original knowledge is not reduced by its being used again, in contrast to all material inputs (machinery, labour, etc.) So increased knowledge intensity of production should boost production around the world, including by small firms. It should therefore promote catch-up by developing countries, making it easy for them to combine modern knowledge with low-cost labour and other inputs.

The paradox of modern capitalism is that strong intellectual property rights (IPR) regimes in developed countries have enabled wholesale privatization of knowledge and the creation of knowledge monopolies in the hands of big, mostly Western-based, global firms. Private property in knowledge has global effects, because it prevents others using that knowledge anywhere in the world where the property rights can be enforced—even though others using the knowledge do not curb the knowledge usable by the first user. In contrast, private property in tangibles—machinery, land—has local effects that do not prevent use by others elsewhere of a similar machine or similar land. So knowledge monopolies are driving intense concentration of corporate wealth and power—and holding back global income catch-up, making the Rise of the Rest an exaggeration (Pagano, 2014).

Indeed, to refer to developed economies as 'free-market economies' is even more misleading today than in the 1960s, when it was already substantially misleading (as shown by J. K. Galbraith (1967), *The New Industrial State*). Developed economies have become, strangely enough, 'closed-knowledge' economies, even though they are highly integrated into global trade, finance, and investment. Science has also moved from 'open' towards 'closed'—closed behind patent and copyright protection. Closed-science and closed-knowledge economies make for a more unequal kind of capitalism very different from the usual understanding of modern capitalism as 'free-market capitalism'.

The fundamental change in the character of modern capitalism since the 1990s tends to constrain catch-up by developing countries, not to mention the prospects for 'decent work' in developed countries. The change is captured by several measures:

(1) *Intangible assets now dominate tangible assets in corporate balance sheets.* In 1982, about 62 per cent of the total assets of the S&P 500 firms based in the United States were tangibles (buildings, machines), leaving intangibles at 38 per cent (patents, copyright, trademarks). By 1999, intangibles had jumped to 84 per cent of total assets, leaving tangibles at 16 per cent (Pagano, 2017).

(2) *The distribution of the global total of patents in each of several sectors is very unequal between countries.* Evidence on the distribution of global patents comes from a study of the between-country distribution of the total patents in five key growth sectors: electrical engineering, chemistry and pharmaceuticals, mechanical engineering, instruments, and process engineering.

In 1980 the Gini coefficient of distribution between countries of patents in each of these sectors varied between 0.82 and 0.85. By 2015, the five sectors all had roughly the same—and much higher—Gini coefficients of just under 0.95. So companies headquartered in a tiny number of the world's 180-plus countries hold just about all the patents in these key sectors for economic development.[4]

(3) *Global profits in each of many sectors are highly concentrated in a tiny number of countries.* Global profits are also highly concentrated in a few countries (Starrs, 2014). *Forbes Global 2000*, an annual list of the world's biggest 2,000 publicly traded companies (by assets, market value, profits, and sales) gives the share of different countries (the share of companies headquartered in different countries) in total global profits in each of twenty-five sectors, such as heavy machinery, electronics, aerospace, banking, health care equipment and services, and media. In 2013 US companies had the biggest share of global profits in eighteen sectors, 72 per cent of the total; and between 2007 and 2013 their profit share increased in ten sectors, including those classed as the technologically most sophisticated.[5]

(4) *China.* The only developing country with more than a toehold in the global distribution of profits is China, which in 2013 ranked in the top five countries by profit share in twelve of the twenty-five sectors (Starrs, 2014). But other data show how far behind China is. In personal computers, for example, China became the world's biggest market in 2011, overtaking the United States. But Chinese companies' share of profits in computer hardware and software amounted to only 2 per cent, compared to the United States' 72 per cent. In autos, China became the world's biggest auto market in 2009; but the profit share of Chinese companies in the auto, truck, and parts sector was only 5 per cent, while the combined share of the United States, Japan, and Germany was over 50 per cent. In electronics, China has been the biggest exporter since 2004, but its profit share of the exports is 3 per cent, compared to Taiwan's 25 per cent and the United States' 33 per cent. Or take China's role in innovation, proxied by triadic patents (registered with the European Patent Office, Japan Patent Office, and US Patent and Trademark Office). In 2010, US and Japanese companies held about 60 per cent of the world's triadic patents; Chinese companies, 1.8 per cent.

[4] Google, Amazon, Apple, Facebook, and Microsoft combined applied for 52,000 patents between 2009 and early 2017. They are diversifying far beyond their original sector. Amazon has applied for a patent on devices which identify people according to blood flow and heart rate. Apple has applied for a patent within autonomous vehicle technology, for 'collision avoidance of arbitrary polygonal obstacles' (CBInsights, 2017).

[5] The knowledge rents earned by the ICT giants are measured and explained in Cooper (2016).

2.6 Finance is in the Driving Seat of the World Economy and Exposes EDEs to Volatile Growth

The financial sector has acquired such power in advanced countries that UNCTAD refers to the current era as 'finance-driven globalization' (to which we might add 'barge-driven globalization' and 'knowledge-monopoly globalization'). In most respects the Western financial system is even more powerful than before 2008. While the big banks are, on average, holding more capital than before the crisis,[6] they remain heavily indebted and interconnected, and because of a wave of mergers during the last crisis the banking industry as a whole is even more concentrated than before. They—and everyone else—know that in the event of another 2008-style panic they would probably be bailed out, as before. This confidence gives them even more power.

Robert Rubin, US Treasury Secretary in the Democrat-led government of Bill Clinton (and before that, twenty-six years in Goldman Sachs), celebrates this development. As Treasury Secretary he and his deputy Larry Summers engineered the repeal of the Glass–Steagall Act (1933), which had separated investment banking and retail banking, and strongly and successfully opposed measures to regulate the derivatives industry (which became an engine of the 2008 crash). David Rothkopf, author of *Power, Inc.* (2012), interviewed Rubin for the book, well after the crash, and asked whether he thought that having a sector of big banks 'too big to fail' was a problem that should be fixed. Rubin replied:

> No, don't you see? Too big to fail isn't a problem with the system. It *is* the system. You can't be a competitive financial institution serving global corporations of scale without having a certain scale yourself. The bigger multinationals get, the bigger financial institutions will have to get. (quoted in Sharpe, 2012)

In other words, 'the system' requires big banks to be propped up regardless of their performance. As Mike Sharpe says, reviewing Rothkopf's book, 'This is socialism for the rich, free enterprise for everyone else.' After Rubin left government service he worked part time for Citigroup for ten years, and received US$126 million in remuneration (Wikipedia, 2018).

The dominance of finance causes the management of for-profit companies to give priority to short-term success targets such as profits, dividends, and share prices; so it is these indicators—not ones measuring customer experience or even long-run growth—that weigh heavily in senior executive compensation packages.

[6] The chair of the US Federal Deposit Insurance Corporation from 2006 to 2011, Sheila Blair (2018), said:

> US politicians, with some help from regulators, are trying to weaken these rules [designed to constrain excessive borrowing by 'systemic' financial organizations], setting a dangerous global precedence. Both Republicans and Democrats supported legislation giving the three largest US custody banks an average of a 20 per cent reduction to their leverage ratios.

The effects of financial dominance in service industries are the subject of a 2017 front-page column in *The New York Times (International)*:

> Relentless pressure on corporate America is creating an increasingly Dickensian experience for many consumers as companies focus on maximizing profit. [According to a veteran public relations executive], 'There's always been pressure from Wall Street. But I've been watching this for 30 years, and it's never been as intense as it is today.' Rich bonus packages for top executives are now largely tied to short-term income targets and fatter profit margins instead of customer service. (*New York Times (International)*, 2017)

The *New York Times* titles this column, 'Discomfort of Air Travel Starts with Wall Street'. It relates how the prevailing corporate mindset hit a low point when airline staff violently dragged an unlucky and unwilling passenger—chosen at random—off an overbooked United Airlines flight in Chicago in April 2017. But Wall Street loves the result: United Airlines' stock sold for US $25 per share in 2012; today it sells for US$80 per share. United's profit margins are up from 3.7 per cent to 13.6 per cent over the same period. The average profit margin for the US airline industry rose from 5.2 per cent to 16.3 per cent over this period.

International financial markets are organized hierarchically. New York and London are the top financial centres, and the United States, issuer of the top currency, enjoys great privilege and power over countries with lower-ranked currencies (Kaltenbrunner and Painceira, 2018). US monetary conditions and monetary policy affect monetary conditions around the world, thanks to the US dollar being the most liquid international store of value and the most widely used unit of account.

Southern countries, on the other hand, face monetary subordination: they are unable to borrow internationally in their domestic currency, they are under strong pressure to maintain completely open capital accounts, and they depend on short-term portfolio inflows of finance to cover external deficits and a lot of domestic investment. The low position of their currencies in the international currency hierarchy means that they must offer higher interest rates or profitable exchange rate movements in order to attract foreign capital and prevent capital flight. A rising portion of 'investment' tends to be financial investments, crowding out 'real' investments to raise production capabilities.

The result: the high interest rates lower domestic capital accumulation and economic growth; and the volatility of capital flows and exchange rates makes their economic growth subject to high levels of external vulnerability, which recurrently tips into debt crises, further subordinating them in the international 'real' and 'financial' economy. No surprise if they remain in the 'middle-income trap'.

To spell out the mechanism in more detail: EDEs' domestic asset and credit markets are now heavily populated with foreign investors and financial organizations (raising the economy's external liabilities), thanks to their governments (complying with Western wishes) putting few regulations and restrictions on:

(a) foreign capital inflows and outflows;
(b) foreign financial establishments in their territory; and
(c) residents' access to foreign financial markets as borrowers and investors.

Also, their own non-financial corporations have borrowed heavily in international financial markets, with most repayments in US dollars, further raising the economy's external liabilities. The Institute of International Finance calculates that corporate debt in foreign currencies is now at the highest level ever. Turkey is especially exposed. Its companies borrowed US dollars to fund factories, shopping malls, and the Istanbul skyscrapers; and now, as the lira plunges, a growing number of companies are declaring that they cannot repay their (foreign) loans. This has the potential to spread far and wide. American investors own nearly 25 per cent of outstanding Turkish bonds and more than half of publicly traded Turkish stocks (Thomas, 2018).

These trends expose EDEs to boom–bust cycles in the major advanced countries, the United States above all (Akyüz, 2017)—boom–bust cycles driven by rising income and wealth concentration at the top in the United States, the United Kingdom, and several other major advanced countries, and now also China. In the advanced countries, most of the population has been on stagnant incomes even as average productivity rises, and the wage share of national income has fallen dramatically. Most of the gain in income from economic growth accrues to people at the top, who get much of their income from returns to capital while they sleep.

These economies therefore face a demand gap, a shortfall of demand relative to supply potential. To boost demand even as income concentration at the top is high, many governments, notably the Anglo ones, have adopted a debt-led growth model. They support arrangements which facilitate the ability of people with modest incomes to borrow in order to spend—and close the demand gap with borrowed finance. This can generate a credit and asset boom (property, stocks), which can produce moderate or even fast growth—for a while. But meantime people's ability to repay debt out of income (as distinct from the putative value of their asset, when house prices are rising) tends to fall, the economy becomes more financially fragile because dependent on continued rises in asset values, and the fragility can easily tip into financial instability and crisis. The Roman playwright Plautus captured the point when he had one of his characters declare (around 300 BCE), 'I am a rich man—until I have to repay my creditors.'

In the United States this debt-led mechanism produced a series of booms and busts: savings-and-loan cycle in the 1980s, dot.com cycle in 1990s, sub-prime cycle in the 2000s, and the 'quantitative easing' (QE) cycle since 2008. All but the last (so far) ended in financial crisis with far-reaching economic and political damage.

The United States now relies heavily on monetary policy to regulate economic activity, because fiscal policy is either regressive (tax cuts for the rich) or politically paralyzed. The US central bank, the Federal Reserve, makes its decisions to serve the US economy, with little regard for effects on the rest of the world. (In 1971 US Treasury Secretary John Connelly informed his astonished counterparts at a G-10 meeting in Rome, 'The dollar is our currency but it's your problem.') When US central bank interest rates are very low, as all through the 2000s to date, finance and financial establishments tend to head—without restrictions—to EDEs (like Turkey), where interest rates and other returns are higher: to their markets for equities, bonds, property, and credit. When US rates go up and/or US growth goes up, the trend reverses (as in 2017–18). The inflows and outflows can have destabilizing effects on the exchange rate, investment, productivity growth, and long-term GDP growth of EDEs.

US monetary policy swings can be expected to be large into the future, with big spillover effects in the rest of the world, as long as monetary policy continues to be the United States' main stabilization tool and the US dollar remains the main international currency. And as of 2017–18, shadow financial markets in the United States are frothing, repeating the run-up to the 2007–8 crash as regulators flout the Dodd–Frank Act (passed after the crash to make a repeat crisis less likely) and the US Congress has partially repealed the Act.

Note in passing that other large advanced countries, notably Germany and Austria, have adopted an export-led growth model, which depends on selling into debt-led countries. The two models are complementary and both are fragile, which underlines Germany and Austria's irresponsibility in urging deficit countries of the European Union, notably Greece, to 'be like us' and become net exporters (Goda and Sanchez, 2017).

To understand better the mechanism producing EDE vulnerability we need to disaggregate EDEs' integration into the world financial system by distinguishing different types of assets (Akyüz, 2017). First, *foreign exchange reserves*. As they experienced—or saw others experience—financial crashes, EDEs increased their foreign exchange reserves many times over, mostly in low-yielding reserve assets issued by advanced countries, especially the US Treasury. As of 2014, about two-thirds of total EDE exchange reserves were held either by China or by the fuel exporters. The other third was mostly borrowed, and matched by an increase in EDE external liabilities. So their attempt to self-insure gives them a lot less protection than the exchange reserve figures suggest.

Second, *foreign direct investment* accounts for a large share of the external liabilities of EDEs. Contrary to common belief (which says that FDI + GVCs is the magic formula for EDE economic development), the large stock of FDI in EDEs substantially raises their vulnerability. A large part of total FDI in EDEs since 2000 is in service sectors, with low exports; and even in manufacturing, the import content of FDI manufactured exports is high. Typically, the export earnings of

FDI operations in EDEs do not cover both their imports and their income transfers (in the form of profits, royalties, licence fees, and interest paid on loans from the parent company). This means that, typically, FDI makes a negative contribution to the balance of payments.

At the same time, host governments face more difficulties than before in putting performance conditions on FDI operations or in other ways extracting positive spillovers (e.g. technological), because (a) the companies tend to be footloose ('barge economics'), (b) they have strong intellectual property protection, which limits learning by residents, and (c) governments are constrained in extracting positive spillovers by free trade agreements or bilateral investment treaties.

Third, *bonds*. Many EDEs have opened the door wide to foreign buyers of sovereign bonds issued in local currency. This means the bonds are repaid in local currency, so foreign buyers take the exchange rate risk, which should avoid the currency mismatches that triggered many financial crises in Asia and Latin America in the 1990s and early 2000s. But Yilmaz Akyüz reports that there is no comprehensive data on non-resident holdings of local currency bonds—which means that the sovereign debt of many EDEs is probably underestimated, more internationalized than reported, and more is held by—fickle, flighty—private entities than by official bodies (like the World Bank). But note that China and India wisely continue to restrict non-resident purchase of domestic bonds.

2.7 Conclusion

Six bottom-line points. First, EDEs as a category have acted in line with consensus advice in the Western-dominated international development community to integrate the national economy to a high degree into the international economy, including in finance and investment. In thus exposing their growth to shocks in the international economy, they make it prone to zoom up and down like a rollercoaster.

Stephen Broadberry and John Wallis (2016) argue that the 'great escape upwards' of Western countries during the nineteenth and twentieth centuries—the emergence of a Western core and non-Western lagging periphery tied to the core—reflects a long-term pattern of fairly stable and moderate growth in the core and more volatile growth in the periphery, meaning fairly fast expansion followed by prolonged shrinkage. They elaborate what they call 'shrink theory' as distinct from 'growth theory'.

Recent research shows how persistent long-run dollar cycles affect economic development in EDEs. Dollar appreciation (as during 1981–5, 1995–2002, 2008–9, and 2012–15, when the data set ends) is associated with (a) fall in commodity prices, (b) fall in EDEs' GDP growth, and (c) rise in the number of EDEs experiencing external crises (due to large foreign currency debt and sharp exchange rate depreciations) (Druck et al., 2015; Chow et al., 2015).

The second bottom-line point is that the institutional structure of the international economy into which EDEs integrate contains a basic impediment to their development: from the mid-1940s beginning of the Bretton Woods architecture till today, the mechanism for curbing countries' external deficits and surpluses puts all the adjustment pressure on deficit countries to reduce their deficits, and no symmetrical pressure on surplus countries to reduce their surpluses (think Germany). Yet developing countries undertaking heavy investment in infrastructure and production capacity should be able to run sizeable deficits safely, and this would be more feasible if surplus countries ran smaller surpluses.

Third, the combination of global value chains, knowledge monopoly, and financialization makes for slow or no long-run convergence upwards of the majority of EDEs towards the average income and productivity of advanced countries: in fact, it makes for the continuation of the core–periphery structure of the world economy, with persisting large gaps in average income and productivity. Again, China is the great exception, thanks partly to it having being a poor pupil of the Washington Consensus.

Fourth, the core—the West—depends heavily on rental income accruing from ownership of financial assets, patents, brands, and copyrights on software, movies and the like. Western, especially American, firms occupy the commanding heights of GVCs; and within these commanding heights the top positions are occupied by a small number of financial firms, which control the 'real economy' firms through shareholdings and debts, and which drive each GVC towards the goal of shareholder (not stakeholder) value maximization, generating unpaid-for costs for the living planet and for the insecure workforce in EDEs (an example is Foxconn) (Vitali and Battiston, 2014). In this structure producers in low-income countries (such as Bangladesh and Cambodia in Asia) can certainly get a foothold in entry-level industries like textiles as costs rise in China; but rising into higher value-added activities, even within textiles, is much more difficult.

Fifth point: Neoclassical economics is a misleading guide to development policy. It thinks in terms of curves, not step changes. And it makes no distinction between activities (or sectors) according to their growth potential—it treats each unit of GDP as having equal potential for future growth. Yet the governments of virtually all the successful catch-up countries recognized that they had to nurture 'superior' or 'star' economic activities by means of trade protection, subsidies, and regulations, buffering them from—but not insulating them from—competitive pressures.

Erik Reinert (1994) calls this the 'List-cum-Smith strategy' (Friedrich List with Adam Smith). The British government followed it when it closed down the prosperous woollen cloth industry in its colony of Ireland starting in 1699, and when it closed down the fledgling cotton textile industry in its colony of India starting in 1814. And it helps to understand why the English economist David Ricardo, in the early nineteenth century, was happy to provide—and generations of economists were happy to believe—a theory of comparative advantage which apparently demonstrated scientifically that England should specialize in textiles and Portugal should specialize in wine. This at a time when wine making was technologically stagnant and textiles was a prime site of mechanical and organizational innovation.

Friedrich List summarized the English strategy for economic dominance: 'The principle, sell manufacturers, buy raw material, was during centuries the English substitute for an economic theory' (1844: 12). But as just noted, the English Ricardo did provide the justifying theory purporting to show that England's specialization in textiles and Portugal's in wine was in their mutual interest, and the theory has been taught as the bedrock of neoclassical economics ever since.

Finally, for an EDE to escape the periphery and move into the core of the world economy is in some ways even more difficult now than in the past. The rise of the North-east Asian economies has shrunk the room to industrialize for late-late industrializers in Africa or re-industrializers in Latin America. At the same time, the room for trade management and industrial policy has been shrunk by (a) more liberal trade rules and (b) deregulated capital markets across borders. Digital innovation and robotization will accelerate productivity growth, while generating massive technological unemployment or employment in precarious jobs as distinct from 'middle-class' jobs. And all this in a more carbon-constrained world facing major disruption in fossil-fuelled capitalism. This puts a premium on national governments creating effective 'direction-setting' agencies, centrally placed in the state and with top-level political commitment, to navigate through the complexities.[7]

References

Akyuz, Yilmaz (2017) *Playing with Fire: Deepened Financial Integration and Changing Vulnerabilities of the Global South.* Oxford: Oxford University Press.

Blair, S. (2018) 'The US Must Hold Firm on Bank Capital Rules.' *Financial Times*, 2 October.

Broadberry, Stephan and John Wallis (2016) 'Shrink Theory: The Nature of Long-run and Short-run Economic Performance.' Available at http://www.econweb.umd.edu/~davis/eventpapers/WallisShrinkTheory.pdf.

[7] Wade (2004) contains several chapters outlining the organization and politics of Taiwan's several steering agencies.

Bowles, S. and W. Carlin (2017) 'The New Paradigm for the Introductory Course in Economics.' VOX, 7 September, http://voxeu.org/article/new-paradigm-introductory-course-economics.

CBInsights (2017) 'The 2017 Global CVC Report.' New York: CBInsights.

Chow, J. T. et al. (2015) 'Spillovers from Dollar Appreciation', IMF Oikuct Discussion Paper No. 15/02. Washington, DC: International Monetary Fund.

Cooper, M. (2016) 'Overcharged and Underserved: How a Tight Oligopoly on Steroids Undermines Competition and Harms Consumers in Digital Communications Markets.' Roosevelt Institute Working Paper. Available at: http://rooseveltinstitute.org/wp-content/uploads/2017/02/Overcharged-and-Underserved.pdf.

Deaton, A. (2013) *The Great Escape: Health, Wealth, and the Origins of Inequality*. Princeton, NJ: Princeton University Press.

Deaton, A. and A. Heston (2010) 'Understanding PPPs and PPP-national Accounts', *American Economic Journal: Macroeconomics* 2(4): 1–35.

Druck, P. F. et al. (2015) 'Collateral Damage: Dollar Strength and Emerging Markets' Growth.' IMF Working Paper No. 15/179. Washington, DC: International Monetary Fund.

Engel, J. and D. Tagliari (2017) 'Measuring and Analysing the Impact of GVCs on Economic Development', in World Bank, WTO, OECD, 2017, *Global Value Chain Development Report*, ch. 5.

Fischer, A. (2015) 'The End of Peripheries? On the Enduring Relevance of Structuralism for Understanding Contemporary Global Development', *Development and Change* 46(3): 700–32.

Frank, T. (2012) *Pity the Billionaire*. London: Harvill Secker.

Galbraith, J. K. (1967) *The New Industrial State*. Princeton, NY: Princeton University Press.

Goda, Thomas and Santiago Sanchez (2017) 'Market and Disposable Top Income Shares Adjusted by National Accounts Data', Working Paper No. 1711, Post Keynesian Economics Society.

Kaltenbrunner, A. and J. P. Painceira (2018) 'Subordinated Financial Integration and Financialisaton in Emerging Capitalist Economies: The Brazilian Experience', *New Political Economy* 23(3): 290–313.

Lerner, A. (1972) 'The Economics and Politics of Consumer Sovereignty', *American Economic Review* 62 (2): 258–66.

List, F. (1844) *The National System of Political Economy*. New York: Augustus Kelley.

Lucas, R. (2004) 'The Industrial Revolution—Past and Future.' 2003 Annual Report Essay, Federal Reserve Bank Minneapolis, May.

Mayer, F. and Nicola Philips (2017) 'Outsourcing Governance: States and the Politics of a Global Value Chain World', *New Political Economy* 22(2): 134–52.

Millberg, W. and D. Winkler (2013) *Outsourcing Economics: Global Value Chains in Capitalist Development*. Cambridge: Cambridge University Press.

Nayyar, D. (2013) *Catch Up: Developing Countries in the World Economy*. Oxford: Oxford University Press.

New York Times (International) (2017) 'Discomfort of Air Travel Starts with Wall Street', 30 May, p. 1.

Pagano, U. (2014) 'The Crisis of Intellectual Monopoly Capitalism', *Cambridge Journal of Economics* 38(6): 1409–29.

Pagano U. and M. Rossi (2017) 'The Knowledge Economy, the Crash and the Depression', in D. Tyfield et al. (eds) *Routledge Handbook of the Political Economy of Science*. London: Routledge.

Palley, T. (2018) 'Globalization Checkmated: Political and Geopolitical Contradictions Coming Home to Roost.' PERI Working Paper Series No. 466. Amherst: University of Massachusetts.

Reinert, E. (1994) 'Catching up from way behind: A Third World Perspective on First World History', in J. Fagerberg, B. Verspagen, and N. Tunzelman (eds) *The Dynamics of Technology, Trade and Growth*. Cheltenham: Edward Elgar.

Rothkopf, D. (2012) *Power, Inc.: The Epic Rivalry between Big Business and Government—and the Reckoning That Lies Ahead.* New York: Farrar, Straus and Giroux.

Sharpe, M. (2012) 'The corporation and the state against the public', *Challenge* (May–June): 137–41.

Slobodian, Q. (2018) *Globalists: The End of Empire and the Birth of Neoliberalism*. Cambridge, MA: Harvard University Press.

Starrs, S. (2014) 'The Chimera of Global Convergence', *New Left Review* 87 (May–June): 81–96.

Thomas, L. (2018) 'Turkey's Financial Crisis Surprised Many. Except This Analyst', *New York Times,* 11 August.

Tooze, A. (2008) 'Beyond the Crash', *Guardian*, 29 July.

Uchitelle, L. (2002) 'Challenging the Dogmas of Free Trade', *New York Times*, 9 February.

UNCTAD (2013) *Trade and Development Report*. Geneva: UNCTAD.

Vitali S. and S. Battiston (2014) 'The Community Structure of the Global Corporate Network', PLoS One 9(8): e104655. Available at https://www.ncbi.nlm.nih.gov/pmc/articles/PMC4134229/.

Wade, R. (1996) 'Japan, the World Bank, and the Art of Paradigm Maintenance: The East Asian Miracle in Political Perspective', *New Left Review* 217(May/June).

Wade, R. (2004 [1990]) *Governing the Market: Economic Theory and the Role of Government in East Asia's Industrialization*. Princeton, NJ: Princeton University Press.

Wade, R. (2017) 'Global Growth, Inequality, and Poverty: The Globalization Argument and the 'Political' Science of Economics' in John Ravenhill (ed.) *Global Political Economy*. Oxford: Oxford University Press, pp. 319–35.

Wikipedia, 'Robert Rubin'. Available at: https://en.wikipedia.org/wiki/Robert_Rubin.

Wolf, M. (2004) *Why Globalization Works*. New Haven, CT: Yale University Press.

World Bank (1993) *The East Asian Miracle*. Washington, DC: World Bank.

World Bank (2013) *China 2030: Building a Modern, Harmonious, and Creative Society*. Washington, DC: World Bank.

3

Learning from East Asia

Catch-up and the Making of China's Developmental State

Daniel Poon and Richard Kozul-Wright

3.1 Introduction

As China celebrates its fortieth year since the start of its reform period, a strong backlash against globalization has gained traction. China, as the pre-eminent economic success story of the last four decades, is inevitably caught up in this backlash. Western policymakers, in particular, having held up China as an example of what happens when policymakers embrace 'an open liberal economy' and attract foreign investment (Blair, 2005) now brand it a 'strategic competitor' that has abused the rules of that same open liberal economy and distorted global markets (USTR, 2018).

This is not, however, the first time that a successful late industrializer has gone from economic paragon to political pariah. After four decades of rapid and sustained growth from the end of the Second World War, Western attitudes towards Japan turned from extoling its virtues on the right side of the Cold War political divide to seeing it as a model of unfair competition exploiting a dangerous combination of protectionist practices, underhand state support for its corporations, and financial repression.

Reducing these success stories to a simple binary narrative around state versus market and open versus closed economies is, however, seriously misleading. This point was made by Chalmers Johnson (1982) in his seminal book, *MITI and the Japanese Miracle* (1982), who emphasized the role of the 'developmental state' in Japan to push policy discussions at the time beyond the black-and-white contrast between American and Soviet economies. Johnson (1999: 32) would later write about the 'enormous ideological resistance in the English-speaking countries' to his work, a resistance which, as Cohen and DeLong (2016) have shown, goes against parts of their own ideological history.

In attempting to understand China's remarkable development path, this chapter follows Cohen and DeLong in arguing both that 'getting the political economy right is and has been of overwhelming importance in producing prosperity' (23) and that 'the Asian development model is about nothing if not national boundaries' (18).

From this perspective, we show that it is China's pragmatic experimentation with an East Asian-style developmental state configuration that has managed those boundaries and shaped its interaction with the global economy. This should not be a great surprise, as it is well known that China's leaders actively drew lessons from development experiences in the region (and beyond), particularly from Japan and the newly industrialized economies (NIEs) of Republic of Korea (ROK), Taiwan, and Singapore (Johnson, 1999; Nolan, 1996).[1]

Like East Asian countries that came before it, China's rise is stirring controversial questions about the roles of comparative advantage, industrial policy, foreign direct investment, state-owned enterprises (SOEs), technology transfer, and other trade policy performance requirements in the process of economic development. Also, and as was the case in the earlier East Asian development episodes (Amsden, 1994; Wade, 1996), the mix of policy instruments and institutional mechanisms underpinning its rapid growth have not been widely appreciated and at times have been obscured by the wider international community. Conversely, it was not uncommon, for example, for Japan's Ministry of International Trade and Industry (MITI) to shroud its strategic activities in secrecy and to manage information in ways that gave its firms a competitive advantage (Johnson, 1999: 45). Moreover, it took several decades, and the World Bank's misrepresentation of the East Asian 'miracle', before Japan felt sufficiently confident to offer its own account of its economic success.

This chapter assesses China's developmental state orientation based on a closer reading of key features as postulated by the authors associated with the term's origination. With the international policy community gradually progressing from the 'why' of industrial policy to the 'how' of implementing it, the analysis focuses on forms of what Johnson (1982) regarded as 'market-conforming methods of state intervention', which Wade (2010) later called 'open economy' industrial policy, and Amsden (2001) referred to as 'reciprocal control mechanism'.[2]

Section 3.2 sets out the main elements of the developmental state as formulated by scholars that played important roles in documenting the developmental state in Japan, ROK, and Taiwan. These elements are used as a rough guide to highlight institutional experimentation and learning in China's gradual refinement of the role of the state in economic management in the industrial and financial sector, which has combined an export push with targeted policies to promote production capacity in strategic sectors. The chapter concludes with remarks on the implications

[1] Several studies have explored the extent to which China's rapid catch-up growth follows the East Asian developmental state model; using different metrics the studies have presented a varied picture, often reflecting the time and place of the authors concerned—see Zhang, 2018; Knight, 2014; Boltho and Weber, 2009; Baek, 2005; Pearson, 2005; Lee et al., 2002; Breslin, 1996.

[2] Similar to these concepts, Gunnar Myrdal used the term 'operational controls'. See Kozul-Wright and Poon (2018).

of China's developmental state trajectory and the transferability of policy lessons from its experience to other developing countries.

3.2 Elements of the East Asian Developmental State

Chalmers Johnson's account of Japan's rapid post-war catch-up growth laid the foundations of the East Asian 'developmental state' concept on which later authors would further build. In adopting this term, Johnson was consciously creating a taxonomy of 'how the government intervenes and for what purposes' (1982: 18). He classified the Soviet centrally planned economy model as 'plan-ideological', whereas capitalist economies came in two broad forms: 'plan-rational', associated with Japan's developmental state; and 'market-rational', associated with the US regulatory state.

Plan-ideological economies essentially exhibited a disconnect between the 'how' of government intervention and the 'what' of achieved outcomes. Policy instruments of centrally planned economies, such as state ownership of the means of production, wide-ranging state planning, and strict bureaucratic goal setting, were treated as not simply tenets of sound economic management but objectives in their own right; evidence of inefficiency or ineffectiveness that put these tenets into question was deemed heretical.

In contrast, the distinction between the two capitalist-type economies is related to different approaches to managing private economic activities and the state's priorities in economic policy. A market-rational state relies on regulatory powers to set the rules of the game of market competition, but generally does not concern itself with finer-grained details of domestic industry structure or firms. A plan-rational state, however, actively sets social- and economic-oriented goals, places its highest priority on 'development functions' linked to policies of industrialization, and focuses on domestic industry structure and firms to enhance the nation's international competitiveness. By extension, these different approaches entail different policy tools: in particular, whereas a market-rational state prefers using horizontal non-selective policies to achieve efficiency, a plan-rational state pragmatically leverages the use of both horizontal and selective instruments to prioritize degrees of policy effectiveness, over pure efficiency concerns (Haggard, 2018: 20; Johnson, 1982: 18–22; Wade, 2018: 11).[3]

It is because of these distinctions and the primary focus of a plan-rational state on progressing through stages of industrialization that the developmental state is

[3] Although Johnson argued that a market-rational state usually does not have a formal industrial policy because this would imply a strategic goal-oriented approach to the economy, he qualified this statement with 'or, at any rate, will not recognize it as such' (1982: 19). In this way, he may have been hinting at the apparent 'covert' use of industrial policy in many developed countries (Block, 2008; Chang, 2010: 85–6).

often associated with managing the process of capital accumulation to address failures in market structure and coordination that can weaken the investment process (Wade, 1990). In this vein, a key common feature among East Asian development experiences (including China's) was relatively high levels of domestic investment rates (Singh, 1996; UNCTAD, 1996), which are, in turn, associated with the creation and management of economic rents (UNCTAD, 2016) along with higher rates of learning, technical progress, and structural change (Ocampo, 2005: 16). Similarly, for Amsden (2001: 125), the four main functions performed by the developmental state are tilted towards issues linked to production capabilities: development banking, local content management, strategic and selective opening, and national firm formation.

While Johnson knew well that Japan's developmental state would be hard to emulate, he recognized that it was not impossible for a different society to configure its own socio-political arrangements in ways similar to post-war Japan by giving highest priority to industrialization objectives and incentivizing public–private-sector cooperation. As such, Johnson distilled four essential elements of the developmental state to provide an abstract model of Japan's catch-up growth experience which other countries could use as a rough guide to inform their own policymaking and concrete implementation (1982: 314–15).[4] These four elements are: (i) a small but high-quality bureaucracy composed of the best managerial talent available in the system, able to select and support strategic sectors including through supervised competition; (ii) a political system which allows the bureaucracy sufficient scope to take initiatives and to operate effectively; (iii) market-conforming mechanisms of state intervention with discretionary power both to guide private interests and strike a balance with public interests and able to improve their own effectiveness in these tasks through learning by doing and repeated interactions (both cooperative and conflictual) with the private owners of strategic sectors; and (iv) a lead role for a pilot, or apex, organization—such as Japan's MITI—endowed with strategic capacity to implement industrial policy, indirect control of government funds, and 'think-tank' functions (Johnson, 1982: 315–20).

Over time, these key elements were elaborated and refined by authors also closely associated with developmental states in the Asia region. In his comparative analysis involving South Korea, Peter Evans (1995) coined the term 'embedded autonomy' to highlight the nature of the state's utilitarian need for close working relationships with private-sector firms, while also maintaining the ability to discipline these actors in aligning the interests of capital with those of the state—instead of vice versa.

[4] Foreshadowing similar reactions to the rise of the NIEs, and more recently China, Johnson (1999: 40) lamented that 'the "learn-from-Japan" craze then sweeping the United States was dangerously ahistorical and simple-minded'. At the same time, he also acknowledged that perhaps the single most important question about Japan's developmental state was: 'Is it duplicable? Is there really a Japanese model? What are the general, culture-free lessons to be learned from the Japanese case?'

Amsden also emphasized embedded autonomy features in her concept of 'reciprocal control mechanism', which involved a set of institutions that impose discipline on economic behaviour, such that 'recipients of subsidies were subjected to *monitorable performance standards that were redistributive in nature and results-oriented*' (2001: 8). Importantly, Amsden believed that fostering industrial development by using reciprocal control mechanisms in the areas of science, technology, and innovation constituted the 'neo-developmental state' (2000: 6, 13) under stricter multilateral rules of international trade.

Keeping in mind Johnson's idea of market-conforming mechanisms of state intervention (the third element), Wade, Amsden, and others argued that the cases of Taiwan and ROK were distinguished not by their resort to a wide range of policy tools of intervention, but by the imposition of performance criteria on which state support was made conditional. Firms receiving preferential state policies had to meet performance metrics related to, for example, targets for exporting, or local content requirements, or advances in domestic production capacity. On this last metric, conditions were tied to closing the price and quality gap between imports and domestic substitutes by a certain time period, or to pushing forward the technological frontiers of domestic production (Amsden, 2001; Wade, 2018).

More specifically, Wade regarded East Asian industrial policy as consisting of two kinds: 'pulling the market' and 'pushing the market'.[5] The first kind involved cases where the government clearly made an investment decision that private investors would not have otherwise made. The second kind involved cases where the government supported investment directions made by private firms, but pushed them to advance the domestic technological frontier in these areas, as well as other areas where these firms might profitably invest next. These two kinds of economic interventions, but especially the second kind, are what Wade called 'open economy' industrial policy—which strategically blends an export push with explicit consideration of import substitution activities (Wade, 2010: 155–6; Amsden, 2004).

Wade illustrates Taiwan's 'pushing the market' institutional mechanism in the form of a fiscal incentive scheme for which domestic or foreign firms were eligible, provided that they invested in production capacity that met certain product specifications. Over time, production capacity was increased by adjusting upwards the product-specific technical threshold at which firms would be eligible to receive benefits (Wade, 2010: 156; 2018: 14).[6]

[5] For conceptual clarity, these terms are re-formulations of Wade's original concepts of: 'leading the market' and 'following the market'.

[6] The formulation and adjustment of technical specifications found in the scheme were facilitated by selective use of foreign consultants as part of a process of building domestic production capabilities. Through the provision of US aid, much of the industrial planning and screening in Taiwan in the 1950s was done by J. G. White Engineering Corp. of New York. In the early 1960s, it was the Stanford

Over time, as the production capacity of domestic firms improved, the product-specific technical threshold at which firms were eligible for fiscal incentives would be raised to push firms to upgrade and diversify their production capacities. The ratcheting-up feature of this incentive mechanism applied to specific product-level technical standards within and across different industrial sectors as domestic capabilities progressed from light-industry goods to medium- and high-technology goods. Also, Taiwanese policymakers resisted appeals to make the product list of the fiscal incentive scheme broad and unselective and, over time, the product lists became more precisely defined. As these product lists were used over the course of decades, they were updated regularly to avoid quickly becoming out of date (Wade, 2010: 155–6; 1990: 183–4). This bureaucratic capacity was located in the Industrial Development Bureau within Taiwan's Ministry of Economic Affairs, which provided an industrial extension service parallel to the agricultural extension service, mostly staffed with engineers (Wade, 2018: 15; Amsden, 2004).

Thus, East Asian developmental states conducted both kinds of 'pulling the market' (from the top down) and 'pushing the market' (from the bottom up) industrial policies, 'in a way that generates pressure for upgrading and diversifying national production' (Wade 2003: 636). Getting at the heart of open-economy industrial policy practice, domestic firms were granted a range of incentives to replace imports, but they were not fully insulated: industrial policies provided domestic producers a limited buffer from international competitive pressure 'until such time as the producers succeeded in (almost) matching the price and quality of competing imports, or failed to do so' (Wade, 2018: 14).

Sections 3.3 and 3.4 delves into China's processes of institutional and policy learning in the transition from a plan-ideological state to a plan-rational developmental state model, with a focus on industrial and financial sector reforms and, in particular, the use of 'open economy' industrial policies in pushing and pulling domestic production capacities towards upgrading and diversification.

3.3 China: Transition to Plan-Rational State

China's experience of navigating the transition from a centrally planned economy to a market-economy model has been forty years in the making. Previously, the government's role in economic planning, coordination, and resource allocation

Research Institute that helped detail next steps in industrialization, while in the 1970s and 1980s, the government employed the services of Arthur D. Little International Inc. for the same purpose (Wade, 1990: 211). Similarly, in the Republic of Korea, it was noted that, 'the star of technology transfer to Korea is the short-term independent consultant. Typically such a figure is Japanese, either retired or still in the permanent employment of a Japanese enterprise, consulting in Korea on an ad hoc basis' (Amsden, 1989: 234).

effectively supplanted market mechanisms, but with the onset of reforms in the late 1970s, Chinese leaders wanted to improve economic performance and to replicate the achievements witnessed in the East Asia region.

On the eve of reform in 1978, Chinese leaders did not have a detailed blueprint that foresaw all the twists and turns of reform for the next four decades. Rather, policymakers adopted a gradual and strategic approach to economic reform and integration into the global economy, premised on a pragmatic agenda that sought practical evidence-based policy lessons for the country's economic problems. The idea was not to quickly liberalize the economy, in hopes that market mechanisms would sprout automatically, but to maintain stability while gradually putting in place market-supporting institutions that would drive reforms and economic growth. In doing this, China's leaders maintained a healthy scepticism of mainstream economic theory and policy advice emanating from advanced industrialized nations (El-Erian and Spence, 2008; Perkins, 1988). In particular, China's gradual approach has been characterized by a strong emphasis on experimentation with microeconomic-level measures to adjust institutional arrangements that improve incentives, which, in turn, eased accumulated distortions and imbalances at the macroeconomic level (Heilmann, 2008; Hofman, 2018; Lin and Wang, 2008).

This section focuses on China's industrial-sector reforms, but to fully appreciate the institutional and policy learning processes, it is important to recognize the origins of Chinese reforms in the agricultural and rural sectors. It is in these areas that China's pragmatic experimentation to transition from planned to mixed economy began and led to its 'dual-track' reform approach, through the household responsibility system (HRS), which jump-started the country's sustained economic performance and became a hallmark of its overall reform-policy mindset (Lin, 1992). Moreover, as was common to (later) reforms in other sectors, agricultural reforms were at times fitful and reversed due to government concerns over loss of control and unanticipated outcomes, but these were expedient detours rather than a return to pre-reform practices (Sicular, 1988). This approach paid close attention to political economy dynamics whereby a market track provided the incentives for economic actors to enhance productivity, but on condition that they fulfil their obligation to the plan, while the plan track represented implicit transfers to compensate economic actors who could be worse off from market liberalization by maintaining existing rents and subsidies under the plan (Gilson and Milhaupt, 2011; Qian, 2003).

A second stage of reforms from 1985 onwards allowed a greater role for markets in guiding agricultural production as state plans were phased out. This stage was marked by progressive market liberalization as procurement programmes and quotas were replaced by a combination of contract and market purchases. The supply of other agricultural inputs, such as credit and chemical fertilizers, also increased substantially during the reform period (Lin, 1992). State control over procurement and prices of farm inputs were relaxed only gradually during the reform era, beginning in the mid-1980s with machinery, pesticides, and plastic film, and in the early 1990s extended to key inputs such as chemical fertilizers (Huang et al., 2008).

3.3.1 Industrial and Financial Sector Reforms

Under central planning, SOEs were the main economic agents in the non-agricultural sectors responsible for the production and distribution of goods: on the one hand, they exerted little autonomy over key decisions of their operations as these were determined by government plans; on the other hand, they provided essential social services (such as housing, health care, education) to employees and their families. Prices and profits played essentially no role in resource allocation as competition was circumscribed and most SOEs were allowed monopoly power over a given local or provincial market. Monopoly prices, in turn, created profits that were in large part surrendered to the state and accounted for the bulk of government revenue (Yusuf et al., 2006).

Broad-based success in boosting output and productivity in agriculture provided momentum to extend reforms to the industrial sector. By the mid-1980s, an enterprise responsibility system (ERS) was enacted, based on the HRS, to improve the economic performance of SOEs by formalizing the relationship between SOEs and the responsible government agency. Like HRS, initial reforms focused on the incentive structure of firms, followed by reforms to the overall market environment in which firms operated. ERS required firms to abide by state plans and output quotas, and in return allowed them greater autonomy over issues such as production decisions, use of retained earnings (and other sources of financing), employee compensation and recruitment practices, staffing levels, and purchase of inputs. Moreover, a dual-track system was established as plan-track products (using inputs provided at planned prices) were sold at state prices, while market-track products were sold at market prices (using inputs purchased at market prices). By the end of 1988, the ERS applied to 93 per cent of SOEs, and, over time, as the number of industrial goods subject to state-set prices was reduced, market competition increased incrementally as the two tracks converged (Rawski, 1994; Song, 2018).

Increased competitive pressures were complemented with measures to relax industry entry barriers and to foster non-SOE enterprises, particularly in labour-intensive downstream sectors. These changes resulted in significant shifts in China's structure of production in the 1980s and early 1990s, with the previously dominant role of SOEs reduced by increasing output shares by industrial collectives, particularly township and village enterprises (TVEs), and foreign-funded firms, primarily investors from Hong Kong, Macau, and Taiwan. These trends are shown in Table 3.1; by the mid-1990s, SOEs were no longer the dominant

Table 3.1 Gross industrial output by ownership category, 1995–2011 (percentage of total)

Ownership category	1995	2001	2006	2011
SOEs*	34.0	18.1	9.7	7.9
Collective	36.6	14.6	4.3	2.0
Private	12.7	9.2	21.2	29.9
Joint-stock	3.0	29.6	33.0	33.1
Foreign**	11.7	28.5	31.6	25.9
Other	1.9	0.1	0.2	1.2
Total	99.9	100.1	100	100

Notes: *Defined as wholly owned state enterprises. **Includes foreign-invested enterprises from Hong Kong, Macau, and Taiwan.

Source: Authors' elaboration based on China Statistical Yearbook (various years).

industrial producer, surpassed by collectives whose share then proceeds to decline, as these are converted into other ownership categories, particularly private and joint-stock enterprises, whose shares of industrial output rises alongside that of foreign-invested firms.

Despite much diversity in the ownership and management of TVEs, some broad generalizations are applicable. Most TVE industrial output is produced by firms that are controlled by local governments, rather than formal worker cooperatives. TVEs are perhaps best understood as an institutional adaptation to China's transition to markets: by the late 1980s, markets and market prices existed for nearly all commodities (product markets), but factor markets for land, labour, and capital would only slowly emerge in the 1990s. Although many would later be privatized, TVEs were the expedient policy solution that allowed rural communities to translate control over assets into income streams despite the absence of asset markets and conventional property rights enforced by a legal system and at the same time helped boost local fiscal revenues (Gilson and Milhaupt, 2011: 263–4; Naughton, 1994).

In contrast, the state generally concentrated on sectors that were not deemed appropriate to other ownership types, such as natural monopolies (capital intensive), pillar industries (capital goods), national defence industries, and other high-technology areas (Nolan and Wang, 1999: 185). This is consistent with views held by Chinese policymakers at the time that sectors in the middle-level technological range should be given stronger state support since these sectors provide inputs that are used by the export sector, and a sole focus on labour-intensive industry based on existing comparative advantage could ultimately place a ceiling on economic development (Baek, 2005: 488–9).

These initial reform measures increased domestic market competition, but SOEs' soft budget weaknesses remained a problem and growing losses by SOEs in the 1990s motivated deeper reforms. Further ownership diversification was signalled with Deng Xiaoping's open show of support in 1992 for the country's experiments with special economic zones, known as Deng's 'southern tour'. At that time, the basic legal infrastructure to support private exchange was enacted, such as corporate, foreign investment, bankruptcy, competition, commercial banking, central banking, insurance and securities laws (among others). Overall, Chinese leaders sought to establish the institutional framework for a modern enterprise system based on Western corporate models adapted to the 'socialist market economy': in most cases, the laws were not designed to support private-sector activity per se, but aimed to facilitate state-sector reform. The 1993 Company Law, for instance, provided the framework for SOEs to be re-organized as corporate entities, which helped to streamline previously ill-defined shareholding control structures in the state-owned sector (Heilmann, 2018: 94–6; Yusuf et al., 2006: 72).

Although Table 3.1 clearly shows the reduced role of the state in industrial output, the process of corporatization in the 1990s sought to further diversify ownership patterns to enhance enterprise economic performance and oversight, but retain a significant, albeit adapted, role for the state (Nolan and Wang, 1999: 188–9; Yusuf, 2006: 87–9). This can be observed by examining the composition of fixed-asset investment by ownership category: as China pursued investment-led growth that rose from 29.4 per cent of GDP in 1980 to over 40 per cent after the global financial crisis, the structure of types of enterprises contributing to total fixed-asset investment has clearly diversified, especially since the mid-2000s. In contrast to Table 3.1 showing the industrial output share of SOEs declining to less than 10 per cent, Figure 3.1a presents a different picture: by 2016, the share of total fixed-asset investment attributed to SOEs was 21.3 per cent, and to private-sector enterprises was 32.9 per cent. In 2016, the largest share, 44.4 per cent, was accounted for by a 'mixed' ownership category.

The composition of this mixed ownership category is revealed in Figure 3.1b, with a growing proportion for the 'joint-stock' enterprises: by 2016, this type of enterprise accounted for 81.7 per cent of fixed-asset investment within the 'mixed' category of Figure 3.1a, while foreign-invested enterprises (including those from Hong Kong, Macau, and Taiwan) accounted for 9.7 per cent. Many of these joint-stock firms, it should be noted, include state-holding enterprises (majority state-owned share) or state-controlled enterprises (state-owned share less than 50 per cent) (Milhaupt and Zheng, 2016: 4; Szamosszegi and Kyle, 2011).

The process of SOE corporatization would become known as 'grasp the large, and release the small', and was adopted as government policy in 1995. By 1997, the government embarked on a more forceful round of state-sector consolidation and ownership diversification, while also allowing large numbers of workers to be laid

(a)

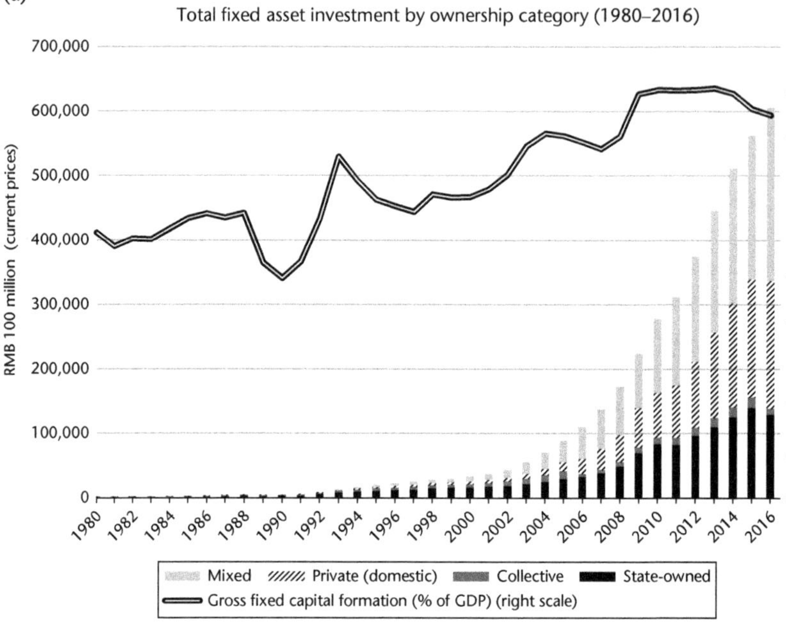

(b)

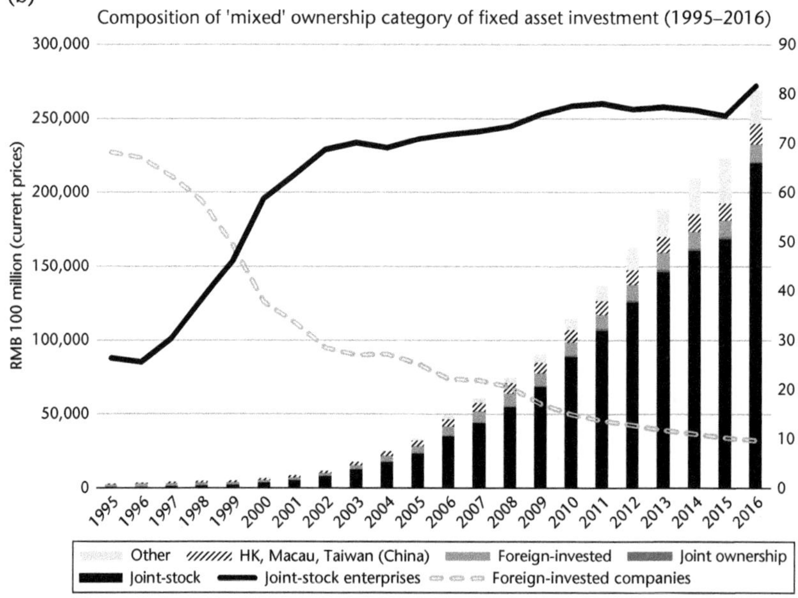

Figure 3.1 Components of China's fixed-asset investment

Note: The 'joint-stock' category includes limited liability companies and shareholding companies.

Source: Authors' elaboration based on *China Statistical Yearbook* (various years) and UNCTADstat

off. The idea of privatization was still deemed politically sensitive, but SOE corporatization took a multitude of forms: mergers, employee and management buyouts, stock exchange listings, open sales, bankruptcy, leasing, and joint ventures with foreign enterprises. Overall, the goal was to keep the number of remaining large central SOEs between five hundred and a thousand. These reforms gained further political impetus with the onset of the Asian financial crisis of 1997–8, as Chinese leaders sought to address a key vulnerability—since state banks were the primary source of lending to SOEs, weak SOEs resulted in a banking sector burdened with non-performing loans (NPLs) (Poon, 2014: 10–12; Song, 2018: 351–2; Yusuf et al., 2006: 78–81).

SOE corporatization was intertwined with three institutional reform initiatives that would be the foundations for an emerging regulatory state. First, in the late 1990s, China's economic bureaucracy was streamlined with many line ministries downgraded in rank or eliminated, which allowed the space for a growing number of regulatory commissions to supervise healthy industrial structure at the sectoral level to be created in the 1990s and early 2000s, such as for financial services (securities, insurance, and banking) and infrastructure sectors (telecommunications, aviation, and electric power). Second, as part of bureaucratic restructuring, incumbent business monopolies were spun off from the ministries that previously controlled them, creating conditions for 'limited' market competition—ideally two or three large SOEs complemented by a handful of smaller upstart local players. Third, a clearer rationale for the role of the state in the economy and its division of labour with non-state firms (Naughton, 2010: 444–5; Pearson, 2005: 302–4).

Overall, these reform measures helped remaining large SOEs boost retained earnings, and by 2003 the government established the State-owned Assets Supervision and Administration Commission (SASAC) to own, oversee, and manage state assets at the central level, which was replicated with SASAC bureaus in local government. At the beginning, SASAC was responsible for 196 of the largest SOEs, with the objective of reducing the number to 80–100 by 2010. By the end of 2013, 113 central SOEs remained under SASAC's ownership; by 2018, the number was reduced to ninety-six. Most of these central SOEs are in 'strategic' natural monopoly sectors in which SASAC will maintain sole ownership or absolute control, but also in competitive downstream 'pillar' manufacturing and service sectors in which SASAC will maintain strong control and influence. While natural monopoly sectors are often considered 'strategic' in other countries, the identification of 'pillar sectors' is less common. China's pillar sectors include: equipment manufacturing (machinery), automobiles, information technology, construction, iron and steel, non-ferrous metals, and chemicals (Lin and Milhaupt, 2013; Poon, 2014: 10).[7]

[7] In 2016, SASAC announced the reorganization of SOEs into three functional categories: 1) those operating in competitive and commercial industries; 2) those involved in national security and in key

These variations in the diversification of ownership hint at traces of 'China's institutional ecology' (Milhaupt and Zheng, 2016: 20), or the use of various 'institutional bridging' mechanisms through which the state has embedded itself within the private sector, through 'the pervasive use of personnel-rotation systems, linked equity-ownership structures, and strategic forms of cooperation, such as joint ventures, which serves to unite separate components of the state sector' (Lin and Milhaupt, 2013: 701–2). In the more recent context, reform of the state sector continues to carefully proceed along the lines of a 'mixed ownership' economy, with the outcome uncertain (Milhaupt and Zheng, 2016; Naughton, 2018). But as some have observed, 'party documents specify that the market's "decisive role" is in *resource allocation*. In other words, in China the market is a mechanism for setting prices but not for reassigning control of assets' (Kroeber, 2016: 6).

With the onset of the reform period, China's financial system changed from a mono-banking to a plural-banking system. In 1984, four state-owned specialized banks were spun off from the People's Bank of China (PBoC) to better differentiate between commercial and central bank functions. Thus, the 'big four' state banks were created: the Agricultural Bank of China, Bank of China (BoC), China Construction Bank, and Industrial and Commercial Bank of China (ICBC). Further reforms in 1994 sought to enhance the independence of the central bank and to separate commercial lending from policy lending, by creating three separate policy banks and by converting the state banks to state-owned commercial banks (SOCBs) (UNCTAD, 2016: 26).

In the early 1990s, administrative measures rather than markets still allocated funds for China's economic growth via a credit plan, which was abolished in 1998. SOCBs gained greater autonomy over lending decisions, but PBoC still restricted the total amount of credit available for SOCBs to lend and indirectly intervened through 'window guidance' to control bank lending. At the same time, the government gradually established basic financial markets, such as an interbank bond market, a foreign exchange market, and government and corporate bond markets. Experiments in stock markets began in the 1980s and led to the creation of the Shanghai Security Exchange in 1990 and the Shenzhen Security Exchange in 1991 (Okazaki, 2007: 12–13, 19).

Overall, policymakers maintained a cautious orientation to market mechanisms and capital markets, while introducing improvements in corporate governance and risk management (Chen, 1999; Yi, 2014; Zhao, 2017). For example, because of China's capital account restrictions, foreign investors only gained access to China's capital markets in 2002, through a transitional arrangement called the Qualified Foreign Institutional Investor (QFII) scheme that included

industries/areas considered the 'lifeline' of the economy; and 3) industries that provide public goods. See SASAC (2016).

qualification requirements and investment quotas that were only relaxed over time (SSE, 2015). For the most part, stock markets have been an instrument to provide SOEs with other capital-raising channels, rather than for fundamental changes to Western-style corporate governance (Walter and Howie, 2011: 146–7; Yusuf et al., 2006: 71–2). Growth of bond markets has been relatively slow, but by the end of 2017, the total value of outstanding issuance was around 63 per cent of GDP, with state or policy banks accounting for over 80 per cent of total issuance (Wright and Rosen, 2018: 11–12). Only in July 2017 were foreign investors allowed to trade in mainland interbank bond markets using Hong Kong accounts under a streamlined process (International Capital Market Association, 2018). A similar propensity for institutional learning and experimentation can be discerned in China's approach to venture capital markets (Lin, 2015).

The financial system has gradually diversified, but banks still accounted for 81 per cent of all assets held by financial institutions in China at the end of 2017 (Wright and Rosen, 2018: 11). A key turning point occurred in the late 1990s, as authorities sought to address high levels of accumulated NPLs by injecting capital, transferring NPLs to asset management companies, selling minority stakes to foreign strategic investors, and raising new funds through stock market listings in Hong Kong. By 2003, Central Huijin Investment was formed to recapitalize financial institutions, and in so doing became a controlling shareholder for state banks, policy banks, and other financial entities (Central Huijin, 2017). Central Huijin is considered the financial sector equivalent to SASAC in terms of ownership of state assets. Regulatory and supervisory functions over banking and financial institutions, however, were placed under the China Banking Regulatory Commission (CBRC), also created in 2003. By 2007, the China Investment Corp. (CIC) was established with an initial US$200bn to diversify use of foreign exchange reserves—a third of the amount would be used to purchase Central Huijin (Wu and Seah, 2008: 47, 52).

Returned to financial health in the late 1990s, plans to place policy banks on a more commercial footing were ultimately shelved, particularly with the onset of the 2008 global financial crisis (Kozul-Wright and Poon, 2018: 18). Going forward, indications suggest that China will 'make full use of the advantages of development finance' in supporting the country's ambitious foreign economic policy focused on regional infrastructure building known as the 'Belt and Road' initiative (PBoC, 2018; UNCTAD, 2018). More recently, further financial sector opening was announced, such as allowing foreign investors 51 per cent shareholdings for securities, fund management, futures, and personal insurance companies—with this foreign equity restriction to be removed in three years (Zhu, 2018).

For the purposes of this chapter, it is clear that Chinese leaders have made substantial progress in institutional and policy learning in gradually refining the role of the state in economic development: from centralized, direct, and blunt forms of control and planning, to relatively decentralized, indirect and more nimble forms of 'guidance planning' (Heilmann, 2018: 137, 151–2). In this transition from plan-ideological to plan-rational state, policymakers have maintained control through adjustments in 'incentive alignment' that enabled China's pragmatic institutional policy experiments—this has drawn surprising parallels with the corporate venture capital model in which venture capitalists invest in start-ups to experiment and learn outside established corporate norms and organizational boundaries (Gilson and Milhaupt, 2011: 270).

To further make the case for China's developmental state orientation, Section 3.3.2 briefly examines features of its inward foreign direct investment (FDI) regime and the 'Made in China 2025' plan, which appear to actively use 'open-economy' industrial policy tools to push for upgrading and diversification.

3.3.2 Open-economy Industrial Policy Features

China's strong export push and ability to attract FDI inflows since the early 1990s has been subject to much policy analysis and debate in terms of the developmental impact of joining global value chains. Thus, while China's export orientation is widely known, its efforts to simultaneously and selectively conduct import substitution activities has received little attention. These latter aspects have been an important part of China's overall development strategy and can be found in its so-called *Foreign Investment Industrial Guidance Catalogue* (guidance catalogues), which provides for different treatment of FDI inflows in different sectors in terms of incentives, market access, and ownership restrictions. Long recognized as a key instrument in China's industrial policy toolbox (Poon, 2014: 24; USTR, 2018), most existing studies examine the guidance catalogues from a narrow commercial, legal, or national security perspective, rather than for the purposes of understanding China's processes of institutional learning related to catch-up economic development.

First introduced in 1995, the FDI catalogues were issued amidst rising FDI inflows and have been revised seven times: in 1997, 2002, 2004, 2007, 2011, 2015, and 2017. The guidance catalogues are unlike most other policy documents insofar as they consist only of line after line of production learning objectives of varying technical specificity. Each 'line item' is organized by classification (encouraged, restricted, prohibited) and by industry (agriculture, manufacturing, services) sub-sector. Put simply, encouraged sub-sectors are eligible for policy incentives, whereas restricted or prohibited sub-sectors are deemed too sensitive and are generally closed to FDI inflows. Activities not found among line items under the three classifications are considered 'permitted' (neither provided incentives nor protected).

Table 3.2 highlights two features of the guidance catalogues: line items that contain foreign equity ownership ceilings (Table 3.2A), and line items that contain

Table 3.2 FDI guidance catalogue: ownership and production capacity features

A. Line items with foreign equity restrictions by classification (1995–2017)

Classification	FDI guidance catalogues							
	1995	1997	2002	2004	2007	2011	2015	2017
Encouraged with foreign equity ceilings	20	20	41	42	61	50	21	0
Restricted	111	111	74	77	86	79	38	35
Prohibited	28	28	32	33	39	38	36	28
Total	159	159	147	152	186	167	95	63

B. Electronics: Integrated circuits

Line item	FDI guidance catalogues							
	1995	1997	2002	2004	2007	2011	2015	2017
Design and large-scale manufacture of integrated circuits with line width of: (microns)	<0.35	<0.35	<0.35	<0.35	<0.18	<0.18	<0.028	<0.028
Catalogue classification	Encouraged							
Equity restrictions	None							

C. General machinery: Truck cranes

Line item	FDI guidance catalogues									
	1995	1997	2002	2004	2007	2007	2011	2011	2015	2017
Manufacture of truck cranes with lifting capacity of (tons):	<50	<50	<50	<50	<300	>300	<400	>400	>400	>400
Catalogue classification	Restricted					Encouraged	Restricted	Encouraged		
Equity restrictions	No FDI allowed		Joint venture						None	

D. Special-purpose machinery: bulldozers

Line item	FDI guidance catalogues									
	1995	1997	2002	2004	2007	2007	2011	2011	2015	2017
Manufacture of bulldozers, horsepower	<320	<320	<320	<320	<320	>520 (+design)	<320	>520 (+design)	>520 (+design)	>520 (+design)
Catalogue classification	Restricted					Encouraged	Restricted	Encouraged		
Equity restrictions	No FDI allowed		Joint venture		None					

Source: Poon (2019).

production capacity features (Table 3.2B, 3.2C, 3.2D). In terms of the former, line items classified as restricted and prohibited are considered as implying foreign equity ceilings (if not explicitly outlined), but line items classified as encouraged can also have foreign equity ceilings explicitly included. As seen in Table 3.2A, adding these together provides a sense of total foreign equity ceilings in each version of the guidance catalogues over the years: the number rises to a peak of 186 in 2007, before declining rapidly to sixty-three in 2017, with the number of encouraged line items with foreign equity ceilings dropping to zero. Although these ceilings remain for line items in restricted and prohibited sectors, it was over twenty years before ceilings in encouraged line items were completely dropped.

Tables 3.2B, 3.2C, and 3.2D provide a sense of individual encouraged line items that also contain production capacity specifications. These tables are a compilation of a single line item from an individual industrial sub-sector across each version of the guidance catalogues, along with associated classification and explicit ownership limits. This aspect of the guidance catalogues draws a close comparison with Taiwan's use of fiscal incentive schemes to promote diversification and upgrading of production capacities over time by raising the product-specific technical threshold at which foreign-invested firms would be eligible to receive policy incentives.

The most straightforward cases are line items that involve sophisticated technologies in pillar sectors where Chinese production capacities have been limited, or in 'strategic' sectors with high levels of state ownership. Table 3.2B shows the rising product-specific technical thresholds for foreign investment in the design and large-scale manufacture of integrated circuits (ICs). The line item is only 'encouraged' throughout all the guidance catalogues with the technical threshold increasing in capability in 2007, when production of ICs with line width of 'less than 0.35 microns', was raised to IC production with line width of 'less than 0.18 microns' (and raised again in the 2015 guidance catalogue). Due to limited indigenous Chinese production capacities, there were no foreign ownership equity ceilings included with this line item.

More complex examples of individual line items can be found in pillar industries where there is already significant existing domestic production capacity. Tables 3.2C and 3.2D compile the respective line items related to the manufacture of track cranes with specified lifting capacity (in tons), and to the manufacture of bulldozers with specified earth-moving capacity (in horsepower). As seen in Table 3.2C, from the 1995 to the 2004 guidance catalogue, the manufacture of truck cranes of 'less than 50 tons' is under the restricted classification. In the 2007 guidance catalogue, the technical threshold is raised to 'greater than 300 tons' for this line item under the encouraged classification, while investment in truck cranes with lifting capacity of 'less than 300 tons' is restricted. By 2011, this arrangement is maintained but the technical threshold is increased to greater/less than 400 tons. The 2015 and 2017 catalogues maintain the same technical threshold for this line item under the 'encouraged' classification, while that previously under the 'restricted' classification is removed. In terms of foreign equity ceilings, no FDI is permitted for this line item in the 1995 and 1997 guidance catalogues, which is changed to a joint-venture requirement in the 2002, 2004, 2007, and 2011 versions. The 2015 and 2017 guidance catalogues include no ownership restriction for this line item.

In December 2016, the State Council, NDRC, and MOFCOM amended the 2015 guidance catalogue and further reduced the ninety-five line items with foreign equity ceilings. Moreover, all remaining foreign equity ceilings will be converted into an FDI 'negative list' (MOFCOM, 2016). The adoption of the negative list format was formalized in the 2017 FDI guidance catalogue, which removed foreign equity ceilings from all line items under the 'encouraged' classification, and further reduced line items under the 'restricted' and 'prohibited' classifications to sixty-three.

Although the use of the guidance catalogues as an FDI 'positive list' industrial policy instrument seems to have ended, China's practice of open-economy industrial policy can still be seen in guidance planning practices more closely linked to innovation (Cheung et al., 2016; Ray et al., 2016), notably the 'Made in China 2025' (MC2025) economic upgrading plan issued by the State Council in May 2015.

MC2025 reaffirms the importance of the manufacturing sector to China's national security and power, but recognizes that by global standards, China's manufacturing industry is large but not strong, and remains weak in areas such as innovative capabilities, resource utilization rates, industry structure, informatization, quality, and brands. MC2025 is primarily focused on achieving technological breakthroughs in ten key sectors in advanced manufacturing, including: next generation information and communication technologies; high-end numerically controlled machine tools and robotics; space and aviation equipment; advanced rail transportation equipment; new energy vehicles, parts, and components (Poon, 2018: 113–14).

Despite international controversy surrounding explicit import substitution targets found in MC2025 for (domestic and global) market share in the ten key areas (Kozul-Wright and Poon, 2017), further details in MC2025 accompanying documents or sector-specific implementation plans suggest production capacity thresholds found in the foreign investment guidance catalogues are also present in more comprehensive MC2025 key technology and sector road maps, the first version published in 2015, followed by a second version in 2017 (NMSAC, 2015; 2017).[8]

[8] Work on the 2015 road map began in April of that year, lasted five months, and included six drafts. The government assembled over forty-eight academicians and more than four hundred experts and senior managers drawn from enterprises, universities, research institutes, professional and industry associations, and relevant government departments (NMSAC, 2015).

A specific sectoral example of the relatively detailed 'open economy' industrial policy aspects embedded in the CM2025 plan is the road map for hydrogen fuel cell vehicles (one of the three kinds of 'new energy vehicles'), which outlines development objectives for this sector for the period 2020–30. These objectives include technical capacity and cost targets for hydrogen fuel cell vehicles (passenger car, commercial vehicle); key common technologies (hydrogen storage, control technology, critical materials, and fuel cell stacks) and critical components; and hydrogen fuel infrastructure (refuelling stations, hydrogen delivery and supply technologies). Targets are also established for fuel cell system production capacity, and fuel cell vehicle deployment. Separate detailed roadmaps for 2015–30 are further provided in areas such as: vehicle hydrogen fuel cell stacks and key components, and passenger car and commercial vehicle fuel cell system (engine) technologies (SAEC, 2017).

Another less noticed aspect of MC2025 is its financial support policies. In order to reduce the cost of capital for manufacturing firms, the plan seeks to expand financing channels, while outlining specific roles for national development banks: the Export-Import Bank of China will further boost its support for manufacturing firms investing abroad, and the CDB will be encouraged to increase loans as a way to 'guide' other financial institutions to provide innovative products and services for eligible manufacturing firms, including investments from venture capital and private equity funds. This approach suggests that China seeks to achieve MC2025 upgrading and reform objectives by creating a set of purpose-built investment vehicles—so-called government (or industry) guidance funds (GGFs)—that are responsible for allocating public funds (Kozul-Wright and Poon, 2017; Lin, 2015; Naughton, 2018: 385–6). Some consider this more market-based investment approach 'a bold experiment designed to improve the likelihood of success' (Thomas, 2015).

In 2015, there were a total of 780 GGFs with capital of RMB2,183.4bn (US$352.2bn). City-level GGFs were the most numerous, followed by provincial level, district level, and national level. In terms of fund scale, provincial-level GGFs led the way, followed by those at the city level, national level, and district level (Poon, 2018). Exemplifying the GGF approach, China's state-backed Tsinghua Unigroup recently secured RMB150bn in new financing to support upgrading of the country's semiconductor industry. Of that financing, RMB100bn came from CDB and RMB50bn came from the National Integrated Circuit Industry Investment Fund (NICIIF), a national-level GGF created in 2014 with an initial fund of US$19.5bn (Kozul-Wright and Poon, 2017). By 2017, the distribution of NICIIF investment along the integrated circuit production chain was: manufacturing 65 per cent, design 17 per cent, packaging and testing 10 per cent, and equipment material 8 per cent (Wang, 2017: 9). Importantly, the apparent 'guidance' function of China's development finance appears to be similar to the 'signalling effect' used by development banks in East Asian countries to mobilize resources from a wider range of public- and private-sector financial institutions (Stiglitz and Uy, 1996: 265–6).

3.4 Conclusion

No country has made the arduous journey from widespread rural poverty to post-industrial prosperity without employing targeted and selective government policies to shift the production structure towards activities and sectors with higher productivity, better-paid jobs, and frontier technologies. Further, while government capacities to design and implement these policies reflect specific historical legacies, and are subject to political, informational, and technical constraints, these are not fixed; they emerge through acquisition and learning strategies of varying duration and degrees of contestation. China is no different, though that journey has, to date, proceeded at a spectacular pace and has been distinct in having to design and implement such policies as it was shedding the legacy of central planning.

An emphasis on flexibility and experimentation, in the institutions and by the practitioners of policymaking, appears to be crucial in forging a successful path, reflecting the realities of operating in an uncertain world where knowledge of the best ways to promote economic growth and development is limited, and there are diverse forms of success, contingent on national political and social cultures, on historically determined path dependencies, and on the behaviour of ruling elites. Experimentation, together with rules and conventions to ensure that failed experiments are dropped rather than retained, is of particular importance for increasing the probability of success.

The chapter has suggested that 'pragmatic experimentalism' has been a guiding approach in China's success story. In this context, policy goals are rarely of the either/or type—growth or price stability, open or closed economy, state or private ownership, or totally fixed or flexible exchange rates—but of various shades in between. Rather, learning to mix objectives and instruments has been a key to that success. An important point is that the capacities required to underpin a developmental state can be created; they do not emerge effortlessly out of existing or traditional organizations.

There is no single model applicable to all contexts; different institutional forms will suit particular local histories and politics. However, in the case of China, it was able to draw on successful neighbouring experiences with a developmental state and adapt those experiences to its specific challenges. Undoubtedly, its size has influenced that adaptation process and unlike earlier East Asian cases, China has had to devise its industrial strategy under the more stringent rules governing international trade and investment in the WTO era. At the same time, China's own success impacts on those rules and alters the environment facing a new generation of late-industrializing economies—particularly as China expands its outward economic engagement. Yet, generalized lessons from China's catch-up growth can provide valuable insights into the processes of industrialization and structural transformation, just as the previous cohort of East Asian countries were often held up as reference models of successful heterodox economic policymaking.

References

Amsden, A. H. (1989) *Asia's Next Giant: South Korea and Late Industrialization.* Oxford: Oxford University Press.

Amsden, A. H. (1994) 'Why Isn't the Whole World Experimenting with the East Asian Model to Develop?: Review of *The East Asian Miracle*', *World Development* 22(4): 627–33.

Amsden, A. H. (2000) 'Industrialization under New WTO Law.' Prepared for UNCTAD X High Level Roundtable on Trade and Development: Directions for the Twenty-First Century. Bangkok, February.

Amsden, A. H. (2001) *The Rise of 'the Rest': Challenges to the West from Late-Industrializing Economies.* Oxford: Oxford University Press.

Amsden, A. H. (2004) 'Import Substitution in High-Tech Industries: Prebisch Lives in Asia!', *CEPAL Review* 82: 75–89.

Baek, S. W. (2005) 'Does China Follow "the East Asian Development Model"?', *Journal of Contemporary Asia* 35(4): 485–98.

Blair, T. (2005) 'Tony Blair's Conference Speech 2005.' Available at https://www.theguardian.com/uk/2005/sep/27/labourconference.speeches

Block, F. (2008) 'Swimming against the Current: The Rise of a Hidden Developmental State in the United States', *Politics & Society*, 36(2): 169–206.

Boltho, A. and M. Weber (2009) 'Did China Follow the East Asian Development Model?', *The European Journal of Comparative Economics* 6(2): 267–86.

Breslin, S. G. (1996) 'China: Developmental State or Dysfunctional Development?', *Third World Quarterly* 17(4): 689–706.

Central Huijin (2017) Investments, December. Available at http://www.huijin-inv.cn/.

Chang, H.-J. (2010) 'How to 'Do' a Developmental State', in O. Edigheji (ed.) *Constructing a Democratic Developmental State in South Africa: Potentials and Challenges.* Cape Town: Human Sciences Research Council (HSRC), pp. 82–96.

Chen, Y. (1999) 'Warding off Policy-oriented Financial Risks and Promoting Effective Growth of the National Economy', in Bank of International Settlements (BIS) (ed.) *Strengthening the Banking System in China: Issues and Experience.* Basel: BIS. Available at https://www.bis.org/publ/plcy07.pdf.

Cheung, T. M., T. Mahnken, D. Seligsohn et al. (2016) 'Planning for Innovation: Understanding China's Plans for Technological, Energy, Industrial and Defense Development.' Report prepared for the US-China Economic and Security Review Commission (USCC), July.

Cohen, S. and J. Bradford DeLong (2016) *Concrete Economics: The Hamilton Approach to Economic Growth and Policy.* Cambridge, MA: Harvard University Press.

El-Erian, M. and M. Spence (2008) 'Growth Strategies and Dynamics: Insights from Country Experiences.' World Bank Commission on Growth and Development Working Paper No. 6: 1–33. Washington, DC: World Bank.

Evans, P. (1995) *Embedded Autonomy: States and Industrial Transformation*. Princeton, NJ: Princeton University Press.

Gilson, R. and C. Milhaupt (2011) 'Economically Benevolent Dictators: Lessons for Developing Democracies', *American Journal of Comparative Law* 59(1): 227–88.

Haggard, S. (2018) *Developmental States*. Cambridge: Cambridge University Press.

Heilmann, S. (2008) 'Policy Experimentation in China's Economic Rise', *Studies in Comparative International Development* 43(1): 1–26.

Heilmann, S. (2018) *Red Swan: How Unorthodox Policy Making Facilitated China's Rise*. Hong Kong: Chinese University Press.

Hofman, B. (2018) 'Reflections on 40 Years of China's Reforms', in R. Garnaut, L. Song, and C. Fang (eds) *China's 40 Years of Reform and Development 1978–2018*. Canberra: Australian National University Press, pp. 53–66.

Huang, J., K. Otsuka, and S. Rozelle (2008) 'Agriculture in China's Development: Past Disappointments, Recent Successes, and Future Challenges', in L. Brandt and T. Rawski (eds) *China's Great Economic Transformation*. Cambridge: Cambridge University Press, pp. 467–505.

Johnson, C. (1982) *MITI and the Japanese Miracle*. Stanford: Stanford University Press.

Johnson, C. (1999) 'The Developmental State: Odyssey of a Concept', in M. Woo-Cummings (ed.) *The Developmental State*. Ithaca: Cornell University Press, pp. 32–60.

Knight, J. B. (2014) 'China as a Developmental State', *The World Economy* 37(10): 1335–47.

Kozul-Wright, R. and D. Poon (2017) 'Learning from China's Industrial Strategy', *Project Syndicate*, 28 April.

Kozul-Wright, R. and D. Poon (2018) 'Asian Development after the Asian Drama.' WIDER Working Paper No. 2018/135, October.

Kroeber, A. (2016) 'Reform of Prices, Not Ownership', in S. Kennedy (ed.) *State and Market in Contemporary China: Towards the 13th Five-Year Plan*. Washington, DC. Center for Strategic and International Studies, pp. 5–8.

Lee, K., D. Han, and J. Lin (2002) 'Is China Following the East Asian Model? A "Comparative Institutional Analysis" Perspective', *The China Review* 2(1): 85–120.

Lin, J. Y. (1992) 'Rural Reforms and Agricultural Growth in China', *The American Economic Review* 82(1): 34–51.

Lin, J. Y. and Y. Wang (2008) 'China's Integration with the World: Development as a Process of Learning and Industrial Upgrading.' World Bank Policy Research Working Paper No. 4799, December.

Lin, L. (2015) 'Re-engineering a Venture Capital Market: The Case of China.' National University of Singapore (NUS) Law Working Paper No. 2015/007, July.

Lin, L. and C. J. Milhaupt (2013) 'We Are the (National) Champions: Understanding the Mechanisms of State Capitalism in China', *Stanford Law Review* 65(4): 697–760.

Milhaupt, C. J. and W. Zheng (2016) 'Why Mixed-ownership Reforms Cannot Fix China's State Sector.' Paulson Policy Memorandum, January.

Ministry of Commerce (MOFCOM) (China) (2016) 'Foreign Investment Industrial Guidance Catalogue: Announcement of the Revised Draft for Public Comment' [in Chinese], December. Available at http://wzs.mofcom.gov.cn/article/n/201612/20161202088897.shtml.

Naughton, B. (1994) 'Chinese Institutional Innovation and Privatization from below', *The American Economic Review* 84(2): 266–70.

Naughton, B. (2010) 'China's Distinctive System: Can It Be a Model for Others?' *Journal of Contemporary China* 19(65): 437–60.

Naughton, B. (2018) 'State Enterprise Reform Today', in R. Garnaut, L. Song, and C. Fang (eds) *China's 40 Years of Reform and Development 1978–2018*. Canberra: Australian National University Press, pp. 375–91.

NMSAC (2015, 2017) *Made in China 2025 Key Technology Road Map 2015* [in Chinese], October. Available at: http://www.cm2025.org/uploadfile/2016/0321/20160321015412313.pdf and http://www.cm2025.org/uploadfile/2018/0307/2018030814131234.pdf.

Nolan, P. (1996) 'Large Firms and Industrial Reforms in Former Planned Economies: The Case of China', *Cambridge Journal of Economics*, 20(1): 1–29.

Nolan, P. and X. Wang (1999) 'Beyond Privatization: Institutional Innovation and Growth in China's Large State-Owned Enterprises', *World Development* 27(1): 169–200.

Ocampo, J. A. (2005) 'The Quest for Dynamic Efficiency: Structural Dynamics and Economic Growth in Development Countries', in J. A. Ocampo (ed.) *Beyond Reforms: Structural Dynamics and Macroeconomic Vulnerability*. Washington, DC: UN Economic Commission for Latin America and the Caribbean (ECLAC).

Okazaki, K. (2007) 'Banking System Reform in China: The Challenges of Moving toward a Market-oriented Economy.' Occasional Paper, Rand Corporation.

Pearson, M. M. (2005) 'The Business of Governing Business in China: Institutions and Norms of the Emerging Regulatory State', *World Politics* 57(2): 296–322.

People's Bank of China (PBoC) (2018) Official Launch of China–IMF Joint Capacity Building Centre [in Chinese], April. Available at http://www.pbc.gov.cn/goutongjiaoliu/113456/113469/3518488/index.html

Perkins, D. (1988) 'Reforming China's Economic System', *Journal of Economic Literature* 26(2): 601–45.

Poon, D. (2014) 'China's Development Trajectory: A Strategic Opening for Industrial Policy in the South.' UNCTAD Discussion Paper No. 218, December.

Poon, D. (2018) 'China's Overseas Development Finance: Policy Tools and Mechanisms', in A. Jaguaribe (ed.) *Direction of Chinese Global Investments: Implications for Brazil*. Brasilia: Alexandre de Gusmao Foundation. Available at http://funag.gov.br/loja/download/1232-CHINESE-GLOBAL-INVESTIMENT.pdf.

Poon, D. (2019) 'An Analysis of China's Foreign Investment Guidance Catalogues 1995–2017.' ILO Working Paper (forthcoming).

Qian, Y. (2003) 'How Reform Worked in China', in D. Rodrik (ed.) *In Search of Prosperity: Analytic Narratives on Economic Growth*. Princeton, NJ: Princeton University Press, pp. 297–333.

Rawski, T. G. (1994) 'Chinese Industrial Reform: Accomplishment, Prospects, and Implications', *The American Economic Review* 84(2): 271–5.

Ray, J., K. Atha, E. Francis et al. (2016) 'China's Industrial and Military Robotics Development.' Prepared for U.S.–China Economic and Security Review Commission (USCC), October.

Shanghai Stock Exchange (SSE) (2015) 'What Is QFII and RQFII? Briefing on QFII Scheme and its Development.' Available at http://english.sse.com.cn/investors/qfii/what/.

Sicular, T. (1988) 'Agricultural Planning and Pricing in the Post-Mao Period', *The China Quarterly* 116: 671–705.

Singh, A. (1996) 'Savings, Investment and the Corporation in the East Asian Miracle.' UNCTAD Study 9, March.

Society of Automotive Engineers of China (SAEC) (2017) 'Hydrogen Fuel Cell Vehicle Technology Roadmap.' Strategy Advisory Committee of the Technology Roadmap for Energy Saving and New Energy Vehicles. Available at http://www.sae-china.org/news/society/201711/1667.html.

Song, L. (2018) 'State-owned Enterprise in China: Past, Present, and Prospects', in R. Garnaut, L. Song, and C. Fang (eds) *China's 40 Years of Reform and Development 1978–2018*. Canberra: Australian National University, pp. 345–73.

State-owned Assets Supervision and Administration Commission (SASAC) (2016) 'Implementation Plan for Improving the Functional Classification Assessment of Central Enterprises' [in Chinese]. September. Available at http://www.gov.cn/xinwen/2016-09/26/content_5112309.htm.

Stiglitz, J. E. and M. Uy (1996) 'Financial Markets, Public Policy, and the East Asian Miracle', *World Bank Research Observer*, 11(2): 249–76.

Szamosszegi, A. and C. Kyle (2011) 'An Analysis of State-owned Enterprises and State Capitalism in China.' Report prepared for US–China Economic and Security Review Commission (USCC), October.

Thomas, C. (2015) 'A New World under Construction: China and Semiconductors.' McKinsey & Company article, November, available at: https://www.mckinsey.com/featured-insights/asia-pacific/a-new-world-under-construction-china-and-semiconductors.

UNCTAD (1996) *Trade and Development Report 1996*. New York: United Nations.

UNCTAD (2016) 'The Role of Development Banks in Promoting Growth and Sustainable Development in the South.' UNCTAD Report, December. New York: United Nations. Available at: https://unctad.org/en/PublicationsLibrary/gdsecidc2016d1_en.pdf.

UNCTAD (2018) 'Scaling up Finance for the Sustainable Development Goals: Experimenting with Models of Multilateral Development Banking.' UNCTAD Report.

New York: United Nations. Available at: https://unctad.org/en/PublicationsLibrary/gdsecidc2017d4_en.pdf.

USTR (2018) Finding of the Investigation into China's Acts, Policies, and Practices Related to Technology Transfer, Intellectual Property, and Innovation under Section 301 of the Trade Act of 1974.' March.

Wade, R. (1990) *Governing the Market: Economic Theory and the Role of Government in East Asian Industrialization.* Princeton, NJ: Princeton University Press.

Wade, R. (1996) 'Japan, the World Bank, and the Art of Paradigm Maintenance: The East Asian Miracle in Political Perspective', *New Left Review* 217: 3–36.

Wade, R. (2003) 'What Strategies Are Viable for Developing Countries Today? The World Trade Organization and the Shrinking of "Development Space"', *Review of International Political Economy* 10(4): 621–44.

Wade, R. (2010) 'After the Crisis: Industrial Policy and the Developmental State in Low-Income Countries', *Global Policy* 1(2): 150–61.

Wade, R. (2018) 'Escaping the Periphery: The East Asian "Mystery" Solved.' WIDER Working Paper No. 2018/101, September.

Walter, C. E. and F. Howie (2011) *Red Capitalism: The Fragile Financial Foundation of China's Extraordinary Rise*, Singapore: John Wiley & Sons (Asia).

Wang, Z. (2017) 'National Integrated Circuit Industry Investment Fund: Implementing National Strategy by Means of Marketization' [in Chinese], *Manufacturing Strong Country Research* 18(32): 1–14. Available at: http://www.cm2025.org/uploadfile/2017/1219/20171219094926627.pdf.

Wright, L. and D. Rosen (2018) *Credit and Credibility: Risks to China's Economic Resilience.* Washington, DC: Center for Strategic and International Studies (CSIS).

Wu, F. and A. Seah (2008) 'The Rise of China Investment Corporation', *World Economics*, 9(2): 45–68, April-June.

Yi, G. (2014) 'The Logic of China's Path to Financial Sector Opening' [in Chinese], *China Reform*, October. Available at: https://finance.sina.com.cn/zl/china/20141009/142220493031.html.

Yusuf, S., K. Nabeshima, and D. H. Perkins (eds) (2006) *Under New Ownership: Privatizing China's State-Owned Enterprises.* Washington, DC: World Bank and Stanford University Press.

Zhang, F. (2018) 'The Chinese Developmental State: Standard Accounts and New Characteristics', *Journal of International Relations and Development* 21(3): 739–68.

Zhao, C. (2017) 'China's Financial Mechanisms in Industrial Development with Inspirations for Africa', in *Industrialize Africa: Strategies, Policies, Institutions, and Financing.* Abidjan: African Development Bank, pp. 171–80.

Zhu, M. (2018) 'China Financial Market Re-Opening: Internationalization of the Domestic Market' [in Chinese]. *China Finance* 40, May. Available at: http://www.cf40.org.cn/plus/view.php?aid=12698.

4
Catch-up and Mission-oriented Innovation

Mariana Mazzucato

4.1 Introduction

Innovation has not only a rate but also a direction: the twenty-first century is becoming increasingly defined by the need to respond to major social, environmental, and economic challenges.[1] Sometimes referred to as 'grand challenges', these include environmental threats like climate change, demographic, health and wellbeing concerns, as well as the difficulties of generating sustainable and inclusive growth. These problems are 'wicked' in the sense that they are complex, systemic, interconnected, and urgent, requiring insights from many perspectives. Poverty cannot be solved without attention to the interconnections between nutrition, health, infrastructure, and education, as well as redistributive tax policy. Grand challenge thinking is being applied both in developed and developing countries, with some of the most interesting experiments around sustainability being driven by the needs of emerging economies.

Turning these challenges into concrete problems that drive innovation across multiple sectors and actors, there is much to learn from 'mission-oriented' policies that in the past have been aimed at achieving specific objectives, whether landing a man on the moon, or battling climate change (Ergas, 1987; Mazzucato, 2014, 2017). Such policies require different actors (both public and private) and different sectors to innovate (going to the moon required innovation in aeronautics, robotics, textiles, and nutrition). At the same time, to be successful, they must enable bottom-up experimentation and learning so that the innovation process itself is nurtured through dynamic feedback loops and serendipity (Rodrik, 2004).

Examples of such direction-setting policies abound, including different technology policy initiatives in the United States (Mowery et al., 2010), France (Foray et al., 2009), the United Kingdom (Mowery et al., 2010), and Germany (Cantner and Pyka, 2001). Mission-oriented policies are not just about throwing funds at problems but doing so in specific ways. It is for this reason that it is useful to study how specific mission-oriented agencies and organizations have worked, whether

[1] This chapter is a revised version of Mazzucato (2018), 'Mission-Oriented Policies: Challenges and Opportunities', *Industrial and Corporate Change*, 27(5) (Special Issue: Mission-Oriented Innovation Policy and Dynamic Capabilities in the Public Sector).

in military R&D programmes, or in areas like health (Sampat, 2012), agriculture (Wright, 2012), or energy (Anadon, 2012). In these examples, the relevant organizations made choices on what to fund, going against the more classic position that the point of policymaking is simply to level the playing field. Indeed, these agencies, and the wider programmes around them, tilted the playing field through missions aimed at a public objective, with other policies needing to be introduced to make it more profitable to move in that direction (e.g. the US land grant system, or tax reliefs for green investments) (Mazzucato and Perez, 2015).

In this chapter I focus on the broader lessons from mission-oriented programmes for innovation policy—and indeed policies aimed at investment-led growth. While much has been written about case studies on missions (Mowery et al., 2010), this has not resulted in an alternative policymaking toolkit. Missions—at the least—require those tools to be just as much about market co-creating and market shaping, as they are about market fixing (Mazzucato, 2016; Nelson, 2011).

The chapter first reviews the characteristics of mission-oriented programmes before looking at key features of those programmes that can provide lessons. A discussion follows on how to choose and implement mission-oriented policies, with an example, and the final section concludes.

4.2 From Technological Feats to Wicked Problems

Mission-oriented policies can be defined as systemic public policies that draw on frontier knowledge to attain specific goals, or 'big science deployed to meet big problems' (Ergas, 1987). While the archetypical historical mission is NASA putting a man on the moon, contemporary missions aim to address broader challenges that require long-term commitment to the development of challenges that are as much social as technological (Foray et al., 2012). The active role being taken by governments and transnational organizations to develop strategies for a greener economy can be seen through a mission-oriented lens—as can those being developed to create greater wellbeing for an ageing population, and better jobs for modern youth (European Commission, 2011). In fact, these challenges—which can be environmental, demographic, economic, or social—have entered innovation policy agendas as key justifications for action, providing strategic direction for funding policies and innovation efforts.

However, societal missions are much more complex because they are less clearly defined and indeed must be co-defined by many stakeholders (how to frame the challenge around inequality is more difficult than those around the space race) (Foray et al., 2012). One could add that these challenges also require big regulatory and behavioural changes at the societal/national systems level. Nelson's work *The Moon and the Ghetto* (2011) asked the demanding question of why innovation has resulted in such difficult feats as landing a man on the moon, and yet continues to be so terribly disorganized and technologically unsavvy in dealing with the more earthly problems of poverty, illiteracy, and the emergence of ghettos and slums. He argued that while politics was partly the culprit, the real problem was that a purely scientific and technological solution could not solve such problems. Even at the disciplinary level there is a greater need to combine understandings of sociology, politics, economics, and technology to solve these problems, as well as to make the conscious decision to point innovation towards them. This is exactly what a well-designed mission can achieve.

The so-called Maastricht Memorandum provides a detailed analysis of the differences between old and new mission-oriented projects (Table 4.1).

Although the memorandum specifically focuses on mission-oriented programmes that tackle environmental challenges, its analysis applies to other contemporary challenges (water and food supply, energy efficiency and security, disease, demographic change, etc.). This is because these challenges all present similar characteristics, particularly that new technological solutions to address them will require long-term commitment from both public and private agents, and increasingly those in the non-profit sector. They will in most cases also require changes in regulation and tax policies. And the diffusion of solutions to

Table 4.1 Characteristics of old and new mission-oriented projects

Old: Defence, nuclear, and aerospace	New: Environmental technologies and societal challenges
Diffusion of the results outside the core of participants is of minor importance or actively discouraged	Diffusion of the results is a central goal and is actively encouraged
The mission is defined in terms of the number of technical achievements, with little regard to their economic feasibility	The mission is defined in terms of economically feasible technical solutions to particular societal problems
The goals and the direction of technological development are defined in advance by a small group of experts	The direction of technical change is influenced by a wide range of actors including government, private firms, and consumer groups
Centralized control within a government administration	Decentralized control with a large number of agents involved
Participation is limited to a small group of firms due to the emphasis on a small number of radical technologies	Emphasis on the development of both radical and incremental innovations in order to permit a large number of firms to participate
Self-contained projects with little need for complementary policies and scant attention paid to coherence	Complementary policies vital for success and close attention paid to coherence with other goals

Source: Modified version of Table 5 in Soete and Arundel (1993: 51).

a broad base of users requires as much attention to demand-side policies as to supply-side ones.

The six characteristics of contemporary missions identified in Table 4.1—diffusion of technologies, economic feasibility, shared sense of direction, decentralized control by public agencies, development of both radical and incremental innovations, and enabling complementary policies—are of pragmatic importance for the promotion and implementation of mission-oriented policies.

A mission-oriented approach highlights the need to make a precise diagnosis of the technological, sectoral, or national innovation system that an innovation policy wishes to transform. The alignment of different types of capabilities is key for the success of any mission-oriented policy. These can be described as follows (Mazzucato and Penna, 2016a):

- *Missions should be well defined.* More granular definition of the technological challenge facilitates the establishment of intermediate goals and deliverables, and processes of monitoring and accountability. When governance is too broad, it can become faulty, and there is a risk of being captured by vested interests.
- *A mission does not comprise a single R&D or innovation project, but a portfolio of such projects.* Because R&D and innovation is highly uncertain, some projects will fail and others will succeed. All concerned should be able to accept failures and to use them as learning experiences. Furthermore, stakeholders should not be punished because of failures derived from good-faith efforts.
- *Missions should result in investment across different sectors and involve different types of actors.* In order to have highest impact, missions should embrace actors across an entire economy, not just in one sector and not just in the private or public realm.
- *Missions require joined-up policymaking,* whereby the priorities are translated into concrete policy instruments and actions to be carried out by all levels of the public institutions involved. While these missions should involve a range of public institutions, it is crucial that there is a strategic division of labour amongst them, with well-defined responsibilities for coordination and monitoring.

These considerations point to the need to adopt a pragmatic approach to defining missions. Chosen missions should be feasible, draw on existing public and private resources, be amenable to existing policy instruments, and command broad and continuous political support. Missions should create a long-term public agenda for innovation policies, address a societal demand or need, and draw on the high potential of the country's science and technology system to develop innovations.

4.3 Key Lessons from Mission-Oriented Policies

Mission-oriented policies can transform the policymaker's tool kit. The next section reviews ways in which mission thinking requires an alternative lens for policymaking.

4.3.1 From Picking Winners to Picking the Willing

Missions are about setting concrete directions, which of course must be picked, that is, chosen strategically. The choice is not whether or not to pick but *how*: picking directions is not the same thing as 'picking winners' in the sense of picking individual firms or sectors. It is about deciding that a transformation must occur in society—and making it happen. The direction will require different missions, which provide a focusing device for the different actors and sectors to collaborate in order to concretely achieve it. Thus missions require picking the willing: those organizations across the economy (in different sectors, including both the public and private spheres) that are willing to engage with a societally relevant mission.

Missions are a new way to frame 'vertical policies'. Industrial and innovation policies require both horizontal and vertical policies working together systemically. Traditionally, industrial strategy has often focused on (vertical) sectoral interventions. Until the end of the 1970s this consisted of various measures ranging from indicative planning to outright nationalization of entire industries (e.g. steel, coal, shipbuilding, aerospace).

Although certain sectors might be more suited to sector-specific strategies, there are good reasons for avoiding a sectoral approach—particularly when private lobbying interests may prevail in negotiating specific provisions with the government (Buchanan, 2003), negatively influencing the industrial strategy with indirect measures (e.g. tax credits) that potentially waste public funds and create little if no additionality in terms of new investment. The patent box tax policies being adopted in many countries are an example of these misconceived policies since there is no reason to lower tax on monopoly profits and it has been shown to have little effect on additional research investment (Griffith et al., 2010).

A mission-oriented approach uses specific challenges to stimulate innovation across sectors. Through well-defined missions—focused on solving important societal challenges related to climate change and environmental quality, demographic changes, health and wellbeing, mobility issues, etc.—governments have the opportunity to determine the direction of growth by making strategic investments throughout the innovation chain and creating the potential for greater spillovers across multiple sectors, including low-tech sectors (Foray et al., 2012).

Germany's *Energiewende* is an interesting case of the use of an integrated strategy that addresses several sectors and technologies in the economy and enables bottom-up learning processes. With its missions to fight climate change, phase out nuclear power, improve energy security by substituting imported fossil fuels with renewable sources, and increase energy efficiency, *Energiewende* is providing a direction to technical change and growth across different sectors through targeted transformations in production, distribution, and consumption.

This has allowed even a traditional sector like steel to use the 'green' direction to renew itself. While the steel industry in many countries remains relatively low tech and subsidized, it was the *Energiewende* policy that placed pressure on steel to lower its material content. It did so through the use of a 'reuse, recycle, and repurpose' strategy (BMUB, 2016). In this sense, mission-oriented policies should be focused on ways to provide sectors with transformation policies—fewer subsidies and more focused policies that reward investment and innovation that meet a need.

4.3.2 From Fixing Markets to Actively Co-shaping

Missions do not fix existing markets but create new markets. Indeed, this transformation ambition can be seen in the explicit remit of mission-oriented organizations. Examples below from three classic mission-oriented agencies exemplify the point: the organizations are not about fixing existing markets but creating new landscapes:

- *NASA*: to '[d]rive advances in science, technology, aeronautics, and space exploration to enhance knowledge, education, innovation, economic vitality, and stewardship of Earth' (NASA 2014 Strategic Plan).
- *DARPA*: 'Creating breakthrough technologies for national security is the mission of the Defense Advanced Research Projects Agency'.
- *National Institute of Health (NIH)*: to 'seek fundamental knowledge about the nature and behaviour of living systems and the application of that knowledge to enhance health, lengthen life, and reduce illness and disability.'

By breaking new ground, and bringing together different players, they are better able to attract top talent as it is an 'honour' and interesting to work for them. By actively creating new areas of growth they are also potentially able to 'crowd in' business investment by increasing business expectations about where future growth opportunities might lie (Mazzucato and Penna, 2015).

This proactive approach, whereby the state leads and business follows, is different from the traditional approach where the state is at best a fixer of markets. The market-fixing approach has its roots in neoclassical economic theory, which asserts that competitive markets will bring about optimal outcomes if left to their own devices. This theory justifies government 'intervention' in the economy only if there are explicit market failures, which might arise from the presence of positive externalities (e.g. public goods like basic research, which require public-sector spending on science), negative externalities (e.g. pollution, which requires public-sector taxation), and incomplete information (where the public sector may provide incubators or loan guarantees).[2] On top of this, the literature on systems of innovation has also highlighted the presence of system failures—for example the lack of linkages between science and industry—requiring the creation of new institutions enabling those linkages (Lundvall, 1992).

And yet missions exemplify a more proactive approach to policy than fixing suggests. It has required public organizations to be responsible for actively shaping and creating markets and systems, not just fixing them; and for creating wealth, not just redistributing it.

In a market failure framework, *ex ante* analysis aims to estimate benefits and costs (including those associated with government failures), while *ex post* analysis seeks to verify whether the estimates were correct and the market failure successfully addressed. In contrast, a mission-oriented framework, which actively co-creates new markets, requires continuous and dynamic monitoring and evaluation throughout the innovation policy process. The notion of public value becomes a more useful term than a public good since missions may be transformative across the entire value chain and not be limited to narrow areas where positive and negative externalities exist.

4.3.3 From Fearing Failure to Welcoming Experimentation

Systemic mission-oriented policies must be based on a sound and clear diagnosis and prognosis (foresight). This requires not only the identification of missing links, failures, and bottlenecks—the weaknesses or challenges of a national system of innovation—but also recognition of the system's strengths. Foresight is necessary in order to scrutinize future opportunities and identify how strengths may be used to overcome weaknesses. This diagnosis should be used to devise concrete strategies, novel institutions, and new linkages in the innovation system (Mazzucato, 2016a).

In its most general form, the mission-oriented framework differentiates between public policies that target the development of specific technologies in line with state-defined goals ('missions') and those that aim at the institutional development of a system of innovation (Ergas, 1987). The state must therefore be able to learn from past experiences in mission-oriented innovation policy.

[2] Reviews of the impact of positive externalities and incomplete information on innovation financing are provided in Hall (2002), Hall and Lerner (2010), and more recent evidence is reviewed in Kerr and Nanda (2015). The role for government in the face of negative externalities (climate change) is laid out in Jaffe et al. (2005).

Systems and eco-systems of innovation (sectoral, regional, and national) require the presence of dynamic links between the different actors and institutions (firms, financial institutions, research/education, public-sector funds, intermediary institutions) as well as horizontal links within organizations and institutions (Freeman, 1995). What should also be emphasized, and has not been thus far in the literature on innovation systems, is the nature of the actual actors and institutions required for innovation-led growth (Mazzucato, 2016a).

In order to stimulate the innovation process by shaping and creating technologies, sectors, and markets, missions require dynamic relationships to be developed which create trust between actors. It is essential in this process for lead public organizations to galvanize the interests of relevant actors and organize themselves so that they have the 'intelligence' to think big and formulate bold policies that create a sense of ownership amongst diverse public, private, and academic stakeholders. It is also crucial to be able to implement the policies by coordinating the efforts of this network of stakeholders through the state's convening power, brokering of trust relationships, and use of targeted policy instruments.

Because innovation is extremely uncertain, the ability to experiment and explore is key for a successful entrepreneurial state (Hirschman, 1967; Rodrik, 2004, Mazzucato, 2013). Therefore, a crucial element in organizing the state for its entrepreneurial role is absorptive capacity or institutional learning (Cohen and Levinthal, 1990; Johnson, 1992). Government agencies learn in a process of investment, discovery, and experimentation that is part of mission-oriented initiatives. This requires 'dynamic capabilities' in the public sector.

Other authors have referred to processes of experimentation and learning process as 'smart specialisation' (Foray et al., 2009).[3] However, smart specialization is most commonly used in connection with a market failure framework, meaning that it is seen as a discovery process for the identification of bottlenecks, failures, and missing links (that is, market failures or market gaps). Smart specialization would be more usefully employed in connection with a systemic perspective on innovation policies.

Key to mission-oriented innovation is the exploration of the characteristics of innovation agencies that must be in place so that they can welcome uncertainty and build explorative capacity. Breznitz and Ornston (2013) focus on the role of peripheral agencies, arguing that when they become too central and well funded they lose their flexibility and ability to think outside the box. While flexibility is undoubtedly important, it is also true that some of the most important innovation agencies in Europe and the United States were not so peripheral, as can be seen from DARPA's continued success in recent years. What seems to be more important for these organizations is a degree of political independence. Indeed, Italy's public holding company IRI (the Istituto per la Ricostruzione Industriale

[3] See also also Foray (2018).

established in 1933) had its most successful phase before the 1970s when it was public. The key lesson is that it is not about public or private, but what kind of public and what kind of private.

4.3.4 From a Focus on Quantity of Finance to a Focus on the Quality

If we focus on the market-making role, rather than the market-fixing one of missions, it also becomes clearer why they have required public investments by mission-oriented institutions along the entire innovation chain, not just basic upstream research. Institutions like the National Science Foundation (NSF) have been critical to basic research, institutions like DARPA and Advanced Research Projects Agency-Energy (ARPA-E) to translational research, and institutions like the Small Business Innovation Research (SBIR) to long-term finance for companies. Block has called this distributed network of different state actors the 'developmental network state' (Block and Keller, 2011). Better understanding of the distribution of public agencies, their positioning across the innovation chain, and the balance between directive and bottom-up interactions is a key area for future study.

From 1936 to 2016, cumulative R&D expenditure by NIH amounted to more than US$900 billion (in 2015 dollars), and since 2004 has exceeded US$30 billion per year. Perhaps unsurprisingly, research shows that around 75 per cent of the most innovative drugs on the market today (the so-called 'new molecular' entities with priority rating) owe much of their funding to the NIH (Angell, 2005). Moreover, NIH's share in total US federal outlay on R&D has increased year on year over the past fifty years. This suggests that the surge in absolute NIH-related R&D expenditure cannot simply be conceived as resulting from a generalized and proportional increase in total R&D expenditure by the government during downturns, or as simply levelling the playing field. Instead, it appears a deliberate and targeted choice on where to direct public R&D funding.

Due to the short-term nature of private finance, the role of public institutions is often to provide longer lead times and the willingness to engage with high uncertainty. While in some countries this has occurred through public agencies, such as DARPA and NIH mentioned above, in others, patient finance has been provided through other institutions including publicly owned development banks, otherwise known as state investment banks. State investment banks (SIBs) have their historical roots in the monetary agreements of Bretton Woods and the reconstruction plans for Europe following the Second World War. The idea was to create an institution that promoted financial stability through a permanent flow of finance to fund the reconstruction plan and unleash agricultural production potential, thus preventing the deleterious effects that speculative private finance could have on post-war economic recovery (World Bank, 2015).

While the traditional functions of SIBs were in infrastructure investment and counter-cyclical lending during recession when private banks restrained credit (a classic Keynesian role), they have, over time, become more active as key players in the innovation system. They have provided the patient capital for innovative firms, and also focused on modern societal challenges with technological 'missions'. For example, SIBs have notably filled the vacuum left behind by private commercial banks since the financial crisis, more than trebling their investments in clean energy projects between 2007 and 2012 (Mazzucato and Penna, 2016b; Fried et al., 2012). A report by Bloomberg New Energy Finance finds that in 2013 SIBs were the largest funders of the deployment and diffusion phase of renewable energy (Mazzucato and Semieniuk, 2017), outpacing investment from the private sector (Louw, 2012). Examples of 'mission-oriented' investments include: the European Investment Bank's €14.7 billion commitment to sustainable city projects in Europe (Griffith-Jones and Tyson, 2012), the efforts of KfW to support Germany's *Energiewende* policies through the greening and modernization of German industries and infrastructures, China Development Bank's investments in renewable energies, and the technology fund put in place by BNDES (2012) to channel resources toward selected technologies in Brazil (FUNTEC).

4.3.5 Engagement

Understanding how the definition of missions can be opened up to a wider group of stakeholders, including movements in civil society (as discussed by Leadbeater, 2018), is a key area of interest. Indeed, it was to a large extent the green movement in Germany (including but not restricted to the Green Party) that led to a slow cumulative interest in society about tackling green missions, which was subsequently represented in the *Energiewende* agenda.

Understanding more democratic processes through which missions are defined and targeted is tied to rethinking the notion of public value. Indeed, part of building a market-shaping and -creating framework that can guide mission-oriented thinking beyond the market failure framework involves rethinking public value beyond the notion of the 'public good'. Too often the public good concept has been used to limit and constrain the activities of public actors, creating a static distinction between activities for business and those for policy. This means that ambitious policies—daring to reimagine the market rather than just fixing the public good problem—have then been accused of 'crowding out' private activity, whether the accused are innovation agencies, public banks, or the BBC (Mazzucato and O'Donovan, 2016).

But similarly, achieving public value cannot be the work only of the public sector; hence opening up this process to include a wider set of stakeholders—involved in the definition of missions as well as the serendipitous process of how to achieve them—will be an exciting new area of analysis linked to twenty-first-century innovation policy targeting grand challenges.

4.3.6 From De-risking to Sharing Both Risks and Rewards

Missions require a vision about the direction in which to drive an economy, focusing investment in particular areas, not just creating the horizontal (framework) conditions for change. Even if this is not about 'picking winners' in the classical sense, but more about 'picking the willing' (those organizations across the economy interested and willing to help achieve a mission), crucial choices must be made on which organizations to support, the fruits of which will create some winners, but also many losers. For example, as part of Obama's drive to create green growth, the US Department of Energy provided guaranteed loans to two green-tech companies: Solyndra (US$500 million) and Tesla Motors (US$465 million). While the latter is often glorified as a success story, the former failed miserably and became the latest example in the media of a government being inefficient and unable to pick winners (Wood, 2012). However, any venture capitalist will admit that for every winning investment (such as Tesla) there are many losses (such as Solyndra).

And these types of investments are often those that private venture capitalists are not willing to make due to their exit-driven model that seeks short-term returns (usually three-to-five-year cycles). In many sectors, venture capitalists have entered only after decades of public investment (e.g. NIH in biotech, or the role of SBIR in other areas, as discussed in Block and Keller, 2011). And some have argued that it is precisely this short-termism that has caused problems in sectors like biotechnology (Lazonick and Tulum, 2011; Pisano, 2006).

But there is another side to the story. If public funds do act as public forms of venture capital (VC), then there is reason to argue that the rewards should be proportional to the risks actually taken. In making their downstream investments, therefore, governments can learn from portfolio strategies of venture capitalists, structuring investments across a risk space so that lower-risk investments can help to cover the higher-risk ones. In other words, if the public sector is expected to compensate for the lack of private VC money going to early-stage innovation, it should at least be able to benefit from the wins, as private VC does. Otherwise, the funding for such investments cannot be secured. It may be desirable to allow the state to reap some of the rewards from its investments for a number of other reasons (Mazzucato and Wray, 2015). Matching this type of spending with the corresponding return would provide a measure of efficiency, holding policy-makers accountable; government net spending has limits dictated by the real resource capacity of the economy; and voters will be more willing to accept the (inevitable) failures if they see that these are compensated by important successes.

As discussed in Mazzucato (2013) and Laplane and Mazzucato (2018), the public sector can use a number of return-generating mechanisms for its investments, including retaining equity or royalties, retaining a golden share of the IPR, using income-contingent loans, or capping the prices (which the taxpayer pays) of those products that emanate, as drugs do, from public funds (Mazzucato, 2013).

4.3.7 In Sum, a New Approach to Policymaking

The principles above can be summarized in four big questions, encapsulated by the provocative acronym R-O-A-R. Policy must ROAR in order to lead with an ambitious challenge, nurturing organizational capabilities, new forms of assessment, and a better sharing of rewards so that innovation-driven growth can also result in inclusive growth (Mazzucato, 2016a):

- *Routes and directions*: how to use policy to actively set a direction of change; how to foster more dynamic (bottom-up) debates about possible directions to ensure enduring democratic legitimacy; and how to choose and define particular missions concretely, but with sufficient breadth to motivate action across different sectors and actors in an economy.
- *Organizations*: how to build decentralized networks of explorative public organizations that can learn by doing and welcome trial and error, with the confidence and capability to lead and form dynamic partnerships with private and third-sector partners; how to manage and evaluate progress, learning, and adaptation; and how to use a portfolio approach to balance inevitable failure with success.
- *Assessment*: how to evaluate the dynamic impact of public-sector market-creating investments, going beyond the static ideas embodied in cost/benefit analysis and ideas of 'crowding in' and 'crowding out', based on a richer conception of public value creation; how to develop new indicators and assessment tools to aid decision-making.
- *Risks and rewards*: how to structure new types of deals between public and private sectors so that rewards are shared as much as risks taken.

These questions provide a starting point for the new categories of thought that are needed, with many more questions following in relation to application in particular contexts.

4.4 Choosing and Implementing Mission-Oriented Policies

Missions should be broad enough to engage the public and attract cross-sectoral investment; and remain focused enough to involve industry and achieve measurable

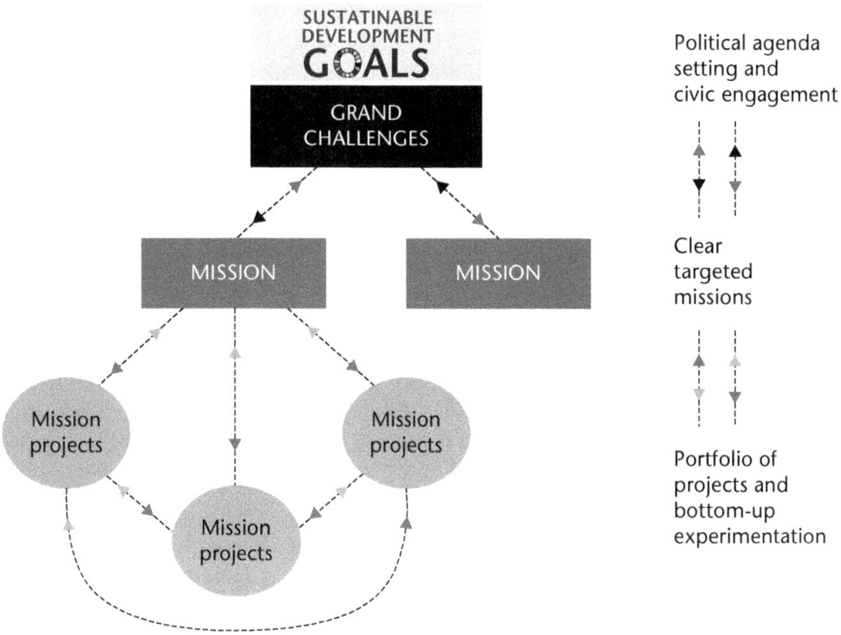

Figure 4.1 From challenges to missions
Source: Based on Mazzucato (2018)

success. By setting the direction for a solution, missions do not specify how to achieve success. Rather, they stimulate the development of a range of different solutions to achieve the objective. As such, a mission can make a significant and concrete contribution to meeting a sustainable development goal (SDG) or societal challenge.

For example, SDG 14, 'Conserve and sustainably use the oceans, seas and marine resources for sustainable development', could be broken down into various missions, for example 'a plastic-free ocean' (European Commission, 2018). This could stimulate research and innovation in ways of clearing plastic waste from oceans, or reducing use of plastics, innovation in new materials, research on health impacts of micro-plastics, and behavioural research and innovation to improve recycling or drive public engagement in cleaning up beaches. Each of these areas can be broken down into particular 'projects'. Missions must be chosen. Yet their success will depend on the bottom-up processes that nurture innovation while 'getting there'. A culture of experimentation and risk-taking is a crucial element in the philosophy of missions. There must be incentives to 'think outside the box' to come up with new solutions to address the mission objective. This requires a portfolio approach, based on different solutions, and a broad range of different interactions. The objective should be addressed by multiple actors, stimulating cross-disciplinary academic work, with a strong focus on the intersection between natural sciences, formal sciences, social sciences, and humanities; collaborations across different industries; and new forms of partnership between the public sector, the private sector, and civil society organizations. Innovation itself is often characterized by feedback effects, trial and error, and serendipity (the search for one thing leads to the discovery of another)—picking missions that have different possibilities for solutions will enhance the innovation dynamic itself.

How should missions be picked? The following five criteria build on the issues raised above and are clearly set out in the European Commission report on missions that will be framing the new (FP) Horizon programme (Mazzucato, 2018):

(1) *Bold, inspirational with wide societal relevance*

Missions should engage the public. They should make clear that through ambitious, bold action at the European level, solutions will be developed that will have an impact on people's daily lives. To do this, missions must outline exciting opportunities for bold innovation—while being connected to debates in society about what the key challenges are, like sustainability, inequality, health, climate change, and increasing the quality of the welfare state.

(2) *A clear direction: targeted, measureable, and time-bound*

Missions need to be very clearly framed. While enabling long-term investments, they need a specific target that can either be formulated in binary ways (as clearly as whether man has reached the moon and returned back safely) or quantified (as clearly as whether a certain percentage reduction in carbon emissions against a baseline has been reached across manufacturing). In addition, they will need a clear time frame within which actions should take place. This needs to be long enough to allow the process to grow, for actors to build relationships and interact, while at the same time being time-limited. Without specific targets and timing, it will not be possible to determine success (or failure), or measure progress towards success.

(3) *Ambitious but realistic research and innovation actions*

Mission objectives should be set in an ambitious manner (taking risks), centred on research and innovation activities across the entire innovation chain, including the feedback effects between basic and applied research. Ambitious objectives will ensure that researchers and innovators are challenged to deliver what would otherwise not be attempted ('additionality' in research). Yet, the objective should be framed to be on the one hand high risk but also realistically feasible, at least in theory, within the given time period. Setting the technical objectives unrealistically high will result in a lack of buy-in, while setting the objective too low will not incentivize extra efforts—or provide inspiration.

(4) *Cross-disciplinary, cross-sectoral, and cross-actor innovation*

Missions should be framed in such a way as to spark activity across, and among, multiple scientific disciplines (including social sciences and humanities), across different industrial sectors (e.g. transport, nutrition, health, services), and different types of actors (public, private, third sector, civil society organizations). Missions need to be chosen to address clear challenges that stimulate the private sector to invest where it would not have otherwise invested ('additionality' in business). With a problem-focused and not a sectoral lens, problems related to sustainability, for example, will not just involve renewable energy, but could also involve transport, strategic design, and new digital solutions, amongst others. Similarly, problems related to health will involve innovation not only in pharmaceuticals but also in such areas as nutrition, artificial intelligence, mobility, and new forms of digitally enhanced public service provision.

Missions connect all relevant actors through new forms of partnership for co-design and co-creation by focusing on targets that require multiple sectors and actors to solve. Thus, mission-oriented innovation has the possibility of leading to system-wide transformation.

(5) *Multiple, bottom-up solutions*

Missions should not be achievable by a single development path, or by a single technology. They must be open to being addressed by different types of solutions. A mission-based approach is clear on the expected outcome. However, the trajectory to reach the outcome must be based on a bottom-up approach of multiple solutions—some of which will fail or have to be adjusted along the way.

4.5 Conclusion: A Practical Approach to Implementing Mission-Oriented Innovation Policies

The chapter opened with the observation that governments are increasingly seeking economic growth that is smart (innovation-led), inclusive, and sustainable. We need to see this in the context of grand social challenges such as tackling climate change, improving public health and wellbeing, and adjusting to demographic changes.

Missions cannot happen without new toolkits. We have discussed the need for policy itself to be seen as market making and shaping rather than just fixing, and the need for particular tools including the use of patient finance, and the ability of state actors to experiment, explore, and build capacities for learning.

It is clear that such capacity will be required at different levels. These include:

- *Scientific-technological capacity*: an appropriate scientific and technological knowledge base in the education and research subsystem;
- *Demand capacity*: latent or effective (public or private) market demand, in terms of both purchasing power and need;
- *Productive capacity*: an appropriate business base (e.g. existing firms or entrepreneurs willing to take risks to establish an innovative firm) in the production and innovation subsystem;

- *State capacity*: appropriate knowledge inside the public organizations formulating and executing policies about the problem and solution being targeted and/or knowledge about who-knows-what-and-how;
- *Policy capacity*: appropriate supply-side and demand-side policy instruments (strategically deployed), supported by complementary policies;
- *Foresight capacity*: a fine-tuned diagnosis of the problem and solution, including an analysis of the current situation and future prospects for targeted technologies and sectors, formulated in terms of a well-defined mission and vision.

Successful mission-oriented policy experiments require all six factors in place. They require a more dynamic framing of key questions: less about picking or not picking, and more about the institutional and organizational capacity of forming broadly defined directions, through strategic deliberation. Less about static cost–benefit metrics which so often result in accusations of 'crowding out' and more about dynamic assessment criteria that can nurture and evaluate market-shaping processes and capture the spillovers that are created across sectors.

Mission-oriented innovation policy has a major part to play in delivering better-quality growth while addressing grand challenges, but the changes in mindset, theoretical frameworks, institutional capacities, and policies required are by no means trivial.

Mission-oriented innovation policy is far from being a step into the unknown. As set out in this chapter, substantial theory, evidence, case studies, and experience have been accumulated over many decades of successful practice. It is also important to understand the challenges associated with gathering the necessary political commitment and public legitimacy behind such ambitious policies.

To reap the substantial benefits from this approach, what is needed is to abandon the ideology that often informs, and misinforms, the role that the state can play in the economy. Public, private, and third-sector actors can work together in new ways to co-create and shape the markets of the future. We can learn from practical policy experiences to foster a more coherent and cohesive framework across sectors, institutions, and nations. Only in this way can investment-led growth not only help address the growth problem but help solve the wicked twenty-first-century challenges ahead.

References

Anadon, L. D. (2012) 'Missions-oriented RD&D Institutions in Energy: A Comparative Analysis of China, the United Kingdom, and the United States', *Research Policy* 41(10): 1742–56.

Angell, M. (2005) *The Truth about the Drug Companies: How They Deceive Us and What to Do about It*. New York: Random House.

Block, F. L. and M. R. Keller (eds) (2011) *State of Innovation: The U.S. Government's Role in Technology Development.* Boulder, CO: Paradigm Publishers.

BMUB (2016) 'German Resource Efficiency Programme II.' Available at: http://www.bmub.bund.de/fileadmin/Daten_BMU/Pools/Broschueren/german_resource_efficiency_programme_ii_bf.pdf.

BNDES (2012) 'Apoio À Inovação.' Rio de Janeiro: BNDES.

Breznitz, D. and D. Ornston (2013) 'The Revolutionary Power of Peripheral Agencies: Explaining Radical Policy Innovation in Finland and Israel', *Comparative Political Studies* 46(10): 1219–45.

Buchanan, J. M. (2003) 'Public Choice: The Origins and Development of a Research Program', *Champions of Freedom* 31: 13–22.

Cantner, U. and A. Pyka (2001) 'Classifying Technology Policy from an Evolutionary Perspective', *Research Policy* 30(5): 759–75.

Cohen, W. M. and D. A. Levinthal (1990) 'Absorptive Capacity: A New Perspective on Learning and Innovation', *Administrative Science Quarterly* 35(1): 128–52.

Ergas, H. (1987) 'Does Technology Policy Matter?' in *Technology and Global Industry: Companies and Nations in the World Economy.* National Research Council. Washington, DC: National Academies Press, pp. 191–245.

European Commission (2011) 'Green Paper–From Challenges to Opportunities: Towards a Common Strategic Framework for EU Research and Innovation Funding.' Brussels: European Commission.

European Commission (2018) 'European Strategy for Plastics.' Available at: http://ec.europa.eu/environment/waste/plastic_waste.htm.

Foray, D. (2018) 'Smart Specialization Strategies as a Case of Mission-oriented Policy—a Case Study on the Emergence of New Policy Practices. *Industrial and Corporate Change, 27*(5), 817–832.

Foray, D., P. A. David, and B. Hall, B. (2009) 'Smart Specialisation: The Concept.' Knowledge Economists Policy Brief (Expert group on Knowledge for growth) No. 9.

Foray, D., D. Mowery, and R. R. Nelson (2012) 'Public R&D and Social Challenges: What Lessons from Mission R&D Programs?' *Research Policy* 41(10): 1697–902.

Freeman, C. (1995) 'The "National System of Innovation" in Historical Perspective', *Cambridge Journal of Economics* 19(1): 5–24.

Fried, L. S., S. Shukla, and S. Sawyer (eds) (2012) 'Global Wind Report: Annual Market Update 2011', Global Wind Energy Council, March.

Griffith, R., H. Miller, and M. O'Connell (2010) 'Corporate Taxes and Intellectual Property: Simulating the Effect of Patent Boxes.' IFS Briefing Note No. 112, Institute for Fiscal Studies.

Griffith-Jones, S. and J. Tyson (2012) 'The European Investment Bank and its Role in Regional Development and Integration', in M. A. Cintra and K. D. R. Gomes (eds), *The Transformations of the International Financial System.* Brasília: IPEA.

Hall, B. H. (2002) 'The Financing of Research and Development', *Oxford Review of Economic Policy* 18(1): 35–51.

Hall, B. H. and J. Lerner (2010) 'The Financing of R&D and Innovation', in B. H. Hall and N. Rosenberg (eds) *Handbook of the Economics of Innovation*, Vol. 1. Amsterdam: North-Holland, pp. 609–39.

Hirschman, A. O. (1967) *Development Projects Observed.* Washington, DC: Brookings Institution Press.

Jaffe, A. B., R. G. Newell, and R. N. Stavins (2005) 'A Tale of Two Market Failures: Technology and Environmental Policy', *Ecological Economics* 54(2–3): 164–74.

Johnson, B. H. (1992) 'Institutional Learning', in B.-Å. Lundvall (ed.) *National Systems of Innovation: Towards a Theory of Innovation and Interactive Learning*. London: Pinter, pp. 23–44.

Kerr, W. R. and R. Nanda (2015) 'Financing Innovation', *Annual Review of Financial Economics* 7: 445–62.

Lazonick, W. and Ö. Tulum (2011) 'U.S. Biopharmaceutical Finance and the Sustainability of the U.S. Biotechnology Business Model', *Research Policy* 40(9): 1170–87.

Leadbeater, C. (2018). 'Movements with Missions Make Markets'. UCL Institute for Innovation and Public Purpose Working Paper Series (IIPP WP 2018-07). Available at https://www.ucl.ac.uk/bartlett/public-purpose/wp2018-07.

Louw, A. (2012) 'Development Banks: Less for Green in 2013?' Renewables Research Note, 2012, Bloomberg New Energy Finance.

Lundvall, B.-Å . (1992) 'Introduction', in B.-Å. Lundvall (ed.) *National Systems of Innovation: Toward a Theory of Innovation and Interactive Learning.* London: Pinter, pp. 1–20.

Mazzucato, M. (2013) *The Entrepreneurial State: Debunking the Public vs. Private Myth in Risk and Innovation.* London: Anthem Press.

Mazzucato, M. (2014) Think Piece: 'A Mission-oriented Approach to Building the Entrepreneurial State.' Paper commissioned by Innovate UK-Technology Strategy Board November 2014T14/165. Available at: https://www.gov.uk/government/news/long-term-growth-innovations-role-in-economic-success.

Mazzucato, M. (2016) 'From Market Fixing to Market-Creating: A New Framework for Innovation Policy', Special Issue of *Industry and Innovation:* 'Innovation Policy—Can It Make a Difference?' 23(2): 140–56.

Mazzucato, M. (2017) 'Mission-oriented Innovation Policy: Challenges and Opportunities.' UCL Institute for Innovation and Public Purpose Working Paper (2017-1). Available at https://www.ucl.ac.uk/bartlett/public-purpose/publications/2018/jan/mission-oriented-innovation-policy-challenges-and-opportunities.

Mazzucato, M. (2018) 'Mission-oriented Research and Innovation in the European Union: A Problem-solving Approach to Fuel Innovation-led Growth.' Brussels: Directorate-General for Research and Innovation, European Commission. Available at: https://publications.europa.eu/en/publication-detail/-/publication/5b2811d1-16be-11e8-9253-01aa75ed71a1/language-en#.

Mazzucato, M. and C. C. R. Penna (eds) (2015) *Mission-oriented Finance for Innovation: New Ideas for Investment-Led Growth.* London: Policy Network/Rowman & Littlefield.

Mazzucato, M. and C. Penna (2016a) 'The Brazilian Innovation System: A Mission-oriented Policy Proposal.' Report for the Brazilian Government commissioned by the Brazilian Ministry for Science, Technology and Innovation through the Centre for Strategic Management and Studies, (06/04/2016). Available at: https://www.cgee.org.br/the-brazilian-innovation-system.

Mazzucato, M. and C. Penna (2016b) 'Beyond Market Failures: The Market Creating and Shaping Roles of State Investment Banks', *Journal of Economic Policy Reform* 19(4): 305–26.

Mazzucato, M. and C. O'Donovan (2016) 'The BBC as Market Shaper and Creator', in N. Seth-Smith et al. (eds), *Rethinking the BBC: Public Media in the 21st Century.* Commonwealth Publishing. Available at: http://commonwealth-publishing.com/shop/rethinking-the-bbc-public-media-in-the-21st-century/.

Mazzucato, M. and G. Semieniuk (2017) 'Public Financing of Innovation: New Questions', *Oxford Review of Economic Policy* 33(1): 24–48. https://academic.oup.com/oxrep/article/33/1/24/2972707/Public-financing-of-innovation-new-questions.

Mazzucato, M. and C. Perez (2015) 'Innovation as Growth Policy', in J. Fagerberg, S. Laestadius, and B. R. Martin (eds), *The Triple Challenge for Europe: Economic Development, Climate Change, and Governance.* Oxford: Oxford University Press, pp. 229–64.

Mazzucato, M. and L. R. Wray (2015) 'Financing the Capital Development of the Economy: A Keynes-Schumpeter-Minsky Synthesis.' Working Paper, No. 837, Levy Economics Institute. Available at: http://www.levyinstitute.org/pubs/wp_837.pdf.

Mowery, D. C., R. R. Nelson, and B. R. Martin (2010) 'Technology Policy and Global Warming: Why New Policy Models Are Needed (or Why Putting New Wine in Old Bottles Won't Work)', *Research Policy* 39(8): 1011–23.

Nelson, R. R. (2011) 'The Moon and the Ghetto Revisited', *Science and Public Policy* 38(9): 681–90.

Pisano, G. (2006) 'Can science be a business?' *Harvard Business Review* 10: 1 12.

Rodrik, D. (2004) 'Industrial Policy for the Twenty-First Century.' John F. Kennedy School of Government Working Paper Series rwp04-047.

Sampat, B. N. (2012) 'Mission-oriented Biomedical Research at the NIH', *Research Policy* 41(10): 1729–41.

Soete, L. and A. Arundel (1993) *An Integrated Approach to European Innovation and Technology Diffusion Policy: A Maastricht Memorandum.* Luxembourg: Commission of the European Communities, SPRINT Programme.

Wood, R. (2012) 'Fallen Solyndra Won Bankruptcy Battle but Faces Tax War', *Forbes*, 11 June. Available at: http://www.forbes.com/sites/robertwood/2012/11/06/fallen-solyndra-won-bankruptcy-battle-butfaces-tax-war/.

World Bank (2015) 'History'. Available at: http://go.worldbank.org/65Y36GNQB0.

Wright, B. D. (2012) 'Grand Missions of Agricultural Innovation', *Research Policy* 41(10): 1716–28.

PART II
EMPIRICAL PERSPECTIVES

5

Meiji Japan

Progressive Learning of Western Technology

Kenichi Ohno

5.1 Introduction

Learning for catch-up by any nation and in any age exhibits globally common features as well as locally unique characteristics. Japan's encounter with the powerful West in the nineteenth century and its subsequent rise as the first non-Western industrialized society is already a thing of the distant past, but the combination of universality and uniqueness was clearly visible there. Meiji Japan's development was not a story from a different planet. Despite the fact that its industrialization took place in very different internal and external contexts from those facing today's latecomers, certain basics which are still relevant today were fulfilled as preconditions for successful catch-up. With a proper distinction between what was time invariant and what was specific to this particular case, and with appropriate selectivity and modification, developing countries in the twenty-first century can still gain valuable insights from Meiji Japan's experiences. No developmental model should be copied directly and without adjustments by any other country, whether it is Japan in the nineteenth century, Korea in the late twentieth century, or Ethiopia at present. In this sense, the lessons of Meiji Japan carry fundamentally the same value and quality as other model nations.

Catch-up always takes place in an international context where a nation is confronted with diverse stimuli and formidable pressure from without. Certain foreign things and systems must be adopted as concrete benchmarks for climbing up the ladder. Broad and pragmatic learning that covers technology, institution building, and policy formulation is required at all levels in the private and public sectors. Moreover, to be successful, catch-up must go beyond just government propaganda to become a national passion embraced by all firms and citizens and driven by a mixture of pride and humiliation. All these features were present in Meiji Japan's industrialization.

Certain key elements must be present for catch-up regardless of country or age. These constants include competent industrial human resource, competitive domestic enterprises, industrial infrastructure, proper business institutions, and constructive engagement between the state and the private sector. The Meiji government created or strengthened all of these elements. But *how* these were implemented was quite unique to Meiji Japan. The two prominent features are discussed below. Additionally, the government endeavoured to establish a modern and friendly business environment and macroeconomic stability as a background for industrial catch-up in the context of the late nineteenth century—not perfectly but with a fair amount of success.[1]

However, external circumstances surrounding Meiji Japan were very different from those of today. This was the age of imperialism and colonialism. Japan's global integration was forced by the show of American military power, not by the friendly counsel of a well-meaning international organization. There were no donor countries to help latecomers with knowledge acquisition or infrastructure building. All costs for foreign advisers and turnkey projects were borne on the Japanese side which led to a desire for 'import-substituting' engineers and technicians as quickly as possible. Under Western pressure, free trade was imposed with tariff rates set to a uniform 5 per cent. Thus, there was little scope for infant industry protection until 1911 when tariff rights were regained. FDI and external borrowing were available, but Japan resisted both for fear of foreign dominance (except for borrowing for war purposes). Investment funds had to be generated domestically. Meanwhile, reverse engineering and copy production were frequently practised until 1900 when the commercial law was revised to protect Western intellectual property rights. Meiji industrialization had to proceed with more self-reliance and greater caution against foreigners' hostile intentions than is the case today.

Another unique feature of Meiji Japan was the high absorptive capability of Japanese people, enterprises, and government which facilitated rapid technology transfer and internalization with proper local adjustments. Technology learning progressed from simple to complex, and from foreigner dependent to Japanese owned. A large part of this chapter is devoted to describing how this was done in concrete projects, business decisions, and policy measures. Possible reasons for Japan's high absorptive capacity are explored from a historical perspective. Within fifty years of forced opening, Japan, formerly a backward agro-society, emerged as one of the most advanced economies of the world by the early twentieth century. This internal capacity of Meiji Japan was truly remarkable, and offers a compelling reason for not copying its policies to another developing country, apart from the obvious differences in age and international conditions.

[1] Business climate and the macroeconomy of Meiji Japan are beyond the purview of this study. Suffice it to say that the Meiji government rapidly introduced a large number of Western systems including the metric standard, banking, business education, commercial law, joint-stock companies, and the stock exchange. Inflation surged in early Meiji, and it took many years for the government to settle on the type of monetary system most suitable for Japan. The Bank of Japan was created as a sole central bank in 1882 and the silver standard was replaced by the international gold standard in 1897.

5.2 Rapid Industrialization and Westernization

From the early seventeenth century to the middle of the nineteenth century, Japan was ruled by the samurai (warrior) government of the Tokugawa family which governed from Edo (present-day Tokyo). Japan then was an internationally isolated feudal society[2] with its production mainly based on peasant agriculture. As the nineteenth century dawned, Western powers began to approach Japan for diplomacy and trade but the samurai government refused to deal with them. Then, in 1853, an American military fleet (the Black Ships) commanded by Commodore Matthew C. Perry entered the Bay of Edo to demand the opening of Japanese ports with a display of cannon fire. The following year, Japan was obliged to sign treaties of 'amity' with five Western powers which permitted port calls by foreign ships. Four years later, in 1858, Japan was forced to conclude 'unequal' commercial treaties with the West under which it lost the right to set its own tariff rates or charge foreigners with criminal offences. Through this humiliating experience, Japan found itself a backward nation which was no match for Western economic or military might. A decade of political struggle and military conflicts ensued, which toppled the samurai government and established a new one that considered rapid Westernization and industrialization as paramount national goals. The new Japan was officially ruled by Emperor Meiji but actually was run by former young samurais who ended the Tokugawa rule by military means.

Meiji Japan (1868–1912) set itself the targets of political modernization, industrialization, military build-up, and correcting the unequal commercial treaties. All of these were eventually attained. In less than half a century after the forced opening of ports, it succeeded in vigorously importing Western systems and technology, transforming itself into a 'modern' state boasting a Western-style constitution, parliament, laws, courts, cabinet, ministries, military, police, and local governments (Banno and Ohno, 2010, 2013). In the economic arena, an industrial revolution in light manufacturing was achieved in the 1890s (Minami, 1986; Hara, 1999). By the early twentieth century, Japan had overtaken the United Kingdom as the world's top exporter of cotton textile products. In the military sphere, Japan defeated the Qing Dynasty of China (1894–5) and the Romanov Dynasty of Russia (1904–5), and secured control over Korea and a small part of North-eastern China. As Japan's political, economic, and military standing rose, Europe and America agreed to revise the unequal commercial treaties in steps with the complete restoration of tariff and court rights achieved in 1911. After the

[2] There is a debate regarding whether the Edo society should be classified as feudal. Here, we define feudalism simply as a leader–follower relationship based on provision of land to govern. The Tokugawa shogun, wielding unrivalled power, freely allocated and reallocated land to govern to regional samurai lords (*daimyo*) and in turn required absolute loyalty and obedience from them.

First World War (1914–18), Japan was invited to major international conferences as one of the Big Five along with the United Kingdom, the United States, France, and Italy.

Meiji Japan's emergence from an agro-based backward latecomer to one of the most advanced nations in the world was accompanied by a fast and broad absorption of Western technology and its local adjustments, and high-quality human capital which made this possible.

More specifically, as domestic capability steadily rose, one prominent aspect of Meiji Japan's technology absorption was progression from easy to complex in both content and method of technology learning (Uchida, 1990). This situation will be amply and concretely demonstrated in the rest of this chapter. Another essential feature was a happy blend of strong private dynamism and (mostly) appropriate industrial policy. This was true not only in the late nineteenth century, but also in the post-Second-World-War period when Japan recorded another rapid growth, this time based on heavy industries and high technology (Ohno, 2018). In both periods, private dynamism was the main engine of growth while policy played an important supporting role. Another unique factor was the long co-existence of traditional and modern industries and their parallel development and interaction (Nakamura, 1997; Odaka, 2000). Old industries from the Edo period were not wiped out by the intrusion of superior Western technology. This was possible partly because Japan and the West belonged to entirely different cultural spheres with dissimilar food, clothing, and housing, and also because Japanese traditional industries selectively adopted new technology to improve and scale up production.

5.3 Historical Background

The natural question is: where did Japan's private dynamism and relatively wise government come from? For this, a historical perspective is crucial. The answer must be found in the periods leading up to the Meiji period, not just in what the Meiji government did in terms of technology transfer or engineer training. Before delving into concrete ways of technology learning, this section reviews the preconditions for the Japanese industrial revolution which had been prepared before Meiji. It also explains why today's developing countries are advised not to directly copy the policy menu of Meiji Japan, not only because external conditions have changed greatly since the late nineteenth century but also because many of the latecomers today lack the internal preparation for technology learning which Meiji Japan had.

Umesao (2003) advances a hypothesis that Japan's unique geographical position generated social dynamism throughout its recorded history of almost two millennia. According to him, Japan—just like Britain—is physically separated from the Eurasian Continent by a narrow strait. This allowed it to import the culture and systems of high civilization with relative ease while avoiding or minimizing military invasion from outside. Enjoying external stimuli under efficient defence, society could evolve continuously without being destroyed or severely damaged by foreign invaders. The Japanese state, which first emerged in the fourth century CE, evolved sequentially from strong central power to decentralization, feudalism, the rise of local economic activities, and finally capitalism, unlike societies on the Eurasian Continent which were prone to attacks and even annihilation by violent nomadic peoples every few centuries. Umesao believes that Japan's unique geography and the resulting cumulative history prepared conditions for strong economic growth, and that its industrialization proceeded in parallel with that of the West rather than by just copying others.[3]

Shiba, in historical essays published over 1986–96, points to Japan's status as an island nation as the major factor shaping the Japanese people, making them curious and eager to accept foreign ideas and objects but only after adjusting them to Japanese tastes and mindset. The other key shaping force identified by Shiba is the samurai spirit whose highest value is honour, not personal gain or family prosperity. Japanese people want to live and die honourably, avoiding shame.

Maegawa (1998) observes that, in general, an encounter with the powerful West often weakens or even destroys an indigenous society but it may also lead to its activation and dynamism. In the world system, the centre (large nations and international organizations) imposes its rules on the peripheries (latecomers), forcing them to adopt the norms created by the strong. The peripheries look helpless and passive in the face of external pressure. However, Maegawa argues that a latecomer is not really weak if it controls the type, terms, and speed of the importation of foreign things, using them to stimulate the existing society for new growth. Even as foreign elements are added, the basic structure of the indigenous society can and should remain intact. A nation that does this is said to manage global integration adroitly. Meiji Japan is regarded as a prime example of this feat, which Maegawa calls *translative adaptation.*

What is the mechanism by which long and evolutionary history forges a nation capable of absorbing foreign elements effectively without losing national identity? Umesao is reticent on this question, and we can list only some hints (Ohno, 2018). Frequent mergers of domestic and foreign elements make the society unafraid of and resilient to external shocks, and at the same time flexible enough to change. It will also learn appropriate methods and procedures for mixing two cultures.

[3] Umesao's hypothesis was first presented in a Japanese article published in 1957. He terms it an 'ecological view' but, as explained here, it is more concerned with Japan's particular geography which permitted an uninterrupted social evolution. The view that Japan's long history, especially the existence of feudalism prior to Meiji, prepared conditions for industrialization is echoed by two oriental scholars of Western origin, Karl Wittfogel (1957) and Edwin Reischauer (1978).

Moreover, the mindsets of both the ruler and the ruled are inculcated by the institutional memory of the long past to admire behaviours that preserve the nation against short-term crises. Heroic deeds are told and re-told through books, poems, songs, and theatrical arts in which the hero laments the cruel fate but selects the action that best serves the nation and its future generations. Japanese people adore Yoshitsune, a young and splendid samurai leader in the twelfth century who won dazzling victories but was cornered by his jealous brother to his tragic death, as a model samurai who performed duties without clinging to self-interest. There are many other heroes and heroines remembered by all generations. Spiritual values such as hard work, honesty, perseverance, high aspiration, sacrifice, and long-term vision are esteemed. Japanese national leaders, government officials, and business people are naturally affected by this socio-cultural tradition.

When feudal Japan was confronted by Western powers in the middle of the nineteenth century, this historically generated national mindset was fully at work.

In politics, the previously uncontested authority of the Tokugawa family began to crumble after the unequal commercial treaties were signed with the West without the emperor's approval, and domestic opponents of the treaties were brutally suppressed through execution and imprisonment. From around 1860, the legitimacy of the Tokugawa government was openly challenged, leading to several years of intensive debates and fights over new political leadership and the wisdom of foreign trade. Even in this fierce competition, opposing camps often cooperated over a common goal of avoiding colonization by modifying strategies and re-forming partnerships rather than clinging to their original positions with an unwavering determination for mutual annihilation (Banno and Ohno, 2010; Ohno, 2013). The transition from feudal Edo to modern Meiji was achieved with surprisingly low casualties of about ten thousand warriors and soldiers. In contrast, the French Revolution and the Napoleonic Wars resulted in five million deaths, and post-Second-World-War conflicts in Korea, Vietnam, Nigeria, Cambodia, Afghanistan, Mozambique, and Sudan each claimed over one million lives. One Meiji journalist wrote: 'Although both [Japan and France] go from one extreme to the other, our people do so within certain bounds while the French do so outside these bounds' (Tokutomi, 1889).

Moderation in political and military showdown had several causes. Fights over political leadership and international trade were restrained by the rise of National Study (*kokugaku*) which strengthened Japanese national identity,[4] nationalism against foreign colonizers, the emerging rich and intellectual classes who preferred moderation to extremism, and popular discontent with the outdated policies and

[4] Historically, Japanese academic research had long been dominated by imported ideas of Buddhism and Chinese philosophy. In the Edo period, however, respect for and study of Japan's ancient beliefs and literature emerged with Keichu, Kamono Mabuchi, Motoori Norinaga, and Hirata Atsutane as leading scholars. When the US Black Ships arrived in 1853, *kokugaku* quickly turned from academic research to the political ideology 'respect Emperor and repel foreigners' (*sonno joi*).

governance of the Tokugawa rule. These in turn were the results of the peaceful and steady development of Edo society which nurtured the sense of national oneness for common goals. For these reasons, nineteenth-century Japan could maintain a subtle balance between fierce political competition (dynamism) and ultimate national unity (stability) in the midst of a severe external crisis.

In the socio-economic arena, Edo Japan spawned many important developments which facilitated technology learning and industrialization in the subsequent Meiji period. First, smallholder family agriculture grew in both cultivated area and land productivity. There were active public and private projects for opening new fields and water management, and new farming methods, tools, and organic fertilizers (dried fish) were introduced to boost quality and yields. Second, nationally integrated markets and transport systems for rice (tax base) as well as various cash crops and manufactured products developed. It can be safely said, as price data show, that Edo Japan's domestic market was highly integrated. Third, commerce, finance, and a wealthy merchant class emerged with Osaka as a national economic centre. Fourth, a large number of pre-modern manufactured goods such as sake, kimonos, ceramics, cutlery, processed food, and natural dye were produced in virtually every *han* through private effort and public support. Fifth, some regional lords even succeeded in systematically promoting agriculture and manufacturing in their domains and increased tax revenue, even though the central Tokugawa government was largely uninterested in and incapable of such promotion (Ohno, 2018).

On top of all this, education became a national fad from top samurai to commoners. For adults, official and private courses were offered in ancient Chinese literature and philosophy as well as, in later years, Western languages, medicine, and navigation. For children aged roughly seven to thirteen, around twenty thousand unregulated for-profit private primary schools (*terakoya*) emerged all over Japan where self-appointed teachers taught reading, writing, and arithmetic (abacus) with flexible and individualized curriculums.

Thus, when Japan was prised open for diplomacy and trade in the 1850s by the American Black Ships, its people and institutions were ready to absorb and internalize new technologies and systems presented by the West. It can be said that Japan's re-encounter with the advanced West occurred just at the right time, when Japanese society had evolved sufficiently and was willing to take up the new challenge of transformative growth. The old policies and systems imposed by the Edo government had become constraints on new growth.

5.4 Early Attempts at Technology Learning

In 1854, the Edo government made its first conscious effort to import pragmatic foreign technology by installing Western-style armaments for coastal defence.

Some *hans* also tried to replicate foreign technology by building furnaces to smelt metals for casting cannons. Scholars of Dutch studies and traditional craftsmen built such furnaces relying solely on descriptions in imported Dutch books, which however were already outdated by the time they were translated.[5] Haphazard copy production of steel and arms generally failed. Some *hans* also test produced Western-style ships and steam engines from Dutch texts, but the technology gap between their results and actual foreign ships visiting Japan was so great that this effort had to be abandoned. Realizing the limitations of learning technology only from books, the central government and some *hans* reverted to directly importing ships and firearms manufactured in the West after Japan opened up for international trade in 1859.

The results were not so disappointing in cases where technology was transmitted in the presence of foreign instructors. The construction in 1854 of a Western-style wooden ship at Heda port in the Izu Peninsula, where Japanese carpenters worked under Russian naval officers and shipwrights to build a new vessel for Russians to return home, can be regarded as the first successful attempt at on-site technology transfer. The Japanese carpenters absorbed the technology so well that they later became skilled workers in Japanese naval arsenals and private shipyards.

Another notable case was the Nagasaki Naval Training Centre. Established in 1855, it trained the crew of Japan's first Western-style battleship, the *Kanko Maru*, which was a gift from the Dutch government. This training project was a joint undertaking of the Dutch navy and the Edo government with daily management entrusted to the former. Five Dutch naval officers trained 167 samurais who had been competitively selected from all over Japan. Courses focused on standard naval training such as navigation, artillery, and the care and maintenance of steam engines. The Japanese crew also received on-the-job training with navigation exercises to Kagoshima. Between 1860 and 1870, the Edo government and a number of *han* governments imported a total of 166 ships from the West. It was the graduates of the Nagasaki Naval Training Centre and two similar centres subsequently set up in Edo and Hyogo who operated them. The importation of different types of ships enabled the Japanese to compare and enrich their knowledge of warships, engines, and artillery. Similarly, the army of the Edo government acquired skills both through the artillery it imported and the foreign military advisers who trained students.

The Edo government also built the Nagasaki Steel Mill and Shipyard in 1857 and the Yokosuka Steel Mill in 1866 as ancillary facilities for the Nagasaki Naval Training Centre. These facilities, which later became Mitsubishi Nagasaki Shipyard

[5] During the Edo period, the Netherlands was the only Western nation permitted to trade with Japan under the strict control of the central government and only at Nagasaki. The only other country that was granted trading rights with Japan was China. For this reason, Western technology entered Japan through Dutch books and products.

and Yokosuka Naval Arsenal, replicated Western mechanized factory production and transferred technology to the Japanese under the supervision of foreign engineers and technicians. Kagoshima Spinning Mill, established in 1867 by Satsuma Han, adopted a similar approach. These early factories became a model for the Meiji government's programme which hired foreign advisers for construction and to guide factory operation.

5.5 Foreign Experts and Turnkey Projects

In the early years of Meiji, the new government hired from 300 to 600 foreign advisers in any year on a project contract basis, at considerable fiscal cost, to establish Western-style state-owned enterprises in railways, telegraphy, and silk reeling (Umetani, 1968). Some foreign advisers received salaries higher than that of the Japanese prime minister. Each project recruited a team of foreigners, usually of the same nationality, with various functions, who imported virtually all the materials required to create an exact replica of a foreign model (Kasuya, 2000). These were turnkey projects with a foreign director supervising his fellow countrymen and Japanese workers, with the Japanese side taking over operation and maintenance after project completion.[6] Yokosuka Shipyard, Tokyo-Yokohama Railway, Imperial Mint, and Ikuno Silver Mine were examples of such projects. Foreign advisers were also hired individually to fill specific technological needs at government bureaus and agencies as well as industrial, mining, and agricultural projects run by the Home Office and the Hokkaido Settlement Agency. Such individual employment required greater ownership and involvement on the Japanese side than projects entirely entrusted to foreign teams.

These turnkey projects hired Japanese workers only for unskilled or auxiliary tasks. The Imperial Mint was directed by William Thomas Kinder who was dispatched, along with other experts, by the British Oriental Bank to create and manage the mint under a Japanese government contract. Its annual reports were published in Kinder's name. The official report of the Ministry of Industry's Telegraphic Service, however, was submitted in the name of the Japanese second-in-command. The Japanese edition of the report claimed that Japanese and foreigners shared duties equally but the English edition stated that the Japanese worked under the supervision of foreigners. The latter was probably

[6] Technology transfer at state-run enterprises under turnkey projects proceeded on a trial-and-error basis rather than as a well-planned process. Masahide Yoshida, a former samurai serving the Edo government, recounted that he had been recruited as one of the first Japanese staff of the Telegraphic Bureau in 1869 simply because he was studying English in Yokohama. On the third day he was asked to send and receive telegrams, of which he had no previous knowledge. He somehow learned the skill but eventually chose to become an interpreter for the foreign adviser laying telegraphic cables between Tokyo and Nagasaki (Uchida, 1990).

closer to the truth, while the former version was designed to please senior ministry officials.

The primary aim of establishing a mint, telegraphic service, railways, and shipyards was to rapidly introduce modern industrial infrastructure comparable to Western models. Given the speed at which the Meiji government wished to build them, it is not surprising that these enterprises were run by a large number of foreigners who managed them in the same way as establishments at home. These early projects did not always consciously aim at transferring technology to Japan.

Western countries also considered it highly desirable for Japan to build infrastructure to Western standards. For foreign diplomats, merchants, and shipping companies, Nagasaki and Yokosuka Steel Mills were indispensable for the repair of their ships. Nagasaki Kosuga Dock and Takashima Coal Mine were additionally created to repair foreign ships and replenish fuel (charcoal) under the management of British merchant Thomas B. Glover. A request for the construction of lighthouses and the telegraph service was made by British Consul General Harry Smith Parkes to the Meiji government. By 1874, British engineer R. H. Branton was commissioned, who assembled an eighty-eight-man strong team of British, Chinese, and Filipino workers that included builders, lighthouse keepers, and boat crews. Branton undertook construction and maintenance with all costs borne by the Meiji government. These lighthouses ensured safe passage for foreign and Japanese ships alike.

In the area of telegraphy, the Edo government signed an agreement with the French government to build a telegraph service in 1866. However, this decision was overturned by the Meiji government which chose, through the mediation of the British Consul General, a domestic service provider. The Danish-owned Okita Telegraph Company was awarded a contract for sole agency. By 1866, two international telegraph lines had been laid from Europe to the Far East via Russia and via the Indian Ocean, with Japanese telegraphic cables connecting them at the end and extending them to Nagasaki and Yokohama, the two port cities with large foreign settlements. This enabled foreign diplomats and merchants in Japan to have easy contact with home.

Japanese government orders for machinery, equipment, and materials brought handsome profits to foreign merchants, who also mediated technology transfer. Jardine Matheson & Co. and the Oriental Bank competed over an order to build and equip the Imperial Mint. When the latter won the contract, it not only imported second-hand equipment from the Hong Kong Mint and sold gold and silver for minting but also provided Japan with management expertise by hiring a British team headed by Kinder. For any such project, foreign merchants would act as middlemen for the import of management and technology by mobilizing engineers and technicians from the home country.

International migration of Western engineers was also behind the prevalence of turnkey projects abroad. As much British industrial infrastructure had been completed by the 1850s, the pace of building railways, ports, and other facilities slowed down, producing a surplus of civil engineers in Britain. Needing work, many chose to migrate to the Continent, then to British colonies and foreign lands such as Canada, India, Australia, South Africa, and South America. Machinery and equipment makers also turned to overseas markets. For British railway contractors, it was customary for a supervisor who received an overseas order to secure all equipment and materials needed, such as train track and locomotives, at home, hire subcontractors and a team of skilled workers, then travel with them to his destination. In 1857, a team of 160 Britons travelled to Argentina to build a railway. A similar team came to Japan thirteen years later to lay the first railway between Shimbashi and Yokohama.

As noted above, technology transfer was not the main purpose of turnkey projects, but the method did provide a good training ground for Japanese workers. It fostered new machine operators, steam engine drivers, steelworkers, and electricians. They often migrated from state-owned enterprises to the private sector or set up their own factories, spreading Western technology that they had acquired and contributing to the creation of Japanese enterprises with modern management knowledge from the 1880s onwards.

As the absorption of Western technology and management progressed, turnkey projects conducted by large foreign teams came to an end in the relatively early years of Meiji. From around 1875, state-owned enterprises stopped hiring such teams and, by 1880, foreign engineers had disappeared from all but a few workplaces. Factories and facilities that had been created under management contracts were now run by Japanese. This shift resulted partly from the strong desire of the Meiji government to 'import substitute' engineers so it no longer had to foot the expensive bill. But more important was the speed with which Japanese workers absorbed new practical skills. Japanese enterprises did not need continued foreign help to operate modern and complex equipment which the country had only seen a decade or so before. There were already competent Japanese managers and engineers who could easily replace foreigners.

5.6 Engineering Education

After the departure of the foreign advisers, Japanese engineers assumed the role of internalizing and diffusing Western technologies in Japan. They understood the core Western technology and could put this knowledge to practical use. They collected the latest technical information from abroad and instructed appropriate models to purchasing missions to be dispatched to European and American manufacturers. After a factory was built, they supervised its operation. This smooth transfer of Western technology owed much to the fact that Meiji Japan trained a large number of Japanese engineers to an exceptionally high standard in a short period, a feat that few latecomer countries have been able to emulate. Apart from the turnkey projects mentioned above, industrial training was realized by sending students abroad as well as by establishing domestic institutions for technical education and training.

Early engineers studied Western technology before a formal university and technical education system was established. They can be divided into three types. First, there were Dutch studies scholars from the late Edo period who relied on imported technical books and journals. They worked for Western-style establishments owned by the Edo government or various *hans*, and later served as engineers for the Meiji government. Oshima Takato, who built the first blast furnace in Japan, Takeda Ayasaburo, who built the star-shaped fort in Hakodate, and Utsunomiya Saburo, who became Japan's first cement manufacturer, were among them.

Second, there were graduates from technical schools managed and taught by foreigners. They included the Nagasaki Naval Training Centre (1855), the Yokosuka Shipyard School (1870), the Telegraphic Service Technical Training College (1871), the Imperial Naval Academy's Institute for Maritime Studies (1873), and the Railway Engineering Training Centre (1877). These institutions taught in a foreign language—usually English and sometimes German—and transmitted the knowledge necessary to perform assigned functions so workers could run the business after foreign management left. The graduates later worked as foremen or junior technicians in the Japanese army, telegraphic service, railways, and shipbuilding. For instance, in 1878–80 graduates from the Railway Engineering Training Centre supervised and successfully completed the construction of a railway from Kyoto and Otsu which included tunnelling through Osaka Mountain.

The third group of early Meiji engineers were those who were sent abroad to study by the government. The Ministry of Education and the military selected the best graduates from educational or training institutions for continued study abroad. They proved to be extremely good and hardworking students despite the meagre stipends provided by the government. Returning to Japan, they worked as senior technical experts for government ministries or for the private sector. The very first overseas students were seven men sent to the Netherlands by the Edo government to learn military navigation in 1862. The navy later sent many trainees abroad from the Yokosuka Shipyard School and the Naval Academy to learn shipbuilding and arms manufacture. There were also some who chose foreign education at their own expense, and even others who went abroad without official permission.

By the end of the 1880s, as far as the records show, the government had dispatched around eighty students abroad to be trained as engineers. Of these, twenty-one studied shipbuilding, seventeen mechanical engineering, thirteen civil engineering, ten mining and metallurgy, six arms manufacture, and four studied chemistry. By destination, twenty-eight were sent to the United Kingdom, twenty to the United States, fourteen to France, nine to Germany, and eight to the Netherlands (excluding unknowns, Uchida, 1990). They not only took formal courses at universities but also went to renowned technical schools, received on-the-job training at factories, or had private lessons to broaden their knowledge.

Not many Western universities at that time offered practical technical education or acknowledged its value. In the United Kingdom, only universities in Scotland and London had mechanical and civil engineering chairs prior to the 1840s. It was customary for a British engineer to be trained on site, first working as an apprentice and then as an assistant. Many of the British engineers who migrated abroad had been trained in this way. In France, there were some notable technical institutions such as École Polytechnique, École d'Application, and École Centrale. In Germany, each state boasted a number of technical and vocational schools, including the mining school of Freiberg established in 1765. In the United States, there were few technical education institutions until the first half of the nineteenth century. Boston Tech, which later became Massachusetts Institute of Technology, was founded in the 1860s, and at around the same time Columbia University and Cornell University first offered civil, mechanical, mining, and materials engineering courses. However, these technical institutions and courses were still considered to rank below universities until the end of the nineteenth century. It can be said that the first wave of Japanese overseas students were sent to the right institutions for absorbing practical technical knowledge, and received first-class training on a par with European and American engineers. It is no surprise that they could easily replace foreigners on their return to Japan.

Meiji Japan accepted engineering, along with medicine and law, as one of the new subjects to be studied vigorously. Unlike Western Europe, it did not look down on engineering as an inferior subject of lower academic quality. The early establishment of faculties of engineering at Japanese universities contributed greatly to the country's technological advance. Meiji Japan selectively imported the latest and best of the engineering education which the West had created through a century of trial and error, and combined them for the best practical—not academic—results. This was initiated with the founding of the Institute of Technology (Kobu Daigakko) in 1871, and courses in applied science and civil and mechanical engineering at the University of Science.

The Institute of Technology was established by the Ministry of Industry to train a cadre of engineers for its mining, railways, telegraphy, and construction bureaus.[7] As the ministry did not possess the required technical expertise, it hired Henry

[7] In 1871, Kogaku Ryo (School of Engineering) was created within the Ministry of Industry and upgraded to a university in 1873. The university was renamed Kobu Daigakko in 1877. It was merged with the University of Science to become the Faculty of Engineering of the Tokyo Imperial University under the Ministry of Education in 1886.

Dyer, a British engineer, to run the Institute under a management contract. As rector of the Institute, Dyer was in the fortunate position to be able to design a programme which he considered ideal by integrating theory and practice, a feature that British engineering education lacked. The six-year programme of the Institute included basic training in English and mathematics in the first two years, specialized classroom instruction in the next two years, and internship at various bureaus of the Ministry of Industry under the supervision of foreign engineers in the final two years. On graduating, young engineers were expected to assume positions within the Ministry of Industry. At the University of Science, a smaller number of graduates found employment at the Home Ministry, the Imperial Mint, and other establishments. Three other imperial universities founded in the Meiji period—Kyoto, Tohoku, and Kyushu—were equipped with a faculty of engineering from the outset.

These faculties of engineering were not research oriented but dedicated solely to transmitting Western engineering knowledge to Japanese soil. Textbooks were all foreign, and many of the lectures and examinations were conducted in English or German. The journals published by the Societies of Industrial, Mechanical, and Electrical Engineering devoted many pages to overseas mission reports and excerpts from foreign journals.

Establishment of schools to supply mid-level industrial instructors and factory supervisors was proposed by Gottfried Wagener, a hired German engineer, and Tejima Seiichi, a Ministry of Education official. Tokyo Shokko Gakko (Tokyo Craftsmen School, later renamed Tokyo Kogyo Gakko or Tokyo Industrial School) was the first to be established in 1881. It selected students aged 16 to 17 through exams and school records. Courses were first offered in mechanical engineering and chemical engineering with other subjects added later. In early years, special courses were also taught on how Western technologies should be adapted to upgrade indigenous Japanese industries such as textiles, ceramics, and brewing. Unlike the Institute of Technology, all the instructors were Japanese except Wagener who taught ceramics and glass making. The school initially faced administrative and financial problems but these were overcome around 1890 as Tejima took over the top management role. In 1897, under the Technical Schools Act, it was formally recognized as an industrial high school. Tokyo Kogyo Gakko became Japan's leading institute for producing industrial instructors, factory managers, engineers, and entrepreneurs. When its campus in central Tokyo was destroyed by the Great Kanto Earthquake in 1923, the school relocated to O-okayama where the Tokyo Institute of Technology is today.

Apart from the Tokyo campus, publicly run industrial schools were created in Osaka (1901), Kyoto (1902), Nagoya (1905), Kumamoto (1906), Sendai (1906), Yonezawa (1910), and Akita (mining course only, 1910), making a total of eight schools by the end of Meiji. Subsequently, twenty-three more industrial schools were opened by the 1940s. After the Second World War, most of them were converted to faculties of engineering of national universities, and many privately run industrial schools were also established. Education offered at industrial schools was more limited in scope than that offered at the faculties of engineering at universities, but student quality was high. They attracted good students who could not afford to attend a university. While university graduates normally assumed official or academic positions, industrial school graduates went to factories and became core engineers.

Table 5.1 shows the number of Japanese engineers by type of education from 1880 to 1920. In early Meiji, the number of recognized engineers was fewer than a hundred which caused a severe shortage of experts who could understand and adopt Western technologies. Subsequently, university-educated engineers and industrial school graduates grew greatly in number. By the turn of the century, engineers employed in the private sector outnumbered those in government offices.

The sectoral distribution of engineers tells us about the leading industries of Meiji. At the end of the Meiji period in 1911, among all engineers employed in the private sector 513 (18.0 per cent) were in the mining sector, 300 (10.6 per cent) were in textiles, 250 (8.8 per cent) were in shipbuilding, 231 (8.1 per cent) were in power and gas, 186 were in commerce (6.5 per cent), 149 (5.2 per cent) each were in railways and food processing, 106 (3.7 per cent) were in general machinery, and 104 (3.7 per cent) were in electrical machinery,

It is noteworthy that the commercial sector also employed engineers. During Meiji, *sogo shosha*, or general trading houses such as Mitsui, Okura, and Takada played a crucial role in transferring technology to Japanese corporate customers. They made foreign trips, established overseas branches, collected technical information from academic journals, helped their customers to choose appropriate technologies and foreign manufacturers, and assisted in ordering, transporting,

Table 5.1 Number of Japanese engineers by type of education

Employer	Category of engineer	1880	1890	1900	1910	1920
Government departments and agencies	Early Meiji-era engineers	61	72	–	–	–
	University graduates	25	183	474	1,075	1,795
	Industrial school graduates	–	45	263	1,160	1,999
	Subtotal:	86	300	737	2,235	3,794
Private organizations	Early Meiji-era engineers	–	17	54	34	–
	University graduates	–	131	385	846	3,230
	Industrial school graduates	–	34	389	1,963	7,138
	Subtotal:	–	182	828	2,843	10,368
Total	Early Meiji-era engineers	61	89	54	34	–
	University graduates	25	314	859	1,921	5,025
	Industrial school graduates	–	79	652	3,123	9,137
	Grand total:	86	482	1,565	5,078	14,162

Source: Uchida (1990), p. 281.

installing, and operating the equipment. They also mediated technical cooperation agreements between Japanese and foreign firms, as explained in Section 5.7. To perform these roles, general trading houses needed many industrial engineers.

5.7 Machinery Import and Foreign Partnership

In middle to late Meiji, Japan began to expedite technology transfer by learning from imported machinery as well as through technical cooperation agreements. With a growing number of Japanese engineers, it became possible for enterprises owned and operated solely by Japanese to absorb sharply targeted foreign technologies. Some specific examples are given below.

To set up a national telephone network, engineers at the Ministry of Communications, including Oi Saitaro, a graduate of the Institute of Technology, collected publicly available technical information, visited the United Kingdom, the United States, and Germany to compare their telephone systems, negotiated with foreign telephone equipment makers, and selected the kind of system suitable for Japan. Advanced equipment had to be imported, but Japanese engineers and workers laid the lines and managed operations without any foreign assistance. By comparison with the introduction of telegraph services through a turnkey contract in early Meiji, its capacity as a receiver of foreign technology had improved remarkably.

In the navy, early Meiji-era engineers trained in Britain and France, as well as shipbuilding and armaments engineers graduating from naval technical schools, were similarly instrumental. Throughout the Meiji period, the principal battleships were imported mostly from the United Kingdom, with Japanese naval shipbuilding and armaments engineers travelling to Britain as observers while state-of-the-art battleships were built and readied for delivery. This provided them with ample opportunity to learn about ship design and construction from the British navy and shipyards. Their knowledge proved invaluable to the domestic production of arms and support vessels by Japanese naval arsenals. Over time, Japan acquired capacity to build even principal ships. Private shipyards such as Mitsubishi, Kawasaki, Osaka Steel Works, and Ishikawajima also gradually improved their ability to construct steel-hulled ships by importing machinery and equipment. These enterprises relied on imported steel materials and components that could not be produced domestically. Sometimes they also procured designs from Britain (Arisawa et al., 1994).

In the textile industry, the government imported ten sets of cotton spinning machinery, each equipped with 2,000 spindles, from the United Kingdom. After installing and test running the equipment at state-owned mills in Aichi, the government sold these concerns off to the private sector as ten separate cotton mills. Engineers and technicians from the Ministry of Agriculture and Commerce assisted with commercialization of these factories. Graduates of the Institute of

Technology, employed as master engineers, built and managed Owaribo and Miebo, two dominant mills of that early period. In the next phase, the large-scale private cotton mills of Osaka, Amagasaki, and Kanebo were built. For this, university-educated engineers designed factory plans, and travelled to the United Kingdom to purchase machinery and acquire the practical skills and technology needed (Hanai, 2000).

As these examples illustrate, technology transfer from middle Meiji onwards occurred mainly through the import of machinery and acquisition of know-how that accompanied such machinery. As Table 5.2 shows, machinery imports rose significantly throughout the Meiji period. It should also be noted that foreign machinery entered Japan at the uniform low tariff of 5 per cent imposed by the 'unequal' commercial treaties until Japan regained tariff rights in 1911.

Alongside machinery imports, domestic production of machinery had also emerged. Not surprisingly, Japanese machinery in the Meiji period was inferior in quality to Western. Moreover, in design, nearly all machines manufactured in Japan were copies of imports. In this way Japanese producers acquired technology arduously, gradually, and through trial and error, leading in some cases to commercially viable domestic production.

Table 5.2 Machinery imports in the Meiji period (in 1,000 yen)

	1878–82	1883–7	1888–92	1893–7	1898–1902	1903–7	1908–12
Telegraphic and telephone equipment	11.8	19.3	35.8	43.1	65.1	113.5	78.0
Railway carriages	–	29.0	355.8	518.5	1,045.6	1,771.7	2,336.0
Locomotives	–	72.2	408.2	1,505.4	1,963.5	1,705.8	1,156.8
Steamships	81.9	718.5	841.7	4,744.5	3,562.2	4,692.1	2,215.6
Steam engines	–	81.7	329.1	586.2	759.8	1,208.8	797.2
Internal combustion engines	–	–	–	–	102.5	262.2	873.9
Dynamos and electric motors	–	–	–	–	322.6	1,546.0	2,275.4
Machine tools	–	3.0	4.5	106.1	649.1	2,404.2	2,687.9
Spinning machines	–	71.9	784.5	3,012.1	1,330.3	1,840.8	3,608.0
Looms	–	25.6	99.0	206.1	199.8	391.5	1,060.8
Total	1219.2	12,066.4	5,755.0	16,427.7	19,145.1	30,354.8	37,381.6

Note: Import of steam engines for 1883–7 does not include the value for 1883.

Source: *Nihon Boeki Seiran* (Japanese Statistics of International Trade), Toyo Keizai Shimposha (1935).

The early days of electrical equipment production provide examples. Tokyo Light Company, a distributor of imported electrical machinery, tried to encourage domestic production of dynamos and light bulbs which it was procuring. The company's Senju Power Plant test purchased dynamos from Ishikawajima Shipyard that were designed and copy produced from a catalogue under the supervision of a certain professor, but the heat they generated distorted their shape. Similarly, Miyoshi Electric Machine, a pioneer firm in electrical machinery, supplied dynamos to Kobe Light Company and tram motors to the municipality of Kyoto. In both instances the products were returned as defective. Through such failures, Japanese industries learned that they could not rely on amateur copy production and that Western technology had to be absorbed more systematically with repeated trial production until it was successfully internalized.

From the 1900s, technical cooperation agreements offered a new way of transferring relatively new technology from large foreign firms of various nationalities. In some cases, such as Japan Steel Works, Nippon Electric Company (NEC), Tokyo Electric, and Shibaura Engineering Works, these contracts included establishment of joint-stock companies between Japanese owners and the foreign firm.

Let us look at the case of steam turbine technology. This was a new technology invented in 1884 by Charles Parsons in the United Kingdom. Within a decade, the technology spread to ship engines and thermal power plants throughout the West. Meanwhile, Japanese navy yards and private shipyards were producing their own reciprocating steam engines and boilers. In 1905 the Japanese navy learned that the British navy planned to adopt steam turbines in their principal ships for increased speed. This news prompted the Japanese navy to import Curtis turbines from the United States and install them on the *Ibuki* and the *Aki*, battleships that were under construction at the time. The navy also acquired the patent for turbine technology from Curtis and encouraged Mitsubishi Shipyard to acquire the Japanese patent for Parson's turbines. Thereafter, Mitsubishi and the Japanese navy began their own turbine production for future ships while continuing to import turbines for ships under construction. This was a complex way of technology transfer combining learning from imported products, the rights to patent execution, and copy production.

Steelmaking was an area in which the Ministry of Industry had difficulties transferring technology during the 1870s and 1880s. State-owned steel works at the (later privatized) Kamaishi Iron Mines did produce pig iron and steel with the assistance of hired foreign engineers, but the quality was not up to expected standards. By that time, the United States and Germany had improved technology greatly with open-hearth furnaces and basic oxygen furnaces which permitted the construction of large integrated mills combining iron making, steelmaking, and rolling processes. A strongly worded petition from the Japanese military urged the government to import a complete set of integrated steel mills. In 1901, the state-owned Yawata Ironworks, with technology from the German company

Gutehoffnungshütte, was constructed. This was a turnkey contract consisting of commercially confidential mill design, imported machinery and equipment, and provision of German engineers and technicians. However, unlike turnkey projects in the early Meiji period, the metallurgy engineers were Japanese. Moreover, the Japanese side chose the factory site and the type of technology to be adopted, and made the decision to procure raw materials from China. When initial operations using the German technology failed, it was Japanese engineers who adjusted the technology to local conditions and enabled the mill to operate successfully (Suzuki, 2000).

The creation in 1907 of Japan Steel Works, a joint-stock company owned by Mitsui and two British companies, Armstrong and Vickers, also originated from a request by the Japanese military for domestic production of armour plating and large-calibre guns for its lead ships. In this case, equipment and know-how were entirely British, but the Japanese engineers and skilled workers, who came mostly from naval munitions factories, quickly learned and assimilated the technology transferred.

In electrical machinery, the following three historical circumstances led to the establishment of joint ventures with American firms. On the Japanese side, the revision of commercial treaties with the West around 1900, based on the principle of equal treatment of domestic and foreign nationals, permitted foreign direct investment in Japan for the first time. Furthermore, as the modified Japanese law guaranteed the patent rights of foreigners, Japanese manufacturers were no longer allowed to copy produce the latest imported goods for free. On the American side, leading electrical equipment manufacturers had adopted a strategy of manufacturing new products at overseas subsidiaries.

In 1896, the Japanese government decided to adopt the American Telephone & Telegraph (AT&T) system under its First National Plan to Expand Telephony. As the government intended domestic production of telephone equipment, Western Electric, which was the manufacturing arm of AT&T, first tried to form a joint venture in Japan by acquiring the stock of Oki Electric Industry. However, negotiations with Oki failed, prompting Western Electric to establish Nippon Electric Company (NEC) in 1899, holding 54 per cent of the shares. NEC was the first subsidiary of a foreign firm in Japan. Western Electric and NEC were bound by a technical cooperation agreement that gave NEC the right of sole agency in Japan and a monopoly on future patent re-execution rights. Western Electric offered technical guidance to NEC, for which the latter paid roughly 2 per cent of its sales revenue. NEC initially distributed imported telephones, then built a manufacturing plant with design and equipment imported from Western Electric, and produced telephones by using materials and processes satisfying international standards under the supervision of an American foreman. All internal documents were written in English. Thus, the products and production methods of NEC were identical to those in the United States.

In 1905, General Electric (GE), another American giant, concluded a technical cooperation agreement with Tokyo Electric which was similar to the one between Western Electric and NEC, with GE acquiring 51 per cent of Tokyo Electric's shares. The latter had evolved from Hakunetsusha, a light-bulb manufacturer established in 1890. As the company had been unable to establish a viable production technology or compete with imported light bulbs from Germany, it sought management assistance from GE, a world leader in the industry. GE's policy of allowing its subsidiaries to produce light bulbs under their own patents was another reason why Tokyo Electric selected GE as a business partner. Equipment and materials were imported from GE, and American engineers came to Japan to teach manufacturing methods. Tokyo Electric's engineers were well trained and able to quickly master any frontline technology developed by GE. Unlike NEC which was newly founded, Tokyo Electric was an existing company acquired by GE as an overseas factory. But the technology transfer method was quite similar in both cases.

Business collaboration between GE and Shibaura Engineering Works in 1907 was different from the above two cases, however: it was partial and more incremental. GE acquired only 24 per cent of Shibaura's shares while the remainder was held by Mitsui. Technical assistance was provided through patent licensing agreements, supplemented by sharing of R&D results, exchange of engineers, and access to the blueprints for production equipment. In return, Shibaura paid royalties amounting to 1 per cent of sales revenue. Mitsui opted for this technical cooperation to catch up with rapid technological advances abroad under the constraint of the Universal Patent Convention that now protected the patents of foreign manufacturers in Japan. Through this collaboration, Shibaura was able to design heavy electrical equipment by executing its rights on the GE patent and obtain new technical information through the exchange of engineers. But this did not give Shibaura a great technology leap, unlike the cases of NEC and Tokyo Electric. GE's technology was added to Shibaura's existing technology without fundamentally changing the character of the latter. Large dynamos continued to be imported from GE which competed with Shibaura products. This was a case of a patent licensing agreement supplemented by a purchase contract for machinery and know-how.

These cases provide examples of how the latest Western technology was introduced to Japan in the late Meiji period. Whether technical cooperation agreements entailed an acquisition of dominant shares by foreigners depended largely on the corporate strategy on the foreign side. Some transfers of technology were selective and partial while others were guided by foreigners in every respect. The latter may look like a repetition of the wholesale purchase of Western technology practised in early Meiji, but there were important differences. First, by the end of Meiji, Japan was importing frontline technologies which were simultaneously being developed and adopted in the West rather than buying common and mature technologies as in the early Meiji period. Second, the existence of competent domestic engineers and technicians allowed Japan to take a significant lead in selecting, adjusting, and internalizing imported technologies instead of remaining a passive student.

References

Arisawa, Hiromi, Kazuo Yamaguchi, Kazuma Hattori et al. (eds) (1994) *Nihon sangyoshi 1 (History of Japanese Industries, Vol. 1)*. Nikkei Bunko: Nihon Keizai Shimbunsha.

Banno, Junji and Kenichi Ohno (2010) 'The Flexible Structure of Politics in Meiji Japan.' Developmental Leadership Program Research Paper No. 07, April.

Banno, Junji and Kenichi Ohno (2013) *Meiji ishin 1858–1881* (*Meiji Restoration 1858–1881*). Tokyo: Kodansha Shinsho.

Hanai, Shunsuke (2000) *'Keikogyo no shihon chikuseki'* ('Capital Accumulation of Light Manufacturing'), in K. Ishii, A. Hara, and H. Takeda (eds) *Nihon keizaishi 2: sangyo kakumeiki* (*Japanese Economic History 2: Period of Industrial Revolution*). Tokyo: University of Tokyo Press, pp. 111–89.

Hara, Akira (1999) *Nihon keizaishi* (*Economic History of Japan*). Revised edition. Tokyo: University of the Air Press.

Kasuya, Makoto (2000) *'Kindai kigyo no ishoku to teichaku'* ('Introduction and Internalization of Modern Industries'), in K. Ishii, A. Hara, and H. Takeda (eds) *Nihon keizaishi 1: bakumatsu ishinki* (*Japanese Economic History 1: End of Bakufu and Meiji Restoration*). Tokyo: University of Tokyo Press, pp. 103–52.

Maegawa, Keiji (1998) 'The Continuity of Cultures and Civilization: An Introduction to the Concept of Translative Adaptation', in Kenichi Ohno and Izumi Ohno (eds) *Japanese Views on Economic Development: Diverse Paths to the Market*. London: Routledge, pp. 166–76.

Minami, Ryoshin (1986) *The Economic Development of Japan: A Quantitative Study*. Basingstoke: Palgrave Macmillan.

Nakamura, Takafusa (ed.) (1997) *Nihon no keizai hatten to zairai sangyo* (*Japanese Economic Development and Indigenous Industries*). Tokyo: Yamakawa Shuppansha.

Odaka, Konosuke (2000) Shokunin no sekai, kojo no sekai, shinban (*The World of Craftsmen and the World of Factories*, new edition). Tokyo: NTT Publishing.

Ohno, Kenichi (2013) *Learning to Industrialize: From Given Growth to Policy-aided Value Creation*. London: Routledge.

Ohno, Kenichi (2018) *The History of Japanese Economic Development: Origins of Private Dynamism and Policy Competence*. London: Routledge.

Reischaur, Edwin O. (1978) *Japan: The Story of a Nation*. Third edition. Clarendon, VT: Tuttle.

Shiba, Ryotaro (1986–96). *Kono kuni no katachi* (*The Shape of This Nation*). Historical essays in six volumes. Tokyo: Bunshun Bunko.

Suzuki, Jun (2000) 'Jukogyo kozangyo no shihon chikuseki' ('Capital Accumulation of Heavy Industries and Mining'), in K. Ishii, A. Hara, and H. Takeda (eds) *Nihon keizaishi 2: sangyo kakumeiki (Japanese Economic History 2: Period of Industrial Revolution)*. Tokyo: University of Tokyo Press, pp. 199–256.

Tokutomi, Soho (1889) *Kokumin no tomo* (*Companion of the People*), 50: 2 (11 May). Minyusha.

Uchida, Hoshimi (1990) *'Gijutsu iten'* ('Technology Transfer'), in N. Shunsaku and T. Abe (eds) *Nihon keizaishi 4: sangyoka no jidai 1 (Japanese Economic History, Vol. 4: The Age of Industrialization 1)*. Tokyo: Iwanami Shoten.

Umesao, Tadao (2003) *An Ecological View of History: Japanese Civilization in the World Context*. Melbourne: Trans Pacific Press.

Umetani, Noboru (1968) *Hired Foreign Advisors, Vol. 1*. Tokyo: Kajima Research Institute Publishing House.

Wittfogel, Karl (1957) *Oriental Despotism: A Comparative Study of Total Power*. New Haven, CT: Yale University Press.

6
Catch-up and Learning in Taiwan
The Role of Industrial Policy

Wan-wen Chu

6.1 Introduction

Taiwan's post-war economic performance has been extraordinary. Its real PPP per capita income was only US$916 in 1950,[1] less than one-tenth that of the United States. By 2008, Taiwan's real per capita income had increased 22.8-fold, and by 2017 it had reached 84 per cent of the United States' and was ranked nineteenth in the world in terms of PPP per capita GDP.[2]

When the Japanese colonialists withdrew from Taiwan following their country's defeat in 1945, Taiwan was still a typical colonial economy, mainly exporting sugar and rice to the protected Japanese market. Industrialization under colonialism was limited; it supported Japanese military activities, and the plants were mostly owned and managed by the Japanese.[3] At the end of 1949, the Nationalist regime in mainland China was defeated by the Communists and had to retreat to Taiwan. Fortunately, Taiwan was able to embark on a path of sustained industrialization, rapidly reducing its reliance on primary exports. The share of rice and sugar in Taiwan's exports declined from 74 per cent in 1952, to 47 per cent in 1960, and a mere 3.2 per cent in 1970,[4] indicating the fruits of industrialization in the first twenty post-war years.

Taiwan managed to sustain the rapid pace of development throughout the post-war decades, and has grown from a low-income to a high-income economy. Its GDP and per capita GNP grew at an average annual rate of 9.2 and 6.3 per cent respectively in the first thirty post-war years, 1951–80, and 5.7 and 4.9 per cent from 1981 to 2016 (see Tables 6.1 and 6.2). It faced various challenges along the way, but facilitated by suitable and adaptive industrial policies, it managed to adapt to the new environment and transform itself at every turn. For example, its

[1] This is from Maddison (2010). The unit was 1990s International Geary-Khamis dollars.
[2] According to the IMF World Economic Outlook (July 2018), Taiwan's PPP per-capita GDP was US$50,293, about 84 per cent of the United States' (US$59,501), in 2017. http://www.imf.org/external/datamapper/PPPPC@WEO/OEMDC/ADVEC/WEOWORLD.
[3] For discussion of the Japanese colonial period, see Ho (1978) and Cumings (1984).
[4] See Chu (2017: 68).

Table 6.1 Major economic indicators (I), 1951–2016

Year	Average annual growth rates of					Export	CPI
	Real GDP	Population	Real GDP per capita*	Gross capital formation**	Industrial population***		
1951–60	8.1	3.6	4.5	14.1	11.9	22.1	9.8
1961–70	9.7	3.1	6.8	15.4	16.5	26	3.4
1971–80	9.8	2	7.7	13.9	13.8	29.5	11.1
1981–90	7.6	1.4	6.4	7.9	6.2	10	3.1
1991–2000	6.3	0.9	5.1	8.2	5.1	10	2.6
2001–16	3.3	0.4	3.1	0.8	3.7	4.7	1.0
1951–2016	7	1.7	5.4	9.1	9.1	15.9	4.6

Note: * Figures were deflated by indexes with 2011 as the base. ** Figures before 1969 were deflated by indexes with 1986 as the base; those afterwards were by indexes with 2011 as the base. *** Figures for 1995 and before exclude quarrying.

Sources: 1. DGBAS, http://www.dgbas.gov.tw/mp.asp?mp=1; http://61.60.106.109/task/sdb; http://www.dgbas.gov.tw/ct.asp?xItem=9522&ctNode=2857; 2. CEPD, *Taiwan Statistical Data Book*, various years. 3. DGBAS, http://www.dgbas.gov.tw/ct.asp?xItem=9522&ctNode=2857.

high-tech industry has become the major manufacturer of ICT (information and communications technology) products in the world in the last two decades.[5]

This chapter will examine how and why Taiwan developed its economy successfully in the post-war era. It will first discuss conditions at the beginning of the

Table 6.2 Major economic indicators (II), 1952–2016

Year	GDP per capita (US$)	Gross fixed capital formation as % of GDP	Exports as % of GDP	Trade balance (US$ million)	GDP by Industry (%)		
					Agriculture	Industry	Service
1952	213	11.3	8	−71	32.2	19.7	48.1
1960	164	16.6	11.5	−133	28.5	26.9	44.6
1965	229	17	19.4	−106	23.6	30.2	46.2
1970	393	21.7	30.4	−43	15.5	36.8	47.7
1975	978	31.3	39.9	−643	12.7	39.9	47.4
1980	2385	30.7	52.6	78	7.7	45.7	46.6
1985	3290	19.5	52.5	10,678	5.7	44.6	49.7
1990	8124	23.1	44.5	12,639	4	38.9	57
1995	12,918	25.7	46.3	9330	3.3	33.1	63.5
2000	14,704	24.4	52.2	11,218	2	30.5	67.5
2005	16,051	21.9	61	15,817	1.7	31.3	67.1
2010	18,503	20.7	71.5	23,364	1.6	31.1	67.2
2016	22,540	20.9	62.8	49,753	1.8	35.1	63.1

Sources: 1. DGBAS, http://www.dgbas.gov.tw/mp.asp?mp=1; http://61.60.106.109/task/sdb; http://www.dgbas.gov.tw/ct.asp?xItem=9522&ctNode=2857. 2. CEPD, *Taiwan Statistical Data Book*, various years.

[5] See Amsden and Chu (2003).

post-war era, and then review the various stages of development in chronological order, from import-substitution industrialization in the 1950s, through export promotion and upgrading in the 1960s and 1970s, to entry into the high-tech sector from the 1980s, and to liberalization and globalization subsequently.

6.2 Factors Favourable to Development

The Nationalist government that took over Taiwan in 1945 after fifty years of colonial rule encountered difficulties because state and society did not understand each other. Though Taiwan's economy had been badly affected by the war, however, there were some factors that were favourable to economic development in the early post-war period.[6] The Japanese colonialists had built modern infrastructure and laid the foundations for subsequent modernization. US military and economic aid provided crucial political support and much needed resources to stabilize the economy and the regime. But it was up to the Nationalist government to build up the infrastructure to make post-war growth possible. This confirms the structuralist theory of development which argues that it is necessary for the state to play an active role to substitute for the deficient market mechanism in a latecomer country.

Stabilizing the economy made implementing industrial policy feasible after 1949. In the post-war years on the mainland, the Nationalist government had mishandled the economy, causing hyperinflation, which contributed greatly to its defeat. The political leaders learned the hard way that it was crucial to maintain macroeconomic stability. A key factor in Taiwan's early success in promoting industrialization were the many highly motivated officials with experience in economic planning on the mainland who built up the bureaucratic organization required for effective industrial policy. The government appointed the National Resource Commission (NRC) to help restore major industrial production (especially Taiwan Sugar and Taiwan Power).[7] A new set of institutions and policies to promote industrialization effectively emerged.

Moreover, Taiwan was fortunate in having the scope to practise industrial policy during the early post-war period. Japan's economic forces, with their superior productivity, had to leave Taiwan after the defeat of 1945. However, US political and military aid stemming from Cold War considerations enabled the Nationalists to intervene in the economy to promote development. Associated US economic aid provided crucial foreign exchange to support the currency, reduce the fiscal deficit, and stabilize prices and the economy. The aid agency also

[6] This section draws much from Chu (2017).

[7] Facing the imminent threat of Japanese military invasion, the Nationalist government set up the National Resource Commission in 1935 to build up military supply and related industrial production. NRC was responsible for basic wartime industrial production, and continued to train relevant personnel in preparation for post-war industrial recovery and construction. See Chu (2017: 172–98).

coordinated with the local economic bureaucracy so that the right to allocate US aid became an industrial policy tool. Nevertheless, US aid played a positive role in Taiwan's development only because the local government used it in the right way. Where this was not the case, as often occurred elsewhere in the developing world, US aid did not necessarily produce favourable results.

What was the private business sector like at that time? During the colonial period, exporting sugar and rice to the Japanese market had brought steady growth to the local economy, but colonial policy had limited industrialization to a Japanese enclave. Some local businessmen accumulated wealth by participating in trade. After the war, from 1945 to 1949, small plants emerged producing light industrial consumer goods. After 1949, land reforms implemented by the government discouraged the elite from living on agricultural rent. Locals who had been discouraged from engaging in modern industries during the colonial era found the new investment environment enticing, and their behaviour was strongly influenced by industrial policy. Sensing the government's resolve to promote industrialization, the private sector responded by learning about and investing in modern industrial production.

6.3 Economic Recovery and Import Substitution in the 1950s

Taiwan's post-war industrialization was undoubtedly very much a state-led development, with the Nationalist government having almost all the essential policy tools at its disposal and using them to promote economic development resolutely.[8]

Nevertheless, they faced formidable odds of political uncertainty, large-scale immigration from the mainland, persistent fiscal and balance of payment deficits, and chronic shortages of foreign exchange and material resources.[9]

The government needed large amounts of material resources to restore economic stability, relying first on gold reserves and then on US aid to shore up the currency. From 1950 to 1965, economic aid amounted to about US$1.5 billion, which was almost equal to the total balance of payment deficit.[10]

In a series of land reforms, the Nationalists implemented the 'Land to the Tiller' programme in 1953. The compensation given to landlords partly consisted of shares in the four industrial state-owned enterprises (SOEs). To ensure the lasting success of the land reform, the government paid careful attention to the agriculture sector, assuring farmers an adequate supply of necessary inputs for production. In

[8] For discussions of major policies, see Amsden (1979), Ho (1978), Wade (1990), Gold (1981), and Chu (2017).

[9] This section draws on Chu (2017: 198–220).

[10] Chao (1985: 8).

addition, the newly emerged industrial sector provided opportunities for the elite who had to leave the rural sector. The rise in agricultural productivity and output helped to secure an ample food supply for the enlarged population and to keep industrial wage levels low. It also contributed to an improvement in income distribution.

Moreover, to successfully industrialize, the government needed to extract surplus from a very productive agricultural sector. The fact that the agricultural sector had made significant gains in productivity, and the land reform had redistributed income in the tenants' favour, made the sector better able to bear the heavy fiscal burden. The former tenants' newly acquired land could be turned into capitalized assets in the modernization process. In a way, the success of the land reform started a virtuous cycle.

In addition to its pursuit of economic recovery, in the 1950s the government promoted import-substitution industrialization due to severe foreign exchange constraints. During 1951–3, it kick-started the main target industry, cotton textiles, by bearing most of the risks and responsibilities itself. A few other industries, including utilities, fertilizer, and some consumer essentials, were also targeted and enjoyed prioritized allocation of resources.

Instead of expanding the SOE sectors, the Nationalists promoted private enterprise. Though most of the non-agricultural US aid went to support the large SOEs, especially utilities and transportation, a significant part of it was used to promote new manufacturing industries, mostly in the private sector. Here the government acted as entrepreneur, drafting the investment plans from scratch and handling them all the way up to handover to the would-be private industrialists. The share of private enterprise s in manufacturing output, therefore, increased from 41 per cent in 1952 to 70 per cent in 1966.[11]

Despite retreating to Taiwan, Chiang Kai-shek intended eventually to 'recover' the mainland. Paradoxically this provided the strong political will necessary to support post-war developmental projects. The economic bureaucracy enjoyed great autonomy in promoting industrialization under authoritarian rule, and the pathway to industrialization has continued to the present day. Section 6.4 will discuss subsequent changes in policy.

6.4 Policy Reform and the Start of Export-Led Growth in 1958

The scale of the domestic market was obviously too small to realize economies of scale in industry and to sustain growth. For example, the cotton textile industry reached self-sufficiency within just two years and began to accumulate excess capacity. However, the foreign exchange regime was designed to facilitate import

[11] CEPD, *Taiwan Statistical Data Book*, various years.

substitution, and had overvalued exchange rates and a complicated set of multiple exchange rates. To help lessen the foreign exchange constraint and encourage firms to export,[12] the government had to design schemes, such as 'getting the prices wrong'.[13]

With hindsight, the switch to an export-promotion policy regime seemed a logical next step for a government eager to find ways to sustain growth and push industrialization. However, due to fear of unforeseen risk and resistance from vested interests, the Foreign Exchange Reform was implemented in 1958 only after a prolonged round of heated debate among the economic bureaucrats and the ruling elite. In a two-stage process the multiple exchange rates were converted to a unitary rate, the currency was devalued significantly, and various export promotion programmes were adopted.

Furthermore, to promote overall economic development, the government enacted the 19-Point Programme for Economic and Financial Reform and the important Statute for Encouraging Investment in 1960. The latter remained in effect till 1990 when it was replaced by the Statute for Promoting Industrial Upgrading. It put in place the framework to reduce investment barriers and to provide tax breaks for investors. The policy regime switch was not as drastic as it seemed, however, because the extent of trade liberalization was rather limited, and the domestic market remained to a great extent protected. Nonetheless, exports began to grow very rapidly, led by the textile industry: Taiwan's cotton textile products began to be subject to import restraints in the US market as early as 1962. This occurred long before apparel exports began to take off in the late 1960s, showing the beneficial effects of import substitution.[14]

6.5 Industrial Upgrading

The policy switch did not imply, however, that the government would cease to promote industrialization. As light industry was beginning to grow in the 1950s a secondary import-substitution programme was introduced to set up the upstream production to supply inputs to the exporting downstream industries, though with time limits, and price and quality conditions.[15] A man-made fibre manufacturing plant was established with government help in the mid-1950s. The automobile industry made a start in 1956. Plans for the steel and petrochemical industries also

[12] This section draws on Lin (1973: Chs 4 to 6) and Chu (2017: 273–300).

[13] Amsden (1989) coined the phrase 'getting the prices wrong' in her seminal work on South Korea's post-war economic development. The term means that the latecomer state has to provide subsidies to the disadvantaged latecomer firms so as to alter the prevailing market prices to induce the latecomer firms to embark on the learning process.

[14] Chu (2008).

[15] Chu (2001). This is similar to the Korean case as described in Amsden (1989).

began to be discussed in the 1950s. Due to difficulties in obtaining technology and capital, the first naphtha cracking plant did not begin operation until 1968, and the first integrated steel mill began construction only in the early 1970s. Both were undertaken by SOEs, socializing investment risks deemed unsupportable by the private sector at the time. All these were part of the plan to promote industrial deepening.

In the 1970s, the level of US support, which had been crucial for the survival of the Nationalist government on Taiwan, began to lessen. US–PRC relations started to thaw, though diplomatic relations were not established until January 1979. This created a legitimacy crisis for the Nationalist regime, while around the same time the first oil crisis of 1973 brought an economic crisis. In response, between 1974 and 1979 the government introduced the 'Ten Construction Projects': six major infrastructure projects, one nuclear power plant, and three industrial projects—the integrated steel mill, and expansion of petrochemical plants and shipyards. These helped to stimulate the economy in the short term, and to build up infrastructure and sustain and deepen industrialization in the long term.

6.6 Entry into High Tech

Once plans for heavy industry were in place in the early 1970s, the government began to plan for the next growth industry: electronics. Adopting a different policy approach this time, the government set up the National Science Council and public research laboratories such as the Industrial Technology Research Institute (ITRI). The first integrated circuit (IC) project was started in 1976. Subsequent spin-offs from ITRI, principally the United Microelectronics Corporation in 1980 and Taiwan Semiconductor Manufacturing Company in 1987, now comprise the majority of Taiwan's IC industry.

This policy environment also supported local production of key information technology (IT) components, and with successful industrial upgrading, Taiwan has in recent years become one of the world's largest producers of IT products, semiconductors, liquid-crystal-display units, and man-made fibres. In 2016 Taiwan's ICT products continued to occupy a substantial share of the world market in, for example, notebook computers (83 per cent), motherboards (84 per cent), tablets (38 per cent), servers (36 per cent)[16], IC foundry (71 per cent) and IC design (19 per cent).[17] Taiwan's industrial prowess is largely unseen, however, because its leading firms are mostly subcontractors for firms in advanced countries.

Amsden and Chu (2003) have studied how Taiwan upgraded and entered the high-tech sector. The strategy of Taiwanese firms has been to play second mover

[16] Market Intelligence and Consulting Institute (MIC), 2017, *Information Industry Yearbook 2017*, p. 12.
[17] ITRI, 2017, *Semiconductor Industry Yearbook 2017*, 2–14.

or act as subcontractor. Lacking frontier technology, firms enter when the product becomes mature, and earn profits based on efficient and low-cost manufacturing and timely delivery. They have to absorb the technology and expand production quickly. These firms mostly relied on locally trained engineers, as well as some returnees from abroad. While support of the education system, accumulated manufacturing experience, and local production networks provided the necessary conditions for the emergence of these firms, it was also the government's industrial policy that helped to set up the right environment and the crucial institutions, and assisted the advancement of the industry along the way. As a result, the main players in Taiwan's IT industry are large nationally owned firms, not foreign capital. Domestically, the share of the IT and electronics sector in total manufacturing value added rose from around 18 per cent in 1990 to 54 per cent in 2017 (Table 6.3).[18] Meanwhile, an increasing proportion of offshore production shifted to China, reaching 92 per cent in 2016.[19] This gave Taiwanese firms access to an abundant supply of cheap and efficient labour, allowing them to greatly expand their scale of operations. Despite this trend, total employment in the electronics sector has not declined over the last two decades.

Most of the successful second movers in Taiwan have not pursued R&D-intensive and own-brand strategies to catch up. Second movers expand through accumulated organizational capabilities based on subcontracting manufacturing, which implies path dependence.[20] Thus, the strategy of choice for most has been upgrading subcontracting, cross-industry subcontracting, and then own-brand manufacturing, in that order. Industrial policy has been a crucial structural factor affecting a firm's strategic choices. South Korea has produced successful global brands, supported by the state's national champion policy and long-term commitment to the *chaebŏl*, the Korean conglomerates. China has also adopted a highly ambitious national champion strategy. The fact that the government in Taiwan has never adopted a national champion strategy helps to partly explain the evolutionary path of Taiwan's second movers, and attests to the importance of industrial policy.

6.7 Liberalization and Globalization

With the exception of the high-tech industry, overall industrial policy until 1986 was export promotion, accompanied by secondary import substitution and protection of the domestic market. Most of the banks were publicly owned. The government had successfully maintained macroeconomic stability by keeping the budget mostly in balance and the inflation rate low. Foreign exchange was under

[18] MOEA (2017). [19] MIC (2017: 13). [20] Chu (2009).

Table 6.3 Distribution of manufacturing value added, 1971–2017 (in per cent)

	1971	1975	1980	1985	1990	2000	2010	2017	Changes 1971–2000	Changes 2000–17
Food, beverages, and tobacco	12.8	11.9	7.9	8.4	6.8	7.1	4.2	5.3	–5.8	–1.8
Textile, apparel, and leather	23.2	23.9	18.7	17.5	12.6	6	2.1	1.8	–17.2	–4.2
Wood and furniture	4.3	2.9	2.7	4.3	2.6	1	0.3	0.3	–3.3	–0.7
Paper and printing	3.3	2.6	3.5	3.5	3.6	2.2	1.6	1.5	–1.1	–0.7
Chemicals and products	8.8	9.2	8.9	8.8	9.4	12.8	12.7	9.2	4.1	3.6
Petroleum refining	5.4	4.9	8	5.3	4.8	2.3	2.3	4.4	–3.1	2.1
Rubber and plastics	9.4	8.7	8.4	9.8	9.4	4.6	2.6	2.6	–4.8	–2
Non-metallic minerals	4	3.7	4.3	4	3.8	2.8	1.7	1.2	–1.2	–1.6
Basic metal	6.2	5.3	5.2	6.7	7.6	13.6	10.2	4.8	7.4	–8.8
Metal products	1.1	1.1	5.7	5.2	5.5	8.2	4.4	4.1	7.1	–4.1
Machinery	4.2	3.1	4	3.7	4.8	5.8	5	4.4	1.6	–1.4
Electrical and electronics machinery	11.9	16.8	13.3	13.8	18.6	26.9	48.2	54.2	15	27.3
Transport equipment	4.3	4.7	6.6	5.8	7.1	4.7	3.6	4.1	0.4	–0.6
Miscellaneous	1.2	1.2	3	3.1	3.5	2.1	1.4	2.2	0.9	0.0
Sum	100	100	100	100	100	100	100	100		

Source: MOEA, *Yearbook of Industrial Production Statistics by Taiwan Area, ROC*, various years.

control, the exchange rate remained stable and undervalued, and the domestic market was protected.

However, a great and unavoidable transformation of the Taiwanese economy began in 1986. Though the government tried to guide the process, its hands were forced, and instead of adopting forward-looking policies, it simply made necessary adjustments.

Trade surplus and exchange reserves began to accumulate rapidly from 1980. The protection of the domestic market left increasingly wealthy domestic consumers ever more unsatisfied. The sustained trade imbalance between the United States and East Asia eventually led in 1985 to the signing of the Plaza Accord, which forced the New Taiwan Dollar to appreciate from 1986. Its value had risen 40 per cent against the US dollar by 1989. Under US pressure, the government relaxed foreign exchange controls and began to reduce tariff rates, remove non-tariff trade barriers, and phase out the tariff rebate programme. Substantial asset bubbles began to appear in the local stock and housing markets. Wages began to rise significantly, and industry's share in GDP started to decline (see Table 6.2).

Meanwhile, the government also began to liberalize the internal economic environment. With the lifting of martial law in mid-1987 by President Chiang Ching-Kuo,[21] the government began to open up (to both foreign and local firms) domestic markets in some of which the number of operating licences had previously been limited and more or less frozen since the early post-war period. The most important of these newly liberalized markets were modern services, such as banking, telecommunications, transportation, and mass retailing. Significantly, at the same time, the government began to improve the cross-Strait relationship by allowing citizens to visit relatives on the Mainland for the first time since 1949. Privatization of state-owned enterprises began two years later. Thus, democratization, liberalization, and globalization went hand in hand within a short period of time. It should be stressed that this was a process of managed liberalization, even though the extent of its success is debatable.

In hindsight, the government probably should have implemented these reforms earlier in a more forward-looking way. The change from a developmental state model, in which growth was given priority, to one in which political, social, and economic goals had to be renegotiated and realigned, proved difficult.

The pace of globalization has been swift in Taiwan since the late 1980s. The flow of inward and outward foreign direct investment (FDI) has increased significantly. Inward FDI now mostly flows into the modern service sectors, as entry restrictions continue to lessen. By the time Taiwan entered the WTO in 2002, the domestic market had already become quite open. Outward FDI mostly took place from the late 1980s onward, beginning with the move of labour-intensive

[21] He was the son of Chiang Kai-shek, the Generalissimo who had led the Nationalists from 1920s until his death in 1975.

production, first to the ASEAN countries and later to China. In the last few years, high-tech industry has also begun to move mass production lines to China, with firms under intense pressure to upgrade their operations again. Taiwan's outward FDI has become increasingly concentrated on China. The situation in the export trade is similar.[22]

In sum, though Taiwan's economy has become increasingly globalized, its external relations have been dominated by the cross-Strait relationship.

6.8 Recent Slowdown and Prospects

Taiwan's economy has performed relatively well since embarking on its transformation in the late 1980s. Industry has continued to grow, and unemployment has remained at a moderate level. Although labour-intensive production has moved offshore, electronics has become Taiwan's pillar industry, continuing to upgrade and expand, and maintaining its global competitiveness. Integration with the Chinese economy has provided growth momentum and has helped the second movers expand in scale.

As Taiwan's economy approaches maturity, however, economic growth has been slowing down in the last two decades. At the height of post-war growth, in the 1960s and 1970s, overall annual growth averaged nearly 10 per cent, but from 2001 to 2016 growth averaged only 3.3 per cent, and investment growth has fallen to 0.8 per cent this century (see Table 6.1).

There remain serious challenges. Overall growth is overly reliant on the old export-promotion regime. There are several probable reasons for the recent lack of investment growth: the flow across the Strait remains one way; the growth of domestic consumption lags behind overall growth; and the dominant industry, electronics, has encountered greater competitive pressures. Although economic integration with China continues to grow, political debate persists in hindering rational policy planning. At the same time, globalization has brought an unprecedented increase in the degree of economic inequality. The new rules of political competition have not been conducive to addressing these challenges.

These conflicts remain unresolved, and society is yet to face up to the crucial question of how to fit China into Taiwan's economic future. Only if future political developments promote more productive dialogue within Taiwan and across the Strait will Taiwan be able to formulate a new economic vision for its future development.

[22] CEPD, *Taiwan Statistical Data Book, 2017*, 226–7. In 2016, the share of exports heading to Hong Kong and China amounted to 40.1 per cent of Taiwan's total exports, while that to the United States was 12 per cent.

6.9 Industrial Development Trends

Taiwan still relies very much on its industrial sector to maintain growth and global competitiveness. Industrial production has been the driving force from the beginning of the post-war period. The share of agricultural production in GDP decreased from 38 per cent in 1953 to below 10 per cent after 1978, while manufacturing's share increased from 12.9 per cent in 1952 to 29 per cent in 1970, reached a peak at 39.4 per cent in 1986, and had fallen to 30 per cent by 2016. The share of services remained stable, around 48 per cent, in the first thirty post-war years, and then steadily rose to 63 per cent by 2016 (Table 6.2). The shifting pattern of GDP composition among the primary, secondary, and tertiary sectors in Taiwan closely resembles that of more advanced countries, of course, indicating the steady advance of Taiwan's economy. The changes in employment composition are similar to those of GDP. The total number of employees in the manufacturing sector has remained around 2.4 million during the last two decades. Several industry trends are observable in Taiwan. Its exports mainly consisted of labour-intensive products in the earlier post-war period and technology- and capital-intensive products in the later period. Taiwan's exports came mainly from small and medium enterprises (SMEs) in the earlier period and from large-scale firms in the later period. During both periods, subcontracting has been the dominant business model. At present, the leading industrial enterprises in Taiwan are high-tech subcontractors and medium-tech upstream input producers. Very few large-scale firms have their own brands, and Taiwan's few global brands are mostly owned by non-major firms.[23]

Part of the reason why Taiwan has been able to maintain healthy growth over the last sixty years is that its industry has been very adaptive, with new growth industries emerging as its comparative advantage has shifted. In the early post-war period, the leading sector was the textile and apparel industry. At its peak in the early 1970s, it contributed over 23 per cent of manufacturing value added. Since then its share has continued to decline, reaching a mere 1.8 per cent in 2017.

The changes in each sector's share in total manufacturing value added during 1971–2000 and 2001–17 are shown in Table 6.3. In the former period, the declines in textiles and plastics were offset by increases in chemicals, basic metals, and electronics. The more traditional industries gradually moved their operations overseas. In the latter period, however, almost all sectors except electronics experienced decreases in their shares of total manufacturing value added. The share of the electronics sector rose steeply from 26.9 per cent in 2000 to 54.2 per cent in 2017, and the share of the top three industries now accounts for 68.7 per cent.

[23] Chu (2009).

6.10 The Role of Small Firms in Taiwan's Development

It is often argued that small firms played a key role in Taiwan's development, unlike the case of Korea. For example, Feenstra and Hamilton (2006) believe Taiwan's post-war development was a case of bottom-up industrialization. They argue that after the war, SOEs took over Japanese firms and remained dominant till the early 1970s. Only then did Taiwan's economy set off on a trajectory of genuine development. The dynamic export sector, dominated by small firms, created demand for intermediate goods, and that allowed large firms to grow and transform themselves. Thus, they argue, it was small firms that began to lead the entire economy starting from the late 1960s.

Chu (2017), however, finds an alternative explanation. After the war, the SOEs which took over Japanese firms did not expand much beyond their domain. Private enterprises, fostered by the government's industrial policy, took advantage of the Japanese departure and immediately began to grow rapidly. SOE share in industrial production began to decline in the early 1950s, falling below 50 per cent in 1958, when the government changed its policy from import substitution to export promotion. It also began to push import substitution of upstream input production right at the beginning of the export promotion stage. Entrepreneurial small firms, eager to engage in exports, were helped by changes in industrial policy that made exports profitable, granted subsidized export loans, and promoted import substitution of intermediate inputs. In short, Taiwan's trajectory of genuine development started early, from the 1950s, and was not characterized by sudden emergence as postulated in Feenstra and Hamilton (2006). Moreover, the government played a key role in changing the environment and leading development.

Amsden and Chu (2003) present a pointed and well-documented case, disputing Feenstra and Hamilton's (2006: 210) argument that 'the small firm tail of Taiwan's economic organization wags the entire economy'. Amsden and Chu (2003: 67–76) find that it was large firms that played the leading role in recent industrial upgrading. They show that although small firms in Taiwan increased their share of employment both in total manufacturing and in the electronics sector from 1986 to 1996, their share of value added remained at a much lower level. In the important electronics industry, the disparity between employment and value added was even greater. The relative efficiency (valued added per worker) of large firms in this industry increased during this period, while that of small firms declined, reflecting their deficiency in skills and investment. Amsden and Chu (2003) show that although the numerous small firms constituted a dense production network in most of Taiwan's industries, they provided mainly passive low-tech components to the leading firms at arm's length. Leading firms, however, cooperated with ITRI to transfer key technology from foreign suppliers.

Chu's (2015) updated data on value added and efficiency by firm size of Taiwan's manufacturing and electronics industry shows that the small firms' share of value added dropped to only 9 per cent in 2011 in the electronics industry, while their relative efficiency has been declining since 2001.

In her first study of Taiwan's machine tool industry, Amsden (1977) found that small firms in a latecomer country, unlike advanced countries, tend to lack skills, investment, and frontier technology. Hence they cannot be the agent of industrial upgrading.

6.11 Comparison with South Korea

The overall development pattern in the post-war period has been extremely similar in Taiwan and South Korea. However, there has been a distinct difference in policy on big business and national champions.[24] In Taiwan, establishing national champions has never been a priority. The Nationalist government has prioritized stability over growth, and shied away from pursuing a high-risk national champion strategy. Through its control over the banks, the state has kept the debt–equity ratio relatively low throughout the half century of post-war growth. Lacking firm long-term commitment from the state, most of Taiwan's leading firms found the branding strategy too risky to pursue. The state's pursuit of industrial deepening from the 1970s was comparable to Korea's Heavy and Chemical Industrialization Plan, but Taiwan's private firms were unwilling to undertake the projects.[25] It was therefore state-owned enterprises rather than *chaebŏl* that undertook industrial deepening. Institutional arrangements in Taiwan differ from those of South Korea, because of their different strategies for big business and national champions.

There are two possible reasons for the Nationalist government's pursuit of this strategy. The Nationalists' top priority was economic stability, probably because they believed that the failure of their economic policies, which caused hyperinflation and widespread discontent, contributed greatly to their defeat by the Chinese Communists in 1949. It may also have to do with their particular kind of nationalist vision. In the early post-war period, they still believed they could realize their grand plan to modernize China after retaking the mainland, and thus planned Taiwan to be a model province. In this context a risky national champion strategy might jeopardize its economic stability.

[24] Cheng (1990).

[25] In these projects, the state solicited but failed to obtain participation from private firms. Thus, for example, China Steel, an SOE, undertook the integrated steel project, while semi-public firms, United Microelectronics and TSMC, were set up with mainly state funds to undertake the electronics projects. See Chu (2001).

In South Korea, when the Park regime began to promote economic development in the 1960s, it clearly designated *chaebŏl* as the agents of industrialization and used various policy tools to help them. It was understood between the state and *chaebŏl* that Japan was the model to be emulated and *chaebŏl* should strive to be national champions with prominent positions in the global market. This type of policy regime, especially long-term subsidized loans to the *chaebŏl*, helped to finance fast *chaebŏl* growth and industrial deepening, but also led to an extremely high debt–equity ratio that came to characterize all large Korean firms before the 1997 Asian financial crisis. Though some *chaebŏl*, such as Samsung and LG, finally managed to become global brand-name companies, this high-risk national development strategy undoubtedly brought high volatility to the firms, the industries, and the overall economy. Of the top thirty *chaebŏl* before 1997, half have either gone bankrupt or have undergone reorganization.[26]

The state's policy on big business has significant implications for the scope remaining for small firms. Unlike the Korean government, the Nationalists did not privatize the large Japanese firms but kept them as SOEs. They also ensured a favourable policy environment for small firms by facilitating export production, granting subsidized export loans, and so on. By indirect facilitation, restraining the SOEs and not promoting big business, therefore, the Nationalist government allowed some room for small firms to grow.

6.12 Policy Lessons

At each stage of Taiwan's post-war development the government sought to improve the policy environment for all sectors, but with limited resources it was only able to actively promote certain targeted industries, such as textiles, chemicals, and electronics. These industries played the role of growth engine, pulling related sectors to grow together. The pattern of industrial development in advanced countries has been used as a road map. In addition, products ranked by import value can indicate potential targets for import substitution at various stages of development. Fortunately, some of the choices, though not all, have borne fruit.

Moreover, industrial policy had to adapt to the changing environment. Different policy measures were required to promote different target industries. For example, SOEs were tasked with setting up the first petrochemical and integrated steel plants. However, the government changed tactics when promoting

[26] For discussion of industrialization in the earlier period, see Amsden (1989). Woo (1991) discusses the importance of the state's financial leverage in the Korean model. For more recent upheaval, see Shin and Chang (2003).

electronics. It set up public research labs, such as ITRI, to assist with the introduction and development of technology. It established science parks to promote industrial clusters. It helped to set up a venture capital industry to promote IC-related industries in the 1980s. It also made ITRI spin-offs semi-private firms, not SOEs, so that they would have more autonomy in management.

Throughout Taiwan's industrialization, economic officials sought to maintain economic stability and remove obstacles to industrial investment. When growth began to slow under the import-substitution regime, the policy was switched to promotion of exports and upstream inputs. The foreign exchange system was reformed into a single exchange rate regime. Time limits and performance requirements are considered the key difference between the protection regimes in East Asia and Latin America, and relevant legislation continued to be revised to improve the investment environment. Various agencies were set up to help enterprises raise productivity.

In the early period, economic development also brought about some beneficial social results, which in turn were helpful to subsequent development. Land reform contributed to social and income equality. Labour-intensive export production provided ample jobs for young people leaving the agricultural sector. Industrial districts were quite widely dispersed until recently when the electronics boom concentrated new jobs in the north of the island. Implementation of industrial policy relied partly on SOEs, leaving room for SMEs, unlike the case in South Korea.

Education policy emphasized mass education in the early period, vocational education in the later period, and higher education only recently. In the earlier period, education policy served economic development well by supplying a large number of good-quality unskilled and semi-skilled workers, and an ample supply of competent engineers. The higher education system has been greatly expanded since the 1990s. Education reform and further liberalization plans have been the subjects of heated debate in recent years.

Heath policy focused on public health in the early period, emphasizing control of the spread of communicable diseases and implementation of a birth control programme. The health programme has expanded alongside economic progress through the years. A universal health care plan came into effect in 1998, and remains the major social welfare programme in Taiwan today.

In recent years, however, democratization, liberalization, and globalization have posed challenges to Taiwan's original development model, in which growth was given priority. Industry faces increasing global competitive pressure to continue to upgrade. Political, social, and economic goals have to be renegotiated and realigned in the new environment. It remains to be seen how successfully Taiwan will transform itself in the future. As always, economic policies will have to adapt to the changing environment.

References

Amsden, Alice H. (1977) 'The Division of Labor Is Limited by the Type of Market: The Case of the Taiwanese Machine Tool Industry', *World Development* 5(3): 217–33.

Amsden, Alice H. (1979) 'Taiwan's Economic History: A Case of Etatisme and a Challenge to Dependency Theory', *Modern China* 5(3): 341–80.

Amsden, Alice H. (1989) *Asia's Next Giant: South Korea and Late Industrialization.* Oxford: Oxford University Press.

Amsden, Alice H. and Wan-wen Chu (2003) *Beyond Late Development: Taiwan's Upgrading Policies.* Cambridge: MIT Press.

Chao, Ji-chang (1985) *The Utilization of the US Aid in Taiwan.* Taipei: Linking Press. (in Chinese)

Cheng, Tun-jen (1990) 'Political Regimes and Development Strategies: South Korea and Taiwan', in G. Gereffi and D. Wyman (eds), *Manufacturing Miracles: Paths of Industrialization in Latin America and East Asia.* Princeton, NJ: Princeton University Press, pp. 139–78.

Chu, Wan-wen (2001) 'The Effects of Taiwan's Industrial Policy: A Preliminary Evaluation', *Taiwan: A Radical Quarterly in Social Studies* 42(June): 67–117. (in Chinese)

Chu, Wan-wen (2008) 'The Early Development of Taiwan's Cotton Textile Industry', *New History,* 19(1): 167–227. (in Chinese)

Chu, Wan-wen (2009) 'Can Taiwan's Second Movers Upgrade via Branding?' *Research Policy* 38: 1054–65.

Chu, Wan-wen (2015) 'Latecomer Upgrading in Taiwan', *Journal of the Asia Pacific Economy* 20(3): 369–84.

Chu, Wan-wen (2017) *The Causes of Taiwan's Postwar Economic Growth: The Why and How of Late Development.* Taipei: Academia Sinica and Linking Press. (in Chinese)

Cumings, Bruce (1984) 'The Origins and Development of the Northeast Asian Political Economy', *International Organization* 38(1): 1–40.

Council on Economic Planning and Development (CEPD) (various years) *Taiwan Statistical Data Book.* Taipei: CEPD.

Directorate General of Budget, Accounting, and Statistics (DGBAS) (2015) http://www.dgbas.gov.tw.

Feenstra, R. C. and G. G. Hamilton (2006) *Emergent Economies, Divergent Paths: Economic Organization and International Trade in South Korea and Taiwan.* New York: Cambridge University Press.

Gold, T. B. (1981) 'Dependent Development in Taiwan.' PhD dissertation, Harvard University.

Ho, Samuel P. S. (1978) *Economic Development of Taiwan, 1860–1970.* New Haven, CT: Yale University Press.

Industrial Technology and Research Institute (ITRI) (2017) *Semiconductor Industry Yearbook 2017*. Hsinchu: ITRI.

IMF (2018) *World Economic Outlook*, April. Available at http://www.imf.org/external/datamapper/PPPPC@WEO/OEMDC/ADVEC/WEOWORLD.

Lin, Ching-yuan (1973) *Industrialization in Taiwan, 1946–72: Trade and Import-substitution Policies for Developing Countries*. New York: Praeger.

Maddison, Angus (2010) 'Historical Statistics of the World Economy: 1–2008 AD.' Available at http://www.ggdc.net/maddison/oriindex.htm.

Market Intelligence and Consulting Institute (MIC) (various years) *Information Industry Yearbook*. Taipei: Institute for Information Industry.

Ministry of Economic Affairs (MOEA) (2015) *Yearbook of Industrial Production Statistics, 2015*. Taipei: MOEA.

Shin, J.-S. and H.-J. Chang (2003) (various years) *Restructuring Korea Inc.* London: Routledge Curzon.

Wade, Robert (1990) *Governing the Market: Economic Theory and the Role of Government in East Asian Industrialization*. Princeton, NJ: Princeton University Press.

Woo, Jung-en (1991) *Race to the Swift*. New York: Columbia University Press.

7

The Origin of Absorptive Capacity in Korea

How Korean Industry Learnt

Keun Lee

7.1 Introduction

The concept of absorptive capacity (AC) was introduced and defined in an influential article by Cohen and Levinthal (1989, 1990) as the ability of a firm to identify, value, assimilate, and exploit knowledge from the environment. AC is also recognized as an important binding constraint in the development of latecomer economies. Borensztein, Gregorio, and Lee (1998) perform a country panel regression and find that foreign direct investment will produce a growth effect only if a country has a certain level of AC. Fagerberg (1988), and Fagerberg and Verspagen (2002), similarly argue that AC is proxied by the total research and development (R&D) of a country as a fraction of its gross domestic product (GDP). Hammerschmidt (2009) and Griffith et al. (2003) consider AC as a function of total R&D efforts at firm or sector levels.[1]

Although several empirical studies emphasize the importance of absorptive capacity by considering in-house R&D or human capital as proxy (Keller, 1996; Mowery and Oxley, 1995), a recent finding indicates that AC cannot be appropriately proxied by R&D or staff quality alone (Flatten et al., 2011; Lane et al., 2006). Moreover, the earlier studies fail to discover the origin of AC aside from formal R&D or education. This recognition introduces two important questions: What is the origin of AC? How can we tell whether this capacity is established in a firm? These questions are particularly relevant in the context of latecomer countries in which firms are usually uncertain about conducting their own R&D and continue to rely on imported technology by specializing in assembly-type production. Scholars studying Korea as an example of a successful latecomer economy have emphasized the importance of AC in enabling Korean firms to

[1] This chapter is a non-technical re-writing of the author's previously published article, Chung and Lee (2015), 'How Absorptive Capacity is Formed in a Latecomer Economy: Different Roles of Foreign Patent and Know-how Licensing in Korea', *World Development* 66: 678–94.

learn and assimilate external knowledge (Evenson and Westphal, 1995; Keller, 1996; Pack, 1992).

The two-step approach of Zahra and George (2002) to AC helps address our questions by differentiating 'potential' from 'realized' AC: the former involves the acquisition and assimilation of externally generated knowledge, whereas the latter guarantees the successful application of such knowledge for transformation and exploitation. Chung and Lee (2015) used a similar two-step quantitative analysis to answer the two questions. The first step investigates factors encouraging a latecomer firm to conduct its own in-house R&D. The second step determines whether or not such firms establish AC in house by investigating the factors driving them to generate their own innovation outcomes.

This two-step approach is similar to that of Kim (1998), who observes that AC requires learning capability and problem-solving skills; the former is the capacity to assimilate knowledge (for imitation), the latter the capacity to create new knowledge (for innovation). However, these definitions of AC may overlap with the general definition of technological capabilities: the knowledge, skills, and even experience required to acquire, assimilate, use, adapt, change, and create technologies or, in short, to generate and manage technical change (Bell and Pavitt, 1993; Dosi, 1988). While the AC of a firm can be regarded as part of its technological capability, the key difference lies in its origins or sources (Cohen and Levinthal, 1989). Given that AC includes the ability of firms to exploit knowledge from the environment, one means of confirming whether or not a firm has AC is to check whether it generates any outcomes, such as patents, from its exploitation activities.

Several studies have observed that access to external knowledge is especially important in the technological development and AC of latecomer firms (Bell and Pavitt, 1993; Kim, 1997; Laursen and Meliciani, 2002; Lee, 1996; Park and Lee, 2006). Using data from Japanese firms, Kiyota and Okazaki (2005) examine the effect of foreign technology acquisition (formal licensing) on the commencement of own R&D and the generation of own patent applications. In Korea, Lee (1996) conducted cross-section analysis of the effect of technology import as represented by the level of 'technological cooperation with developed countries', which is a broad concept.

Our study is distinctive in terms of its emphasis on the role of know-how acquisition, which involves technical services and training together with relevant documents on basic operational skills and elementary process technology. Many foreign technology licensing contracts in Korea, especially during the early days, involve know-how (a form of tacit knowledge), which is different from the licensing of patent rights (a form of codified or explicit knowledge) to advanced technologies. Furthermore, we perform a dynamic analysis of the effects of foreign technology acquisition over time, as we have a unique data set of 3,141 foreign technology acquisition contracts filed between 1970 and 1993, classified into three categories: know-how-only, know-how-and-patent-rights, and patent-rights-only acquisitions.

This chapter contributes several new findings. First, we find that it is know-how licensing, rather than patent licensing, that encourages firms to start in-house R&D. Second, we find that both in-house R&D and know-how licensing, rather than patent licensing, help these firms to file their patents successfully for the first time, which we take as evidence of consolidation of AC. Our findings verify those of Lane et al. (2006) that the building of AC involves a learning process that cannot be confined to R&D. This notion is consistent with those of other qualitative studies that find that leading firms in Korea generally begin learning operational skills and elementary process technologies before starting their own relevant capital investment (Enos and Park, 1988; Kim, 1997) and that since the mid-1980s these companies have learnt, assimilated, and adopted foreign technologies before starting their in-house R&D.

The chapter proceeds as follows. We first discuss the institutional context of foreign technology acquisition in Korea, before explaining the three types of foreign technology acquisition and relating them to the specific empirical hypotheses that are to be tested. We then provide a summary explanation of the data and discussion of the regressions results of Chung and Lee (2015) before offering conclusions in the final section.

7.2 Foreign Technology Acquisition Trends in Korea

Cohen and Levinthal (1989, 1990) introduce AC as an important concept in management studies as well as a by-product of the R&D efforts of a firm. However, given that AC is derived from other sources as well as formal R&D, the requirements for conducting in-house R&D and generating innovative outcomes (patent applications) must be thoroughly investigated. This question is particularly relevant for latecomer countries where building independent capacity and relinquishing dependence on foreign technology pose a great challenge to firms. Cohen and Levinthal (1990) as well as Kim (1998) identify two important elements of AC: prior knowledge base and intensity of effort. The former consists of knowledge available within the organization, so access of latecomer firms to a foreign knowledge base is critical. Therefore, this study attempts to determine the origin of AC in a latecomer economy based on its acquisition of foreign technologies.

As a latecomer economy, Korea has successfully transformed itself from a technology-importing to a technology-generating country. Korean firms only began to conduct in-house R&D in the mid-1980s after undergoing a period of learning, assimilating, and adapting foreign technologies (OECD, 1996; Lee, 2013). Figure 7.1 shows that the number of foreign technologies acquired by Korean firms

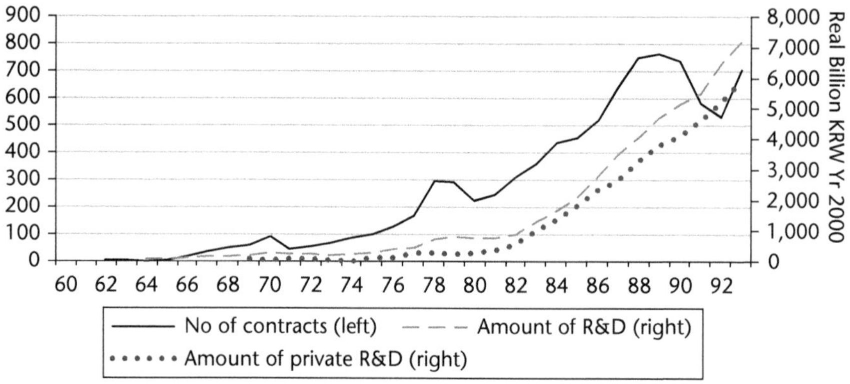

Figure 7.1 Foreign technology acquisition and R&D trends in Korea
Sources: Korea Industrial Technology Association, 1995; National Science and Technology Information Service (http://sts.ntis.go.kr), Tables 1A and 1B

increased from as early as the late 1960s, followed by an increasing trend towards private R&D two decades later. In other words, a significant increase in foreign technology inflow preceded local R&D efforts and innovation outcomes in Korea. Many researchers assert that access to external knowledge is especially important in the development of latecomer firms (Bell and Pavitt, 1993; Kim, 1997; Laursen and Meliciani, 2002; Lee, 1996; Park and Lee, 2006).

Leading firms in Korea generally acquired various forms of know-how, such as operational skills and elementary process technology, before starting their own capital investment (Enos and Park, 1988; Kim, 1997, 1998). These firms built their basic technology proficiency during building and testing of their production facilities, enabling Korean engineers to assume responsibility for daily operations as soon as possible.

In 1960, the government addressed two objectives relating to foreign technology acquisition with the Foreign Exchange Control Act. The first was to ensure that foreign exchange, which became scarce after the Korean War, would only be used for critical technologies. Second, the government wanted to use acquired technology as a stepping stone on which Korean firms could build their own technological capabilities (Korea Development Bank, 1991). The scarcity of foreign exchange during the 1960s compelled Korean firms to seek government approval prior to signing a contract with a foreign counterpart if they wanted to receive technical assistance for a year or longer and if they paid their counterparts in foreign currencies. All applications were scrutinized by the Ministry of Commerce and Industry (Korea Development Bank, 1991).

Korean industries attempted to build production and export capabilities in labour-intensive or light industries, such as textiles, wigs, rubber footwear, and stuffed toys, from the 1960s and into the 1970s. However, during the 1970s firms realized that these industries had low profit margins and insufficient cash inflow to produce the necessary foreign debt services. Therefore, both the government and the private sector wanted to integrate backwards into intermediate goods. If intermediate goods could be secured within the country, the need for foreign exchange should decrease in the long run. Under the Economic Development Plan, a series of legislation was enacted to promote the general machinery, electronics, oil refinery and petrochemicals, transport equipment, steel, and shipbuilding industries (Byun and Park, 1989). The approval procedure for the acquisition of foreign technologies in these target sectors was also simplified.

By the late 1970s, many of the initial entrants into the 'heavy' industries were acquiring both physical capital and relevant technology from foreign sources. Westphal, Kim, and Dahlman (1985: 190–1) reported that more than a quarter of gross domestic investment in Korea from 1977 to 1979 was spent on foreign capital goods. In 1978, an automatic approval system for the acquisition of foreign technology was introduced in general and electric machinery, shipbuilding, chemicals, textiles, and finance under the following conditions: (1) the duration of the contract must be three years or shorter; (2) the down payment must be US$30,000 or less; (3) the running royalty rate must be 3 per cent or lower; and (4) the fixed fee must be US$100,000 or less. From 1979 onwards, most sectors, except weapons, explosives, and nuclear power, were granted automatic approval for their projects subject to satisfying the conditions.

The deregulation process continued in the 1980s and the 1990s until the filing requirement was eventually abolished in 1994. The approval process was simplified to a filing-and-confirmation process from 1984. From 1988, foreign exchange banks were assigned to handle foreign technology acquisition applications under certain scales (Korea Development Bank, 1991; Korea Industrial Technology Association, 1995: 6).

The Korea Industrial Technology Association, a semi-government agency, published a data book, KOITA (1995), covering foreign acquisition in the period 1970–93. The value of this unique data set lies in the fact that all contracts are reported and classified into three categories: know-how-only acquisition, know-how-and-patent-rights acquisition, and patent-rights-only acquisition. Know-how-only acquisition typically consists of technical services and training that are bundled with relevant documents. Know-how-and-patent-rights transfer consists of technical services, training, and documentation protected by the patent system. Patent-rights only consists of patent-right licensing.[2] From this database, we have extracted 3,813 contracts filed by listed firms. Tables 7.1 and 7.2 and Figure 7.2 show several examples of the data.

[2] We follow Kiyota and Okazaki (2005) in using the term, 'foreign technology acquisition'.

Table 7.1 Three types of technology acquisition, 1970–93

Year	Number of					Number of listed firms acquiring				
	Listed firms	Technologies acquired	Know-how-only acquired	Patent-rights-only knw how acquired	Patent-rights-only acquired	Foreign technology	Know-how-only	Patent-rights-know-how	Patent-rights-only	Average number of technologies acquired per firm
1970	35	29	26	3	0	17	16	2	0	1.7
1971	36	13	10	3	0	10	8	3	0	1.3
1972	43	19	12	6	1	18	12	6	1	1.1
1973	126	15	12	3	0	13	10	3	0	1.2
1974	217	25	20	5	0	21	16	5	0	1.2
1975	292	39	16	18	5	28	14	16	5	1.4
1976	313	47	26	20	1	30	18	16	1	1.6
1977	316	37	25	12	0	23	15	11	0	1.6
1978	314	96	45	48	3	49	23	32	3	2
1979	303	94	44	48	2	62	37	31	2	1.5
1980	300	93	43	42	8	60	32	30	3	1.6
1981	295	96	49	36	11	70	40	32	6	1.4
1982	315	156	67	76	13	84	41	32	7	1.9
1983	344	151	79	66	6	96	62	48	4	1.6
1984	423	186	102	78	6	105	71	46	4	1.8
1985	537	196	83	98	15	105	61	50	7	1.9
1986	578	220	100	109	11	119	67	55	10	1.8
1987	605	260	132	113	13	116	85	63	10	2.2
1988	605	334	165	142	27	143	101	60	14	2.3
1989	613	356	175	164	15	131	87	77	9	2.7
1990	639	409	209	181	19	134	85	72	7	3.1
1991	644	297	153	119	23	118	78	78	10	2.5
1992	675	275	135	114	26	109	74	60	11	2.5
1993	671	370	178	163	26	113	81	55	10	3.3

Note: These figures include acquisitions made by non-financial listed firms in the sample between 1973 and 1993. The firms that are scheduled for IPO within the next three years are included in the sample because of the availability of data. Patent-rights know-how is equivalent to the term 'know-how-and-patents licensing' used in the main text.

Source: Tabulated using data from Korea Industrial Technology Association (1995); originally from Chung and Lee (2015).

Table 7.2 Number of technology acquisition contracts concluded by listed firms

Industry	Number of concluded contracts					Share (%)				
	1970 to 1975	1976 to 1981	1982 to 1987	1988 to 1993	1970 to 1993	1970 to 1975	1976 to 1981	1982 to 1987	1988 to 1993	1970 to 1993
Electric and electronics	22	83	349	869	1,323	15.7	17.9	29.9	42.6	34.7
Chemicals	35	85	275	356	751	25	18.4	23.5	17.4	19.7
Transport equipment	17	57	111	192	377	12.1	12.3	9.5	9.4	9.9
General machinery	28	39	86	149	302	20	8.4	7.4	7.3	7.9
Other	38	199	348	475	1,060	27.1	43	29.8	23.3	27.8
Total	140	463	1,169	2,041	3,813	100	100	100	100	100
Know-how-only	96	232	563	1,015	1,906	68.6	50.1	48.2	49.7	50
Know-how-and-patent-rights	38	206	540	883	1,667	27.1	44.5	46.2	43.3	43.7
Patent-rights-only	6	25	64	136	231	4.3	5.4	5.5	6.7	6.1
Total	140	463	1,167	2,034	3,804	100	100	100	100	100

Source: Korea Industrial Technology Association (1995), National Science and Technology Information Service (http://sts.ntis.go.kr), and Korea Intellectual Property Rights Information Office (http://www.kipris.or.kr/); originally from Chung and Lee (2015).

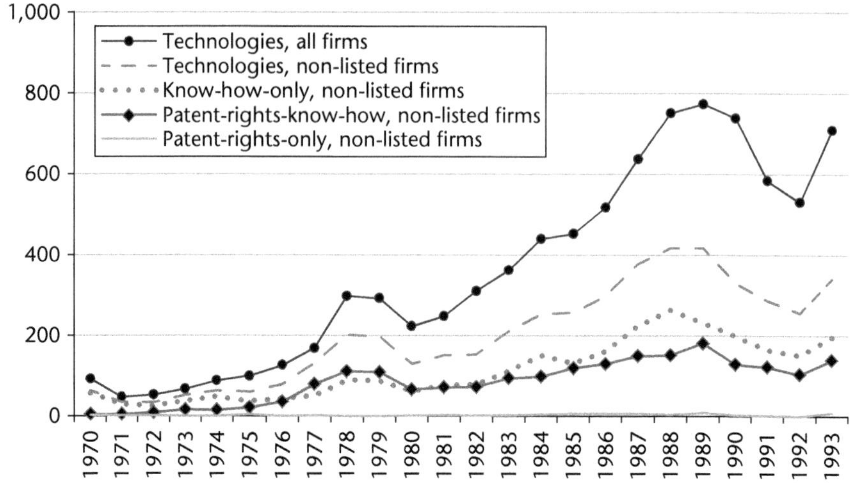

Figure 7.2 Trends in the three forms of foreign technology acquisition
Source: Korea Industrial Technology Association, 1995; National Science and Technology Information Service (http://sts.ntis.go.kr); Tables 1A and 1B

The first finding from these data is that contracts for know-how licensing dominated in the early years, whereas contracts that involve patents followed later. Table 7.1 shows that less than ten firms acquired patent-rights-only contracts before the late 1970s, whereas forty-five and forty-eight firms secured know-how-only and know-how-and-patent-rights contracts, respectively, in 1978. The shares of know-how-only, know-how-and-patent-rights, and patent-only contracts during the period 1970–5 were 69 per cent, 27 per cent, and 4 per cent, respectively. However, these shares amounted to 50 per cent, 45 per cent, and 5 per cent between 1976 and 1981, reflecting the subsequent increase in know-how-and-patent-rights licensing. This pattern may imply that those firms that successfully assimilated basic operation skills and elementary process technology through know-how acquisition advanced to the acquisition of technologies that involve patent rights at later stages. These contracts include not only printed information and blueprints, but also technical services and training information. Expatriate engineers usually come to Korea to ensure that the initial operation of new facilities goes according to plan. Selected Korean engineers are sometimes sent abroad for training, which emphasizes the importance of human capital investment in building AC,[3] as demonstrated by leading firms in Korea, such as Hyundai Motors (Kim, 1998) and POSCO (Pohang Steel Co.) (Song, 2002).

[3] Such investment can be represented by diverse factors, such as the number of engineers and technicians who are hired by the firm and their years of schooling, attendance in capacity-building

Various types of training, particularly overseas and on-site training, were arranged or provided by the firms' foreign suppliers of facilities and equipment. For instance, after Hyundai entered into an agreement with Ford to assemble compact cars on a semi-knocked-down basis, Ford transferred 'packaged' technologies to Hyundai with an accompanying set of explicit knowledge, such as blueprints, technical specifications, and production manuals. Ford also provided tacit knowledge to Hyundai, sending ten Ford engineers to Hyundai and training Hyundai engineers at Ford sites in procurement planning, procurement coordination, production engineering, process engineering, production management, welding, painting, after-service, and marketing (Kim, 1998). In the case of POSCO, the company sent thirty-nine engineers to Japan in1968–9 and 1,861 staff members abroad from 1968 to 1983 during the construction of its first mill (Song, 2002: 128).[4]

The second finding from these data (see especially Table 7.2) indicates that the acquisition of foreign technologies is dominated by four capital-intensive sectors—electrical and electronic equipment, chemicals, transport equipment, and general machinery—rather than by labour-intensive sectors. These findings reflect the industrial policy of the Korean government and the effort of firms to enter these sectors from the early 1970s. The contracts in these four industries comprised more than 70 per cent of the total contracts filed in the sampling period and throughout each sub-period in Table 7.2.[5] This finding indicates that the state's control over foreign technology acquisition was critical for structural transformation of Korean industries from labour intensive to capital intensive, which has ultimately helped them achieve industrial upgrading. The pillar companies of Korea, such as Samsung Electronics, Hyundai Motors, and POSCO, were all established around 1970.

The entry of Korean firms into these industries typically involved the manufacture of products that were new to Korea yet common in the developed world. According to a survey by the Korea Development Bank (1991) on foreign technology acquisition in the 1980s, 55 per cent of such acquisitions by Korean firms related to mature technologies in developed countries, whereas 70 per cent related to the expansion of product mix. Given that Korean firms found the knowledge embedded in manufacturing facilities insufficient for their operations, they sought

programmes, vocational schools, and training in production facilities of the know-how provider. However, we do not have data for all of these factors.

[4] These foreign-trained engineers played very substantial roles in the early days of POSCO as their share in the workforce in charge of facility operation and maintenance reached as high as 62 per cent and 24 per cent, respectively (Song 2002: 128).

[5] However, this case was not evident during the period from 1976 to 1981, when the heavy investment in social overhead capital increased the demand for technology in cement and utility firms, such as electricity.

additional services and training (or know-how-and-patent licensing) from firms in developed countries at an appropriate price.

From the suppliers' point of view, concealing mature technologies was pointless because providing know-how was a way of exporting large manufacturing facilities. The Japanese government's decision to move away from 'pollution-prone', 'natural-resource-consuming' heavy and chemical industries in 1971 provided a favourable environment for Korean firms (Enos and Park, 1988). Selling unnecessary technologies proved profitable for Japan (Enos and Park, 1988: 34), consistent with the 'flying geese' pattern of economic growth in East Asia, where Japanese companies serve as leaders to their follower firms from Korea or Taiwan by transferring their technologies or relocating their factories abroad (Akamatsu, 1962; Kojima, 1973). In this regard, as noted by several scholars including Kiyota and Okazaki (2005), Korean industries followed a similar path to those of Japan, with foreign technology acquisition in the form of licensing rather than FDI nurturing their domestic absorptive capacity and improving their performance (Lee and Kim, 2010).

Table 7.1 also shows that the number of foreign technology acquisitions in the form of patent-right licensing increased during the later period, exceeding fifteen cases a year after the late 1980s. According to the Korea Development Bank (1991), technologies that were bundled with patent rights were more expensive or had a higher value than those that were only bundled with know-how. This arrangement suggests that Korean firms may have demanded something more than the mere operation of manufacturing facilities after stabilizing their daily production. Patented technologies may have been adopted as a means of completing the assimilation and improvement processes that are initiated by investment and know-how acquisition.

7.3 Building Absorptive Capacity through Assimilation of Foreign Technology

Foreign technology acquisition is an interaction rather than an event. Silverberg (1991) and Cimoli and Dosi (1995) emphasize that the imitation and diffusion of technology are part of the innovation process that essentially results in creativity. Process implies a certain passage of time. Even successful firms require sufficient time to accumulate experience and to move 'from imitation to innovation' (Kim, 1997). In line with Von Hippel (1994) and in contrast to other studies that focused on technology spillover from imported capital goods, the current chapter focuses on the contribution of know-how-only contracts concluded along with capital investment contracts in the Korean context. Imported capital goods have been considered among the most important forms of technology transfer in Korea (Lee and Kim, 2010; OECD, 1996). However, these goods become ineffective without the transfer of technology, and especially of tacit knowledge, through know-how-only contracts. Thanks to frequent on-site training by foreign expatriate engineers, Korean engineers quickly learnt to manage their daily operations efficiently. If the knowledge were deemed insufficient, the turnkey contractor and/or other sources, including R&D specialty companies or equipment providers, were contacted for additional information. Enos and Park (1988) argue that even in the most successful cases, such as POSCO and Hanyang Chemicals, time and effort were necessary for Korean firms to become able to use foreign technologies effectively.

Sections 7.3.1, 7.3.2, and 7.3.3 differentiate and discuss the three types of foreign technology acquisitions in Korea to formulate specific hypotheses. The three types of technology transfer are know-how only, know-how and patent rights, and patent rights only.

7.3.1 Know-how Only

Some examples of know-how only included lubricant, cigarette filter, and epoxy resin paint manufacturing, the know-how for TV, radio, lift, and escalator assembly, and the know-how for piston ring, railway brake, boiler, and pump production (Korea Industrial Technology Association, 1995). Know-how only sometimes provided critical knowledge, such as operating skills for naphtha cracking centres, high- and low-density polyethylene and vinyl chloride monomer (VCM) production facilities, and diesel engine facilities. The most valuable and fundamental technologies were generally bundled together with large-scale turnkey projects.

The acquired know-how was transferred by foreign expatriates to Korean engineers on a person-to-person basis. Such transfer usually occurred during the years when the transferee firm was just beginning to adopt a production process without the capability to decipher the tacit contents that underlie documented sources. The primary purpose of foreign technology acquisition during this stage was to generate efficient and effective investment and to achieve the desired operating ratio as soon as possible. Although know-how or tacit knowledge often constitutes the core competitive advantage of leading firms worldwide (Cohen et al., 2000), the non-patented know-how that is transferred from a leading firm to an unrelated party in a latecomer country generally includes basic operational skills and elementary process technologies that are already mature and widely known in the industrialized world. This is confirmed by the Korea Development Bank survey (1991). Hoekman (2005) suggests that leading firms transferred elementary process technology to Korean firms in their early years of development because such technology was considered 'off the shelf', common, and of low value from the perspective of industrialized countries. Korean firms often acquired know-how only as part of large-scale turnkey investment projects. Leading foreign firms found that agreeing to deliver such turnkey projects at a reasonable price was more profitable than turning them down. For instance, even if Gulf Oil refuses to transfer some of its technology to a Korean company such as Hanyang Chemicals, a rival company, such as Dow Chemicals, may agree to the transfer, leaving Gulf Oil with no reason to turn down a turnkey project with Korean firms and to keep a well-known or mature knowledge to itself. Only the price and the conditions of the transfer matter in this situation (Enos and Park, 1988: 62).

7.3.2 Know-how and Patent Rights

Some examples of know-how-and-patent-rights transfer include the licensing of acrylic fibre, TPA (raw material for polyester), cassette player, printed circuit board, excavator, crane, and automobile clutch production (Korea Industrial Technology Association, 1995). Approximately 44 per cent of all foreign technology acquisition contracts of listed Korean firms comprised know-how-and-patent-rights contracts. The ratio of know-how-and-patent-rights contracts to foreign technology contracts significantly increased in the mid-1970s when the basic manufacturing operation of early-mover firms into 'target' industries, such as electrical and electronic equipment, chemicals, iron and steel, and transportation equipment, began to stabilize.

Know-how-and-patent-rights transfer represents a stage in foreign technology acquisition in which Korean firms continued to rely on external sources of tacit knowledge for upgrading their production processes, and yet had accumulated a certain amount of shop-floor experience in the operation of newly imported foreign production facilities. As latecomers, Korean firms were under constant pressure to attain a minimal level of productivity in order to survive in the international market. Economies of scale and scope were the two main sources of productivity improvement for Korean firms in the 1970 and 1980s (Amsden, 2001: 197). Economy of scale was critical in the productivity of target industries, such as iron and steel, petrochemicals, general machinery, electrical equipment, and transportation equipment. Economy of scope was sought as a means of generating profits without hitting the technological ceiling (Amsden, 2001: 197). Korean firms thus tried to invest more in the manufacture of existing products or in the creation of novel product lines. However, they soon realized that tacit knowledge about a product or process that was required by these facilities was no longer regarded as mature or widely known even in advanced economies, and that the owners of the technology tended to be less willing to transfer the knowledge. They therefore moved on to acquire patented foreign technology involving both patent and know-how licensing.

7.3.3 Patent Rights Only

Some examples of patent-rights-only transfer include the patent-rights-only licensing for polycarbonate (a highly sophisticated engineering plastic resin), automobile cooling systems, colour TV, personal computers, and PC graphics software production (Korea Industrial Technology Association, 1995). As shown in Table 7.2, only 6 per cent of foreign technology acquisitions comprise patent-rights-only contracts whereby a latecomer firm is provided with the legal right to use a certain technology, based on patent documents.

However, patent documents often do not contain sufficient information for the manufacture of a new product or the design of a new process. Therefore, patent-rights-only acquisitions imply that the transferee is already equipped with a certain level of R&D capability and does not require expatriate engineers to provide a detailed account of the production process. The latecomer possesses all or almost all the necessary knowledge for adopting a new production process. The R&D capability may entail formal activities that are performed in well-established institutes as well as tacit knowledge accumulated from continuous improvement of imported production processes.

In our cases, most patent-rights-only contracts were concluded by firms in the electrical or electronic equipment sectors. This situation can be interpreted in two ways. First, these sectors produce a large number of patentable products. However, as latecomers, Korean electrical or electronic equipment firms were not the first to file the relevant patents and licences to produce such products. Second, these firms had been highly successful in approaching the technological frontier. Although not the first to develop the relevant technology, Korean firms had the capacity to develop and use such technology without requiring tacit knowledge from other parties.

To summarize, there was a sequence for foreign technology acquisition in Korea. Korean firms began with simple, mature technologies before moving to complex, advanced ones. Most firms, especially in the 1960s and the 1970s, preferred to acquire know-how that could help them construct and operate unfamiliar manufacturing facilities. A typical know-how bundle comprised printed technological contents as well as related on-site training and services provided by expatriate engineers. Korean engineers were sometimes sent to the know-how transferor firm to learn about the implementation process. Korean firms found manuals and blueprints insufficient for learning because of their lack of background knowledge. An expert therefore had to visit these firms to teach the employees how to operate the new technology. Technologies that were inclusive of patent rights emerged after Koreans improved their capacity to decipher the codified content of patents. Firms more capable of deciphering the information reduced their reliance on expatriate engineers over the years. The achievements of these firms grew as they gained more operational experience.

Enos and Park (1988) point out that employees of POSCO and Hanyang Chemicals learnt the tacit contents of process-related technology at an increasingly fast pace as the acquisitions were repeated. The number of mature, and patented, technologies decreases, and increases, respectively, as these companies acquire more foreign technologies. The experience of Korean engineers in managing production facilities helped them learn about foreign technologies at a faster rate. Formal R&D activities usually began after firms had accumulated a certain amount of experience assimilating foreign technology and conducting several know-how-only acquisitions.

In-house R&D became more important than foreign technology acquisition as the technological capabilities of Korean firms progressed because (1) foreign firms became increasingly reluctant to provide core technology to their potential competitors in Korea, (2) labour cost-based competitiveness gradually disappeared, and (3) government support for private R&D increased (OECD, 1996: 91–2). Private R&D activities have achieved nationwide significance since the late 1980s. However, there was significant variation across firms in importance of in-house R&D.

Table 7.3 shows the dates and sequence of the three forms of foreign technology acquisition, in-house R&D, and own-patent applications of the leading firms in Korea. Hyundai Motors contracted know-how licensing in 1968, a year after its establishment, followed by know-how-and-patents and patent-only licensing in 1977 and 1986, respectively. The company reported its first R&D expenditure in its 1975 financial statement (seven years after its first know-how licensing and eleven years before its first patent-only licensing), and filed its first patent application in 1983. Although this sequence seems typical of most companies listed in Table 7.3 and in the entire sample, different sequences and intervals between events are observable in several firms. For instance, several firms waited more than five or ten years after their initial acquisition of foreign technology before starting their R&D, whereas others started their R&D in the same year as the acquisition. We find that 385 of the 764 firms in our sample (50.4 per cent) have contracted foreign technology, 233 of which 233 (60.5 per cent) have acquired know-how only as their first type of technology.

Table 7.4 shows the mean and median number of years that the sample firms spend between technology acquisition, R&D, and innovations. A one-year median interval (with a mean of 0.62 years) was observed between the know-how-only acquisitions and in-house R&D of these firms, which might be shorter than expected. A zero-year median interval (with a mean of minus 0.25 years) was observed between the know-how-and-patent acquisitions and in-house R&D of these firms. Table 7.4 also shows a negative median (−3.0) or mean interval (−3.6) between patent-only acquisitions and R&D, which indicates that firms usually conducted in-house R&D before contracting for patent-only licensing.

Table 7.3 From the acquisition of foreign technologies to the application of patents and in-house R&D: selected Korean firms

Name	Year of establishment	Industry	1st know-how-only contract	1st patent right + know how contract	1st patent right-only contract	1st R&D	1st patent application
Samsung Electronics	1969	Electric and electronics	1969	1975	1972	1976	1978
LG Electronics	1959	Electric and electronics	1966	1967	1975	1976	1976
Daewoo Electronics	1971	Electric and electronics	1968	1982	1975	1975	1982
Hynix Semiconductor	1949	Electric and electronics	1983	1983	1986	1983	1985
Hyundai Motors	1967	Transport equipment	1968	1977	1986	1975	1983
Kia Motors	1944	Transport equipment	1966	1967	N/A	1975	1979
LG Semiconductor	1989	Electric and electronics	1983	1980	1992	1989	1985
Samsung SDI	1969	Electric and electronics	1985	1978	1983	1974	1976
POSCO	1968	Iron and steel	1970	1971	N/A	1983	1977
Samsung Electro-Mechanics	1973	Electric and electronics	1982	1983	N/A	1975	1982
Kolon	1957	Chemical	1972	1980	1983	1980	1976
LG Chemicals	1947	Chemical	1970	1971	1979	1975	1970

Source: Chung and Lee (2015).

Table 7.4 From the acquisition of foreign technologies to the application of patents and in-house R&D: interval in years between events, pair-wise and by sequence of the events Years of interval between events by pair-wise and sequence of the events

Number of years between the events	Mean	Median	Min	Max	Number of firms
From know-how licensing to R&D	0.62	1	−16	16	296
From know-how-and-patent-rights licensing to R&D	−0.25	0	−14	17	240
From patents-only licensing to R&D	−3.6	−3	−17	16	39
From R&D to own patent applications	2.8	3	−20	18	245
From know-how to own patents	3.6	4	−19	22	146
From know-how-and-patents licensing to own patents	3.1	3	−14	19	122
From patents-only licensing to own patents	−1.2	−3	-9	13	15
		Share 1%	Share 2%		
Total sample firms	764	100.00			
Number of firms with ever-acquired foreign technologies	385	50.40	100.00		
Number of firms that started with know-how-only	233		60.50		
Number of firms that started with know-how-and-patents	135		35.10		

Notes: The mean value of 0.62 in the first row, 'From know-how licensing to R&D', indicates that the firms have taken an average of 0.62 years to move to in-house R&D after contracting for know-how transfer abroad.

Source: Chung and Lee (2015); the original authors' calculations.

As regards generating innovations, a three-year median (or a mean of 2.8 years) was observed between the in-house R&D and first-time patent applications of these firms. A four-year median interval (with a mean of 3.6 years) was observed between the know-how-only acquisitions and the patent applications of these firms. A three-year median (or a mean of 3.1 years) was observed between the know-how-and-patent acquisitions and the generation of innovative outcomes. A −3-year median (or mean of −1.2 years) was observed between the patent-only acquisitions and own-patent applications of these firms, indicating that many firms generated their own patents several years before contracting for patent licensing.

Two inferences can be obtained from these data. First, in-house R&D activities began a relatively short time (or one year) after the initial foreign technology acquisitions of a firm, depending on the type of acquisition. Conducting in-house R&D does not necessarily mean that a firm has AC, but rather denotes that it is beginning to build such capacity. Second, firms took an average of three to four years to generate patent applications after starting their R&D or acquiring know-how-based technologies. Therefore, the ability of a firm to generate its own patents may serve as the final proof of their AC or may signify the end of their AC-building process.

These inferences form a two-stage hypothesis about the origin of AC: that the possession of AC can be verified by the capacities of a firm to conduct R&D and to generate patents.

Our first hypothesis states that the acquisition of the three forms of foreign technology motivates them to start in-house R&D. We test this hypothesis by estimating a probit model with conducting R&D (or not) as the dependent variable. In other words, we define the first step of AC as the capacity of a firm to conduct in-house R&D. We hypothesize that those firms that have acquired foreign technology through licensing can promote their AC and subsequently conduct in-house R&D. We suspect the existence of several differences among the three forms of acquisition, specifically between those acquisitions that involve know-how-only and patent-only licensing, because patent licensing and in-house R&D may substitute each other; firms with licensing for foreign patents may be discouraged from conducting their own R&D to develop such technologies. Numerous firms have also conducted R&D before contracting for patent licensing. As shown in Table 7.4, patent licensing usually follows in-house R&D with a three-year median interval.

Our second hypothesis seeks to determine whether these firms can achieve innovations that can be measured based on their patent applications. We use patent applications as evidence of the successful consolidation—or second step—of AC. Econometrically, we hypothesize that in-house R&D activities are primarily responsible for the capacity of firms to generate patent applications. We likewise examine the direct links between the three forms of acquisition and the generation of patents. We hypothesize that although a positive link exists between the acquisition of know-how or know-how and patents, and patent generation, patent-only licensing will not lead firms to generate their own patents. This hypothesis is consistent with the results in Table 7.4, which show that although firms have taken three to four years to apply for a patent after contracting for know-how-only or know-how-and-patent licensing, they had been applying for their own patents three years before contracting for patent-only licensing. This test is conducted using a probit model with patent applications as a dummy variable.

The suitability of patent applications as evidence of a firm's innovation may be questioned. Patents tend to reflect and express non-tacit yet codified knowledge. However, as verified by Jung and Lee (2010), tacit knowledge-oriented sectors and firms likewise generate patents, although not as many per unit of R&D expenditure as in explicit knowledge-oriented sectors. Therefore, we apply a probit estimation method with a dummy variable that takes the value of one for any positive number of patent applications rather than applying regular regressions with the number of patents as the dependent variable. We likewise apply additional regressions with productivity improvement as the dependent variable to determine whether innovation increases productivity.

7.4 Data and Econometric Analysis in Chung and Lee (2015)

7.4.1 Data and their Sources

Chung and Lee (2015) combined three distinctive sets of data to examine the relationship between foreign technology acquisition and the performance of listed companies. These were: (1) foreign technology acquisition data from 1970 to 1993 collected by Korea Industrial Technology Association and recorded in KOITA (1995); (2) typical financial statement data from 1973 to 1996 compiled by Korea Information Service (KIS), Korea Stock Exchange, or Korea Listed Companies' Association; and (3) patent application data from 1973 to 1996 provided by Korea Intellectual Property Rights Information System (KIPRIS).

KOITA presents a summary of all foreign technology acquisition contracts filed before 1994, when the compulsory filing requirements were abolished. This data set is complete in the sense that all firms were required to report the conclusion of foreign technology acquisition contracts in which foreign currency payments were made. Over half of the data set comprises know-how-only contracts, in which tacit knowledge is the technology of interest. Know-how acquisitions relating to the construction of POSCO steel mills, petrochemical complexes, and Hyundai gasoline engine facilities are all documented in the KOITA data set. This data set tends to represent larger companies that preferred to purchase foreign technology at arm's length to enhance their knowledge-based assets. These companies dominate technological advancements in Korea (Amsden, 2001; Kim, 1997).

7.4.2 Estimation Method and the Main Results

The analysis used a probit model with random effects and followed specifications similar to those of Bernard and Jensen (1999) as well as Kiyota and Okazaki (2005) to examine the effects of foreign technology acquisition on the formation of innovation and AC. The aim is to determine the factors that cause firms to conduct in-house R&D. Conducting R&D is captured by a binary variable that takes the value of one if a firm conducts in-house R&D activities. The key independent variable, or the key variable of interest, is the variable that represents several forms of technology acquisition (licensing), as well as the in-house R&D dummy in the case of patent application equations. Technology acquisitions are entered as dummies that correspond to know-how only, know-how and patent rights, and patent rights only, respectively. We also experiment with several dummy variables by combining two forms of acquisition.

Other control variables include the following. The first is the value of fixed assets to represent firm size because the asset values, rather than sales or number of employees, may better represent the propensity of a firm towards capital investment. Capital investments often play an important role in the absorption and assimilation of foreign technology. We also control for firm age, which denotes the number of years that have elapsed since the establishment of a firm. This variable influences innovative outcome and productivity (Huergo and Jaumandreu, 2004a, 2004b). Capital–labour ratio indicates not only the level of past investments, but also the type of technology that is employed by a firm before its acquisition of foreign technology (Arrow et al., 1961). Industry dummies are given based on the KSIC two-digit code.

First, the regression results in Chung and Lee (2015) support the hypothesis that tacit knowledge (licensing involving know-how), rather than explicit knowledge (patent-only licensing), matters both in the initial formation of AC or 'potential' AC of Zahra and George (2002), and in the final consolidation of AC or 'realized' AC. Second, the results demonstrate the limited effect of patent-only licensing, which merely reinforces existing AC by contributing to subsequent or follow-up innovations. Although Lee (1996) reports that technological cooperation with advanced countries tends to have a non-complementary relationship with in-house R&D, the current study identifies the cooperation method (patent-only licensing) where the relationship is observed. And third, the study finds that know-how licensing has an inducing rather than a substituting effect on both in-house R&D and innovation generation.

Taking these regression results together allows us to determine how firms from developing countries achieve technological progress, particularly AC. Foreign firms from advanced countries play a fundamental role in the provision of know-how and patents. As hypothesized before, latecomer firms tend to acquire foreign know-how as well as packaged technologies during the early stages of importing foreign production facilities and equipment. These activities mark the first stage of AC building. These firms then go on to conduct in-house R&D activities to assimilate foreign technologies. Later on, latecomer firms begin to generate their own innovations based on the assimilated foreign technologies, although these may initially appear 'imitative'. Therefore, despite eventually reducing their dependence on foreign knowledge, latecomer firms rely on different sources of external and internal knowledge throughout the process. Externally, these sources change from know-how or imported capital goods to patents, whereas internally, they change from on-site training and education to own accumulated knowledge as the firms begin to accumulate 'prior knowledge'. This phase marks the end of the AC-building process.

7.5 Concluding Remarks

The existing literature tends to use in-house R&D as a proxy for AC and fails to reveal the origins of R&D ability. We define AC as the ability of a firm to conduct in-house R&D and to generate innovation outcomes, and then try to explain how it was formed in Korea. We have used unique data from Korea to distinguish three forms of foreign technology acquisition: know-how-only licensing; know-how-and-patent licensing; and patent-only licensing. These data show that the majority of Korean firms began with know-how-only licensing before using patents.

An econometric analysis in Chung and Lee (2015) shows that know-how licensing associated with imported capital led Korean firms to build AC and then to start in-house R&D, whereas patent-only licensing was not significantly related to being able to conduct R&D. Therefore, a substitution effect may be observed between the introduction of foreign patents and the initiation of own R&D activities at the early stages of development. A similar econometric exercise for the second step shows that conducting in-house R&D leads firms to generate innovations, in terms of either patent applications or increased productivity, during the later stages of their development. Moreover, know-how licensing experience tends to be significantly related to firms' first-time patent applications, whereas patent-only licensing helps stimulate the subsequent generation of patents. This study also finds that firms generally spend at least three to four years building their AC, from the first year of know-how licensing to the first year of patent applications.

Chung and Lee's study (2015) was the first to verify the dynamic link between the learning of tacit knowledge and the formation of AC, as well as the first to measure the actual length of time firms taking to build this capacity. This finding verifies the two-step-based differentiation of 'potential' and 'realized' AC that is proposed by Zahra and George (2002), as well as the decomposition of AC into learning capacity and problem-solving capacity by Kim (1998). In contrast to Lee (1996), our view is that the substituting or inducing effect of foreign technology acquisition on indigenous R&D depends on the specific licensing method. Patent-only licensing exhibits a substituting relationship, whereas know-how licensing tends to produce an inducing effect on in-house R&D. Moreover, a learning process that involves foreign technology, especially tacit knowledge in the form of know-how, occurs before firms can conduct in-house R&D and innovation. However, this specific learning process may not be the only way to build AC, given the importance of worker education, on-the-job training, and overseas training.

Lee (2013), arguing that it may be difficult to derive generalizable lessons from the state-versus-market view of Korean economic development, proposed instead a 'capability-based' view and elaborated various modes of capability building that may be useful in other latecomer countries. Chung and Lee's (2015) econometric study provides a microeconomic foundation for a macro-level view of economic development from which several generalizable implications may be derived.

First, the building of AC is a dynamic process that may become more effective when combined with access to foreign knowledge, particularly tacit knowledge (know-how). This suggests that know-how transfer should be an essential element in technology licensing contracts for a latecomer firm. Moreover, the potential substituting effect of foreign patent licensing may interfere with formation of in-house AC, especially if it is not linked to the start of in-house R&D activities or contracting for know-how transfer.

References

Akamatsu, K. (1962) 'The Historical Patterns of Economic Growth in Developing Countries', *Developing Economies* 1(s1): 3–25.

Amsden, Alice (2001) *The Rise of 'The Rest': Challenges to the West from Late-industrializing Economies*. Oxford: Oxford University Press.

Arrow, K. J., H. B. Chenery, B. S. Minhas, and R. M. Solow (1961) 'Capital-Labor Substitution and Economic Efficiency', *The Review of Economics and Statistics* 43(3): 225–50.

Bell, M. and K. Pavitt (1993) 'Technological Accumulation and Industrial Growth: Contrasts between Developed and Developing Countries', *Industrial and Corporate Change* 2(1):157–210.

Bernard, Andrew B. and J. Bradford Jensen (1999) 'Exceptional Exporter Performance: Cause, Effect, or Both?' *Journal of International Economics* 47(1): 1–25.

Borensztein, E., J. D. Gregorio, and J. W. Lee (1998) 'How Does Foreign Direct Investment Affect Economic Growth?', *Journal of International Economics* 45:115–35.

Byun, Hyung-Yoon and Dong Chul Park (1989) 'Development of Capitalism in Korea: Formation and Development of Monopolistic Capital', in Hyung-Yoon Byun (ed.) *Korean Economy*. Seoul: Yupoong Publishing Company. (in Korean)

Cimoli, Mario and Giovanni Dosi (1995) 'Technological Paradigms, Patterns of Learning and Development: An Introductory Roadmap', *Journal of Evolutionary Economics* 5(3): 243–68.

Cohen, Wesley M. and Daniel A. Levinthal (1989) 'Innovation and Learning: The Two Faces of R&D', *The Economic Journal* 99(397): 569–96.

Cohen, W. M. and D. Levinthal (1990) 'Absorptive Capacity: A New Perspective on Learning and Innovation', *Administrative Science Quarterly* 35: 128–52.

Cohen, Wesley M., Richard R. Nelson, and John P. Walsh (2000) 'Protecting their Intellectual Assets: Appropriability Conditions and Why U.S. Manufacturing Firms Patent (or Not).' NBER Working Paper No. 7552, National Bureau of Economic Research.

Chung, Moon Young and Keun Lee (2015) 'How Absorptive Capacity Is Formed in a Latecomer Economy: Different Roles of Foreign Patent and Know-how Licensing in Korea', *World Development* 66: 678–94.

Dosi, G. (1988) 'Sources, Procedures, and Microeconomic Effects of Innovation', *Journal of Economic Literature* 26(3): 1120–71.

Enos, John L. and Woo Hee Park (1988) *The Adoption and Diffusion of Imported Technology: The Case of Korea*. New York: Croom Helm.

Evenson, Robert E. and Larry E. Westphal (1995) 'Technological Change and Technology Strategy', in Jere Behrman and T. N. Srinivasan (eds) *Handbook of Development Economics, Vol. 3A*. Amsterdam: Elsevier Science, pp. 2209–99.

Fagerberg, J. (1988) 'Why Growth Rates Differ', in G. Dosi, C. Freeman, R. Nelson et al. (eds) *Technical Change and Economic Theory*. London: Pinter, pp. 432–57.

Fagerberg, J. and B. Verspagen (2002) 'Technology-gaps, Innovation-diffusion and Transformation: An Evolutionary Interpretation,' *Research Policy* 31(8–9): 1291–304.

Flatten, T., A. Engelen, S. Zahra, and M. Brettel (2011) 'A Measure of Absorptive Capacity: Scale Development and Validation', *European Management Journal* 29(2): 98–116.

Griffith, Rachel, Stephen Redding, and John Van Reenen (2003) 'R&D and Absorptive Capacity: Theory and Empirical Evidence', *Scandinavian Journal of Economics* 105(1): 99–118.

Hammerschmidt, A. (2009) 'No Pain, No Gain: An R&D Model with Endogenous Absorptive Capacity', *Journal of Institutional and Theoretical Economics JITE* 165(3): 418–37.

Hoekman, Bernard M., Keith E. Maskus, and Kamal Saggi (2005) 'Transfer of Technology to Developing Countries: Unilateral and Multilateral Policy Options', *World Development* 33(10): 1587–602.

Huergo, Elena and Jordi Jaumandreu (2004a) 'Firms' Age, Process Innovation and Productivity Growth', *International Journal of Industrial Organization* 22(4): 541–59.

Huergo, Elena and Jordi Jaumandreu (2004b) 'How Does Probability of Innovation Change with Firm Age?' *Small Business Economics* 22(3/4): 193–207.

Jung, Moosup and Keun Lee (2010) 'Sectoral Systems of Innovation and Productivity Catch-up: Determinants of the Productivity Gap between Korean and Japanese Firms', *Industrial and Corporate Change* 19(4): 1037–69.

Keller, Wolfgang (1996) 'Absorptive Capacity: On the Creation and Acquisition of Technology in Development', *Journal of Development Economics* 49(1): 199–227.

Kim, Linsu (1998) 'Crisis Construction and Organisational Learning: Capability Building in Catching-up at Hyundai Motor', *Organization Science* 9(4): 506–21.

Kim, Linsu (1997) *Imitation to Innovation: The Dynamics of Korea's Technological Learning*. Boston, MA: Harvard Business School Press.

Kiyota, Kozo and Tetsuji Okazaki (2005) 'Foreign Technology Acquisition Policy and Firm Performance in Japan, 1957–1970: Micro-aspects of Industrial Policy', *International Journal of Industrial Organization* 23(7–8): 563–86.

Kojima, K. (1973) 'A Macroeconomic Approach to Foreign Direct Investment', *Hitotsubashi Journal of Economics* 14: 1–21.

Korea Development Bank (1991) *Analysis of Effects of Technology Acquisition.* Seoul: Korea Development Bank. (in Korean)

Korea Industrial Technology Association (1995) *Records of Technology Acquisition Contracts: 1962–1995.* Seoul: Korea Industrial Technology Association. (in Korean)

Korea Listed Companies' Association (1976–7) *Public Announcement on Listed Companies.* Seoul: Korea Listed Companies' Association.

Korea Listed Companies' Association (1978–97) *Annual Report of Listed Companies.* Seoul: Korea Listed Companies' Association.

Korea Stock Exchange (1974–5) *Annual Report of Listed Companies.* Seoul: Korea Stock Exchange.

Lane, Peter J., Balaji R. Koka, and Seemantini Pathak (2006) 'The Reification of Absorptive Capacity: A Critical Review and Rejuvenation of the Construct', *Academy of Management Review* 31: 833–63.

Laursen, Keld and Valentia Meliciani (2002) 'The Relative Importance of International vis-à-vis National Technological Spillovers for Market Share Dynamics', *Industrial and Corporate Change* 11(4): 875–94.

Lee, Jaymin (1996) 'Technology Imports and R&D Efforts of Korean Manufacturing Firms', *Journal of Development Economics* 50(1): 197–210.

Lee, K. (2013) 'How Can Korea Be a Role Model for Catch-up Development? A "Capability-based View"', in Augustin K. Fosu (ed.) *Achieving Development Success: Strategies and Lessons from the Developing World.* Oxford: Oxford University Press, pp. 25–49.

Lee, K. and Y. K. Kim (2010) 'IPR and Technological Catch Up in Korea', in Hiroyuki Odagiri, Akira Goto, Atsushi Sunami et al. (eds) *Intellectual Property Rights, Development, and Catch Up: An International Comparative Study.* Oxford: Oxford University Press, pp. 133–67.

Mowery, D. C. and J. E. Oxley (1995) 'Inward Technology Transfer and Competitiveness: The Role of National Innovation Systems', *Cambridge Journal of Economics* 19: 67–93.

OECD (1996) *Reviews of National Science and Technology Policy: Republic of Korea.* Paris: OECD.

Pack, Howard (1992) 'Learning and Productivity Change in Developing Countries', in G. K. Helleiner (ed.) *Trade Policy, Industrialization, and Development: New Perspectives.* Oxford: Clarendon Press, pp. 21–44.

Park, Kyoo-Ho and Keun Lee (2006) 'Linking the Technological Regime to the Technological Catch-Up: Analyzing Korea and Taiwan Using the US Patent Data', *Industrial and Corporate Change* 15(4): 715–53.

Silverberg, Gerald (1991) 'Adoption and Diffusion of Technology as a Collective Evolutionary Process', in N. Nakicenovic and A. Grubler (eds) *Diffusion of Technologies and Social Behavior*. Berlin: Springer, pp. 209–29.

Song, Sungsoo (2002) 'Historical Development of Technological Capabilities in Korean Steel Industry: Posco from the 1960s to the 1990s.' PhD thesis, Seoul National University. (in Korean)

Von Hippel, Eric (1994) '"Sticky Information" and the Locus of Problem Solving: Implications for Innovation', *Management Science* 40: 429–39.

Westphal, Larry E., Linsu Kim, and Carl J. Dahlman (1985) 'Reflections on the Republic of Korea's Acquisition of Technological Capability', in Nathan Rosenberg and Claudio Frischtak (eds) *International Technology Transfer: Concepts, Measures, and Comparisons*. New York: Praeger, pp. 167–221.

Zahra, S. and G. George (2002) 'Absorptive Capacity: A Review, Reconceptualization, and Extension', *Academy of Management Review* 27(2): 185–203.

8
China
Learning to Catch up in a Globalized World

Justin Yifu Lin and Jun Zhang

8.1 Introduction

Despite a recent slowdown, over the past forty years the Chinese economy has maintained an average annual growth rate of 9.5 per cent. No country or region has ever sustained such a long period of growth at such a high rate. Its per capita GDP increased from US$156 in 1978 to about US$8,640 in 2017. China has a population of nearly 1.4 billion, suggesting that in 2017 its total GDP stood at US$12 trillion, second only to that of the United States, and China's share of the world economy has increased from 1.8 per cent in 1978 to around 15 per cent in 2017. Over the same period China's foreign trade has maintained an average annual growth rate of 14.5 per cent in dollar terms. Again, no country has ever been able to move so successfully and so quickly from a closed economy to an open economy. In 2010, China's exports overtook those of Germany and it became the world's largest exporter. More than 95 per cent of its exports were manufactured products, making China a new manufacturing powerhouse after the United Kingdom, the United States, Japan, and Germany, which had successively claimed the title since the Industrial Revolution in the eighteenth century. More importantly, the technological complexity of China's manufactured exports has also increased steadily, narrowing the gap with developed economies dramatically. As a global manufacturing workshop, China has continued to move up the global value chain. With an increased proportion of value added to its manufactured exports, and its rapid technological progress, China is now transforming from a technology imitator to an innovator.

Thanks to rapid economic development, China's urbanization ratio has also been rising at a remarkable pace—from 17.9 per cent in 1978 to 58.5 per cent in 2017, equivalent to 1 percentage point every year. This means more than 10 million new urban residents every year. Through its rapid economic growth, China is also contributing greatly to the world's poverty alleviation efforts. During the same period, more than 700 million people have been lifted over the international poverty line of US$1.25 a day, contributing to more than 70 per cent of the poverty reduction across the world.

These accomplishments are little short of miraculous. From the 1950s to the 1980s, China implemented a planned economy and adopted an import-substitution strategy, prioritizing heavy industries. It gave up its potential latecomer advantages and sought to catch up with developed economies through self-reliant industrialization. Nearly thirty years after the founding of the PRC, however, China was still a large poor country. In 1978, China's per capita income did not even reach one-third that of sub-Saharan African countries, 82 per cent of its people lived in rural areas, and almost 84 per cent lived below the international poverty line.

Prior to 1978, constant political movements almost crashed China's economy. At the National Planning Conference in December 1977, vice premier of the State Council Li Xiannian stated that the loss of national income caused by the decade-long Cultural Revolution was about 500 billion yuan, which is equivalent to 80 per cent of the total value of capital construction investment in the thirty years since the founding of the PRC, and exceeds the total value of fixed assets in China during the same period.[1]

While China's economic success is widely attributed to its economic reform and opening-up policy, it might be better perceived as a learning process. As a latecomer, China has grasped the opportunities to learn both technology and institutions from early developers and has made full use of its advantages. China is without doubt the most successful learner of the past forty years.

In this chapter, we will look at how China kicked off its learning journey forty years ago and why historically it stands out in the process of catch-up. We start with Deng Xiaoping and his vision of a development paradigm shift taking the form of quasi-natural experimentation; special economic zones were created in the southern provinces of Guangdong and Fujian, and a pilot project began for processing low-end exports with incoming capital from Hong Kong and Macau. We then look at the development of the Yangtze River Delta, which accelerated China's integration with the global economy and led to the establishment of joint ventures between foreign and Chinese firms and wholly foreign-owned enterprises. Rapid accumulation of human capital and export processing in the Pearl River Delta benefited this region in the early years of reform and opening up, and the development of the Pudong New Area of Shanghai in 1990 was followed by a series of market-oriented reform policies and a package of FDI-friendly policies which brought China's manufacturing sector into global production chains.

China has successfully pushed the process of industrializing its agrarian economy through technology learning and a comparative advantage-based catching-up approach. At the end of this chapter, following the New Structural Economics conceptual framework developed by Justin Lin, we hope to explain why China has

[1] From Sina Blog, 11 December 2013: http//: blog.sina.com.cn/s/blog_64892f210101m0v7.html.

become a successful learner over the past forty years and what lessons it can offer for late latecomers.

8.2 Kicking off the Change

8.2.1 A Starting Point

1976 was a bad year in China with the deaths of Chairman Mao Zedong and Premier Zhou Enlai, and a devastating earthquake which claimed many lives. The year 1978, however, turned out to be rather unusual. At the age of 74, Deng Xiaoping had just returned to his leadership position after being purged three times due to political movements. Although not holding the highest position, thanks to his seniority and influence, Deng was recognized as the de facto leader of the Chinese Communist Party (CPC) and the state.

Before 1978, China had shut itself off from the rest of the world for more than twenty years. In 1978, Deng Xiaoping encouraged the country's leaders to make study trips abroad, and with thirteen leaders believed to have made twenty trips to foreign countries both in Europe and Asia, 1978 was later named 'the year of foreign travel'. Deng himself made visits to Japan and Singapore in 1978 and was impressed by their technology advancement and high standard of living. In Japan, he and his wife took a ride on the Japanese Shinkansen high-speed train and visited Panasonic. He became deeply concerned about China's backwardness and technology distance from Japan. He also showed great interest in how Singapore was utilizing foreign capital to develop its export manufacturing capability.[2]

In April 1978, China's National Planning Commission and Ministry of Foreign Trade also sent a delegation to Hong Kong and Macau. After returning to Beijing, the delegation submitted a report to the State Council entitled 'Report on the Economy and Trade of Hong Kong and Macau'. The report recommended that two small towns, Baoan County (the predecessor of Shenzhen), bordering Hong Kong, and Zhuhai County, bordering Macau, be designated export-processing bases in order to strengthen economic and trade ties between the mainland and Hong Kong and Macau. Setting up export-processing zones in Zhuhai and Baoan would exploit the comparative advantages of Guangdong in cheaper land and low-cost labour force, combining with those of Hong Kong and Macao in provision of capital and technology.

[2] In a speech in October 1979, Deng Xiaoping said:

> I got some knowledge about how Singapore put foreign capital to use. When foreign investors set up factories in Singapore, Singapore can get multiple benefits: First, the state can get revenue from the 35 per cent of corporate tax; second, labourers can get income; third, it can boost the service industry, which can generate additional income...I think studying the economic issues should focus on how to make full use of foreign capital. If we don't use it, it would be a shame.

Vice premier of the State Council Gu Mu also paid a month-long visit to Europe with his team in May 1978, reporting to senior Party leaders on his return. In West Germany, the automation, modernization, and high efficiency greatly impressed the members of the delegation. They learnt that an open-pit coal mine with an annual output of fifty million tons of lignite in West Germany used only 2,000 workers, while in China to produce the same output needed 160,000 workers—eighty times more. In Bern, Switzerland, they were also shocked by a hydroelectric power station with only twelve employees managing an installed capacity of 25,000kW. They knew that in China, a 26,000kW hydropower station employed about three hundred people, implying labour productivity more than twenty times lower.

Again, reported Gu and his team, France's Marseilles-based Solmer Steel had only 7,000 workers to produce an annual output of 3.5 million tons of steel, while China's Wuhan Iron and Steel (WISCO) employed 67,000 workers to produce an output of 2.3 million tons. At Charles de Gaulle airport, a plane would take off or land every minute, making sixty flights an hour, while at Beijing Capital International Airport in 1978, there were two flights per hour, and Beijing still found the workload overwhelming.

In September 1978, Deng Xiaoping visited North Korea, where at a meeting with his friend Kim Il Sung, he stated: 'Our starting point for modernization is to make use of internationally advanced technology.'[3]

The famous Third Plenary Session of the 11th Chinese Communist Party (CPC) Central Committee was held in Beijing from 18–22 December 1978, preceded by more than twenty meetings at which senior Party leaders had discussed the reports from officials who had made visits abroad. Deng Xiaoping persuaded leaders and Party members to abandon damaging utopianism and dogmatism, and to adopt a pragmatic approach to economic development. The Third Plenary Session decided to end Mao's Cultural Revolution with its frequent and radical political movements and to turn the Party's focus to economic development and opening up.

8.2.2 Initial Experimentation

On 5 March 1979, the State Council approved a proposal from provincial leaders in Guangdong Province to locate export-processing and assembly zones in Baoan and Zhuhai, and agreed to let them absorb capital from Chinese in Hong Kong and Macau to set up joint ventures.

[3] See Liu Jintian's (1996) article in *Literature of the Chinese Communists*.

Coincidentally, the Hong Kong-based China Merchants Group also proposed to set up an industrial zone in the small peninsula of Shekou. The century-old China Merchants Group was founded in 1872 by Li Hongzhang, the Military Minister of the Qing Dynasty. On 6 January 1979, the proposal to set up Shekou Industrial Zone was submitted to the State Council for approval, and a 2.14 km^2 industrial zone was finally approved by the State Council with special policies including preferential tax and customs policies. On 20 July 1979, Shekou Industrial Zone broke ground and became China's first export-processing zone in Guangdong Province.

Inspired by the Asian Tigers' use of foreign capital and technology to accelerate their economic development, Guangdong Province asked the central government for a delegation of authority so that they could take the first pioneering steps in technology transfer. Guangdong asked for Shantou to be included in the pilot export-processing plan in addition to Shekou Industrial Zone, as the Chaoshan area enjoyed geographical proximity to Hong Kong and was home to numerous overseas Chinese. The province sought authority to implement policies in accordance with international best practice to better attract direct investment from overseas Chinese, Hong Kong, and Macau compatriots, and foreign companies. Guangdong planned to experiment with export processing first in Shantou, Baoan, and Zhuhai, which are adjacent to Hong Kong and Macau, to use overseas capital, introduce advanced technology and equipment, engage in compensation trade, processing and assembly, and cooperative running of businesses in China.

Fujian Province, which is close to Taiwan, also proposed the establishment of an export-processing zone in the city of Xiamen. It hoped to take advantage of being the hometown of many Chinese living overseas to absorb their remittances, and aggressively develop export processing.

Recognizing the importance of experimentation to their massive economic reform agenda, the Chinese government decided on 15 July 1979 to let both Guangdong and Fujian provinces move ahead of others to set up export-processing zones in four cities, Shenzhen, Zhuhai, Shantou, and Xiamen, granting them the title of Special Economic Zones (SEZs) and a certain degree of autonomy, and delegating powers to their city governments to attract overseas direct investment and generate exports. Deng Xiaoping recommended that top priority in the trial be given to Shenzhen special economic zone.[4]

In terms of size, these four cities were really nothing compared to the whole of China. Shenzhen SEZ, with a total area of 327.5 km^2, was the largest. The total area of Zhuhai SEZ, Shantou SEZ, and Xiamen SEZ was 6.81, 1.6 and 2.5 km^2

[4] In February 1979, the State Council officially issued Document No. 38, which explicitly stated that an export base and a new type of border city would be established in Baoan. In order to highlight the importance of Baoan, in March 1979, the CPC Central Committee and the Guangdong Provincial Committee decided to upgrade Baoan County into Shenzhen City, which was later further upgraded to the status of a city directly under the province.

respectively. The total area of the four SEZs initially approved was 338.41 km^2. Later, Zhuhai, Shantou, and Xiamen SEZs all expanded. By the end of 1990, the total area of the four SEZs had expanded to 632.1 km^2.

Though all the SEZs were geographically small, the experiment turned out to be extremely valuable for the transformation of the Chinese economy in the early 1980s. The principal purpose of setting up SEZs was to learn from early comers through the use of foreign investment, technology, and management know-how. As drivers of the development paradigm shift, the SEZs were pioneering movers ahead of the rest of China in integrating with the world economy, strategically triggering the learning process and calibrating the institutional distortions of the Chinese economic system. In fact, given the huge distortions and constraints existing in China's economic institutions, it would have been unrealistic in the late 1970s and early 1980s for China to fully open up and integrate all at once into the global economy. Guangdong and Fujian provinces were not the growth poles of China under the planned economy, and therefore the economic cost of policy change was much lower and it was much easier to manage. This is why China did not at that time establish SEZs in big cities with relatively better conditions, such as Shanghai and Tianjin, whose manufacturing production was extremely important to the economy in the 1980s.[5]

8.2.3 Starting Export Processing in Shenzhen

Construction of Shenzhen SEZ started in the second half of 1980. In order to ease the financial constraints at the beginning of the development, Shenzhen decided to set aside legal rules prohibiting transfer of land to foreign investors and collected land use fees to increase its revenue. Shenzhen was the first city to attempt to legalize the practice of land use for a fee. In 1982, Shenzhen published the Interim Provisions on Land Management in Shenzhen SEZ, and took the lead in reforming the land allocation system. Under the Provisions, the industrial land was allowed to be leased out to investors for a maximum of thirty years, commercial land for twenty years, and commercial residential land for fifty years. Land used for education, science and technology, and health-care purposes could be leased for a maximum tenure of fifty years.[6] In the second half of 1987, the Shenzhen SEZ leased the rights to use three pieces of land to overseas investors gained land premium of more than RMB 20 million yuan.[7]

[5] James Kung (1985) was the first to raise this question in this paper.

[6] *Studies on China's Special Economic Zones* (1984), co-authored by the Economics Research Institute of the College of Economics of Jinan University and the Shenzhen Association for Science and Technology, provides a detailed introduction.

[7] This data comes from an article written by Chen Shanzhe (2004) in the *21st Century Business Herald*.

Based on the experience of land use for money, the Shenzhen SEZ Land Management Regulations were officially implemented on 3 January 1988. The Regulations clearly stipulate the separation of land-use rights from land ownership. The government owns the land by law, but the land-use rights can be transferred by the local government, and re-transferred to others. They can also be mortgaged and leased. In April of the same year, the transfer of land-use rights was written into the constitution, which was tantamount to acknowledging the legitimacy of Shenzhen's land system reform. After Deng Xiaoping's famous South Tour speech in 1992, the land lease system was allowed for and widely adopted outside the SEZs, paving the way for the easing of fiscal constraints facing local governments in their public capital formation costs.

Shenzhen was also granted a certain amount of fiscal autonomy and a number of other special policy concessions by central government and Guangdong province. It was allowed to formulate its own package of preferential policies to support infrastructure finance, marketization, direct investment, and technology transfer. This policy package provided guidelines for changes to the employment and wage determination system and to policy restrictions on foreign exchange and the opening of foreign banks. It was also allowed to break away from the province's planned economic and administrative management systems, to encourage liberalization of factor markets for labour, land, and capital.

The new system of labour recruitment and contracts in Shenzhen was first introduced experimentally around 1980 in JVs in Shekou. In 1982, based on the lessons learnt, Shenzhen began to use labour contracts as the main form of employment, including for top management, in all firms in the SEZ. The lifetime employment system which used to be prevalent in state-owned enterprises was finally abolished in Shenzhen. Employment contracts were generally only for two years. The employment reform obviously sparked economic change and led to improved human resources for management, laying the foundations for the establishment of a professional management market and the subsequent transition to the establishment of corporate governance. Shenzhen adopted a dual-track approach to avoid excessive social costs caused by the shift of employment system. Shenzhen also took the lead in establishing a labour insurance fund in collaboration with Chinese insurance companies. This fund, paid into by employer and employees on a monthly basis, paid pensions and benefits to workers who were dismissed.

Having made institutional changes with minimal disruption, Shenzhen was 'ready for take-off' as recipient of direct investment from overseas, including Hong Kong and Macau, and as the export-processing hotspot. A total of 522 investment projects were approved by 1983, with US$2.91 billion of investment, and US$ 399 million paid in. The average annual paid-in FDI was nearly US$100 million. In 1985 alone, the FDI contracts amounted to over US$1 billion, and more than five hundred foreign-invested enterprises (including those invested

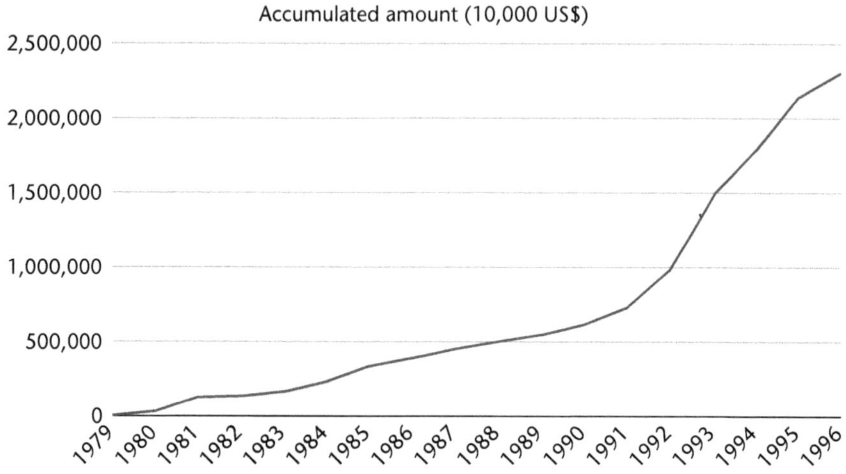

Figure 8.1 Cumulative total of FDI contracts, Shenzhen SEZ
Source: Shenzhen Statistical Yearbook, various years

by capital from Hong Kong and Macau) were approved. Figure 8.1 shows the cumulative total of FDI contracts arriving in Shenzhen. Since the 1990s, as China's commitment to opening up deepened and wholesale structural reform to a market economy accelerated, Shenzhen and other SEZs have become even more significant as FDI destinations.

In the first few years, processing and assembly (P&A) of garments, metal and plastic products for export, with materials supplied from Hong Kong, was developed in Shenzhen. At the time Hong Kong was experiencing severe inflation, with skyrocketing real wages and land prices, greatly increasing production costs for Hong Kong's manufacturing industry and enabling relocation of P&A from Hong Kong to Shenzhen. Table 8.1 gives the detailed composition of exports from Shenzhen between 1987 and 1996. It shows that the P&A with materials supplied or imported was the major export-processing form. Export processing remained a major contributor to Chinese manufactured exports from SEZs in the 1990s. Interestingly and surprisingly, in the early 1980s, thanks to the rise of Shenzhen, the province of Guangdong only accounted for about half of China's total export processing.

Granting tariff exemptions on imported intermediate products and components is of course a common approach adopted by most latecomers to promote exports through learning. In East Asian newly industrializing economies (NIEs), the most popular form of export processing is processing with imported materials (PIM) by local producers. In China, however, largely due to lack of technical equipment and insufficient human capital, export processing in Shenzhen and even the entire Pearl River Delta region in the early 1980s was mostly dominated

Table 8.1 Shenzhen's exports, 1987–96, (in US$ 10,000)

Year	1987	1988	1989	1990	1991
Total	203,520	332,167	433,845	505,152	559,565
1. General trade	68,898	117,416	137,394	139,613	113,790
2. PIM	n.a.	91,847	156,525	222,488	291,094
3. Barter trade	n.a.	76	112	137	66
4. Compensation trade	947	901	788	597	218
5. P&A	78,803	116,483	136,153	140,085	152,954
6. Outward processing	n.a.	361	370	2,228	1,437
7. Other exports	n.a.	5,056	2,511	4	6
Year	**1992**	**1993**	**1994**	**1995**	**1996**
Total	628,362	648,271	888,175	894,089	910,352
General trade	141,932	116,648	235,170	185,756	122,589
2. PIM	333,948	398,497	519,561	583,177	645,535
3. Barter trade	25	917	1375	24	169
4. Compensation trade	88	555	2	346	713
5. P&A	151,661	131,205	130,992	109,239	94,462
6. Outward processing	703	382	169	96	169
7. Other exports	5	67	906	15,451	46,715

Notes: 1. Since 1993, barter trade has replaced the previous small-scale cross-border trade.
2. The data in 1987 were incomplete, and n.a. means not applicable.

Source: *The Shenzhen Statistical Yearbook*.

by P&A, in which even the equipment was provided by foreign investors, and local producers only earned a modest processing fee (Lardy, 1994; Sung, 2001).

Since the 1990s, with Shanghai's Pudong New Area at the head of a new wave of pilots for opening up and reform, China's most advanced and integrated area, the Yangtze River Delta, has had high exposure to foreign direct investment, becoming another destination for continued investment from East Asian economies such as Hong Kong, Taiwan, Japan, South Korea, and developed countries in Europe and America. This new round of rapid FDI inflow together with the continuing shift of technology to China, has allowed the country to quickly move to integration with global production chains and attain the status of a global manufacturing centre. P&A was gradually replaced by PIM, although processing exports still accounted for about half of China's manufactured exports. For example, the proportion of PIM in China's exports in 1992 rose to 28.6 per cent, 10.6 percentage points higher than P&A (Sung, 2007).

Today, Shenzhen, together with its neighborhoods of Dongguan, Foshan, and Zhongshan in Guangdong Province, has become the most innovative and dynamic hub of hard technology on the Chinese mainland, boasting a large cluster of famous global brands such as Huawei, Tencent, BYD, Dajiang, etc. Shenzhen has also been listed as one of China's first-tier metropolises.

8.3 Accelerated Integration with the World Through FDI

8.3.1 Opening Shanghai

It was not until ten years after the establishment of the Shenzhen SEZ that the development of Pudong New Area and the full-fledged opening up of Shanghai was put on the agenda. These developments can be regarded as the output from the learning by early-mover SEZs.

Targeting FDI and export-led growth, Pudong New Area formulated a series of policies, including reduced or zero income tax for JVs, sole proprietorships, and cooperative enterprises, abolition of import tariffs on essential machinery and equipment, vehicles, intermediate goods, and building materials. To encourage foreign investors to invest in energy and transport projects such as airports, ports, railways, roads, and power stations, income tax was set at zero for five years after the first profitable year, and was halved for the next five years. Foreign investors were also allowed to set up foreign banks in Shanghai (including in Pudong New Area). Initially, only finance companies were allowed to enter, but later on, to meet Pudong's development needs, several foreign banks were allowed to set up branches in Shanghai. At the same time, a bonded area was established in Pudong New Area, allowing foreign trade institutions to engage in entrepot trade, and to serve as agents for foreign-invested enterprises importing raw materials and spare parts for production and exporting finished products. A land leasehold policy was implemented in the bonded area and land-use rights extended from fifty to seventy years, so that foreign-funded companies were allowed to bid for plots of land in this area for development.

In order to better promote the land lease pilot scheme, Shanghai took the lead in setting up a Land Resources Management Bureau and a Land Lease Office. These agencies organized land census, survey, confirmation, registration, and distribution of land certificates in urban and rural areas, and established relatively complete land archives and a standardized land management system, laying the foundations for the land lease pilot programme and widespread implementation of land-use reform in Shanghai.

Around the same time, in August 1986, Shanghai dispatched a delegation to Hong Kong to learn about land lease practice and the real estate market in Hong Kong. The delegation also sought advice from Hong Kong on how to attract foreign businesses to rent land in Shanghai. Later on, Shanghai invited Leung Chun-ying (who became chief executive of the Hong Kong Special Administrative Region from 2012 to 2017) and six other Hong Kong professionals to serve as consultants for the land lease programme in Shanghai.[8]

[8] Jun Zhang (2018) reviews this history in the forthcoming revised edition of *The Reform Not in the Public Eye*.

Shanghai's land lease pilot scheme followed international practice as far as possible and focused on land transfer to foreign investors, with international bidding rules and the land premium paid in foreign exchange. On 8 August 1988, Shanghai Hongqiao Economic and Technological Development Zone successfully transferred land-use rights to a foreign investor for fifty years at a bid price of US$28.05 million. Soon after, under the land lease pilot scheme, another piece of land in Hongqiao, the first industrial land, was transferred.

Shanghai also developed China's first local regulation to allow the transfer of land-use rights of state-owned land. On 12 April 1988, the first session of China's Seventh National People's Congress amended the Constitution of the People's Republic of China (Amendment). The stipulation 'the land use rights may be transferred in accordance with the provisions of the law' was added to the original Article 10, paragraph 4 ('Any organization or individual may not seize, trade, or otherwise illegally transfer land'). Since then, 'land lease' has gradually become an important source of finance for local governments, speeding up the process of urban planning, renovating infrastructure, and boosting the urban real estate market.

Largely thanks to the spillover and diffusion effect of opening the Pudong New Area of Shanghai, the pace of industrial transformation and integration into global production chains has accelerated in the Yangtze River Delta region (including Jiangsu province and Zhejiang province). Inspired by Shanghai's opening up and preferential policies, the provincial governments of Jiangsu and Zhejiang learned to catch up and implemented their own strategy for attracting foreign investment. A telling example is that in 1993, the Singaporean prime minister Lee Kuan Yew finally decided to build an industrial park in Suzhou, Jiangsu province. Of all the reasons that Suzhou was eventually selected by Singapore, the most important was the potential spillover effect from the future development of Pudong New Area and Shanghai, to which Suzhou is very close. Other cities on the shortlist were Qingdao and Yantai, both coastal cities in Shandong province, where the infrastructure was even better than Suzhou. However, Lee Kuan Yew considered Suzhou the best choice because of Shanghai's plan to build Pudong International Airport, its fully open stance to foreign investment, and the planned Shanghai–Nanjing (capital city of Jiangsu province) expressway (which opened to traffic in 1996, creating even closer economic ties between Suzhou and Shanghai). In fact, thanks to the Shanghai spillover effect and the manufacturing capacity developed in the 1970s through close connection with Shanghai, the southern part of Jiangsu quickly became a principal destination for FDI. Nearly four hundred Fortune Global 500 companies have settled in Jiangsu Province, including companies from the United States, Europe, Japan, Taiwan, and South Korea. Kunshan County under the jurisdiction of Suzhou and the Singapore Industrial Park in Suzhou also host a cluster of famous consumer electronics producers from Taiwan and Korea.

Similarly, Zhejiang province benefited from Shanghai, accelerating integration into global production chains, with Jiaxing, Hangzhou, and Ningbo becoming favoured destinations for FDI and multinationals because of their proximity to Shanghai. Zhejiang has also become the birthplace of leading Chinese internet companies such as Alibaba and NetEase.

8.3.2 FDI Inflow and Export Growth after the 1990s

Figure 8.2 shows FDI inflow to China between 1984 and 2017. In the initial SEZ development phase in Guangdong and Fujian, FDI was relatively small. With the opening of Shanghai and the Yangtze River Delta as well as China's improved legal and regulatory framework, FDI inflow has significantly picked up, with rapid increases from 1992 to 1998. FDI growth was slow between 1999 and 2000 due to the Asian financial crisis, returning to a fast growth track with China's accession to the WTO in 2001.

FDI always accounted for an absolute majority in China's use of foreign capital. There is no doubt that FDI has contributed greatly to China's integration with the world since the 1990s and to the country's prominence as a world workshop. According to IMF statistics, the proportion of FDI in China's foreign capital was mostly around 60 per cent, and in some years (such as 2009) it was even close to 70 per cent. Moreover, as shown in Table 8.2, almost 90 per cent of the foreign capital was utilized in the manufacturing sector.

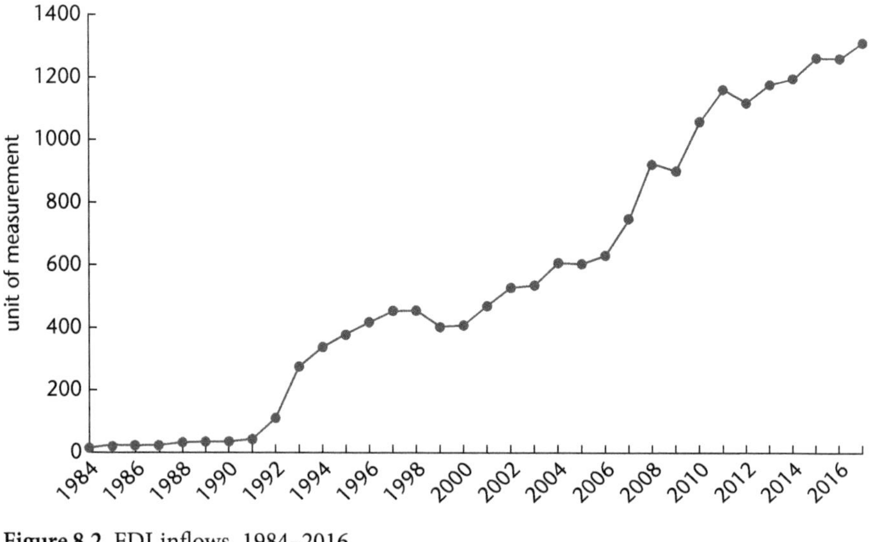

Figure 8.2 FDI inflows, 1984–2016
Source: China Statistical Yearbook

Table 8.2 Distribution of foreign capital in China's industry in 2016 (in US$ million)

Secondary industry	Paid-in FDI	Ratio
Mining	96	0.24%
Manufacturing	35,492	88.26%
Electricity, gas, and water production and supply	2,147	5.34%
Construction	2,477	6.16%
Total	40,213	100%

Source: Ministry of Commerce.

Table 8.3 Spatial distribution of foreign investment, end of 2016 (in US$ million)

Region	Paid-in FDI	Ratio
Eastern region	2,033,125	72.36%
Central region	534,809	19.03%
Western region	187,446	8.61%
Total	2,809,788	100%

Source: Ministry of Commerce.

The distribution of foreign investment has also favoured Chinese coastal regions. Table 8.3 shows that between 1979 and 2016, nearly three-quarters of foreign capital (72.36 per cent) was concentrated in the eastern region, reflecting the fact that FDI tends to be export oriented.

As Figure 8.3 shows, since the 1990s, due to the phenomenal growth in FDI, China's trade has recorded growth higher than that of nominal GDP, causing China's trade-to-GDP ratio to keep rising until 2007, before the global financial crisis. China has since become a major trading country, ranking third globally in terms of trade-to-GDP ratio.

China's higher trade-to-GDP ratio partly reflects the fact that the proportion of processing trade is still relatively high, and also unduly reliant on FDI (Huang, 2003). This phenomenon has not been seen in India and other high-growth economies in East Asia.

In fact, the excessive share of export processing in China should be interpreted as a benefit of the learning process. First, compared to Japan and the four Asian Tigers, China is a latecomer and has had the opportunity to make use of early comers' capital and technology to develop its processing trade. This is a rational choice. Second, in the 1980s when the SEZs were established and the 1990s when Shanghai began to open up, China was to some extent still subject to the planned economy system dominated by state-owned enterprises (SOEs) and administrative control. Under this system, there were still many institutional distortions and

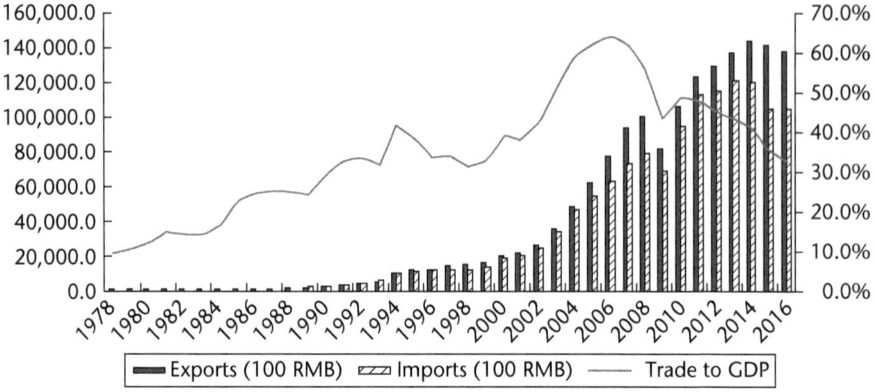

Figure 8.3 China's trade as a percentage of GDP
Source: China Statistical Yearbook

financial discrimination against private enterprise, which greatly limited the ability of Chinese local enterprises to participate in global production. Had it not been for the excessive use of foreign investment under a rigid planned management system, China would not have been able to quickly overcome these obstacles and constraints to participate in the global production chain. So perhaps China's excessive use of foreign capital should rather be regarded as a second-best solution to rapid participation in globalization (Sung, 2001).

Learning curves work in China. From P&A to PIM, Chinese companies learned to catch up. They accumulated knowledge and human capital from the learning process, and continuously improved their manufacturing capabilities. As a result, China's export mix was continuously optimizing (Fu, 2003; Jiang, 2002; Wen, Xian, and Ma, 2009), and the quality of exports continued to improve (Li and Wang, 2013). Moreover, studies have found that the technological sophistication of Chinese exports continued to increase (Xu, 2007; Xu and Lu, 2009), reflecting the technological progress and upgrading of China's manufacturing industry. China is no longer known as a sweatshop and has instead become a global manufacturing powerhouse (Sung, 2007). Furthermore, dependence of China's manufacturing exports on FDI has significantly reduced over the past ten years.

8.4 Paradigm Shift and Institutional Reform

Shortly after the CPC came to power on the Chinese mainland in 1949, China began to build a socialist country modelled on the USSR and implemented a closed command economy system. This was also a typical large-scale experiment in policy learning and technology learning. After completing 156 heavy industry projects with Soviet technical and financial assistance, China decided to embark on a radical development model that promoted import substitution and self-sufficiency, and prioritized heavy and chemical industries. To achieve its goal of catching up with the Great Leap Forward, China chose to build a centrally planned regime, under which the allocation of resources, including employment arrangements, was decided and controlled by a central planning agency (the Planning Commission). China also initiated a collectivization movement in the agricultural sector to deprive farmers of land and freedom of choice so as to support urban industrialization. Agricultural products were procured by the government at a very low price to subsidize urban residents and industrialization. A system of strict urban–rural distinction was implemented: farmers were unable to be freely employed or live in cities, and capital prices were artificially depressed by the nationalization movement.

This approach deviated significantly from the factor endowment structure of China in the early days which featured a lack of capital. Disconnected from the world economy, China, with its abundant labour supply and shortage of capital, could not fully participate in the global industrial chain. As a result, its potential comparative advantage was not tapped and its productivity did not improve at all.

Despite the unique endowments of China's coastal areas (Guangdong and Fujian had a large number of overseas Chinese, and Shanghai before 1949 had close commercial links with Hong Kong, Europe, and the United States), China could not be developed into an economic powerhouse under Mao Zedong's planned economic model and its balance-oriented development strategy. On the contrary, the heavy and chemical industries and the national defence-oriented strategy pursued in the 1960s focused on hinterland provinces and mountainous areas. Because Mao Zedong and his team believed that the international environment was not safe enough for China to develop its coastal areas at that time, he decided to develop inland, abandoning the coastal areas, especially Guangdong and Fujian. (Geographically, China's coastlines are in the east and south, so there is a spatial imbalance between east and west.) This inland-looking development model undoubtedly denied China's comparative advantage.

After the establishment of diplomatic relations with the United States in 1972, Premier Zhou Enlai decided to import a large number of machines from the United States. Unlike most of the machines imported from the USSR, which were sent to the hinterland, half the US machines went to the eastern region, which was more poised for industrialization due to its unique location and endowments. With the establishment of diplomatic relations between China and the United States, Mao Zedong changed his views on the likelihood of a third world war. China's economic policy began to shift from balance oriented to efficiency oriented.

Deng Xiaoping was not interested in the inland development strategy. He believed that Mao Zedong overestimated the probability of a third world war. In 1978, two years after the death of Mao, he insisted that some areas should be allowed to develop first and he turned his attention to Guangdong and Fujian on the east and southeast coast. In 1978, after his visit to Japan and Singapore, he confirmed his determination to develop compensation trade and make use of foreign capital in coastal areas. He was very supportive of the proposal to set up SEZs in Guangdong and Fujian. In order to fight criticism and resistance within the party, he visited Shenzhen SEZ twice showing his endorsement. He was thus regarded as the spokesman of Shenzhen.

The trial-and-error approach of allowing some regions to move first and then replicating their success in other ready regions reflects Chinese leaders' profound understanding of the constraints and conditions facing the country. In 1984, five years after the establishment of the Shenzhen SEZ, the central government decided to carry out systemic reform of the overall planned economy system.

In the years that followed, China's reform was characterized by gradualism and incrementalism. Instead of pursuing large-scale privatization from the outset, SOEs were only allowed to engage in market transactions if they met the planned quota. A 'grandfather policy' was applied in a number of fields, such as employment and housing. Those whose interests were undermined by the reform were compensated by one-off subsidies, keeping resistance to reform to a minimum.[9]

Throughout the 1980s, factor prices, including the price of capital, were not liberalized all at once; a gradualist approach was adopted, with a combination of price adjustments and small-step liberalization according to the relative importance of the factor in question and market equilibrium conditions. One of the upsides of this approach was that private companies began to expand rapidly by leveraging the liberalized market in certain regions or sectors, while SOEs continued to receive support from the planned system. However, with the passage of time and the expansion of the private sector, SOEs inevitably began to face competition from the private sector. Competitive pressures continued to challenge SOEs and change their market environment and profitability, to the extent that in the late 1980s and early 1990s, most SOEs suffered huge losses. This result led to massive sector-by-sector restructuring and governance reform of SOEs in the mid-to-late 1990s.

This dual-track approach provided incentives for state producers to produce more even under the quota system of the planned economy, resulting in significant marginal efficiency improvement in resource allocation and labour productivity. Over time, the proportion of planned production continued to shrink and market-driven production expanded and dominated. Clearly the dual-track reform approach aimed to avoid the economic chaos and social instability of large-scale privatization and radical market-oriented reform—basically a win–win strategy (Lau, Qian, and Roland, 2000; Zhang, 1997).

[9] *The China Miracle: Development Strategy and Economic Reform* by Lin, J. Y. et al. described and analysed how China promoted the reform of the planned economic system; see Lin et al. (1994).

At the end of the 1990s, China shifted its economic reform focus onto macro-economic management and the regulatory framework. This phase can be conceptualized as ending the dual-track system, reshuffling the central–local fiscal relationship, building sound banking and rules-based regulation, and introducing corporate governance of SOEs. This package of reforms paved the way for prolonged macro-economic stability and created institutional conditions favourable to attracting FDI and accelerating China's integration with the world.

These institutional reforms were also important steps on the way to membership of the WTO. After fifteen years of ongoing arduous negotiations, and having gained the support of major developed economies such as the United States, China finally joined the WTO in 2001. In accordance with its commitments to the WTO and the free-trade principle, China over a very short time reformed around two thousand ministerial-level rules and 190,000 local government regulations inconsistent with WTO rules. It also made great changes in IPR protection, national treatment, environmental protection, and market access. In 2013, China decided to introduce a pilot free-trade zone in Shanghai; subsequently a further eleven pilot free-trade zones have been allowed to set up, continuing to deepen the process of opening up and structural reform.

8.5 What can be Learned from China's Catch-up Learning Experience?

According to the World Bank, China's per capita GDP in 1978 was only US$156, less than one-third of that of the sub-Saharan African countries, which was US$490. As in other poor countries, forty years ago, 81 per cent of Chinese residents lived in rural areas, and 84 per cent of Chinese lived below the international poverty line of US$1.25 a day. Today, more than 700 million people have been lifted above the international poverty line, contributing to more than 70 per cent of poverty reduction across the world in the past forty years.

From the 1950s to the 1970s, China was very much a closed economy. In 1978, exports and imports accounted for only 4.1 per cent and 5.6 per cent of GDP respectively (altogether only 9.7 per cent). Moreover, more than 75 per cent of the exports were agri-products or agricultural processed products. Over the past forty years, China's trade with the rest of the world has maintained an average annual growth rate of 14.5 per cent. In 2010, China's exports exceeded Germany's, and China became the world's largest exporter, with manufactured products making up more than 97 per cent of its exports.

From 1978 to 2017, the Chinese economy achieved an average growth rate of 9.5 per cent for forty consecutive years. No country or region in history has sustained such a long period of growth at such a high rate. In 2017, China's per capita GDP reached US$8,640, making it an upper middle-income country.

Meanwhile, although the notion of 'China collapse' has cropped up from time to time, China is the only country in the world that has not experienced a serious economic crisis over the past forty years.

China's economic performance over the past forty years raises many questions for economists. First, why did China achieve such rapid growth over forty years? Second, why was China so poor before the reform and opening up? Third, as China was not the only country that has transitioned from a planned economy to a market economy, why have other economies collapsed, stagnated, and become stuck in crises while China has maintained stable and rapid development? Fourth, what can economists learn from China's transformation process?

To answer the first question, we first need to understand what economic growth is. At first glance, growth appears to be a continuous increase in per capita income, but to achieve increased per capita income, labour productivity needs to be continuously improved. Generally there are two approaches to realizing productivity increase: one is to make technological innovation happen in existing industries so that more and better products can be produced per worker; the other is to upgrade the industrial structure so that resources can be allocated to sectors with higher added value away from those with lower added value. For developed and developing countries alike, both approaches work.

However, as a latecomer, the developing country can easily realize technological progress and industrial upgrading by introducing, digesting, and re-engineering technology from early comers. By leveraging this latecomer advantage, developing countries can achieve technological progress and industrial upgrading at a lower cost and with less risk, achieving faster economic growth than developed countries. This is because the technologies and industries of developed countries are already at the forefront, and only by inventing new technologies and new industries can they sustain technological progress. For developing countries, however, as long as the technology used in the next phase of production is better than the current phase, it constitutes technological progress; the same applies to industrial upgrading.

If China's rapid and prolonged economic growth is reasonably attributed to its advantage as a latecomer, then why did the latecomer advantage not help China before 1978? This leads to our second question.

After the founding of the PRC in 1949, Chinese leaders aspired to build a strong and prosperous country. In the 1950s, the development goal proposed was to catch up with the United Kingdom in ten years and the United States in fifteen. Despite its poverty, China sought to expand its production capacity in heavy industries similar to those of developed countries, in the hope of narrowing the productivity gap as quickly as possible. However, the most advanced industries and the most advanced technologies not only had patent protection, but also were related to national defence and security, so it was impossible to achieve the goal by welcoming transfer of those industries and technologies from the developed world. In these circumstances, China had to be self-reliant in developing these technologies, and therefore had to give up the latecomer advantage.

Advanced industries are extremely capital intensive, and China was then an agricultural country with a severe shortage of capital. To ensure the development of heavy industries during the centrally planned regime, China could only rely on the administrative command and subsidies and distort the prices of resources and factors to reduce the cost of developing heavy industries at the expense of agriculture and light industries. Although the command economy had allowed China to quickly establish an independent and relatively complete industrial system, technical efficiency was rather low. Obviously such a development model was not sustainable for long.

It was not until Deng Xiaoping regained his leadership position in 1978 that China finally and boldly gave up its unrealistic development strategy and dogmatism, changed its development paradigm, and established a development strategy and goal appropriate to its endowment conditions. China decided to implement market-oriented reform and a programme of opening up, consciously encouraging the expansion of industrial sectors with comparative advantage, leading to tremendous growth of manufactured exports. By creating jobs, the export-oriented industrialization shifted huge numbers of surplus labourers from rural and agricultural sectors to labour-intensive industries in the urban areas, achieving rapid growth in labour productivity. The 'grandfather policy' was introduced so that capital-intensive, large-scale state-owned enterprises as well as national security-related industries continued to receive protection and subsidies from governments during the process of structural transformation in order to maintain economic and social stability. The investment in previously suppressed labour-intensive industries was liberalized; SEZs, industrial parks, and export-processing zones have all been set up in a pragmatic manner to vigorously attract FDI and technology transfer, connecting Chinese producers to global production chains and turning the latecomer advantage into a global competitive advantage.

Over time, as physical and human capital has rapidly accumulated, China's comparative advantage has evolved. The former CAD industries have become CAF industries. Previously non-viable companies have become viable. The 'offering fuel in snowy weather' type of protection and subsidies in the transition period have become the 'icing on the cake', creating conditions for the elimination of various market interventions and distortions.

In the 1980s, when China initiated economic reform and opening up, most socialist countries and other developing countries were also transitioning to a market economy. The mainstream view in international academia was that 'shock therapy' was essential for the success of economic transformation, and various government interventions needed to be eliminated all at once, according to the Washington Consensus. Many countries, whether socialist or capitalist, did adopt the 'shock therapy'. However, the Washington Consensus ignored the fact that government intervention was necessary to protect and subsidize heavy industries that defy comparative advantage. Once protection and subsidies were all eliminated, heavy industries would quickly collapse, resulting in mass unemployment, and social and political instability, at least in the short term. Moreover, quite a few heavy industries were related to national defence and security. Even if they were privatized, the state still had to provide protection and subsidies. Private entrepreneurs in these industries would actually have more motivation to ask for government protection and subsidies. Many empirical studies have shown that this is exactly what happened to the former Soviet Union and Eastern European countries.

Fortunately China's economic transformation did not follow any existing doctrines; rather it took note of its own actual conditions. Given the initial political conditions, it would have to take small steps forward and continuously look for opportunities to create new sectors to spark growth. The 'grandfather policy' remained for reasons of economic and social stability, but the focus was on the creation of new sources of growth by shifting surplus labour from agriculture to labour-intensive export manufacturing sectors. In the 1980s and the 1990s, Western mainstream economists believed that the dual-track gradualist transformation adopted in China was perhaps the worst approach, even worse than the original idea of creating a centrally planned economy. However, the result has proved otherwise. China's economic transformation has so far been a great success story. Not only has it successfully undergone structural transformation, but its achievements have amazed the world, even though China still has problems of corruption, income disparity, and environmental pollution.

We believe, considering the similarity of initial conditions, that China's experience as a latecomer and learner might have implications for other developing countries looking to start on the path to industrialization and modernization. After the Second World War, a large number of developing countries aspired to catch up with developed countries. Most socialist countries also wanted to build capital-intensive and modern industries out of their backward agricultural economy. Their problems brought about by the planned economy were similar to those of China. Developing countries such as India, and many in Latin America and Africa, newly independent from colonial powers after the war, also pursued capital-intensive modern industries despite the fact that they were still constrained by lack of capital due to the much lower labour productivity of a backward agricultural economy. A series of market distortions and unwarranted interventions that were essentially the same as China's also cropped up in their economic operations.

By comparing the performance of a handful of successful and a large number of unsuccessful developing economies after the Second World War, we find not a single developing economy that has succeeded by formulating policies in accordance with Western mainstream economics. In fact, the policies implemented by a couple of economies that turned out to be successful were all deemed wrong by mainstream economists. For example, in the 1950s and the 1960s, all developing countries were advised to pursue the goal of modernization and industrialization. At that time, the mainstream economic model for development was structuralism, which proposed an import-substitution strategy, that is, government-led resource allocation to develop modern capital-intensive industries. However, all the economies that pursued this strategy have failed. By contrast, a few successful East Asian economies all started with traditional small-scale labour-intensive industries and pursued an export-oriented strategy rather than import substitution. At that time, such a strategy was considered wrong.

In the 1980s and 1990s, all the socialist and non-socialist countries shifted from a government-led to a market economy. At that time, mainstream neoliberal economics advocated the Washington Consensus and shock therapy to eliminate all kinds of government intervention and distortions in the hope of building a sound market economy system. Countries that took this approach have experienced economic collapse, stagnation, and crises. By contrast, a handful of countries like China, Vietnam, Cambodia, and Mauritius (which began to transform in the early 1970s) that adopted a dual-track gradualist approach, have achieved rapid development.

Mainstream economic theories are based on the experience of developed countries. As developing countries have different endowments and initial conditions, mainstream theories are inevitably problematic for them. Mainstream economists either use developed economies as a yardstick against which to measure developing countries, e.g. structuralism, or propose a growth model based on the experience of developed countries where the model is doing well. However, advocating well-developed institutional arrangements to developing countries is risky, because it ignores the very important fact that developing countries are quite different from developed countries in terms of their initial conditions.

Professor Justin Yifu Lin has been committed to advocating New Structural Economics (NSE) for the past decade (Lin, 2009, 2012). NSE is based on China's own experiences and lessons drawn from the learning process of China and East Asian high-performing economies. It also summarizes the successes and failures of other developing countries and economies after the Second World War. It consciously takes the conditions of developing countries as a starting point for study, and can better explain why China is successful, in what aspects China falls short, and where China should be heading in the future. NSE also has an important reference value for other developing countries.

NSE, the third edition of development economics after structuralism and neoliberalism, is a rethinking tool for revisiting the modern economics derived from developed countries, and aims to build up a new theoretical framework for economic development for developing countries. NSE proposes to use the neoclassical economic approach to study the nature of economic growth and its determinants. NSE underscores the endowment structure in an economy at a given time as a major determinant of industrial and technological structure in the economy at that time; the change in industrial/technological structure is driven by the change in endowment structure. It pays more attention to the role of government in improving both soft and hard infrastructure in the process of structural transformation in an economy.

8.6 Conclusion

China is one of the few economies that successfully achieved rapid growth after the Second World War over a long period of time. Given its population as well as the pace and duration of growth, China's growth is indeed a miracle. Measured by the technological complexity of exports and the speed of technological advancement, China is also one of the fastest technological learners among latecomers. Considering its humble starting point and the widespread poverty in China forty years ago, its success is of particular reference value for late latecomers.

Overall, China's rapid technological progress and economic success would be better attributed to the transformation of its development strategy since 1978. It renounced dogmatism and the unrealistic catching-up strategy, and instead adopted a pragmatic approach to managing the economic transition. For instance, China continued to offer transitory subsidies for CAD industries in the transition process in order to maintain economic and social stability; at the same time, through institutional reform and by encouraging the inflow of FDI, China created market conditions to help CAF industries integrate with global production chains and learn from early comers. With massive accumulation of both physical and human capital through the expansion of CAF sectors with learning and rapid growth, China successfully paved the way to gradually eliminating various distortions and marketizing previous CAD sectors, turning China from a closed economy into a global manufacturing powerhouse.

Another factor in China's successful industrialization and technological advancement may be that China has avoided a top-down, one-size-fits-all industrial policy. China's industrialization process had a strong sense of experimentation. The authorities improved urban planning and physical infrastructure, offered one-stop services, and reduced bureaucracy within the industrial parks and economic zones. Central government created incentives to govern for local officials to focus on and facilitate investment growth and entrepreneurship.

China's experience of economic success, as well as that of East Asian high-performing economies, reveals the points that development economics has so far missed. The catching-up strategy proposed by development economics for latecomers fails to take note of the evolutionary nature of industrial structure, and ignores the importance of initial factor endowments for the success of the industrialization strategy.

The third edition of development economics advocated by Justin Yifu Lin, New Structural Economics (NSE), attempts to draw lessons from the successful catching-up process of high-performing economies, including China. It underscores the importance of technological learning and following comparative advantage in the making of industrial policy. Latecomers should avoid being captured by dogma and should highly respect their initial conditions in triggering economic development. The Chinese case shows that by gradually overcoming various constraints, accumulating physical and human capital by learning from early comers, and expanding CAF sectors, latecomers have a great opportunity of achieving piecemeal rapid economic development and narrowing the income gap with early comers.

References

Chen, Shanzhe (2004) 'A Case in Shenzhen Exposing the Dilemma of the "Time Difference" between the Land Use Right and House Ownerships: Land Use Right Expiration Leading to "Landless" Houses', *21st Century Business Herald*, 8 October.

Economics Research Institute of the College of Economics of Jinan University and Shenzhen Association for Science and Technology (1984) 'Studies on China's Special Economic Zones', internal publication.

Fu, Zhaoyang (2003) 'The Impact of FDI on the Export Growth and Export Mix of China', *Journal of International Trade* 11.

Huang, Yasheng (2003) *Selling China: Foreign Direct Investment during the Reform Era*. Cambridge: Cambridge University Press.

Jiang, Xiaojuan (2002) 'Contribution of Foreign Invested Enterprises to Growth Structure Upgrading and Competitiveness', *Social Science in China*, 6. Available at http://en.cnki.com.cn/Article_en/CJFDTOTAL-ZSHK200206000.htm.

Kung, James (1985) 'The Origins and Performance of China's Special Economic Zones', *The Asian Journal of Public Administration* 7(2): 198–215.

Lardy, Nicholas (1994) *China in the World Economy*. Washington, DC: Institute for International Economics.

Lau, L., Y. Qian, and G. Roland (1998) 'Reform without Losers: An Interpretation of China's Dual-Track Approach to Transition',*Journal of Political Economy* 108(1): 120–43.

Li, Kunwang and Wang Youxin (2013) 'Can FDI Promote China Exports' Quality Upgrading? A Study Based on Dynamic Panel System GMM Method', *World Economy Study* 5.

Lin, Justin Yifu et al. (1994) *The China Miracle: Development Strategy and Economic Reform*. Hong Kong: Chinese University Press.

Lin, Justin Yifu (2009) *Economic Development and Transition: Thought, Strategy, and Viability*. Cambridge; Cambridge University Press.

Lin, Justin Yifu (2012) *New Structural Economics: A Framework for Rethinking Development and Policy*. Washington, DC: World Bank Publications.

Liu, Jintian (1996) '"We Have the Best Mutual Understanding": Deng Xiaoping and Kim Il Sung', *Literature of the Chinese Communists* 6.

Sung, Yun-Wing (2001) 'Export-oriented Foreign Direct Investment in the People's Republic of China: Division of Value Added between Source and Host Economies', in Leonard K. Cheng and Henryk Kierzkowski (eds) *Global Production and Trade in East Asia*. Dordrecht: Kluwer Academic Publishers, pp. 207–25.

Sung, Yun-Wing (2007) 'Made in China: From World Sweatshop to a Global Manufacturing Center?' *Asian Economic Papers* 6(3): 43–72.

Wen, Dongwei, Xian Guoming, and Ma Jing (2009) 'FDI, Industrial Structure Changes and Export Competitiveness of China', *Management World* 4.

Xu, B. (2007) 'Measuring China's Export Sophistication.' Working Paper. Shanghai: China Europe International Business School.

Xu, B. and J. Lu (2009) 'Foreign Direct Investment, Processing Trade and the Sophistication of China's Exports', *China Economic Review* 20(03): 425–39.

Zhang, Jun (1997) *Economics of Dual-Track System: Economic Reform in China, 1978–1992*. Hong Kong: SDX Joint Publishing.

Zhang, Jun (2018) *The Reform Unknown to the Public*. Taipei: Wenjing Press, in press.

9
Learning and Catch-up in Singapore
Lessons for Developing Countries

George Yeo, Tan Kong Yam, and Tan Khee Giap

9.1 Introduction to Learning and Catch-up in Singapore

The overall competitiveness of a state's economy is not just about its ability to mobilize resources to achieve quality economic growth. Promoting greater ease of doing business and improving efficiency are also paramount. For instance, Ethiopia is an example of a developing country that has internationalized its economy by plugging into the globalization network. Key objectives are not only to achieve balanced and equitable economic development across the state through effective use of natural resources to accumulate government surpluses, but also to deliver meaningful employment over time to its people, ensuring social stability and a good quality of life for all in a green, sustainable, and liveable environment.

Effective leadership supported by an efficient civil service with budget sustainability are essential for the successful development of any economy, and such is the hallmark of Singapore's rapid transformation from a third-world to first-world country in only a few decades. To become a competitive, efficient, and equitable economy with a harmonious society requires good governance and efficient public administration, supported by resilient public and private institutions. A government that is to efficiently deliver public services, guided by prudent and sound budgeting principles, needs to implement both hard and soft infrastructure programmes, a prerequisite for creating and redistributing wealth. Furthermore, in macroeconomic dynamics, a fine calibration between external and domestic demand requires the economy to be constantly refashioned in order to stay relevant. Such was the wisdom of Singapore's founding father, Lee Kuan Yew.

9.2 The Neighbourhood Demonstration Effect

Regions need countries with a developmental success story to serve as role models for their neighbours. At the turn of the twentieth century in East Asia, Japan was such a role model.

During the Meiji Restoration period, Japan developed and modernized rapidly, economically as well as socially, both through local innovation and by utilizing technologies from more developed countries in Europe. After the Second World War, neighbouring economies like South Korea, Taiwan, and Singapore acquired ideas and technologies, as well as a psychological boost, from Japan, enabling them to achieve developed status.

In November 1978, senior vice-premier of the People's Republic of China Deng Xiaoping made his first official visit to Singapore, where he met with Lee Kuan Yew and was shown the country's Housing Development Board and the Jurong Town Corporation. Shortly after returning to Beijing, Deng began to spearhead reforms which ushered in more than thirty years of rapid economic growth for China. While there are no official records of their meetings, this piece of history was re-enacted in a state-sanctioned TV drama released in China (see Long et al., 2014). In the series, Lee remarks that China is in a better position than Singapore to develop because of its 'progeny of scholars, mandarins, and literati', to which Deng responds, 'you're right [;] there is no reason for China's economy to be lagging behind'.

The notion of demonstration effect within a region can be put into the African context. In the 2000s, Africa was described by some as the 'hopeless continent'; by 2011, it was more widely recognized as 'rising and aspiring Africa'. According to the International Monetary Fund's (IMF) *World Economic Outlook* in 2018, Ethiopia is among the fastest-growing economies in its region. If Ethiopia develops economically and socially in accordance with this growth, the country could be recognized as a pioneer in the development of sub-Saharan Africa. Just as Meiji Japan played a leading role in the development of East Asia, Ethiopia is in a unique position to lead region-wide confidence in Africa's development: it is one of only two countries in the continent not colonized, with a long and illustrious history and culture.

The chapter is organized as follows. The first section briefly discusses East Asian development experience, before considering in detail the role of the Singapore government in formulating pragmatic public policies and planning longer-term development. Strategic steps towards industrial upgrading and longer-term economic transformation to plug Singapore into the global trading system are then highlighted, followed by analysis of successful and less successful case studies of industry cluster development. The chapter concludes with a look at the Singapore government's updates on its strategic economic roadmaps, with relevant lessons for developing countries.

The East Asian experience shows that an export-oriented strategy of releasing production capacity through comprehensive planned investment to resolve infrastructure underdevelopment is not only a prerequisite for economic take-off but also a useful support in navigating through the middle-income trap (see Tan et al., 2014). For balanced, sustainable, inclusive regional economic integration and social development, provision of both physical and soft infrastructure for greater connectivity is increasingly viewed as a regional public good. Most developing countries, including those from the African continent, however, tend to have weak budgetary conditions. Due to the relatively large capital requirements, the long gestation period, and the longer-term nature of returns on investment for infrastructure projects, the cost of financing tends to be high, and competition with other funding commitments keen, resulting in financing constraints.

In the longer-term roadmap for Africa, it is the stronger economies with comparative advantages that should seek to overcome the infrastructure bottleneck that is causing growth inertia and unbalanced regional development. Emerging economies with an abundant supply of low-cost unskilled labour and adequate financing for infrastructure development through public–private partnerships could bring about a reshuffling of global production networks, achieving significant poverty reduction and improved standards of living for the majority. Effective leadership and good governance will be paramount in harnessing and promoting infrastructure investment.

9.3 Singapore's Track Record: Strong Budgetary Discipline and an Enabling Efficient Civil Service

Two prime attributes are critical to the successful development of any economy: prudent and sustainable budgetary discipline capable of financing strategic economic policies and social development initiatives; and effective leadership supported by an enabling, efficient civil service (see Tan et al., 2015).

The emergence of Singapore as a modern developed city state is partly a historical accident but also owes much to the effective leadership which enabled the economy to thrive under challenging circumstances. Five fundamental principles were recognized by the government as essential to the process of nation building. Hence Singapore's achievements to date are by and large due to the *facilitating role of the government*—which paradoxically is inconsistent with the highly open and globalized city-state economy. The five basic principles are as follows:

1. Singapore will always be more rather than less dependent on external demand, given her small size and limited scope for domestic demand. Thus policies to stimulate domestic demand are likely to be ineffective. The pragmatic approach is to sharpen competitive edge, and build human resource capability and infrastructure capacity to capture and attract external demand.
2. With no natural resource endowment Singapore's only resources are financial and human capitals. Hence continuing wealth accumulation and recruitment of foreign experts are keys to its continued success. Sound and sustainable

budgetary policies thus become the *sine qua non* for creation of government surpluses. Sensitive employment policies providing an appropriate local–foreign workforce mix are vital for continued growth, innovation, equitable social distribution, and stability.

3. While efficiencies can be introduced in education, health care, housing, land use, transportation, water, and electricity supply, these will become increasingly costly without subsidies. Policy subsidies should therefore distinguish target groups and potential benefactors, and should recognize the longer-term financial burden and sustainability.
4. With intensified global competition, trade protectionism, and the disruptive changes caused by digitalization and technological innovation, Singapore has been going through transformational change in an era of growth discontinuity since the 1997 Asian financial crisis and continues to experience rapid economic restructuring. Given widening income gaps and an ageing population, public policy for social mobility and wider social integration needs to take into account the potential fiscal burden of the high dependency ratio.
5. The increasingly uncertain global environment makes 'picking winners' far more difficult than it used to be. The government's new facilitating role in industrial policy instead promotes 'hosting winners'. This requires greater financial resources and a lean and nimble, more transparent and accountable government responsive to closer domestic and international scrutiny.

9.4 Prudent and Sustainable Budgeting

Singapore has adopted a 'workfare' principle under which the government subsidizes the difference between current wage and defined living wage for the unskilled indigenous workforce through the Workfare Income Supplement (WIS) scheme, instead of a conventional welfare system of entitlement to unemployment benefits.

While ensuring that public services such as housing, health care, education, and transport remain efficient and affordable, this principle increases the international competitiveness and productivity of the workforce by directing resources to skills training, industrial internships, and updating the education curriculum rather than to welfare spending for the unemployed.

Table 9.1 shows the trends in Singapore's budgetary structure from 1998 to 2018. The primary budget surplus begun to fall in 1999 and a primary budget deficit has developed since 2002 during the years of slow and low economic growth, although the duration and scale of structural deficits are relatively mild. Faster-than-expected economic restructuring following the 1997 financial crisis significantly altered costs structure and potential output, and competition from emerging global economies has been stronger than expected.

Table 9.1 Singapore's budgetary structure 1998–2018 (US$ million)

	Primary surplus (deficit)*	Special transfers	NII contributions	Overall budget
FY1998	977	52	–	925
FY1999	5,566	682	–	4,885
FY2000	3,531	1,835	2,287	3,983
FY2001	1,190	5,264	1,375	(2,698)
FY2002	(1,683)	1,802	3,675	191
FY2003	(3,184)	603	1,900	(1,887)
FY2004	(1,487)	1,661	3,043	(105)
FY2005	(463)	829	2,777	1,486
FY2006	(549)	3,580	2,845	(1,284)
FY2007	(639)	2,071	2,019	(691)
FY2008	1,600	4,390	3,650	(2,150)
FY2009	(2,344)	4,071	7,006	(819)
FY2010	722	1,505	7,352	980
FY2011	4,514	2,909	7,916	4,003
FY2012	6,811	1.458	7,870	5,821
FY2013	5,292	2,990	8.289	4,988
FY2014	4,151	4,330	8,553	(125)
FY2015	(4,250)	4,540	9,900	(4,880)
FY2016	(2,720)	2,870	14,370	5,180
FY2017	1.240	2.220	14,610	9.61
FY2018**	(7.34)	1.810	15.850	(0.60)

Note: Overall budgetary surplus (deficit) in US$ million = primary position + special transfers + NII contributions;
*primary budgetary surplus (deficits) in US$ million; **estimated.

Source: Republic of Singapore (1998–2018) Annual Budgetary Statements, Ministry of Finance.

Singapore does not follow the conventional IMF budgetary accounting system but adopts a conservative system whereby development expenditure is included as part of total operating expenditure. Revenue from state land sales and returns from the state's investment abroad are both excluded from total operating revenue. From 2000 to 2018, government spending on cash handouts such as New Singapore Shares, Economic Restructuring Shares, cash top-ups on Central Provident Funds, skills development fund, utilities rebates, subsidies, and workfare averaged US$2.3 billion per year (excluding top-ups to endowment and trust funds). This was largely buffered by contributions from net investment income (NII), which amounted to an average of US$6.7 billion per year over the same period, but has since more than doubled to US$15 billion per year from 2016 and 2018.

Singapore's budgetary philosophy has always been to have a balanced budget, on average, over the business cycle, with surplus accumulated during good years and deficit incurred during not-so-good years. It has become the norm for the budget to be supplemented by NII, a timely dividend resulting from early decades of prudent surplus accumulation and investment. NII will help Singapore to put in place further measures to strengthen its competitive tax structure, meet possible increases in spending on defense, social needs, health care, and employment support, and cope with its ageing population.

In the longer term, to build an even more inclusive society, there are only two ways to deal with the potential structural budget deficit. The first option is a 'red ocean' strategy of cutting government expenditure or/and raising taxes for short-term budgetary improvements with marginal financial impacts but longer-term consequences necessarily involving trade-offs. Governments of developing economies often do not have the strong discipline and political will to undertake such painful austerity measures, which gives rise to development inertia caused by financing, infrastructure, and production bottlenecks that exacerbate the vicious cycle of severe structural budget deficit or sometimes insolvency.

With its move into the knowledge-based economy in the new millennium, Singapore adopted the alternative 'blue ocean' strategy: drive for business innovation and transformation; deepen manpower skill sets; and strengthen global trade and investment partnerships with further internationalization of economic activities. This is reflected in the annual budget statements since 2016 when Industry Transformation Maps were first introduced. In the final analysis, having a period of robust and consistent economic growth is the best way to ensure sufficient financial resources and hence the government's commitment to an even more inclusive society.

The second approach to volatile and declining government revenues and expectations of a hike in public spending is broadening the tax base. The global trend of lowering indirect taxes such as corporation tax (CIT) and personal income tax (PIT), together with a more broad-based hike in taxes on direct goods and services (GST), is an integral part of government revenue reforms to ensure a broader and a less cyclical tax base which tends to be outstripped by rising public and social expenditures.

Raising GST, or value added tax (VAT) as it is sometimes termed, alone is clearly regressive since the additional amount of GST, however small, would be a much heavier burden on lower- than on higher-income groups and SMEs. However, the package of tax reforms adopted by the Singapore government in April 1994, which raised GST while also lowering PIT or/and CIT, was progressive because of the extensive and more than one-off GST offsets involving government subsidies and rebates. The ultimate objective was to render the economy more vibrant and competitive, with the economic cake growing over time and everyone benefiting. Developing countries can learn pertinent lessons from the prudent, sustainable budgetary philosophy as follows:

a. Economic restructuring can have a profound impact on public finance, and is thus a necessary but not a sufficient condition for structural budgetary deficit. Given this condition, external shocks or business cycles may trigger a prolonged structural deficit.

b. The instability of government revenue streams can be exacerbated by overheating in one particular sector of the economy, such as bubbles in the property or equity market or both.

c. 'Institutionalized' public spending can hamper economic initiatives and social development plans unless there are fiscal buffers from other sources of investment income derived from accumulated government surpluses.

d. The unpredictability of budgetary conditions underlines the importance of grappling with the budgetary process. It may be useful to lessen the budget burden by outsourcing some social/public services.

e. From the perspective of inter-generational budgetary consideration, it may be critical to avoid the 'spend now and pay later' syndrome and adopt a more responsible 'spend more now and enjoy the pay-off later' paradigm.

f. There should be serious effort to build up or even institutionalize contingency budgetary resources as a hedge against uncertainty and external shocks, due to lack of continuity in government.

Politically, this restructuring may undermine the support of voters who are not prepared to swallow the bitter pill of painful tax reforms. The longstanding political style of the Singapore government, still relevant today, can be found in the classic speech by Minister Mentor Lee Kuan Yew at the 2005 Global Branding Forum:

> I do not believe that popular government means you have to be popular when you govern. I think the best thing to do is to do all the unpopular things when you are governing so that at the end of your term, you have a choice of a date when you feel that they will be most grateful that you have done all these unpopular things and they vote for you.

9.5 The Enabling, Efficient Public Sector and the Art of Public Policy Management

There is no doubt that the prime movers of the Singapore miracle were the nation's visionary and transformational leaders. However, the major institutional vehicle delivering national outcomes was the powerful civil service which prepared development plans, coordinated their implementation, and delivered public services efficiently.

Policies are designed for the long-term good, not short-term populism. This requires strong leadership with a vision and clear direction for the country. The watchwords for policy are flexibility and pragmatic anticipation of change.

Government is regarded as a trusteeship rather than an agency of special interest. Good governance in Singapore is built on three interrelated factors: accountability and transparency, long-term planning, and social justice. For that, a powerful, honest, and efficient civil service is critical.

In a comparison of how talent is selected in Malaysia, Thailand, and Singapore, Poochaoren and Lee (2013) find that Singapore's process of identifying able civil servants is highly selective. The main selection principles are to get the best people, give them a challenge, and pay them well. Candidates are selected by academic results, with ministries often approaching junior colleges and universities for lists of top students. Candidates are also given psychometric tests to determine their suitability for the civil service.

There are also different streams of public service recruitment, including Administrative Service and High Potential (HiPo) programmes singling out those with potential to become administrative officers (AOs) or assume other leadership roles. Within these programmes, there are reporting and ranking systems with a quota-based bell curve designed to incentivize civil servants to work harder. The result is a clear, defined career path for candidates which ensures them a competitive salary. The downside to this system is the potential for an 'us and them' mentality between those deemed to be talented and those who are not. For example, the selection of candidates for HiPo programme is not transparent, while AOs are given a slight preference in the ranking system. Poochaoren and Lee (2013) warns that this might breed cynicism and complacency in the talented and resentment in those who are not.

Singapore's approach to change in public service is described in 'Public Service for the 21st Century: Being in Time for the Future', known as PS21, which has three pillars: to anticipate, welcome, and execute change (see Civil Service College, 2015). The objectives of PS21 are first, to nurture an attitude of service excellence, anticipating and meeting the needs of the public with high standards of quality and courtesy. The essence of anticipating change is scenario planning with alternative possible views of the future. Ideally civil servants should identify driving forces and define critical uncertainties by dealing with known knowns, known unknowns, and unknown knowns, but not with unknown unknowns.

Second, to foster an environment which induces and welcome continuous change for greater efficiency, convincing public officials of the need for change before it becomes critical: evolution in execution yielding a revolution in results. It is crucial to mould public officials' attitudes so as to ensure everyone is an activist for change. These high expectations require leadership, conviction, commitment, and tenacity in seeing through execution.

Third, to formulate and execute public policies cost-effectively by employing modern management tools and techniques, while considering the morale and welfare of public civil servants. Successful management of the civil service requires organizational excellence which must be both people and system oriented.

PS21
IN SUMMARY

• Theme of PS21	Continuous change
• Reason for PS21	Unending uncertainty
• Thrust of PS21	Change as a way of life
• Means of PS21	Harvesting creativity
• End of PS21	In time for the future

Figure 9.1 Singapore's public service: Rising to the challenges of the twenty-first century

Source: Civil Service College (2015) 'Upholding Integrity in Public Service' Institute of Governance and Policy, Singapore

Citizens must therefore be regarded as customers of multiple agencies under the administration of a single government.

PS21 is a programme about change, not change *to* a specific final state but change *as* a permanent state. The thrust is to see change as a superior and necessary way of life and as an instrument for improvement and advancement. The idea is that any organization that effects change only in reaction to circumstances becomes the slave of circumstances, doomed to running around making urgent change after urgent change because it allows circumstances to catch up with it.

PS21 contains strategic imperatives encompassing continuous operational improvement, openness to continuous change, confidence about uncertainty, and superior leadership. These are summarized in Figure 9.1.

Appropriate incentives must be in place for civil servants if effective and efficient provision of public services are to be assured. The bottom line of a company is the profit margin. For the Singapore government, public officials' key performance indicator is linked to GDP growth, which also takes into account events beyond the government's control. This business-oriented mind-set and 'Singapore Incorporated' culture help to attract investment resulting in job creation. Figure 9.2 shows a typical bonus announcement for civil servants in 2017.

9.6 Public Policy Formulations Pioneered by the Old Guard

Singapore has successfully transformed itself from the third to the first world within a few decades. This achievement can be attributed to the public policy formulation pioneered by the country's old guard under the leadership of Lee Kuan Yew, which can be summarized in the following five tenets.

PRESS RELEASE

Civil Service Year-End Payment

Civil servants to get year-end AVC of 1 month. Lower-wage civil servants to get minimum year-end AVC of $1,800.

The Singapore economy grew by 5.2% on a year-on-year basis in 3Q17, higher than the 2.9% growth in the previous quarter. The Singapore economy grew at a faster pace of 3.5% in the first three quarters of 2017, compared to 1.7% over the same period a year ago. Taking into account the global and domestic economic environment, the Ministry of Trade and Industry has forecast that the economy will grow by 3.0% to 3.5% for the whole of 2017.

Against this backdrop, civil servants will be paid a year-end Annual Variable Component (AVC) of 1 month. Lower-wage civil servants will get a minimum year-end AVC of $1,800. This signals the Government's continued commitment to help low-wage workers.

Figure 9.2 Civil service bonus press release, 2017
Source: *Straits Times* (2017) Press Release, Singapore Press Holdings

9.6.1 Pragmatism in Public Policy Formulation—No Reliance on Textbook Cases

Pragmatism is the hallmark of Singapore's unique and innovative policy initiatives. Pragmatism is more than simply being practical; it requires strong adherence to governing with integrity and principles. The affordability of the asset-enhancing public housing scheme through the Housing Development Board (HDB), and the unique Central Provident Fund (CPF) contribution system are examples of pragmatism in policymaking leading to innovation in its formulation.

9.6.1.1 Case Study: Public Housing, Asset Ownership, and Social-political Stability

During one of the frequent riots of the 1960s caused by high unemployment and social tension, Prime Minister Lee Kuan Yew was inspired by the sight of a resident rushing down from his apartment to carry his battered motorbike upstairs to determine that every citizen should have a stake in the stability of the country, this to be achieved by giving them a job and forcing them to save to buy a government-built flat.

Thus a series of highly innovative and interrelated public policies were conceived and implemented. Industrialization created jobs, generated income, and enforced savings. Social stability was restored with a virtuous cycle of economic prosperity, employment, rising standards of living, and improved quality of life for the majority. The CPF and HDB were set up as statutory boards linking citizens' asset ownership to the economy as a stake in the homeland. In 2018, 92 per cent of the population live in this accommodation, with 85 per cent owning their home. Public housing consists of housing estates, which are self-contained satellite towns with schools, supermarkets, clinics, and sports and recreational facilities. There are many different types of flat catering for various housing budgets. HDB flats were built primarily to provide affordable housing for the poor and assisted purchase is available through the CPF.

9.6.2 Industrial Upgrading to Connect Singapore to the Global Trading System

The top priority during the early days of nation building was to reinforce Singapore's strategic location as a regional hub for international trade and services, projecting the republic as a cosmopolitan city state. Faced with limited financial resources after independence, the government prioritized education, concentrating on raising the quality of teaching rather than large-scale expansion of schools or heavy investment in airports and seaports promoting global economic connectivity. Singapore's successful industrial transformation has made it an international hub for world-class financial, aviation, maritime, logistics, and telecommunication and education services.

9.6.2.1 Case Study: Strategic Industrial Upgrading towards a Knowledge-based Economy

In the five decades since political independence in 1965, Singapore has achieved one of the highest rates of economic growth among newly industrialized economies (NIEs). This rapid growth was initially driven by a strategy that leveraged foreign direct investment (FDI). As Singapore's factor costs, especially of land and labour, rose in tandem with rapid economic growth, the government made a concerted effort in the 1990s to shift its policy focus, transforming Singapore from an investment-driven to a knowledge-based economy (see Figure 9.3). This policy shift emphasizes the building of intellectual capital and a vibrant entrepreneurial culture to create value and jobs.

When Singapore separated from Malaysia to gain independence in 1965, the challenge was to develop an economy despite having a small market and no hinterland to rely on. The Economic Development Board (EDB), established in 1961, focused on protectionist policies geared towards a more labour-intensive economy, supported by labour unions who believed that equipment-intensive and innovative industries were worse for workers. However, through legislation such as the Employment Act, the government gave more power to managers and restricted the power of the unions.

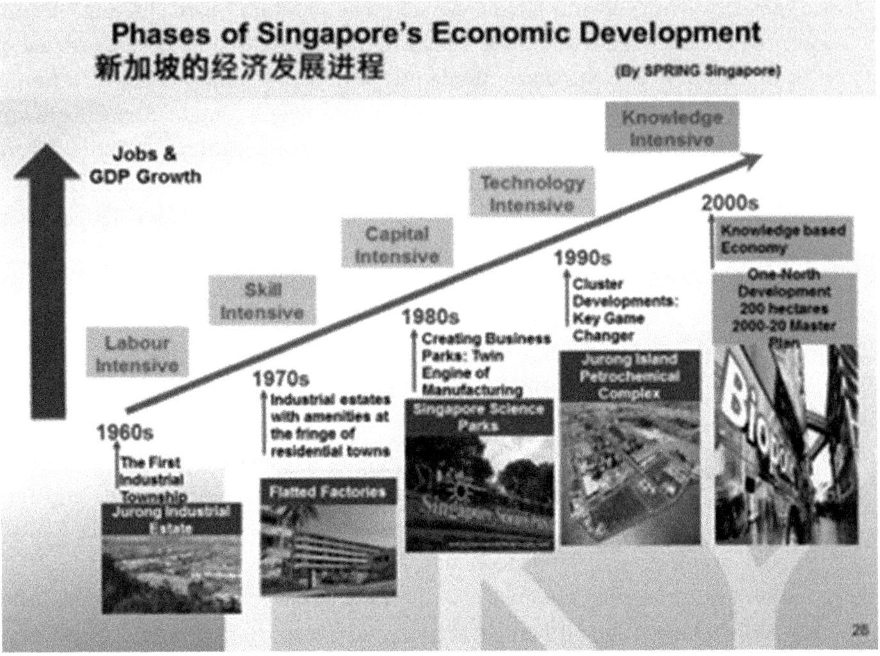

Figure 9.3 Singapore's strategic industrial upgrading
Source: SPRING Singapore, a Singapore Government Statutory Board

In the 1970s, the government removed many tariff restrictions, seeking to promote a more export-oriented economy and attract more MNCs to invest in Singapore. Indigenous firms also lacked productivity measures. FDI-friendly policies placing MNCs at the centre of economic and industrial development enabled a decade of double-digit growth. The EDB then sought to attract foreign and local entrepreneurs to encourage cooperation as well as healthy competition. Singaporeans were sent to the United States, Europe, and Japan to gain technological and technical expertise. The Ministry for Trade and Industry (MTI) set up organizations and statutory boards as spin-offs from EDB specializing in economic and financial activities (see Table 9.2; Republic of Singapore, 1960–2011).

An important industrialization success story relevant for other developing countries is the role of MNCs in helping to develop local industries, domestic entrepreneurs, and the professional class (see Wong, 2008). Several EDB–MNC joint training centres were set up to ensure the availability of skilled workers, including those with Rollei of Germany (optics and precision mechanics) and Philips of Holland (precision machining) in 1973 and 1975 respectively. Workers spent two years at the centre and two years being trained at the plant. Nurturing local supporting industries (LSIs) included support, improving capabilities, and

Table 9.2 Spin-offs from the Economic Development Board

Year	Spin-off	Type	Function
1964	Singapore Institute of Management	Non-profit organization	Management training
1968	Development Bank of Singapore	Publicly listed company	Banking
1968	Jurong Town Council	Statutory board	Industrial estates
1968	Intraco Limited	Government-linked company	Trading
1968	Engineering Industry Development Agency Non-profit organization	Industrial services	
1972	National Productivity Board	Statutory board	Productivity matters
1973	Singapore Institute of Standards and Statutory board	Industrial standards	Industrial Research

Source: Wong, 2008.

facilitating technology transfer to indigenous SMEs. This was a win–win formula for attracting and retaining MNCs, as it helped to lower costs of parts and components, and allowed MNCs to concentrate on final assembly and testing of finished products. An example of the EDB's work under the Local Industry Upgrading Programme (LIUP) is shown in Figure 9.4.

In 1980s, the EDB set out to attract high-tech industries. Mechanization, automation, and computerization required more specialized skills, technical know-how, and production technology. Between 1979 and 1982, EDB set up three Institutes of Technology (ITs) with foreign partners: Japanese-Singapore Institute of Mechatronics, German-Singapore Institute of Production Technology; and French-Singapore Institute of Electro-Technology. They ran three-year courses for diploma-level graduates and four-year skills and craftsman certificate courses. Short courses were provided for supporting electronics industries to enable MNCs to outsource parts- and manufacturing-related services such as moulded stamped parts, surface finishing, printed circuit boards, sub-assembly and testing, tools and die, cartons and packaging, transportation, warehousing, and logistics.

In addition to its consistent upgrading of skillsets and diversification of the economy base, Singapore has coordinated and consolidated a number of different agencies. For example, the EDB attracts investment into Singapore; International Enterprise (IE) Singapore promotes the growth of Singapore-based corporations overseas to smooth the path of international trade; and SPRING Singapore oversees the healthy expansion of small and medium enterprises. On the other hand, Jurong Town Council (JTC) encourages the vigorous growth of the industrial landscape through the development of land and resources, while organizations such as A*Star are centred around high-end science and technology research.

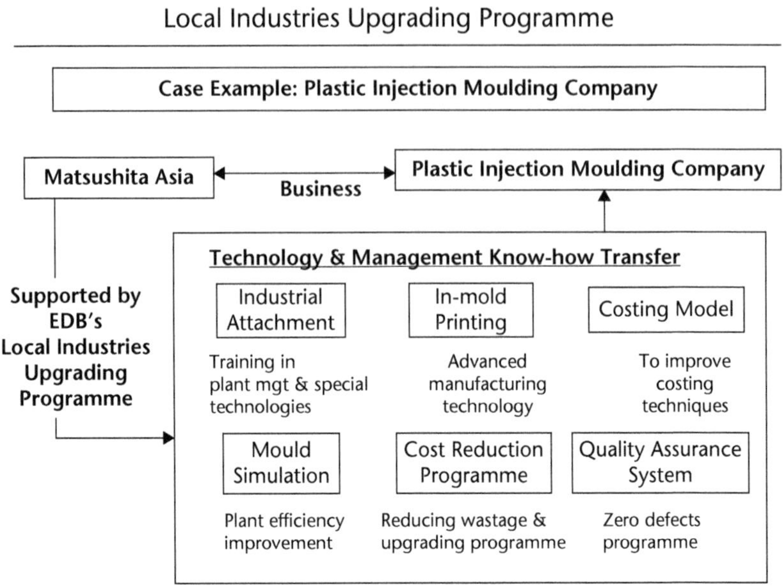

Figure 9.4 Structural framework of plastic injection moulding company
Source: Wong (2008)

The Ministry for Trade and Industry holds monthly ministerial meetings to coordinate overall policies and economic strategies based on regular input from all the various agencies including EDB, IE Singapore, JTC, A*Star, and SPRING Singapore.

Singapore Polytechnic and Ngee Ann Polytechnic were among the early pioneers offering three-year diploma courses in sciences and engineering which became an incubator for indigenous business entrepreneurs such as Wong Ngit Liong, who founded the billion-dollar Venture Manufacturing, and a professional training ground for indigenous managers such as Koh Boon Hwee, who later became chairman of Singapore Airlines. The success of Singapore's committed industrial upgrading can be seen in the near twenty-fold growth of GDP and double-digit sectoral growth summarized in Table 9.3.

9.6.3 Long-term Planning for an Inclusive, Productive, Environmentally Friendly, and Socially Harmonious Cosmopolitan Singapore

As one of the world's most densely populated countries with a multi-racial, multi-religious, multi-cultural, and multi-lingual population of 5.6 million, Singapore's public policies were aimed at an inclusive society from the start of the nation

Table 9.3 Contributions to Singapore's GDP by sector

	1960	1960–70	1970–80	1980–90	1990–2000	2000-11
GDP at constant 2005 prices at end of period ($ million)	6,863	16,567	39,229	82,659	165,245	299,625
Average growth pa (%)		9.3	9	7.8	7.2	5.7
Manufacturing (%)		13.8	11.1	7.3	7.5	6
Construction (%)		16.7	6.4	5.3	10.8	1.8
Services (%)		7.6	8.5	7.9	7.5	5.7
Share in GDP (at end of period)						
Manufacturing (%)	15.2	22.8	27.4	26.3	25.7	27.1
Construction (%)	4.3	8.2	6.2	4.3	5.6	3.7
Services (%)	80.5	69	66.3	69.6	68.6	69.1

Source: Singapore Economic Survey, Department of Statistics, Ministry for Trade and Industry, Singapore.

building process. Given its small geographical area of 720km^2 and lack of natural resources, development policies which maximize land-use value and are inclusive, productive, environmentally sustainable, and socially harmonious are paramount.

Even highly developed economies, however, are today facing worsening income inequality. Although this is frequently said to be an inevitable outcome of globalization, many, including Professor Jagdish Bhagwti and Ben Bernanke, former chairman of the US Federal Reserve, argue that it is the rapid skill-biased technological change rather than the globalization process itself which is causing most of the disparity.

The fundamental social equalizers of education, innovation, and entrepreneurship are critical for an inclusive and productive society. Thus a prolonged period of social stability is an overwhelming priority, without which upward social mobility and a meritocracy-based society cannot prevail. The ultimate solution to worsening income disparity is not state handouts, rebates, or subsidies. Creative policy measures and human resource management are needed that ensure decent-paying jobs and retraining for the lowest-earning 20 per cent of society. As Singapore has moved up the technological ladder to meet the challenge of the new economy, the urgent need to recalibrate the skillset of the indigenous workforce has prompted a restructuring of higher education with the addition of entrepreneurial and industry-relevant dimensions.

Until the end of the 1990s, the National University of Singapore (NUS) followed the traditional British university model with teaching as the primary mission and research as a secondary function, and limited linkages between academia and industry. The major impetus for change came in the late 1990s. Economic slowdown precipitated by the Asian financial crisis led to growing recognition by policymakers of the need to increase the entrepreneurial dynamism of economy. In a speech in August 2002, Dr Tony Tan Keng Yam, deputy prime minister and minister for defence, stated:

> The three primary roles which a world-class university should play in a modern economy and society [are]: i. delivering quality undergraduate education; ii developing graduate education and research; and iii fostering entrepreneurship and industry involvement.

The Singapore government has since embarked on the path of upgrading tertiary education to match the modern economy comparable to those world-class academic institutions prevailing in the west. Tertiary education would now gear toward post-graduate studies with strong emphasis on scientific research. Most of all, the academic curriculum of local universities would now place emphasis on being industry relevant and aiming to produce entrepreneurs who are well versed in the latest technology developments.

With strong support from top political leadership, NUS appointed a new vice chancellor with research leadership experience at leading US universities and corporate experience at a major US corporation. Subsequently highly distinguished and experienced academics from the United States and Europe were appointed vice chancellors at other universities including Nanyang Technological University, Singapore Management University, and Singapore University of Technology and Design.

9.6.4 Planning for a Comprehensive Long-term Vision

The Urban Redevelopment Authority (URA) undertakes long-term planning but its Singapore Urban Development Plan (SUDP) is an example of its ability to actively respond to change. SUDP plots national land allocation for the long term while meeting national needs in the short term, with land allocated to sectors that need it the most following detailed revisions of the Master Plan (see Figure 9.5).

Figure 9.6 shows the structure and function of URA with its mission 'to make Singapore a great city to live, work and play in'. Competing land requirements of housing, commerce, industry, airport, seaport, green parks, water treatment and storage require long-term planning. However addressing short-term needs calls for inter-agency discussion and coordination between agencies including the Singapore Land Authority, National Parks Board, Singapore Tourism Promotion Board, Land Transport Authority, Civil Aviation Authority of Singapore, Maritime Port Authority, Public Utilities Board, Business Chamber of Commerce, and Trade Councils.

Singapore takes a sustainable approach to development which relies on a robust system of good governance, a pragmatic sense of environmentalism, and lastly, a balanced approach to growth and national interests. Figure 9.7 provides an overview

Figure 9.5 Singapore Urban Development Plan: A comprehensive long-term vision

Source: Urban Redevelopment Authority, 'Singapore Urban Development Plan'

Figure 9.6 Structure and functions of the Singapore Urban Redevelopment Authority

Source: Urban Redevelopment Authority, 'Singapore Urban Development Plan'

Figure 9.7 Planning framework of the Singapore Urban Redevelopment Authority

Source: Urban Redevelopment Authority, 'Singapore Urban Development Plan'

of URA's strategic planning framework. The long-term Concept Plan is reviewed every decade and adjusted to suit the national interest. The Master Plan has a detailed medium-term plan for the next ten to fifteen years. A Guiding Plan monitors the actual pace of development based on market demand.

9.6.5 Zero Tolerance of Corruption

Studies by the World Economic Forum and Transparency International have shown a negative correlation between corruption perception and economic competitiveness and attractiveness to foreign direct investment. World Governance Indicators by the World Bank Group have also concluded that political stability is positively related to absence of corruption. A study by Transparency International closely linked corruption with state failure. Singapore continually tops the rankings for being among the least corrupt countries in the world. A strict zero tolerance of corruption, from financial rewards to exchanging power for favours, has been the bedrock of the country's effective public policy formulation and its efficient implementation.

However, as a former colony, Singapore was rife with corruption in its early days. A British-commissioned report found three main reasons: low salaries for public officials, ample opportunities for corruption, and low risk of detection and punishment for corrupt practices (see Quah, 2001, 2017). These factors still prevail in many developing countries. Instability caused by historical and ongoing civil strife or even natural disasters provides scope for corruption. The 'natural resource curse' of many resource-rich developing nations which creates incentives for bribery is another factor. Landlocked countries may have rampant corruption among customs and border officials.

There are three ways to combat corruption. First, strengthening existing anti-corruption mechanisms. This is not feasible for many developing nations because they do not have a strong enough base from which to expand. Second, multiple government anti-corruption agencies (ACAs) that can tackle different types of corruption. Again, this is not recommended because it would create multiple underfunded ACAs competing with each other for resources. Third, as suggested in the literature, a single independent ACA, such as Singapore's Corruption Practices Investigation Bureau (CPIB). Key features of successful ACAs include independence of political whims and police jurisdiction, an effective ACA should be chaired by incorruptible and competent staff. The most important factor enabling an ACA to properly do its job is a conducive environment created by strong political and public support as well as comprehensive anti-corruption laws.

When Singapore took over from the British colonial government, corruption was rife. Prevention was weak: public officials were poorly paid. The population was less well educated and, ignorant of their rights, often resorted to bribery to get things done. The CPIB, founded in 1952 even before Singapore gained independence from the British, is one of the oldest agencies in the world dedicated to handling corruption matters. It works directly under the Prime Minister's Office, and if the prime minister refuses to sign off on an investigation, the CPIB can go to the president instead.

There are four main pillars to Singapore's culture of anti-corruption: effective and all-encompassing anti-corruption legislation; an effective independent ACA; a system that punishes corrupt practices adequately; and efficient government administration (see Figure 9.8). Political will is a key ingredient as it forms that all-important sub-structure upon which all the superstructures of anti-corruption work rest. It provides the soil and the nutrients which allows the seeds of anti-corruption work to germinate and grow. The government has matched its words with deeds as it has mobilized the public and the entire civil service to fight corruption.

Government departments that are prone to corruption, such as police or customs, have their procedures periodically audited to ensure fewer opportunities for corruption. CPIB also can investigate corruption in private enterprises. Through its policy of keeping public-sector jobs economically competitive, the government is able to hire and keep professional staff for the CPIB as well as reduce the chance of other public-sector workers resorting to corruption.

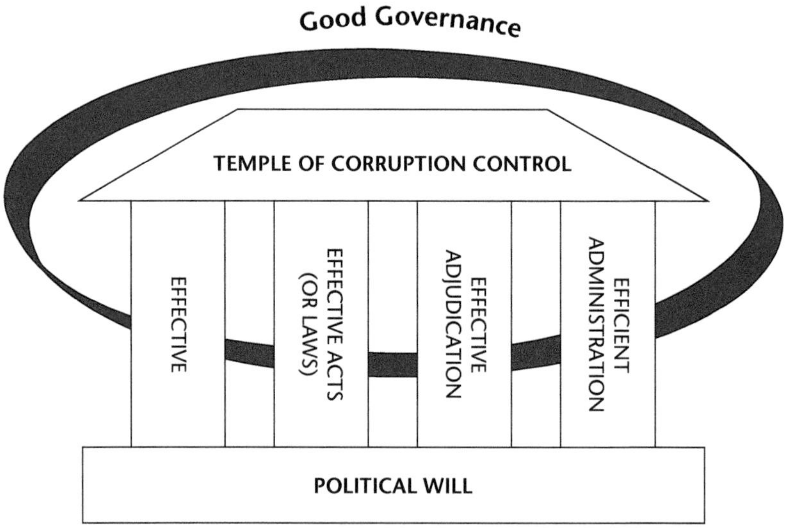

Figure 9.8 Anti-corruption framework in Singapore
Source: Quah (2001)

9.7 Preserving a Democratic Electoral System Allowing for Checks and Balances

Singapore's parliamentary democracy has three pillars: legislation by parliament; governing by the government; and jurisdiction by the courts.

Legislation. Parliament consists of eighty-seven constituency MPs, with a maximum of nine non-constituency (NCMPs) and about nine nominated (NMPs) (see Figure 9.9). Parliament is dissolved and a general election (GE) held every five years. In accordance with legislation passed in 1984, after a general election NCMPs are picked from the highest-polling losing opposition party candidates. Further legislation in 1990 provided for NMPs to be nominated by the Parliamentary Nomination Committee, approved by parliament, and to serve a two-year term.

Government. Following a general election, the president of Singapore appoints the MP who has the majority support of his fellow MPs as prime minister (PM), and on the PM's recommendation other cabinet ministers (CMs) and ministers of state (MOSs) are appointed. The PM, CMs and MOSs are in charge of the various government ministries and collectively report to parliament. The independent Public Services Commission appoints civil servants.

Jurisdiction. The Supreme Court consist of the High Court and Court of Appeal and subordinate courts are district and magistrates courts. The chief justice and high court judges are appointed by the president on the PM's recommendation. Magistrates are appointed by the Legal Service Commission.

The president of Singapore is the supreme head of state and is elected by the citizens of Singapore. The presidential candidate must be a citizen aged 45 or above, not an MP and not belonging to any political party, must have held a significant position in the public or private sector and be of high moral and good social standing. The president normally takes the advice or recommendations of the PM. However, he can act independently in accepting a motion to dissolve parliament, accepting nominations to high positions as required by the constitution, and in proposals to deploy the government's reserves or surpluses.

Fifty years of political milestones for the People's Action Party (PAP) can be summarized as follows. During 1954–9, the old guard was leading the anti-colonial movement. From 1959 to 1963, PAP went through internal party struggles and conflict. Singapore became part of Malaysia and PAP advocated anti-racial politics from 1963 to 1965. Singapore was expelled from Malaysia and became an independent city state in 1965. PAP was elected as the governing party with a two-thirds majority through nine general elections held every five years from 1968 to 2015.

The PAP has the following prime objectives in government: ensuring political stability; delivering robust economic development through meritocracy with

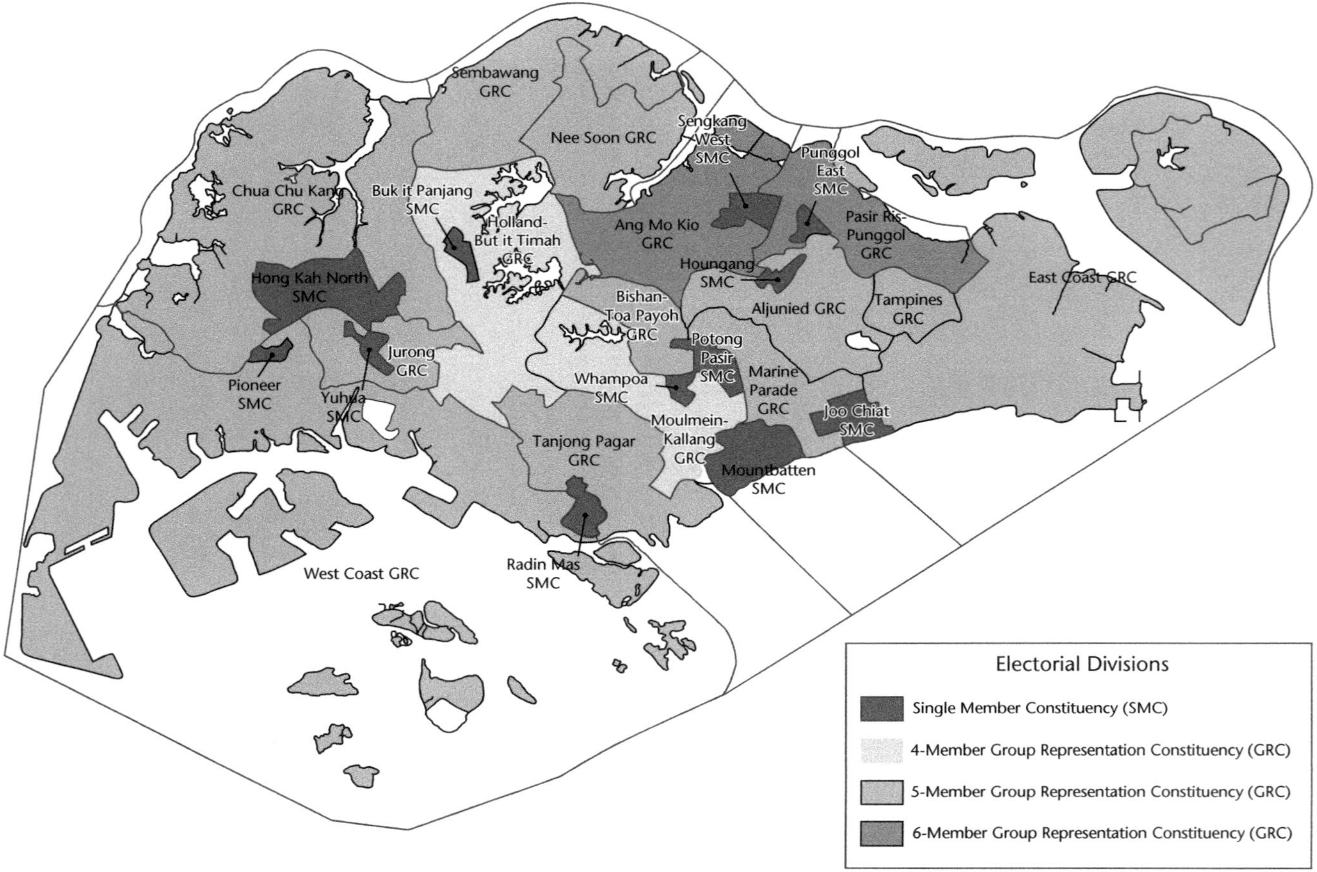

Figure 9.9 Singapore's constituencies in the 2011 general election

Source: *Straits Times*, 'Report on Singapore General Elections 2011', Press Holdings

social mobility; promoting the national interest; forging a united, inclusive, and harmonious community; and cultivating national identity. The guiding principle of national development is the starting point and ultimate end of policy formulation. The PAP won a landslide victory at the 2001 general election which was held soon after the September 2001 terrorist attacks and the collapse of the US tech bubble. In times of crisis, Singaporeans turn instinctively to the trusted hands of the PAP. Ten years later, the 2011 general election was a political watershed for the PAP, which scored only 60.1 per cent of the popular vote, down 15 per cent from ten years previously, and losing five parliamentary seats in a Group Representative Constituency (GPC) and two parliamentary seats in Single Representative Constituencies (SRCs) (see Table 9.4). While GDP growth has been quite respectable over the last ten years, satisfaction levels and confidence in the future seem rather flat, if not negative. The PAP did badly in 2011 because it was out of touch with the grass roots, and was perceived to have become arrogant and deaf to increasing unhappiness over issues such as congestion, rising house prices, and excessive reliance on foreign workers.

Over the period 2011–15, the PAP government worked hard to address the cost of living, issues of housing affordability, public transport, and health care, and significantly reduced the inflow of foreign workers. In the 2015 general election their share of the vote increased by almost ten percentage points. As of today, the ruling party is able to claim the following five significant achievements in public

Table 9.4 Popular votes won by People's Action Party in past ten general elections

Year of election	No of seats won*	% of votes won#
1959	43 (51)	54.08%
1963	37 (51)	46.93%
1968	58 (58)	86.72%
1972	65 (65)	70.43%
1977	69 (69)	74.09%
1980	75 (75)	77.66%
1984	77 (79)	64.83%
1988	80 (81)	63.17%
1991	77 (81)	60.97%
1997	81 (83)	64.98%
2001	82 (84)	75.29%
2006	82 (84)	66.60%
2011	81 (87)	60.14%
2015	82 (88)	69.92%

Notes: *Number in brackets denote the total number of parliamentary seats; # % based on number of valid votes.

Source: 'Summary Report on General Elections', *Straits Times*, Singapore Press Holdings.

services, which are by no means common in many developed or developing countries. First, no Singaporean who wants to work is denied a job unless they are voluntarily unemployed. Second, no Singaporean who wants to study is denied an education because of financial constraints. Third, the majority of Singaporeans will always have a roof over their head and own it as a valuable asset. Fourth, no Singaporean who is unwell is denied basic health care and affordable medical treatment. Finally, public transportation remains affordable for the young, working adults, and senior citizens.

As Lee Kuan Yew, the founding father of Singapore, succinctly put it:

> The government must be clean and efficient, be able to protect the people and to ensure every citizen is able to lead a good life and progress within a stable and disciplined society which must also be capable of ensuring a better life for future generations.

In summary, the five tenets laid down by the political old guard under the leadership of Lee Kuan Yew have underpinned Singapore's public policy formulation for decades and have become a major part of the socio-political contract between the ruling party and the electorate. However, in the post-Lee Kuan Yew era, it is not surprising that the articulation, communication, and implementation of policy will have to take a more consultative approach by engaging in national conversations, and at times, intense debate in terms that resonate with people.

9.8 Singapore's Strategic Transformation to a Knowledge-Based, Innovation-Driven, and High Value-Added Economy

To develop its industries, Singapore adopted a strategy of leveraging global and emerging multinational corporations to encourage cluster development. In particular, Singapore looked to exploit the window of opportunity in the high-tech development and globalization cycle. This strategy required strong support and planning by its ministries and statutory boards, including proactive, targeted FDI promotion policies, geographic agglomeration, and proactive investment in core infrastructure and skills. There was also an opportunity to leverage anchor firms to stimulate development of more specialized resources supporting industries and services.

9.9 Industry Cluster Development Policies: Singapore's MNC Leveraging Strategy

Wong (2008) analyses two case studies—the biomedical tech sector and the offshore marine engineering cluster—of how the Singaporean government worked to strengthen the country's innovation base and knowledge-based industrial clusters.

The biomedical tech sector had to be built from the ground up. This involved attracting foreign talent to train and work in Singapore, developing education institutions to better train locals, international collaboration, and nurturing venture capital for firms in related sectors. In marine engineering the government sought to expand the already strong transport sector towards offshore marine engineering. The difference in strategy between the two sectors illustrates the need to take a tailored approach to developing a knowledge-based cluster that depends on the resources initially available.

Until the mid-2000s, the clusters in Singapore included electronics, computer equipment and peripherals; precision engineering; maritime (ship-building and repair, offshore engineering, port and shipping services); chemical manufacturing; semiconductor assembly and testing; and pharmaceutical manufacturing. However, from the late 2000s, emerging clusters included interactive digital media, water treatment and clean technology, biomedical devices, and life sciences. There are a number of notable examples of industry cluster development. Biopolis is a research and development centre focusing on biomedical, biotechnology, agrobiology, and engineering research. It houses several A*Star institutes and is situated close to universities, creating a technology corridor. Fusionopolis is a research and development complex that focuses on ICT research, media, broadcasting, and solutions for e-business, e-commerce, and the overall development of an intelligent city.

9.10 The Nation's Pillars of Industrialization: Successful and Not-so-successful Case Studies

9.10.1 Case Study of a Successful Industry Cluster: Jurong Island Chemical Hub

Singapore has no oil or gas resources and limited land space. But against all the odds, it has achieved tremendous success in the petrochemical industry. Today, Singapore is the third-largest oil refining centre in the world, the largest bunkering port, one of the top three oil trading hubs in the world, and the price discovery centre of Asia's oil trading industry.

Jurong Island Chemical Hub is today a growing chemical hub in Asia (see Figure 9.10). Its stellar success can be attributed to clever land utilization, adaptability to volatile markets, and adequate attention to safety and security. It is home to almost ninety international petroleum and chemical companies, and has contributed to investments of over US$47 billion. The hub manufactures refined and chemical products from integrated petrochemical complexes of oil majors

Figure 9.10 Jurong Island Chemical Hub: A growing center in Asia
Source: Economic Development Board, a Singapore Government Statutory Board

Exxon Mobil and Shell, intermediate products from chemical producers such as Sumitomo & BASF, to automotive chemicals and agro-chemicals from firms such as Evonik and Solvay.

9.10.2 Case Study of a Not-so-successful Industry Cluster: Biomedical Sciences in Singapore

Singapore's vision for this industry cluster is to project Singapore as a biomedical sciences hub with world-class capability across the whole value chain. The strategy adopted by Singapore included human capital, intellectual capital, and industrial capital elements, and an ethical framework (Figure 9.11).

However, the reality may be different from the vision. First, there is a limited pool of talent in Singapore to develop this sector. Second, there is intense global competition in life sciences. Other larger countries, including the United States and China, have access to financial and human capital resources that impose significant competitive pressures on small countries like Singapore to grow and develop in the life sciences industry. Finally, Singapore lacks a sufficiently large domestic market for the life sciences industry to be able to achieve a critical mass to grow and develop. These three factors have led to the lack of growth in the biomedical and life sciences sector.

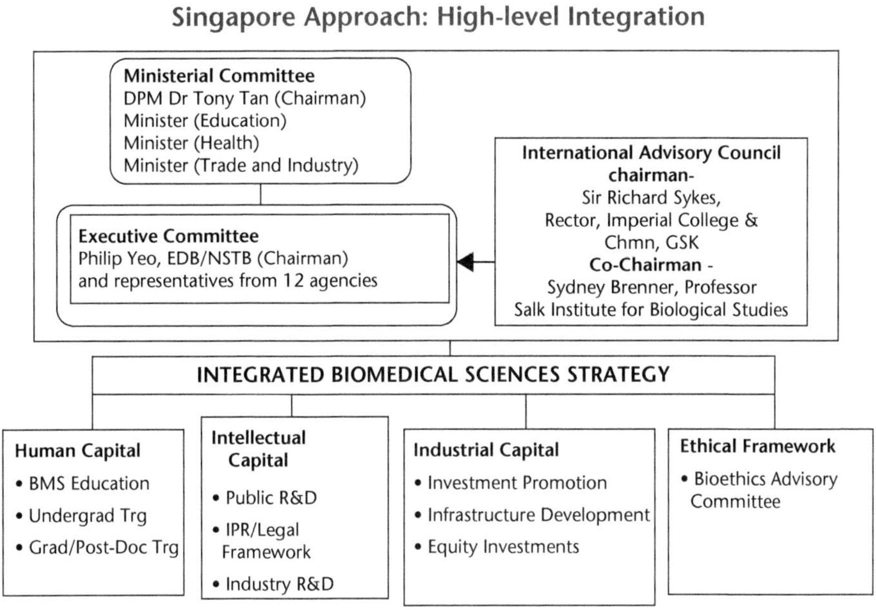

Figure 9.11 Biomedical sciences in Singapore
Source: Wong (2008)

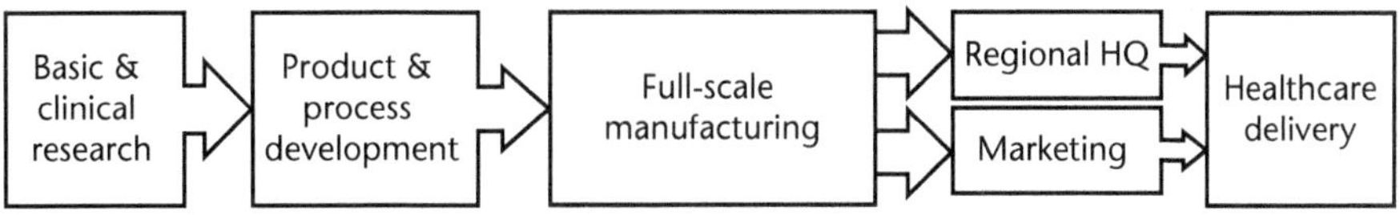

Figure 9.12 Production process for biomedical sciences
Source: Wong (2008)

In 2018, the guaranteed funding for core research activities and overheads of A*Star scientists is set to be cut by up to 20 per cent. The ten biomedical institutes and laboratories, which employ about 1,700 research scientists, engineers, and technicians, had their fixed funding cut to about 70 per cent in 2011. News of another round of cuts in fixed funding has unsettled the biomedical research community. Some scientists are considering leaving for institutes overseas.

Figure 9.12 shows the production process in biomedical sciences. Even after many years of government investment and initiatives, Singapore was not able to make a breakthrough at the first stage of basic and clinical research.

In addition, Singapore's multi-pronged strategy included economic development via investment, recruitment of overseas talent, legal and ethical frameworks, clinical centres of excellence, extramural funding for investigator-based research, research institutes, improvement of the education system, physical infrastructure such as Biopolis, and the development of local human resources such as scholarships for graduate and post-doctoral studies.

9.11 Singapore Government Updates to Strategic Economic Roadmaps

The Singapore Economic Committee was formed in 1985 to examine the longer-term problems and prospects of the Singapore economy, identify new growth areas, and define new strategies for promoting growth. As the Committee studied the problem, it quickly realized that it also had to address the 1985 recession which was caused largely by a slump in commodities' prices and loss of competitiveness. The recession could not be brushed aside as a cyclical difficulty which would eventually disappear by itself. On the contrary, the recession was a manifestation of fundamental problems in the economy. These had to be corrected, with policies changed, not only to overcome the recession, but also to set the correct direction for the country's longer-term growth. Four of the Committee's major recommendations are of particular importance:

1. Undertake competitive and structural wage reforms.
2. Undertake competitive and structural tax reforms.
3. Upgrade business efficiency and productivity.
4. Promote service industries to diversify the economy further.

The Economic Strategies Committee was set up in 2010 to identify key recommendations on seven broad strategies to help sustain Singapore's longer-term growth target of 3 per cent to 5 per cent over the next decade. The seven key strategies are:

1. Growing through skills and innovation.
2. Anchoring Singapore as a global Asia hub.
3. Building a vibrant and diverse corporate ecosystem.
4. Making innovation pervasive, and strengthening commercialization of research and development.
5. Becoming a smart energy economy.
6. Enhancing land productivity to secure future growth.
7. Building a distinctive global city and an enduring home.

The Committee for the Future Economy, formed in 2017, suggests that the national workforce should have deep skills and be inspired to learn throughout their lives. Businesses should be innovative and nimble. The cosmopolitan city should be vibrant and connected to the world by continually renewing itself. The government needs to be well coordinated, inclusive, and responsive. The committee recommended the following moves:

1. Deepen and diversify our international connections.
2. Acquire and utilize deep skills.
3. Strengthen enterprise capabilities to innovate and scale up.
4. Build strong digital capabilities.
5. Develop a vibrant and connected city of opportunity.
6. Develop and implement Industry Transformation Maps.
7. Partner each other to enable innovation and growth.

These collective efforts will allow Singapore's economy to grow by 2–3 per cent per year on average for the next decade, exceeding the performance of most advanced economies, and becoming a value-creating economy that is open and connected to the world, offering a multitude of opportunities, with sustainable wage growth and meaningful careers for all Singaporeans. There is a rising expectation among younger voters of leadership renewal in the next general election, due by 2020 at the latest. A more uncertain global environment and protectionism in trade are to be expected. An ageing population, flagging economic dynamism, and rising health care costs are some of the more challenging circumstances that need to be better prepared for (Republic of Singapore, 1986, 2010, and 2017).

Surrounding the public policy discourse, there are three serious socio-economic challenges that both Singapore's leadership and public will have to deal with: alleviating worsening income disparity; improving upward social mobility; and enhancing social integration by class, ethnicity, religion, and cultural group.

Given the increasing discontent caused by the spread of globalization, more should be done to ensure balanced and inclusive economic growth in order to reduce income inequality. While improving upward social mobility and promoting greater social integration between people from diverse backgrounds may be a daunting task, these goals are paramount, especially in a densely populated city state. The wisdom of the new leadership will be measured by how it approaches issues such as integrated housing programmes, ensuring a level playing field in education, promoting religious harmony, and forging a common national identity that evolves with time.

Singapore took its place on the world stage as the host of the historic Trump–Kim summit in June 2018. In the past Singapore has successfully organized annual meetings of the World Trade Organization, The World Bank Group, and the International Monetary Fund, and will undoubtedly continue to host similar high-level meetings in the years to come. The country's current internationally credible reputation for efficiency has been nurtured over the decades by the Singaporean government under the PAP. However, there will be a host of new social, economic, and political challenges to face as the country moves ahead.

9.12 Lessons for Developing Countries

As the old Chinese saying goes, one should think of potential crisis even if one is at peace or in safety. The Singapore government tends to have a strong sense of crisis to the extent that there is an element of paranoia, which may well be healthy! A perpetual sense of crisis and alertness for the government would mean public policymakers and senior civil servants would always be ahead of the curve. For not only the government but also the population at large to be constantly on guard against complacency, ready for change in anticipation of potential scenarios ahead, would strengthen the public sector's crisis-management capability.

Constant monitoring of an economy's relative global ranking on ease of doing business, reviewing infrastructural competitiveness, investing in research and development, spotting industry and market trends, establishing a committee to crystal-ball gaze into future disruptive changes caused by rapid technological innovation and the imminent replacement of conventional jobs by new skillsets, are paramount for longer-term strategic economic planning.

Developing countries, especially those emerging economies undergoing rapid economic expansion, need to take a balanced approach to national development and be conscious that income disparity, slowing down of upward social mobility, and uneven distribution of opportunities for different social groups could lead to social disharmony and friction within the community.

Promoting robust economic growth, ensuring a balanced government budget over the business cycle, and even generating moderate government surpluses would help to cover the rainy days.

Expanding the middle class through creation of decent-paying jobs is still the optimal way to guarantee adequate and sustainable public services including housing, education, health care, and transportation.

As for existing latecomers to industrialization, the window of opportunity may now be narrower as mechanization, robotization, and digitalization have overtaken much labour-intensive production, so catching up on relevant skillsets becomes a daunting task calling for public-sector initiatives, especially for SMEs. Developing countries are running out of industrialization opportunities sooner and at much lower levels of income than early industrializers, with evidence that both globalization and labour-saving technological progress in manufacturing have been behind these developments. Premature de-industrialization has significant economic and political ramifications, including lower economic growth and democratic failure. The recent round of trade protectionism initiated by the

United States to retaliation by China, Japan, and the European Union is an added cause of concern for global trade and investment. However, there could be another new round of opportunities for developing economies as reshuffling of production value chains begins across the globe from affected economies, notably China, to emerging economies including those in Asia, Africa, and Latin America. Governments of emerging economies need to send out trade and investment missions to actively attract and quicken the pace of production relocations.

References

Civil Service College (2015) 'Upholding Integrity in Public Service.' Singapore: Institute of Governance and Policy.

Long, Pingping, Yazhou Huang, Zhang Qiang, and Wei Ren (2014) *Deng Xiaoping through Meandering of History*. Chengdu: Sichuan People's Publisher.

Poochaoren, Orn-Orn and Celia Lee (2013) 'Talent Management in Public Policy: A Comparative Study of Singapore, Malaysia and Thailand.' Accepted Paper Series No. LKYSPP, 14–15.

Quah, Jon (2001) 'Combating Corruption in Singapore: What Can Be Learnt?' *Journal of Contingencies and Crisis Management* 9(1): 29–35.

Quah, Jon (2017) 'Anti-Corruption Agencies in Asia Pacific Countries: An Evaluation of their Performance and Challenges.' Transparency International.

Republic of Singapore (1960–2011) Department of Statistics, Ministry for Trade and Industry.

Republic of Singapore (1986) 'The Singapore Economy: New Directions.' Report of the Economic Committee, Ministry of Trade and Industry, Republic of Singapore.

Republic of Singapore (1998–2018) Annual Budgetary Statements, Ministry for Finance.

Republic of Singapore (2010) 'High Skilled People, Innovation Economy, Distinctive Global City.' Report of the Economic Strategies Committee, Ministry of Trade and Industry.

Republic of Singapore (2017) 'Pioneering the Next Generation.' Report of the Committee on the Future Economy, Ministry of Trade and Industry.

Tan, Khee Giap, Beng Kai Tan, and Wen Seng Kwan (2015) 'Singapore's Economic Development, 1965–2020: Review, Reflection and Perspective', in *Singapore @50: Reflection and Observations* in COMMENTARY, edited by Victor Savage, published by The National University of Singapore Society, Volume 24, MCI (P) 097/02/2015.

Tan, Khee Giap, Randong Yuan, Wei Cher Wong, and Mu Yang (2014) *Annual Analysis of Competitiveness, Simulation Studies and Development Perspective for 34 Greater China Economies*. Singapore: World Scientific Publishing.

Wong, Kok-Seng (2008) 'Using Foreign Direct Investment and Multinational Corporations to Upgrade Domestic Labor and Firms?' Singapore: Economic Development Board.

PART III
PATHWAYS TO LATE-LATE DEVELOPMENT

10

Industrial Policy and Learning

Lessons from Latin America

Wilson Peres and Annalisa Primi

10.1 Introduction

In the last two decades, the world global economic outlook has profoundly changed. The rise of China, the shifts in the global geopolitical equilibria and the digital revolution are configuring a fast-changing economic landscape in which windows of opportunities open and close at high speed. The South East Asia and the Pacific region dominates the headlines due to its growing global relevance. Africa gathers world attention as the continent where most of global population growth is expected to happen and where local leaderships are standing up with a new, shared vision for the future embedded in the Africa Union Commission (AUC) Agenda 2063: the "Africa We Want", and as a continent for business and investment from traditional and emerging partners. In this context, Latin America appears as a region in slow motion.

Despite progress made in poverty reduction, somewhat better income distribution, increasing access to education and health, advances in digital connectivity, and an emerging regional start-up scene, still the countries in the region remain among the most unequal in the world, and the region seems trapped in some of the challenges of the past (Prebisch, 1949). How to go beyond being a provider of raw materials and commodities to the global economy? How to benefit more from trade and FDI and ensure that the outcomes of increased participation in the world economy accrue to the domestic stakeholders?

This chapter contributes to the understanding of how nations learn by looking at the experience of Latin America. The region is far from being homogeneous. It groups countries at different levels of development, with diverse market sizes and diverse specialization patterns. However, there are similarities in terms of historical and cultural heritages, evolution of policy approaches, and economic performance that make the region a relevant and interesting unit of analysis. The region, as the chapter shows, could have achieved more in terms of development and economic transformation since the 1960s had it exploited at full all the levers through which economies learn and accumulate capabilities (Oqubay and Ohno, this volume). The experience of Latin American countries, despite the limited aggregate outcomes, is rich and offers interesting insights on how and why nations learn, why some learn faster and better than others, and why some don't manage to trigger the profound learning and accumulation mechanisms that are needed for countries to develop.

The chapter, which reviews the experiences of several countries in Latin America, focusing on the most advanced and industrially developed, contains three sections. The first presents some stylized facts about growth and structural change in Latin America. It highlights the limitations of the growth patterns of the countries in the region, the shortcomings in terms of learning opportunities that derive from the prevailing production and trade specialization, and their limited knowledge base. The second section analyses the limited impact of industrial policies in Latin America, discussing their evolution over time and their capacity (or lack of capacity) to foster virtuous learning dynamics. The third section focuses on three areas in which the countries of the region have achieved change and have managed to foster learning in the economy and in policymaking. The chapter concludes deriving lessons for development. The chapter closes by recalling that there is no one-size-fits-all for how nations learn, but that, at the same time, there are some general principles that, when addressed, can trigger virtuous development patterns across all countries and regions.

10.2 A Region in Slow Motion in a Fast-Changing World Economy

While the global economic outlook is changing at a fast speed, Latin America seems to stand out for its slow motion. Latin America's contribution to world GDP is stable at around 7.5 per cent since the 1960s (Figure 10.1). The rise of South East Asia and the Pacific, and in particular China's accelerated growth since the Open Door Policy of the late 1970s, represent a major landmark in the evolution of the global economy outlook. The South East Asia and the Pacific region accounts today for 28 per cent of world GDP, up from 12 per cent in the 1960, surpassing the United States as the world leading economy since 2007.

Latin America stands out for its reduced dynamism. Differently from Africa, China, and South East Asia, over the long run the region is growing less than the world average (Figure 10.2). Despite the increasing demand for its raw materials and the growing middle classes that could have sustained GDP growth through domestic demand, the region is far from recovering the growth rates of its Golden Age. The regional average GDP growth in the last decade is half of what it was during the decades of the 1950s and 1960s, which coincided with the phase of the

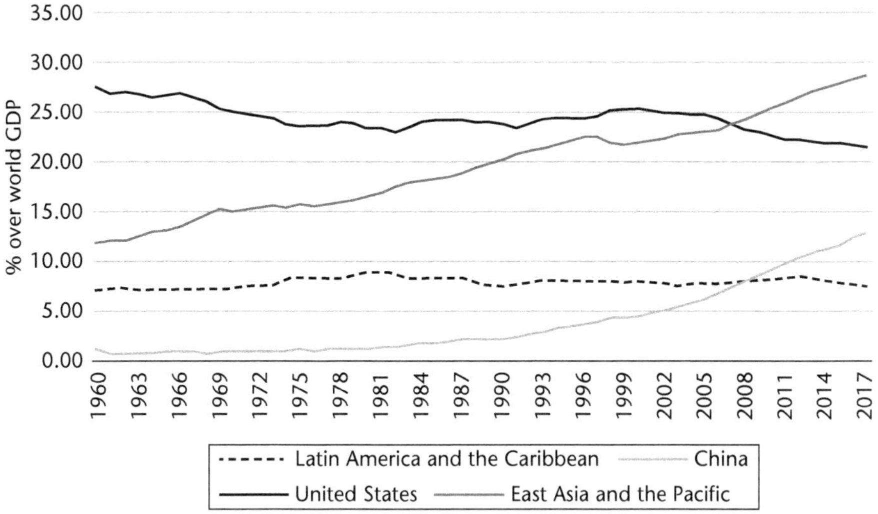

Figure 10.1 Share of domestic GDP in world GDP (US$ constant, 2010), 1960–2017
Source: Authors' analysis based on World Bank Development Indicators

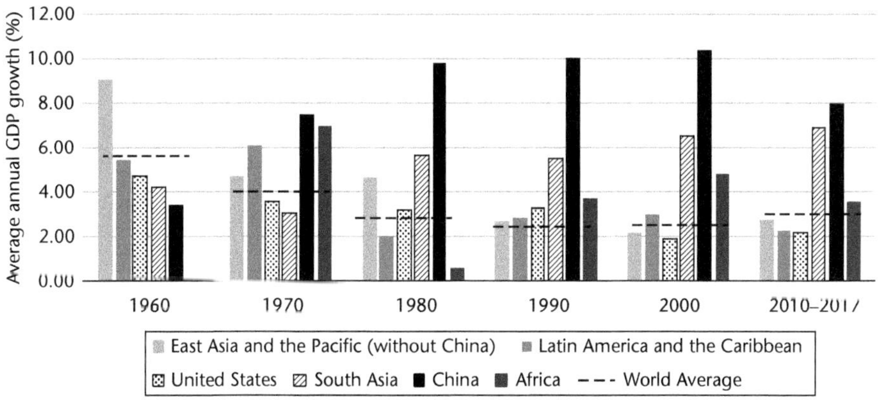

Figure 10.2 Average annual GDP growth (US$ constant, 2010), 1960–2017
Source: Authors' analysis based on OECD (2018f) Main Science and Technology Indicators (https://stats.oecd.org/), UNESCO (2017), Institute for Statistics Database (http://data.uis.unesco.org/)

developmental state and with import substitution policies oriented to build domestic industrial capabilities to compete in the global market.

Learning enables countries to progress; learning is in fact the origin of increases in GDP and productivity (Greenwald and Stiglitz, 2013). Learning takes place at different levels. On the one hand, it happens at the level of policymaking and institutions (see Section 10.2); on the other hand, it happens in production and innovation systems at different levels: sectors and value chains, firms, territorial clusters, and individuals. The limited growth performance of Latin America compared with Asia is associated with the marginal, unidimensional integration into the global economy, the persistent structural inertia of the region, and with the associated limited learning opportunities. On the one hand, Latin America remains anchored to raw materials and commodities and with a limited participation to global value chains (GVCs). While in the success stories from Asia the Hidalgo-Hausmann economic complexity index has risen in the last two decades, it has remained very low in South America, Central America, and the Caribbean (ECLAC-Economic Commission for Latin America and the Caribbean, 2016: 114). Not only have the countries in the region specialized in natural-resource-intensive activities or in assembly functions in GVCs, but many countries in the region have seen their dependency on natural resources increase over time at the expense of their industrial capabilities. In Chile, for example, the share of mining exports over total exports increased from 40 per cent to 50 per cent from 1990 to 2017, and, during the same period, in Colombia the share of oil exports over total exports doubled from 25 per cent to 50 per cent (OECD/UN- Organisation for Economic Cooperation and Development/United Nations, 2018 and OECD/UN/UNIDO 2019).

In Latin America achieving structural change and diversifying economies is still a challenge. Manufacturing, which despite its changing nature due to digitalization is still crucial in terms of its capacity to generate linkages and foster learning and accumulation of capabilities, is losing ground in the region due to growing competition from China and limited investment in research and innovation. Most of the economies of the region share the challenges of low productivity and little diversification of their economic structures. These characteristics are associated with a concentration of opportunities in a few firms, sectors, and territories. For example, in Chile large firms play a dominant role in the economy but they innovate less than their peers in advanced countries. Large firms in Chile are responsible for 73 per cent of business turnover and 57 per cent of total business R&D, while in Germany such firms account for 53 per cent of turnover and for 85 per cent of R&D (OECD/UN, 2018). In addition, economic opportunities tend to be concentrated in a few hubs within each country. In Chile, for example, the Santiago Metropolitan Region generates almost half of national GDP, and accounts for 40 per cent of domestic population. Foreign direct investment concentrates in Santiago and the mining regions of Antofagasta and Atacama, and the creation of new firm clusters in Santiago (OECD/UN, 2018). Something similar occurs in Mexico, where most of modern production and export platforms are located in the northern and central parts of the country.

Despite decades of attempts to increase the technological, innovation, and knowledge base in Latin America, the gap with advanced countries persists and the gap with dynamic developing economies is increasing. A limited knowledge base hampers the capacity to innovate, connect, and learn from others. Most countries in the region suffer a bias towards tertiary education and insufficient vocational and technical training. In addition, quality of education represents a major hurdle. Notwithstanding an average annual investment in education amounting to 3.9 per cent of GDP, countries in the region show poor results in international tests, such as PISA (Programme for International Student Assessment) and TERCE (a large-scale regional study on learning assessment carried out in Latin America by UNESCO, United Nations Educational, Scientific and Cultural Organisation), particularly in science-related areas. In addition, Latin America invests little in innovation and its private sector tends to be more risk adverse than in other areas of the world. On average, Latin American countries devote around 0.8 per cent of their GDP to R&D investments (i.e. R&D intensity), and around 80 per cent of that investment comes from the public sector. Only in Brazil is R&D intensity higher than 1 per cent. These figures are in stark contrast with what happens in advanced economies and in Asia, where countries devote higher shares of their GDP to R&D. On average, OECD countries invest 2.4 per cent of their GDP in R&D, of which almost 62 per cent is financed by the private sector. China has an R&D intensity as high as the OECD average and its private sector finances account for more than 80 per cent of it (Figure 10.3).

Trade and FDI have struggled to deliver on their growth promises in the region. They have contributed to increased export earnings and sustained growth,

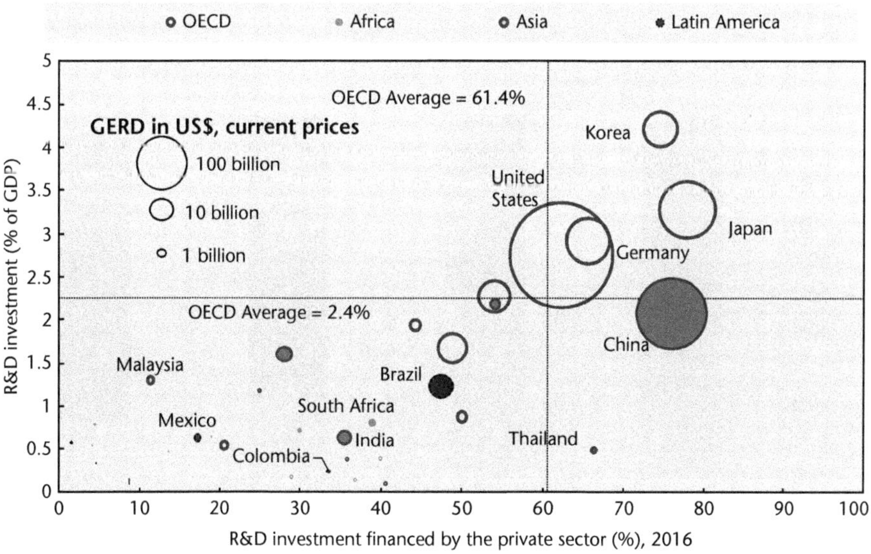

Figure 10.3 Investment in R&D, 2017

Note: GERD: Gross domestic expenditure on research and development.

Source: Authors' analysis based on OECD (2018f) Main Science and Technology Indicators Database, https://stats.oecd.org/, UNESCO (2017)

especially in the phases of growing prices of raw materials, but they have fallen short with respect to opening up widespread possibilities for learning. In Asia, active export-oriented industrialization strategies have sustained the accumulation of capabilities and the development of a domestic entrepreneurial class (Amsden, 1990; Wade, 1990; see also Chapters 7, 8, and 9 in this volume).

In Latin America, trade and FDI have not opened learning opportunities on a par with what has happened in Asia. This can be partially explained by the prevailing production and trade specialization (in Asia trade and FDI have focused relatively more on manufacturing than on natural-resource-based activities) and by the conditionalities included in trade and FDI agreements, which in Asia have tended to contain more effective clauses for local content and domestic linkages. In Asia trade and FDI have been crucial in the setting up of domestic entrepreneurial capabilities, in Latin America this has not been the case. In fact, Latin America stands out, in comparison with Asia, for the lack of home-grown brands, even in industries where the region has attracted FDI and set up trade rules that foster domestic industrial development such as the automotive industry. Latin America also falls short when compared to Asia and Africa with respect to capitalizing on the benefits of regional integration as a way to foster industrialization and learning in the domestic economy. Latin America is the region that trades less within itself than other areas in the world. In Latin America intra-regional exports account for 15 per cent of total exports, while the same figure is up to 23 per cent for Africa and 52 per cent for East and South East Asia (Figure 10.4). The same applies when looking at regional trade in intermediaries, which is a proxy of regional value chains. Only 14 per cent of total exports of intermediate goods from Latin America stays within the region, versus 70 per cent for

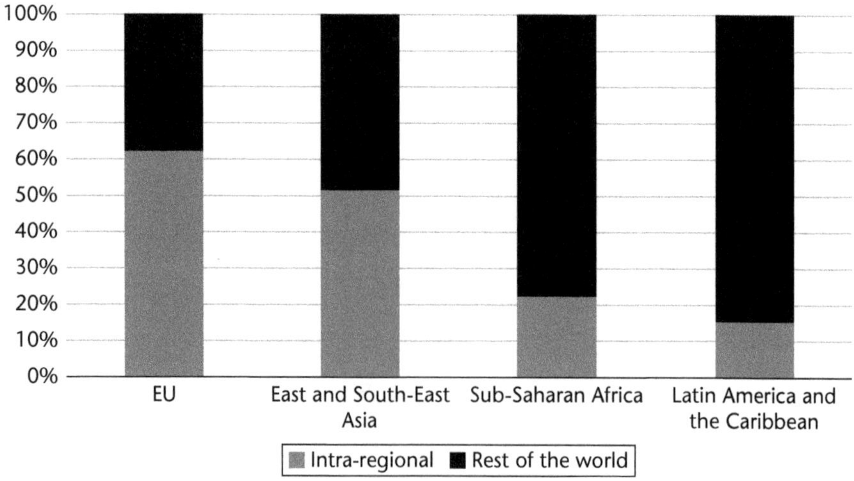

Figure 10.4 Share of intra-regional and extra-regional exports, 2016–18

Source: Authors' elaboration based on UN Comtrade data (2018)

East and South East Asia, according to estimates from the UN Comtrade database. Regional trade can enable learning in developing economies as it tends to be more diversified than global trade (e.g. countries trade a higher number of products within the region than globally) and SMEs tend to participate more in regional trade than in global trade (Dini and Stumpo, 2018). Latin America is also a region where regional trade agreements have struggled to take off, Mercosur is an example while the Central America Common Market, with its more effective integration, represents the exception. In contrast, Asia with the ASEAN (Association of South East Asian Nations) experience shows that regional integration can be highly effective and support industrialization and learning especially when it goes beyond trade and includes cooperation in multiple fields, including scientific and political fields. In this respect, Africa is also showing a bold commitment to sustain the continent's industrialization by boosting intra-regional trade with the signing of the Continental Free Trade Agreement.

10.3 Industrial Policies Struggle to be Pivotal in National Development Strategies

Industrial policies (in different forms and under diverse names) have not been strangers to Latin America since the 1950s (Peres, 2013; Peres and Primi, 2009). However, apart from the period between the 1950s and 1970s, they have struggled to be pivotal in national development strategies. Their destiny has followed a swing that has never recovered the ambitiousness, strength, and investment that they had in the initial phase of the modernization of Latin America, even now that they are back as part of national development strategies (Cimoli et al., 2017; OECD/UN, 2018).

In fact, during the decades of the 1980s up to the 1990s, these policies that had fostered industrialization, learning, and accumulation of capabilities, fell into disrepute. Even though in practice certain industrial policy tools remained active during the liberalization period, they were often disguised under more market-friendly concepts such as competitiveness policies and cluster development policies (Porter, 1990). At that time, the prevailing sentiment towards industrial policies in the region can be effectively summarized by the well-known sentence: 'The best industrial policy is no industrial policy.' An ideological conviction in the superiority of the market as resource allocation mechanism and incentives' setter, fuelled a generalized worry about the perils of active government intervention in the economy, and fostered a soft approach in development strategies to minimize the risks of corruption and capture. Since then industrial policies have come back in the region in different forms and shapes, but their impact has been, apart from some isolated success cases, below expectations (Cimoli et al., 2017; OECD, 2013a; Primi, 2015).

There are many reasons behind the little aggregate impact of industrial policies in Latin America. Among these explanations, the most relevant ones are linked to the fact that various success factors of industrial policies in other areas of the world are not present in the experiences of the different countries of this region. Policies for industrial development in Latin America have always been far from the ambitiousness of the export-oriented industrialization strategies of South East Asian economies, and even further from the whole-of-government approach of preference for the domestic industry and the focus on technology and research that has always prevailed in the United States. And they have not been implemented with the same continuity and budget intensity pursued by successful economies.

Learning in policymaking occurs through two main channels: learning by doing (i.e. by experimenting and implementing new policies) and learning from others (i.e. learning by emulation and by adaptation to the local context of policies and practices applied elsewhere (Reinert, 2009)). The experience of Latin America shows that, while learning from others is crucial, it is not enough. Learning by doing is a more powerful tool to enhance the quality and impact of policy processes. Latin American countries have historically been prone and open to learning from the experiences of other countries. Almost all countries in the region can count many missions to and from more advanced countries with a view to learning from their policy approaches. Many innovation programmes introduced in the region since the 2000s have been designed as a result of looking at the experiences of European countries, and several financial instruments for business start-up and expansion, derive from the experiences of the United States. In their learning from others, in general, governments in Latin America have been always careful to tailor to their realities the experiences of others. However, in some cases they have not been immune to the tendency to 'cut and paste' programmes and institutions from abroad. While peer learning and dialogue matter and can increase the quality and impact of the policymaking process, most of the learning occurs when countries directly experiment with policy design and implementation (Cimoli et al., 2005).

On the one hand, the reason for the limited impact of industrial policies in Latin America is linked to the fact that these policies have never been among the top priorities for governments—at least since the 1980s. Macroeconomic stability and a certain compliance with what was considered to be a respectable and conventional economic policy have been the main shapers of national development strategies. In contrast with the experiences of successful South East Asian economies, in Latin America, even when well designed, industrial policies never had the role of orchestrators of national development strategies (Cimoli et al., 2017; Ocampo, 2017; OECD/UN, 2018, OECD/UN/UNIDO 2019). In South East Asia, activating learning dynamics in the domestic economy and accumulating technological and production capabilities were among the top national priorities; and therefore these policies were able to mobilize investments in bundles and to create the necessary incentives for learning and capabilities accumulation.

On the other hand, industrial polices failed in Latin America because they lacked certain features that characterized the success cases. Overall, they lacked the time and budget consistency enjoyed in other economies, such as the Republic of South Korea and China. But they also differed in specific features that can be grouped in three categories: a) the vision and the strategy; b) the role of private sector and of domestic demand; and c) the implementation mechanisms. Table 10.1 provides an overview of the main characteristics of the policy approaches over the three main historical phases since the 1940s. The Golden Age and the developmental state (1940s up to 1970s), the foreign debt crisis and the liberalization period (1980s and 1990s) and the slow return of industrial policies since the 2000s. Each country has followed different trends and in some countries reforms started earlier than in others, but as an overall overview this periodization is quite accurate for what has happened in the countries of the region.

Latin America has witnessed at least three major changes in visions and strategies for economic development since the 1940s. The changes in the overall policy approach to development from the developmental phase to liberalization and the return of the competitiveness agenda entailed significant ruptures in government funding and regulatory priorities, and also in what concerns the expected role of the private sector and the domestic demand as drivers of growth. These deep changes in the political economy that inspired strategies and policies also resulted in changes in the policy mix, and overall in alterations of the coherence between industrial, technology, and trade policies. Even in countries with the longest and strongest experience in industrial policy, like Brazil, since the 1980s continuity of priorities, investments, and tools was achieved only for a decade (2004–14). Too short to achieve major structural changes and too short to set the basis for private learning processes (ABDI-Brazilian Industrial Development Agency, 2015). In this sense, it is possible to assert that industrial policies have not been part of a strategic development vision in the region, even in the few cases where such vision existed.

Many countries in Latin America struggle when it comes to deciding how to prioritize. The changes in visions and approaches to policies for production transformation that have occurred since the 1940s have generated an ideological bias against government intervention. There is a generalized perception, actually often well-grounded in poor policy experiences, that governments are not well suited to identify priority areas for public and private investment. This fear of government failures, sustained by the temptation of certain policy approaches, backed by product-level analysis, to choose priorities so narrow as to arrive at the granular level of selecting specific products and services, makes it difficult for

Table 10.1 Industrial policies in Latin America, 1940s up to the present

Policies for industrial development and learning			1940s–1970s	1980s–1990s	2000s onwards
Vision and strategy	Priorities		Few, strategic industries of national interest	Horizontal, no selectivity	Multiple, limited selectivity
	Time-frame and budget		Long-term budget and investments	Annual budgeting and programmes	
Role of private sector and domestic demand	National champions		YES (e.g. Embraer)	NO	NO but focus on start-ups
	Domestic demand		Limited, as national consumption gives premium to imported goods and services		
Implementation	Institutions and power structure		Planning and industrial development agencies among top powerful bodies	Planning and strategic functions debilitated. Implementation agencies weakened in the power structure.	Weakness in power structure persist. Implementation agencies regain relevance and capabilities at the territorial level start to be developed
	Quality of civil servants		Limited incentives and control/reward mechanisms		
	Policy mix	Trade and FDI	Aligned and targeted to support domestic capabilities development	Openness and no selectivity	In certain cases return of selective approach to foster upgrading (e.g. Costa Rica electronics, Mexico automotive, Chile mining)
		SMEs	No	YES	YES
		Demand-side	YES	NO	Incipient return [local content and public procurement]
		Skills and innovation	Aligned with industrial development priorities	Horizontal	Incipient return of alignment, but lack of technical skills
	Evaluation as part of policy cycle	Limited	Limited	Limited, when available focused on specific policy tools/instruments	

Source: Authors' elaboration based on interviews with experts and policymakers in the region and revision of official policy documents and available policy evaluations. Consulted background material is available in Peres and Primi (2009); Cimoli et al. (2017); Dini and Stumpo (2018).

countries to 'think big' and identify opportunities beyond the current potential comparative advantages. This is an area, where the difference with the South East Asian approach is remarkable. Successful Asian economies are well known for having developed capabilities, backed by government support, in areas which defeated their initial advantages (Amsden, 1989; Chang, 1994; Lin, 2012; Wade, 1990). Latin America's more gradual approach, (e.g. building technological capabilities in natural resources and agro-food find almost generalized consensus across all political approaches and visions in the region), seems to have made the detour towards learning and diversification longer, and more difficult. In fact, horizontal measures have limited impact in a context characterized by high structural heterogeneity. They tend to foster established interests, and end up being selective in practice. This has been made evident by some analysis of the use of policy instruments in countries of the region. In Mexico, for example, an analysis of fiscal incentives for innovation (a typically market-friendly, horizontal policy tool) revealed that main beneficiaries over time have always been the same large foreign corporations and that these incentives had very limited impact in terms of fostering systemic learning and innovation in industrial clusters in Mexico (Sánchez and Poy, 2019; Unger, 2011).

Prioritizing requires not only a well-grounded, future-oriented vision, it also needs political feasibility. And this is where Latin American governments struggle. The discussion on how ambitious the policy should be and how far from existing assets and competences a country can target are non-consensual issues in the region. Some exceptions in this direction come from small, successful economies such as Costa Rica, which since the early 2010s, started to switch its approach towards a selective approach to attracting FDI, prioritizing knowledge-intensive industries such as ICT and medical devices (OECD, 2012).

This lack of strategic relevance has had a profound impact on policy design and implementation, as well as on governance and institutions. The institutions in charge of technological and industrial development in the region have been debilitated over time and, even in the case of well-respected ones such as CORFO (Chilean Production Development Corporation, an implementing agency affiliated to the Ministry of Economy) in Chile have never recovered their relevance in the domestic power structure of the early developmental days. The vision put forward by CORFO in 2016 on strategic programmes to transform the Chilean economy with a horizon reaching to 2025, leveraging on new technologies, global demand for sustainability, and the uniquenesses of the country, was very innovative and well crafted (OECD/UN, 2018). The vision, and the associated programmes and tools, however, struggled to generate consensus beyond the obvious. Strengthening mining through innovation, local supply chains, and partnerships was well accepted and obtained private funding to back up public investment, building on previous successes of effective cooperation with leading multinationals, domestic and foreign. However, the most transformative aspects of the programme, and the more long-term oriented struggled to find support beyond the administration that proposed the programmes. Investing in digital technologies and in solar energy, both enablers of transformative changes across the whole economy, remained orphan priorities. This is not only happening because the private sector is risk adverse and because market incentives give a premium to natural-resource activities that the current structure of public policy tools is not able to alter in favour of investments in innovation. This is happening also because, from an institutional point of view, there is no agency in charge of strategic planning and thinking for the future. In Chile, the Ministry of Planning ceased its functions in 2011, and has been transformed into the Ministry for Social Development. CORFO, with all its autonomy and reputation, is an implementing agency and is not regarded by the Minister of Finance and the Minister of Economy as the agency in charge of strategic industrial planning.

Many countries in Latin America are actually looking at how to modernize and rehabilitate planning (Primi, 2015). The structural market-oriented reforms packages of the 1980s and 1990s have weakened, when not eliminated, these capabilities. Since the aftermath of the financial and economic crisis of 2008–9, the return of structural growth policies in OECD economies, and the emergence of new technologies and the challenges of digitalization, many countries in Latin America are looking at how to think long term and how to rebuild their planning capacities. In the last two decades, countries such as Argentina, Brazil, Chile, Colombia, Peru, Costa Rica started experimenting with modern ways of fostering long-term thinking by setting up different forms of councils for public–private consultations and for inter-ministerial coordination. The creation of these institutional spaces is not a guarantee of their capacity to operate. In fact, in many instances these councils and commissions lack enforcement mechanisms or decision-making power (as, for example, the National Competitiveness Commission in Chile). However, when supported by presidential commitment, these agencies help in creating spaces for strengthening private–public dialogue and aligning the actions of different ministries to the objective of structural transformation and production upgrading. In certain cases they can help in building trust and alignment with the ministries of finance, which in Latin America often are the most adverse to endorse investments in production transformation strategies.

In addition to the institutional and governance challenges, investments for industrial and technological development in Latin America have often not been up to the ambitions. Chile, for example, with a population four times that of Emilia Romagna (one of the most manufacturing-intensive regions of Italy) invested four times less than that region for industrial development and innovation in the same 2014–17 period (OECD/UN, 2018). While policies for industrial development and innovation in Latin America are often well designed but poorly funded, this is not always the case. Brazil is an exception in this respect. The country, especially since the Production Development Policy (PDP) launched in 2008, has mobilized a sensible amount of public funds for industrial development and innovation. Between 2004 and 2014, Brazil has implemented three consecutive policies for industrial development: the Industrial, Technological, and Foreign Trade Policy (PITCE) of 2004, the Productive Development Policy (PDP) of 2008, and the Greater Brazil Plan (Brasil Plan Maior) of 2011. During those years the financing for production development policy has represented 83 per cent of the total financing disbursed by the National Development Bank of Brazil (BNDES). The BNDES financing of industrial development for the 2004–14 period is estimated to be around US$270 billion, that is, an average of approximately US$ 25.7 billion per year, which rounds up to 1.3 per cent of the country's GDP and close to 15 per cent of domestic manufacturing value added (Table 10.2). During this period, BNDES has also developed new tools to facilitate channelling resources to SMEs (Small and Medium Sized Enterprises). For example, the BNDES has introduced Credit-Card-BNDES that enabled direct access to credit for SMEs, thereby fostering bank usage and reducing the time of access to finance. In addition, BNDES started to introduce new programmes to foster innovation. For example the Innova programme (Inova Empresa) invested more than US$12 billion for innovation; more than 80 per cent of these resources targeted seven priority areas: energy, oil and gas, health-related industries, defence and aerospace, ICT, agribusiness, and the environment (Ferraz et al., 2015).

In Brazil the challenge has not been the limitation of resources, but the capacity to channel the resources to effective uses and to areas and agents that would trigger additional investments from the private sector. In certain cases crowding out of private investment instead of a multiplication effect has taken place, helping to explain the limited aggregate impact of these investments. Industrial policy presented some significant shortcomings in Brazil:

i) Lack of selectiveness. Even for a government structure as large as Brazil's there were too many priority sectors, and their number grew as a result of political pressures and short-term territorial or sectoral development challenges.
ii) Limited coordination with macroeconomic policy. Frequently industrial policy was considered as a means to compensate competitiveness problems caused by domestic currency overvaluation, this being particularly the case during the commodity price boom of the first decade of the century.
iii) Use of industrial policy to address macroeconomic problems. After the 2008–9 financial and economic crisis, industrial policy was used as an instrument of counter-cyclical policy and resources were focused on reducing capital costs to sustain investment.
iv) Scarce evaluation of policy impacts prevented learning and policy adjustments; this problem was compounded with frequent lack of transparency.

Table 10.2 Financing for production development policy in Brazil by BNDES, 2004–14 (yearly disbursements in billions of US$), by industry

Industries	**2004**	**2005**	**2006**	**2007**	**2008**	**2009**	**2010***	**2011**	**2012**	**2013**	**2014****	**Total**
Metal mechanics, electro electronics and health-related industries	4.24	7.81	8.69	8.73	12.65	11.01	15.69	15.84	15.00	15.72	7.22	122,60
Scale intensive	1.40	2.59	4.83	6.68	9.76	11.86	12.96	15.06	13.98	14.98	5.57	99,66
Labor intensive	0.72	1.11	1.29	2.36	4.09	4.65	6.94	8.13	7.99	7.70	2.55	47,52
Total	6,36	11,50	14,80	17,77	26,50	27,51	35,59	39,03	36,97	38,40	15,34	269,79

Notes: * Does not include an operation with Petrobras valued in 24.75 billion reais (about US$8 billion).
** 1st Semestre (Jan–Jun). Data include a slightly different set of sectors. In the source, the yearly total does not coincide with the sum of sector data.

Source: Authors elaboration based on Ferraz et al. (2015).

The peculiar relevance and strategic role of large industrial enterprises in Latin America since the 1940s also contributes towards explaining the lack of pervasiveness of learning processes within the regional productive system. While in early industrializing countries, from the United Kingdom, to the United States, Japan, and Europe, large industrial firms have played an important role in facilitating technological developments and adoption, improvements, and diversification in products and services and in the accumulation and diffusion of new managerial and organizational techniques, in Latin America things have evolved differently.

Large industrial firms have not played a leading role in technological innovation in the region apart from the decades between 1940 and 1970, a period in which the governments of the countries of the region implemented policies targeted to build technological and industrial capabilities in key strategic industries (Ocampo, 2017; Peres and Primi, 2009). On the one hand, the phenomenon of large industrial firms has been limited in number. In addition, only a few of them reached competitiveness in key dynamic, complex, and technology-intensive industries: the Brazilian aeroplane producer Embraer or the Argentinian producer of seamless steel tubes Techint are cases in point. The majority of these large firms is active in natural-resource-intensive industries (such as Ecopetrol in Colombia, Pemex in Mexico, and Codelco in Chile), banking and retail, an area where many *multilatinas* (large enterprises from the region for which a significant portion of their business takes place outside the country of origin, usually within Latin America) do business. On the other hand, especially since the liberalization efforts of the 1990s, political and managerial control of many of these large, state-owned or -controlled firms has been aimed more at reducing their capacity to lobby and capture power, than at fostering their role as catalyzers of learning processes within the overall production structure. Moreover, these firms were badly hit by the debt crises of the 1980s and with more than two decades of the fiscal consolidation programmes that reduced government investments in R&D and in technological progress, many saw their competitive edge declining. Some privatization processes have been successful, such as in the case of Embraer. The company was privatized in 1994; it has managed to resurface and stay innovative and competitive on the global market until now.

In the few successful cases the experience of Latin American countries does not differ from Asian and North American success cases. These large firms, such as Embraer, were set up thanks to government strategic vision and support; they grew by focusing on innovation and on getting ready to compete in the global market and to operate they relied on domestic skilled workforce and capabilities. In practice they acted as engines of growth and development for the local production system and looked at technology and innovation as key competitiveness drivers.

The case of Embraer is emblematic. The company, which nowadays operates at the forefront of global aviation technology and is among the world-leading manufacturers of commercial and executive aircrafts, was set up as a state-controlled enterprise in 1969, and started its first commercial operations in the 1970s. But what was at the origin of its creation? A national ambition that dates back to the early 1940s to develop competences and compete in aeronautics and engineering. An interesting paper by Cassiolato et al. (2002) provides a well-developed and detailed summary of the history of Embraer. The main points are summarized in our own words in the following paragraphs. In 1945, the federal government of Brazil set up an Aeronautics Research Centre, through a partnership with the Massachusetts Institute of Technology (MIT). The Research Centre focused on advancing research in the field through original research and through partnerships with foreign partners. In 1947, the Federal Government inaugurated the Aeronautics Technology Institute to train local engineers and technicians. The building of a solid learning base proceeded in the following years until the mid-1950s, when the federal government set up the Institute for Research and Development. The institute focused on developing aeronautics, aviation, and engineering technologies through basic and applied research and by technology adoption through licenses from more advanced partners, especially from the United States. The main philosophy behind this whole operation and the creation of the research institute was the need for Brazil to achieve technology and knowledge 'independency' by knowing the whole production cycle, even if for productivity reasons they specialized in specific phases and components. The overall objective was to develop a competitive aeronautics company that could design, conceive, and assemble aircraft relying on local engineering and technologies. Embraer, was set up as a state-controlled company in 1969, almost fifteen years after the setting up of the Aeronautics Technology Research Centre. Embraer, as mentioned before, was privatized in 1994 and continues to be a key player in the Brazilian economy. The company has continued to benefit from government support through more market-friendly policy tools such as innovation funds and fiscal incentives for technological development. It is the leading company in the country for technology-intensive exports, a major source of foreign exchange, and a demander of high-skilled employees. Its fortune rests on its innovation-oriented approach that originates from the technology and research focus of its inception back in the 1940s.

If Latin America had more Embraer or Techint type of firms and if its policies for production development had been capable of greater leverage on large industrial firms to engender domestic learning processes, we would probably see a different Latin America today, more diversified and less elite-dominated. On the contrary, since the 1980s the prevailing attitude has been not to back national champions and to control their potential effect in terms of power and rent capture. The focus has shifted to prevent capture by large firms and incumbents, setting aside the tools that could have been used to incentivize these large firms to operate as innovators and groundbreakers.

In parallel with the distrust for national champions, also supported by an effective weakness in competition policy in the countries of the region, Latin American countries have accumulated experience in policies, programmes, and tools for SMEs development (Dini and Stumpo, 2018). These policies gained ground even during the liberalization decades of the 1980s and 1990s. These types of interventions were considered market friendly and in line with traditional market-failure approaches: SMEs face barriers in access to finance, markets, and information, and therefore horizontal programmes were needed to remove (or at least reduce) these barriers and to sustain their competitiveness. In some cases, the SMEs policies have been more successful, as, for example, in Mexico, Chile, Brazil, and El Salvador. Yet most of the domestic firms are small and characterized by low productivity and reduced international competitiveness; moreover, many of them operate in the informal economy.

The attention to SMEs has also evolved into a new approach in policies for economic transformation that takes into account territorial development. Latin American countries are highly heterogeneous when it comes to territorial governance. The region includes federal countries such as Argentina, Brazil, and Mexico and unitary countries, like Chile, where the election of regional authorities is a very recent achievement. Nevertheless, across the whole region there is a growing recognition that policies for industrial development cannot be space blind as they have been in early developmental phases. New tools are being developed to ensure that production and technological opportunities are exploited across the whole territory, regardless of the level of centralization of the country. An assessment of the production development policy of Chile released in early 2018 identified progress towards a place-based approach to industrial development as a key game changer for the country. In addition, the willingness to identify mechanisms to better channel rents from natural resources to foster innovation is also pushing some countries to identify new forms of working with the regions. This is happening, for example, in Colombia where 10 per cent of the royalties from mining are now transferred to regions earmarked for innovation (OECD/UN, forthcoming).

The policy mix for industrial policy in Latin America has also evolved in line with the different waves of policy approaches. While there is disagreement on how to choose the direction of technical change, and who should do it, since the aftermath of the 2008–9 financial and economic crises and taking into account the new digital revolution, there is consensus on the fact that the new context opens opportunities for going beyond the current specialization pattern. This can be done in several ways: by promoting the upgrading and diversification of existing companies; by fostering the creation of new companies; and by strategically interacting with foreign firms. Countries can mobilize different levers for strengthening their domestic capabilities, including financing of S&T development, public procurement, FDI and entrepreneurship promotion. Those instruments are not novel, but they need to be designed in new ways to be in line with the new landscape and to be more effective. Among some of the policy tools that Latin American countries are using nowadays to foster learning and the accumulation of domestic capabilities, it is worth highlighting:

- The incentives enabling a strategic management of FDI and trade. Some countries are trying to attract FDI in a more strategic way linking them to national priorities. A successful case in this respect is Costa Rica, Brazil (especially some states within the country) and Chile are also advancing in setting up strategic partnerships with foreign investors. Chile, according to the information provided by the General Directorate of Foreign Trade of the Ministry of Foreign Affairs, has also recently innovated in its trade policy by introducing a GVCs chapter in future bilateral trade agreements to ensure trade policy is aligned with the objective of increasing participation of domestic firms to GVCs.
- The resurgence in the use of public procurement in areas such as software development, health, defence, infrastructure, and energy. These are businesses where there are high social and economic issues at stake and where in general the state is involved in the research, use, service delivery, and/or production. Managing public procurement is complex and requires transparency. The region has not been exempt from controversies, especially from foreign companies, which claim the application of the WTO principle of equal treatment. More recently, the industrial strategy of the administration that took office on 1 December 2018 in Mexico includes procurement by the federal government to foster local content development as a key policy tool.
- The new set of programmes including financing, service provision, and mentorship to foster start-up development in the region. These programmes have relatively low operation costs and are of relatively high impact. They contribute to placing Latin America under the spotlight of investors in search of innovative projects (OECD, 2013b; OECD, 2016). Since the introduction of Start-up Chile in 2010, similar initiatives have been started in the region, notably in Brazil, Colombia, Mexico, and Peru.
- Financing and research infrastructure for innovation remains the Achilles heel in Latin America's current policy mix. Innovation policy continues to be not aligned with main industrial development priorities and the resources and infrastructure for research are still insufficient with respect to what is happening in South East Asia and in frontier economies. Renewable energies could represent a potential for the region to leapfrog, but bolder public action would be needed in this respect.

Another aspect in which Latin America differs from successful world experiences, is that evaluation is not always conceived as part of the policy cycle and as a tool for policy learning, with the exception of a few cases: the most notable among the recent ones is linked to the quick reforms introduced in the Start-up Chile programme because of monitoring and early-stage implementation evaluation. Since its introduction in 2010, Start-up Chile has been constantly updated to address unintended consequences, such as the bias towards foreign entrepreneurs and the excessive concentration of beneficiaries in the capital region (OECD, 2013b; 2016). In the absence of formal evaluations, some public agencies contribute to increasing awareness of policy objectives and results. For example, in Argentina the Observatory on Employment monitors job and production trends in the country and favours policy fine-tuning by operating in close collaboration with the ministerial level. In Colombia the Observatory for Science and Technology (OCyT), created in 1999 as a public–private partnership initiative, is responsible for the elaboration of qualitative and quantitative indicators to monitor trends and support the process of strategic decision-making (Primi, 2014).

Why are implementation failures so common in the region? On the one hand, there are few policy operators defined as implementing agencies, such as CORFO in Chile and BNDES in Brazil. On the other hand, the policy mix tends to lack powerful instruments. There is a generalized preference for horizontal and soft instruments such as support for meetings, seminars, and services provision, which target a myriad of beneficiaries and have little impact. In addition, sometimes it happens that the political commitments to formulate a policy and release the policy document do not last until resource allocation. In such cases, policies remain merely a propaganda tool to show that governments, at least in theory, care about production development and firms.

10.4 When the Region Takes a Head Start and Learns, Smart Policies are Behind it

As mentioned in the previous section of this chapter, despite Latin America's limited achievements of industrial policies, there are some significant experiences, which show that when effective learning and capabilities accumulation mechanisms take place in the region there are effective institutions and policies behind them. In this section we present lessons learned from three successful recent cases in three different countries in the region: the capacity of an old institution like CORFO in Chile to re-invent its internal procedures and routines to adapt to changing circumstances, the case of the Uruguayan e-government agency (AGESIC), and the experience of Mexico in the automotive industry. These cases have been selected based on two criteria. On the one hand, they entail a learning process at different levels: CORFO and AGESIC provide examples of institutional and policy learning, while the Mexican case focuses on learning dynamics at the firm and cluster level. On the other hand, these cases, even though they all focus on advanced countries in the region, they encompass very different economic realities: a small economy (Uruguay), a medium-sized one strongly specialized in natural resources (Chile), and the second-largest economy in Latin America and the second exporter of high-tech manufacturing in the region (Mexico).

10.4.1 CORFO: The Importance of Renewing Routines

CORFO was created in 1939; it played an important role in the import substitution period from the 1940s to early 1973. Afterwards it kept some of its functions as a holding of state-owned enterprises and since the 1990s it has specialized in promoting entrepreneurship, innovation, and competitiveness, with particular attention to SMEs. CORFO manages several programmes, among them three offer relevant lessons: i) a programme to foster attracting FDI to technology-intensive industries, introduced by lead-managers who had to convince senior leadership of the relevance of the proposal; 2) the setting up of a programme to promote the creation of networks of SMEs to strengthen their competitiveness; and 3) the introduction, with support of top leadership, of a totally new line of action: the creation of Start-up Chile in 2010.

The programme to attract knowledge-intensive FDI aimed at increasing FDI inflows to new industries and making Chile visible to global investors. To reach these objectives, CORFO had to create its own capabilities to formulate and manage the full process of investment promotion: this implied that it had to go beyond its traditional, long-term routines. Its traditional routines were not enough for a new subject for the agency (attracting FDI), particularly because the new task implied direct policy operation, well beyond the elaboration of policy guidelines and the provision of financial resources to firms to which the agency had been used since the early 1940s. Defining and implementing these new routines and procedures required vision and persistency from individual managers, especially because the team in charge had to convince the agency's CEO and the president of the Republic that the new programme was feasible and efficient. A new disruptive team, both at the leadership and operational level, managed the programme. During the first years of operating the programme more than half of the team had to be changed. The successful results contributed to highlighting the need to define targeted programmes to attract FDI and contributed to the upgrading of the domestic institutional governance for attracting FDI. More recently, the Committee for FDI was upgraded and transformed into the Chilean Agency for FDI (InvestChile).

A different logic was behind the second programme under consideration: the promotion of networks to foster SMEs' development. In this instance, the programme was the result of the agency's long-term routines. Its main instruments were grants to hire managers to help sector-based networks of SMEs to implement shared strategies, especially in investment and marketing. The introduction of the new programme was based on the willingness to experiment with new policies in the field of SMEs' development, also based on observation of global trends in the field (especially from Spain). The process of definition and adoption of the new programme involved an open internal debate to ensure consensus and to get feedback from various departments. An initial pilot was approved before the policy was scaled up and introduced into the standard policy tools of CORFO. The piloting phase included: i) the creation of a three-level organizational structure to scale up operations (strategic guidance by CORFO, intermediate policy operators, and beneficiary firms); ii) informal monitoring meetings with policy operators every two weeks; and iii) systematic, structured formal evaluations by independent bodies (universities) and a formal commitment by CORFO to actually use evaluation results to improve policy and instrument design. This programme has been particularly successful (with beneficiary firms increasing sales and employment more than the control group).

In 2010, CORFO introduced a new, disruptive programme in its already big portfolio: Start-up Chile (OECD, 2013b, 2016). Few programmes from CORFO and from Latin America, have had the global resonance that Start-up Chile achieved. Many reasons can explain this success. On the one hand, it was the right programme at the right time. With digitalization exploding and Silicon Valley in need of a different identity, the world was ready to see new start-up hubs emerging globally. Months after the introduction of Start-up Chile similar programmes began to be developed in other countries in the region (Start-up Brazil, Start-up Peru, InnPulsa Colombia, among others). The programme was far from perfect when it was first launched. The initial call offered no repayable contribution only to foreign start-uppers willing to set up a business in Chile. Discontent from stakeholders induced the lead-team to quickly reform the call and eliminate the foreign nationality conditionality. A first early evaluation of results also showed that it was very difficult to scout good proposals and that it was better to split the programme into two phases to avoid waiting time in low-growth unsuccessful business ventures. The programme was, and still is, managed by a disruptive, innovative, and young team (newly recruited CORFO staff) which has been given autonomy to operate faster and in line with the timing of global start-up markets. After an initial pilot phase, Start-up Chile was formally included in CORFO's governance structure, but it maintains a certain managerial flexibility. In addition to contributing to the generation of a critical mass of profitable start-ups in Chile, Start-up Chile has also put pressure on CORFO's operational system to show that it is possible to transfer resources faster to beneficiaries and to improve routines to adapt to the digital economy.

10.4.2 AGESIC: Creating an Agency That Fosters Change

In 2018, Uruguay jointed the D7 collective of world-leading digital governments, which includes Estonia, Israel, the Republic of Korea, New Zealand, the United Kingdom, and Canada. How was it possible for a small Latin American economy to join the network of the world's most advanced digital nations? A significant part of the answer lies in the operation of a strong government agency AGESIC (Agencia de Gobierno Electrónico y Sociedad de la Información y del Conocimiento) which responds directly to the presidency of the Republic and which has been operating since 2007. A set of well-defined priorities, strong governance, and managerial and staff continuity allowed AGESIC to develop and implement an agenda shared by all stakeholders. Within its broad policy agenda, AGESIC is implementing a strategic plan crafted to harness the opportunities provided by blockchain. This involves the development of blockchain-based shared assets to be incorporated into services by public institutions and a platform for the deployment of blockchain as a service (BCaaS) solution. The agency has produced a toolkit through which domestic institutions can assess the convenience of using this technology and determine which type of blockchain would be the most appropriate for their objectives. AGESIC also periodically assesses the political, legal, efficiency, and security implications of blockchain use. At present, blockchain is used for traceability in supply chains. The agency foresees widespread use by 2023. A review of AGESIC's modus operandi reveals the importance of four organizational features: i) a clear objective (in this case, transformation with equity) and efforts sustained for more than a decade; ii) well-defined quantitative goals; iii) the identification of specific implementation bodies; and iv) the practice of quarterly evaluations open to all.

Pragmatism, clear goals, and continuity are at the core of AGESIC's experience. This also helps explain why ICT policies were much more successful than industrial policies in Latin America. The region has been able to expand broadband internet access, sharply reduce tariffs, and connect more than 60 per cent of its population (and almost 75 per cent of millennials living in cities) in the last two decades. Three forces determined these results: i) governments and firms (large, foreign, domestic, and state-owned corporations) worked in partnership; ii) government officials thought of themselves as agents of change and cooperated with their counterparts in other Latin America countries; and iii) all agents worked to foster adaptation to fast exogenous technological change, avoiding actions to defer or prevent its dissemination. The ICT agenda also benefited from a pragmatic approach focused on results and on the willingness to make change possible in the medium term. ICT policies have been freer of the ideological burden that industrial policy carries in the region and therefore enjoyed higher levels of commitment and consensus.

10.4.3 The Automotive Industry in Mexico: Learning from FDI Is Possible, But Home-grown Brands Are Needed to Be Prepared for the Future

Mexico is one of the world's leading producers and exporters of vehicles, although it has no automanufacturers of its own. For more than two decades under the North American Free Trade Agreement (NAFTA), which included Mexico, the United States, and Canada, the country's production of light vehicles grew from 1.1 million units in 1994 to nearly 3.5 million in 2016 and Mexican light-vehicle exports increased from 579 thousand to 2.8 million units during the same period (Klier and Rubenstein, 2017). Although the country has developed some intermediate-level capabilities, its main competitive advantage was being the low-wage country in NAFTA (ECLAC, 2017; Promexico, 2016).

Trade and industrial policies have been determinant in positioning Mexico on the world map of global trade as a cars' export platform. Vehicle assembly in Mexico dates back to the 1920s. During the first half of the twentieth century, Mexicans could only buy cars assembled locally by small-scale plants. After the 1982 debt crisis, the government shifted from import substitution to export promotion. Vehicle producers responded by importing more parts and components from abroad, and by modernizing local factories. NAFTA removed most of Mexico's remaining trade restrictions over a period of ten years. After the end of this transition, a large number of foreign carmakers announced plans to assemble vehicles in the country, due to its competitiveness in terms of low wages, and to trade facilitation measures. Thus, new car companies were set to begin production between 2013 and 2020, raising the number of vehicle producers to eleven, while the number of assembly plants was set to increase from eleven in 2004 to twenty-one in 2020. By 2017 several world-leading companies were operating in Mexico: BMW, Daimler's Mercedes-Benz, Hyundai Motor Group's Kia Motors, Mazda, and Volkswagen Group's Audi subsidiary (Klier and Rubenstein, 2017). Since NAFTA, the auto industry in Mexico has not only became more integrated with the United States and Canada, it has also become more international in nature. According to estimates from the Trade in Value Added (TiVA) database, the domestic value added of gross exports for the automotive industry in Mexico reaches almost 50 per cent, showing a high integration of Mexico in this GVC with quite an important share of local content. These locally generated value added derive from skilled labour and from a well-developed network of research centres that support design, technology development, and the testing of materials and products. As of 2018, Mexico has twenty-eight R&D centres: thirteen private centres connected to large producers, seven connected to academic institutions, seven government centres, and one with mixed capital. Despite significant progress, the Mexican car industry faces limitations. First, there is a limited presence of Tier II and particularly Tier III suppliers, that is, local suppliers struggle in activities where economies of scale matter. Second, and more importantly, the industry is well adapted to the current technological paradigm based on metal-mechanics capabilities but is not prepared for the revolution in production technologies that electric cars and autonomous vehicles will pose. Although many of the most important developers of new car technologies (Tier I suppliers) are located in the country, new research in this field is scant (ECLAC, 2017).

The Mexican experience in the automotive sector shows that a shift from the domestic market to the external market can contribute to fostering learning in the domestic economy if it leads to a large inflow of investment from world-leading firms and their suppliers. However, despite the development of domestic capabilities, it also shows that it is difficult to keep pace with technological change if a country does not have producers of its own. Moreover, the reliance on just one or two markets, as huge as they are, increases uncertainty and may harm investment and innovation, as shown by the unexpected and hard renegotiation of NAFTA, which concluded with a renewed United States–Mexico–Canada agreement in 2018.

The overview of the three experiences presented in this section can be summarized by three main lessons: i) policy design, despite its problems and ideological biases, is the easiest, particularly in a world of open knowledge, the main challenges are in implementation; ii) trial-and-error processes are inevitable, and flexibility to create new routines lies at the heart of successful experimentation; iii) evaluation, although seldom done, is crucial; but what matters most is to actually use evaluations to correct mistakes and improve performance.

10.5 Conclusions

The experience of some of the most advanced and successful countries in Latin America offers relevant insights on how nations learn, or do not learn. Since the 1940s, and despite the changes in policy approaches and the fact that overall the region hasn't actually been able to engender a deep transformative change of its economies and societies, most countries of the region have made progress in the following areas:

- They have realized that having good internal policy processes with the participation of all stakeholders is far more efficient that copying best practices of developed countries and regions.
- Policy design and implementation are learning processes. There are no blueprints for policies, experimentation and trial and error lie at the core of effective policy processes.
- Policies and programmes need to have a limited set of explicit measurable goals. Presenting attractive objectives and somewhat coherent policy lines is

not enough. The apophthegm "if you can't measure it, you can't manage it" may not always be true, but in the case of Latin America it is true.

- Countries in the region have developed a better understanding of the time needed for learning. Governments in Latin America always knew that it takes time to learn and to get tangible results. However, the experience of the last two decades shows that the time needed is much longer than was initially assumed, and definitively longer than the four- to six-year period of a government's administration.
- A plan without a budget is demagogy. Latin American countries, through their own successes and failures, have learned that a policy is a real one only if it is backed up by the financial and human resources to implement it. The private sector tends to interpret small financial commitments as merely acts of public relations and marketing, not as real policies to foster change, and therefore are not interested in collaborating in these small efforts.

Despite progress, some old problems persist in the Latin American approach to industrial development:

- Quite frequently new administrations discontinue previous policies and/or re-brand old plans under new names.
- Often policies for transforming the economy lack prioritization and contain a never-ending shopping list. Announcing dozens of priorities without clear trade-offs among them hampers implementation and is a recipe for failure.
- Many policies, particularly those that consist only of objectives and policy lines, with no quantitative goals and allocation of resources, never go beyond the publication of the policy document.
- Evaluations are still not a common practice and countries seldom use evaluation results to improve policy design and management.
- A new approach to apply leverage on large firms is needed, as with no national champions it is difficult to engender deep learning processes in the domestic production system.

The experiences presented in this chapter highlight that to improve industrial policy design and implementation countries need to pay attention to four issues: i) ensuring the highest political leadership backs the policy; ii) endowing the public sector with managerial and technical capacities to manage these policies; iii) defining a coherent policy mix from trade, to industrial development and innovation that fast-tracks technological change and that does not prevent it; and iv) taking into account all stakeholders from local to regional governments, foreign and domestic firms.

In brief, policy works better when it has clear priorities, when it is capable of getting a constructive dialogue going between the public and the private sector, and when it mobilizes investments in bundles in critical areas, including infrastructure, skills, and finance. Institutions co-evolve with the challenges they are called upon to face and with the policies that they administer and implement. Poor institutional capabilities are no excuse for calling for low state intervention. Investing in institutional strengthening is part of a pro-active policy package.

In a fast-changing global landscape, where digitalization is transforming development opportunities and opening up possibilities not otherwise available, Latin America faces a dichotomy. On one side, such as ICT diffusion and use, the region has registered major advancements, with strong policies designed and implemented and with demonstrable results. When pragmatism was stronger than ideology the region achieved positive results. On the contrary, on the structural side, policies never regained the ambition, continuity, and focus on leading players that they had in early developmental phases. In these areas, the region stands out for its inertia. The Latin American countries discussed in this chapter have made some progress, but their main structural weaknesses persist: little diversification of production and exports, high dependency on commodities and raw materials, little integration into global value chains (apart from the ones linked to natural resources), and poor exploitation of regional integration that hampers development and innovation. To activate learning and fast track development, Latin America needs to modernize its policy approach and learn from its past and more recent successes.

Acknowledgements

The authors thank Arkebe Oqubay and Kenichi Ohno as well as all participants of the workshop hosted by Oxford University Press in Ethiopia on August 2018 for their comments on the first draft of this chapter. The authors thank Mario Castillo, Marco Dini, João Carlos Ferraz, Nicolo Gligo, and Diana Parra Silva for sharing their knowledge on some of the specific policy programmes mentioned in the chapter and Manuel Toselli for research assistance on Latin American trade data.

References

ABDI (2015) *Dez anos de política industrial, balanço & perspectivas 2004–2014*, Brasilia: Federal Government of Brazil.

Amsden, Alice H. (1989) *Asia's Next Giant: South Korea and Late Industrialization.* New York: Oxford University. Press.

Cassiolato, José, Roberto Bernardes, and Helena Lastres (2002) *Transfer of Technology for Successful Integration in the Global Economy: A Case Study of Embraer in Brazil.* Geneva: UNCTAD Publishing.

Cimoli, Mario, João Carlos Ferraz, and Annalisa Primi (2005) 'Science and Technology Policy in Open Economies: The Case of Latin America and the Caribbean.' *Serie Desarrollo Productivo* No. 165. Santiago: ECLAC/CEPAL, United Nations. Available at https://www.cepal.org/publicaciones/xml/3/23153/DP165.pdf.

Cimoli, Mario, Mario Castillo, Gabriel Porcile, and Giovanni Stumpo (eds) (2017) *Políticas industriales y tecnológicas en América Latina.* LC/TS.2017/91. Santiago: United Nation Economic Commission for Latin America and the Caribbean (ECLAC). Available at https://www.cepal.org/es/publicaciones/42363-politicas-industriales-tecnologicas-america-latina.

Chang, H.-J. (1994) *The Political Economy of Industrial Policy.* Basingstoke: Macmillan.

Dini, Marco and Giovanni Stumpo (eds) (2018) *Mipymes en América Latina: un frágil desempeño y nuevos desafíos para las políticas de fomento.* ECLAC, LC/TS.2018/75. Santiago: United Nations Publishing.

ECLAC (2016) *2030: Equality in the Center of Sustainable Development.* Santiago: ECLAC.

ECLAC (2017) *Foreign Direct Investment in Latin America and the Caribbean 2017.* Santiago: ECLAC.

Ferraz, João Carlos, Felipe Silveira Marques, and Antônio José Alves Jr. (2015) 'A Contribuição do BNDES para a Política Industrial Brasileira 2003–2014', in ABDI, *Dez anos de política industrial, balanço & perspectivas 2004–2014*, Federal Government of Brazil, Brasilia.

Greenwald, Bruce and Joseph E. Stiglitz (2013) 'Industrial Policies, the Creation of a Learning Society, and Economic Development', in Joseph E. Stiglitz and Justin Yifu Lin (eds) *The Industrial Policy Revolution I*, International Economic Association Series. London: Palgrave Macmillan.

Klier, Thomas H. and James M. Rubenstein (2017) 'Mexico's Growing Role in the Auto Industry under NAFTA: Who Makes What and What Goes Where', *Economic Perspectives* 41(6): 1–29.

Lin, Justin Yifu (2012) *The Quest for Prosperity: How Developing Economies Can Take Off.* Princeton, NJ: Princeton University Press.

Ocampo, J. (ed.) (2017) *Historia económica de Colombia.* Mexico City: FCE—Fondo de Cultura Económica.

OECD (2012) 'Attracting Knowledge-intensive FDI in Costa Rica: Challenges and Policy Options.' Paris: OECD Development Centre.

OECD (2013a) *Perspectives on Global Development 2013: Industrial Policies in a Changing World.* Paris: OECD Publishing. France.

OECD (2013b) *Start-up Latin America: Promoting Innovation in the Region.* Paris: OECD Development Centre. Available at http://dx.doi.org/10.1787/9789264202306-en.

OECD (2015) *Innovation Policy in Panama: Design, Implementation and Evaluation.* Paris: OECD Development Centre. Available at http://dx.doi.org/10.1787/9789264233447-en.

OECD (2016) *Start-up Latin America 2016: Building an Innovative Future, Development Centre Studies.* Paris: OECD Publishing. Available at http://dx.doi.org/10.1787/9789264265660-en.

OECD/UN/UNIDO (2019) *Production Transformation Policy Review of Colombia Unleashing Productivity.* Paris: OECD Publishing.

OECD/UN (2018) *Production Transformation Policy Review of Chile: Reaping the Benefits of New Frontiers.* Paris: OECD Publishing. Available at http://dx.doi.org/10.1787/9789264288379-en.

Peres, Wilson (2013) 'Industrial Policies in Latin America', in Adam Szirmai, Wim Naudé, and Ludovico Alcorta (eds) *Pathways to Industrialization: New Challenges and Emerging Paradigms.* Oxford: Oxford University Press.

Peres, Wilson and Annalisa Primi (2009) 'Theory and Practice of Industrial Policy: Evidence from the Latin American Experience.' Production Development Policy Series, C/L.3013-P ECLAC. Santiago: United Nations.

Porter, Michael (1990) *The Competitive Advantage of Nations.* New York: Free Press.

Prebisch, Raul (1949) *El Desarrollo Económico de América Latina y sus Principles Problemas.* Santiago: Comisión Económica para América Latina de las Naciones Unidas, CEPAL.

Primi, Annalisa (2014) *Promoting Innovation in Latin America: What Countries Have Learned (and What They Have Not) in Designing and Implementing Innovation and Intellectual Property Policies.* Maastricht: Maastricht University Press.

Primi, Annalisa (2015) 'The Return of Industrial Policy: (What) Can Africa Learn from Latin America?' in Akbar Noman and Joseph Stiglitz (eds) *Industrial Policy and Economic Transformation in Africa.* New York: Columbia University Press, pp. 162–96.

Promexico (2016) 'The Mexican Automotive Industry: Current Situation, Challenges and Opportunities.' Mexico City: Promexico.

Reinert, Erik (2009) 'Emulation versus Comparative Advantage: Competing and Complementary Principles in the History of Economic Policy.' The Other Canon Foundation and Tallinn University of Technology Working Papers in Technology Governance and Economic Dynamics No. 25, TUT Ragnar Nurkse Department of Innovation and Governance.

Sánchez, Arturo and Laura Poy (2019) 'CONACYT benefició a grandes empresas entre 2009 y 2017', *La Jornada*, Mexico City, 18 January 2019.

Unger, Kurt (2011) 'La política de estímulos fiscales a la investigación y desarrollo el México: alcances limitados en el contexto de innovación de las empresas', *El Trimestre Económico* 78(1): 49–85.

Wade, Robert (1990) *Governing the Market: Economic Theory and the Role of Government in East Asian Industrialization.* Princeton, NJ: Princeton University Press.

11

The Journey of Ethiopian Airlines

Technological Learning and Catch-up in Aviation

Arkebe Oqubay and Taffere Tesfachew

11.1 Gate Open: An Introduction to Ethiopian Airlines

This study examines firm-level technological learning and catch-up in Africa, using Ethiopian Airlines (EAL) as a case study.[1] EAL was established in April 1946, barely a year after the end of the Second World War. At the time, sceptics doubted the wisdom of transferring modern technology and management culture into a country that lacked the capabilities to administer them and apply its comparative advantage. In the past seven decades, however, EAL, confounding the sceptics, has evolved from a small domestic airline into a fully integrated, technologically sophisticated, internationally competitive, and highly profitable twenty-first-century aviation company. By 2019, EAL's use of cutting-edge technology and modern organizational and management techniques, has allowed the firm to serve more than 120 international destinations, including more cities in Africa than any other airline.[2]

A July 2018 cover story in the widely read *Airline Weekly* remarked, 'When Ethiopian Airlines started life in 1946, it did so with the help of America's TWA [Trans World Airlines]. Who back then imagined it would be the African airline, not the American one, still alive and thriving 72 years later?' The article, 'Diamond in the Rough,' featured EAL's remarkable success despite being rooted in one of the world's poorest countries: '[In 2017] Africa's strongest airline grew at a lightning pace.'

The prime drivers of this growth were the support of a disciplined state and an obsessive focus on developing technological capability and the intensity of learning, a strategic approach that enabled the company to align itself with the future of the aviation industry. EAL has acquired the technical and operational capability to repair and overhaul the latest commercial aircraft; to train pilots, aircraft

[1] Since the airline's establishment in 1946, its official name has changed several times from, for example, 'Ethiopian Air Lines' before 1965 to 'ETHIOPIAN' to, more recently with the expansion of the range of services, to 'EAG' (Ethiopian Aviation Group). In this study EAL will be used consistently.

[2] See Appendix and EAL 2018a.

engineers, and technical personnel; and to offer intercontinental cargo services in partnership with leading global service providers. In 2011, EAL became a member of Star Alliance, meaning it had narrowed the gap between itself and leading industry players and achieved international best-practice standards. In the past few years, EAL emerged as a major overseas investor and exporter of technical and management services. By early 2019, EAL will have acquired equity in several other African airlines and secured contracts to provide technical, operational, and management services to various other airlines.[3]

This study analyses how EAL acquired and developed these technological and organizational capabilities in a low-income agricultural economy with limited skills, few technological capabilities, and a low knowledge base. Conventional wisdom says that successful technological learning and catch-up require prior development of technical, social, and organizational capabilities by learning by doing through assimilation, adaptation, and mastery of international technologies.[4]

Building these capabilities and 'absorptive capacity' requires considerable investment, intensive learning, specialized skills development, and constant upgrading, especially as economic and technological development progresses.[5] These factors are often cited as distinguishing countries that have caught up (such as Japan, South Korea, and Taiwan) from those that are stuck in the middle-income trap—unable to move beyond a certain level of technological capability—and from those that lag behind, including many low-income African countries that lack even rudimentary technological capabilities.

The EAL experience raises several important research questions. How did EAL acquire the technological and organizational capability to transform itself from a small domestic airline into a global competitor exporting technical, operational, and management services? Why was EAL more successful than other African carriers? Can EAL's learning and catch-up model be emulated by other firms in Ethiopia and other late-latecomer countries in Africa? And what are the implications of EAL's learning and catch-up model for future research in late-latecomer countries?

11.1.1 Learning and Catch-up for Late-latecomers

The pioneering work of Friedrich List and Alexander Hamilton has shed light on the challenges and pathways of technological capability building, and on catch-up

[3] In 2018, EAL was equity shareholder and managing operator in more than six airways (EAL 2018b; *The Economist* 2018).

[4] Cohen and Levinthal (1990). These authors underscore the importance of absorptive capacity for learning and innovation and highlight that 'the ability of a firm to recognise the value of new, external information, assimilate it, and apply it to commercial ends is critical to its innovative capabilities' (p. 128).

[5] Cohen and Levinthal (1990).

by the latecomers of the nineteenth century—the United States and continental European countries such as Germany.[6] In post–Second-World-War economic development discourse, Albert Hirschman and Alexander Gerashchenko advanced the proposition that late starters in industrialization have opportunities to catch up based on 'latecomer advantages'—learning from the frontrunners.[7] Extensive research has studied the dynamics of technological learning and capability building by latecomers and the role of industrial policy in fostering learning capability.[8] A series of firm-level empirical studies focused on the successful learning and catch-up experiences of the newly industrializing East Asian economies.[9] In parallel, other scholars advanced the notion of national innovation systems and viewed technological learning and capability building as an interactive process that goes beyond the firm to the sectoral and national levels.[10]

However, most research on learning and catch-up has focused either on latecomers that have succeeded (the familiar cases in East Asia) and those that gained considerable technological capability but remain far from catch-up, such as Brazil, India, Mexico, and Turkey. Very little research has examined firms and countries in the early stages of technological development and industrialization—which include practically all African countries.[11] The potential for and challenges to their technological learning and catch-up requires further exploration. So does the question whether their being late-latecomers in the twenty-first century constitutes an advantage or a disadvantage.

11.1.2 Ethiopian Airlines against the Odds

In 1946, when most of Africa was still under colonial rule, aviation would have been considered an 'alien industry' for Ethiopia, a poor African country totally reliant on subsistence agriculture with an illiteracy rate of more than 96 per cent. When EAL was first established, Ethiopia had only two secondary schools and no tertiary institution. Influential mainstream economists of the day would have advised that an aviation industry was out of line with Ethiopia's comparative advantage.

Over the past seven decades, more than five thousand airlines have secured International Civil Aviation Organization (ICAO) codes, but only a small number have survived beyond ten years. EAL is one of them. Its journey is thus a rare

[6] Cohen and DeLong (2016); List (1856).
[7] Gerschenkron (1962); Hirschman (1958).
[8] Bell (1984); Freeman (1987); Kim (1997); Lall (1992).
[9] Amsden (1989, 2001); Chang (2003); Kim (1997); Lee (2013); Wade (1990); and others.
[10] Huo (2015); Lundvall (1992); Nelson (1993). See also Fagerberg (2005); Fagerberg and Godinko (2005).
[11] Cramer, Oqubay, and Sender (forthcoming).

African catch-up story, teaching the centrality and complexity of technological learning and the role of a disciplined state in building a national champion. It gives hope to African policymakers that, despite the odds and numerous internal and external constraints, catching up is possible even for late-latecomers in the early twenty-first century.[12]

EAL's story defies the notion of comparative advantage and other conventional nostrums. By 2018, EAL had acquired its 100th airplane—a Dreamliner—and grown its annual passenger count to more than 12 million (Appendix). In the same year, it was voted Best African Airline and was ranked 40th in customer service and 24th in size by the World Airline Awards.[13] Its medium-term vision includes doubling the number of aircraft in its fleet to 200 and increasing the number of annual passengers to 25 million by 2025–30. EAL estimates that its total revenue will also double from the target of US$5 billion in 2019 (more than Ethiopia's projected earnings from merchandise exports) to US$10 billion by 2025–30. EAL expects to transport more than 1 million tons of cargo annually within the next decade, building on a joint venture with DHL Logistics.[14] EAL is also forging partnerships with such leading component and commercial aircraft manufacturers as Boeing, GE, and Airbus and their subcontractors, ultimately aiming to build a new aerospace manufacturing hub in Ethiopia.[15]

EAL developed in three distinct phases. In the first, the airline built absorptive capacity and capability through learning by doing in partnership with TWA, and it pursued a proactive Ethiopianization or localization policy. This phase lasted from EAL's establishment in 1946 until the end of the TWA partnership 1975. In the second phase from 1975 to 2000, by managing a series of externally generated crises, EAL protected and maintained the capability and corporate independence acquired during the first phase and built further capability. In the third phase, which began with the new millennium, EAL has upgraded its capability, improved its processes, diversified its competencies, and caught up.

11.2 Take Off: The Rise of the Ethiopian Aviation Industry (1946–75)

11.2.1 Partnership with TWA: The Genesis

Right after the Second World War, Ethiopia was the only independent African sovereign state, and a founding member of the United Nations.[16] The Ethiopian

[12] Cramer, Oqubay, and Sender (forthcoming).
[13] Skytrax (2018).
[14] Interview with the CEO of EAL, Tewolde Gebremariam (EAL, 2018b).
[15] See Oqubay and Lin (forthcoming).
[16] The only other African country joining the United Nations in 1945 was the Union of South Africa, which was not an independent state but an autonomous dominion within the British Commonwealth.

government, as part of a modernization initiative, committed to establishing a commercial airline to integrate the country politically and economically—the most rational and cost-effective strategy because of the rugged and mountainous terrain and inadequate roads and railways. With the assistance of Swedish Count Eric von Rosen, the Ethiopian government initially approached the Swedish carrier ABA, and an agreement was due to be signed in December 1945.[17] However, in June 1945, the Ethiopian delegation attending the United Nations founding conference in New York met with US State Department representatives and requested technical assistance in establishing a commercial airline, primarily for domestic air service. The state department organized an initial meeting with Brigadier-General T. B. Wilson, board chairman of Transcontinental and Western Airlines (TWA, renamed Trans World Airlines in 1950).[18] The Ethiopian government signed an agreement with TWA in September 1945, and the new airline was founded on 21 December 1945, commencing operation on 8 April 1946 with five war-surplus aircraft.

The agreement creating the TWA partnership was the first critical step in establishing a small domestic air service and later transforming it into a successful international airline. It was the first of five critical agreements signed during the thirty-year partnership to help EAL develop strategic technological capabilities and business competitiveness (see Table 11.1).

The first agreement laid the foundations, giving TWA full authority to establish and manage the new airline.[19] In many respects, the agreement was similar to subcontracting relationships that evolve from joint operations between transnational corporations (TNCs) and local manufacturing firms through original

Table 11.1 EAL–TWA agreements

Agreement	Year	Key content
First	1945	Established EAL, undertook full operation and the procurement of aircraft
Second	1953	Stated clearly the ultimate objective of Ethiopianization
Third	1959	Reinforced the urgency of the Ethiopianization agenda
Fourth	1966	Transferred management from TWA to EAL and appointed an Ethiopian deputy CEO
Fifth	1970	Shifted TWA's role from management to advisory until 1974

Source: EAL–TWA agreements (EAL 2018c).

[17] EAL (1988). Count Eric von Rosen was associated with the initial engagement of the Swedish support for the Ethiopian air force.

[18] John Spencer, foreign affairs adviser to the Ethiopian government, helped facilitate the agreement with TWA.

[19] See Spencer (2006).

equipment manufacturing (OEM) arrangements.[20] Under OEM, the foreign partner initially helps select the technology and equipment needed for production; trains managers, engineers, and technicians; and advises on production, financing, and management.[21] Finished products are initially manufactured according to the specifications of the foreign partner, which markets them under its own brand name. As the local partner learns by doing and imitating, and acquires the capability to manufacture to the TNC's specifications, production is gradually transferred to the local firm. The agreement between TWA and EAL foreshadowed such arrangements. TWA was responsible for selecting and procuring all aircraft and the equipment needed to start an aviation industry. It provided all personnel recruited from abroad, including the CEO, management team, pilots and technicians, finance officers, cabin crew, and staff to perform other functions such as catering. It advised on financial arrangements, including facilitating credit for EAL from US banks. It served as the main interlocutor between EAL and aircraft suppliers. And it provided advisory services for all training and technical facilities established in Ethiopia. For its services, TWA was paid a management fee. It was also offered a minority equity share but never took it up.

From the outset, it was understood that TWA would transfer knowledge and build local capacity so that Ethiopians would gradually take over posts held by foreign (mostly US) staff. The Ethiopianization policy was formalized in the second agreement in 1953, which stated, 'The ultimate aim is that EAL shall eventually be operated by Ethiopian personnel.' The third agreement in 1959 reinforced the localization of expertise, while the fourth in 1966 marked a major milestone, transferring management and appointing as a deputy CEO Semret Medhane, who would become the first Ethiopian CEO in November 1971 on the occasion of the EAL's silver jubilee. The fifth agreement in 1970 articulated the shift of TWA's role from managing to advising. The partnership ended in 1975 when TWA found the venture less attractive. TWA continued to provide services to EAL on request.

11.2.2 Ethiopianization Strategy

The Ethiopianization strategy, which took almost three decades, aimed at the eventual takeover by Ethiopians as pilots, technicians, cabin crew, accountants, and marketing personnel. Execution was challenging, particularly preparing Ethiopians for management roles and, due to safety and operational considerations,

[20] It is important to note, however, that the TWA–EAL partnership predates the concept and practice of OEM. In this respect, it was a precursor in services of an arrangement that subsequently emerged in manufacturing.

[21] Hobday (2000). The OEM model was prevalent in East Asia and, as Hobday shows, contributed significantly to technological learning and catching up in electronics.

replacing pilots and technicians. Constant differences of opinion arose between TWA and the Ethiopian authorities on the pace of Ethiopianization.[22] At a time of widespread racism, Ethiopian trainees had to show exceptional skill and competence before they were allowed to replace US pilots.[23] Developing a pool of Ethiopian recruits was a major challenge due to the lack of higher education. At the time, the only institutions that could provide potential recruits were public colleges, the School of Commerce, and the Technical School, which offered pre-tertiary education. To alleviate the skill constraints, an aviation school was established under the Ethiopian Civil Aviation Authority with assistance from TWA.

The difficulties were eased by recruiting the first Ethiopian pilots and technicians from the Ethiopian Air Force. They had been trained well in Ethiopia and the United States and had built a tradition of excellence. Even the candidates for CEO and other positions came from the air force. Key to the success of Ethiopianization was the young Ethiopian staff's exceptional commitment and sense of mission and the board's strong commitment and close follow-up. TWA was also committed to building competence and achieving Ethiopianization because of the implications for its own reputation and credibility. TWA staff's reluctance to compromise on standards contributed to a tradition of excellence, and fostered the ability to operate in the seemingly impossible situation of practically non-existent infrastructure. Two CEOs in particular, Walden Gene Colien and Vic Harell, played a critical role in instilling a spirit of excellence. Although initially aircraft manufacturers and suppliers played a smaller role, later on Boeing was instrumental in building EAL's technological capability, especially after supplying jets in the early 1960s.[24]

Corporate governance during the TWA partnership included a board with two members from TWA and two members representing the Ethiopian government, while the Ethiopian transport minister served as president and board chair. From the start, the US State Department followed EAL's development closely, and this political support no doubt contributed to the project's success.

11.2.3 Capabilities and Operational Performance

11.2.3.1 Technology Selection

An important element of technology and know-how transfer from TWA to EAL was in the selection of technologies appropriate to the unique local operational requirements and conditions. In 1946, Ethiopia had no runways, and TWA

[22] EAL (1988).
[23] EAL (1988).
[24] See *Christian Science Monitor* (1988) and *The Economist* (1987).

advised the purchase of DC3 (Douglas C-47) war-surplus aircraft, which had a proven record of operating in rugged terrain and difficult conditions. The fleet was then expanded with a dozen new aircraft (DC 6B and CV-240), which were capable of regional and international flights and could handle more passengers. In 1962, after completion of the new Bole airport, EAL became the first African airline to incorporate Boeing 720B jets into its fleet. EAL's entering the jet age had considerable implications for its technological advancement. Its ability to select technologies served it well over the years, as evidenced by its continuing strategic and pioneering decisions in acquiring new commercial aircraft technologies.

11.2.3.2 Capability-building Facilities

The new aircraft required improved facilities, new skills, and certification and standards. In the first two decades of EAL's existence, TWA helped it establish a range of capability-building assets to boost its absorptive capacity. The Ethiopian Aviation Academy was founded in 1956, and the Pilot School in 1964. Pilot training commenced in 1970 for both Ethiopians and trainees from other African countries.[25] An aircraft maintenance and technical facility was opened in 1957, and the first overhaul of jet engines was conducted in 1964. From the beginning, the aviation academy and its technical facility provided training and maintenance for carriers from Africa and the Middle East, thereby developing strategic technological capabilities and business opportunities. Accreditation and certification met a high standard.

11.2.3.3 Operational and Marketing Capability

The corporate and management qualities and capabilities EAL acquired proved beneficial during the early expansion into regional markets and the later multiple crises following the establishment of a socialist regime in 1975. From the early days, TWA instilled in EAL a culture of corporate independence, a need for intensity of learning, and the importance of a strategic approach to marketing. Consequently, EAL's marketing of both domestic and international destinations was aggressive from the start. For instance, EAL surveyed West Africa as early as 1949.[26] In the early 1960s, EAL found that it needed an expanding regional and international flight network to build economies of scale, improve technology, and remain profitable. Consequently, it extended its routes within Africa and to Europe. Soon EAL's annual passenger numbers exceeded 260,000, while its total revenues reached almost ETB 70 million (about US$125,000) by 1971/72 (Appendix). Throughout the 1960s, EAL focused on continuous improvement and took the immense challenges posed by rapid growth as opportunities for accelerated learning, primarily through learning by doing, to ensure survival and sustain the growth

[25] EAL (1971).
[26] EAL (1988).

momentum it had built up. EAL thus vigorously developed its operations and market capability, with TWA as the main driver and as an effective mentor.

11.3 Cruising Altitude: Sustaining Corporate Independence in Turbulent Times, 1975–2000

11.3.1 Crisis Management and Survival, 1975–91

The last quarter of the twentieth century tested EAL with the crises that engulfed Ethiopia, creating instability and economic uncertainty. The airline achieved only modest growth. But its survival in the face of operational challenges and political crisis is testimony to its remarkable progress during the early stage of learning and building absorptive capacity.

Between 1972 and 1975, EAL had already begun the transition to Ethiopian executives and personnel, and after the partnership with TWA was officially terminated in 1975, EAL was managed and operated by Ethiopians.

The first challenge of the period was the dramatic political instability created by two regime changes. Following the toppling of the emperor in the February 1974 revolution, the Derg—a totalitarian military regime—came to power in 1975. The Derg's socialist economic doctrine was a major obstacle to EAL. Derg officials intervened in the airline's internal corporate affairs, dismissing Semret Medhane and appointing a military general as CEO solely on political grounds.[27] The government also interfered in labour relations, compromising EAL's performance, staff discipline, and conformity with industry practice, which later led to major financial losses that brought EAL close to bankruptcy.[28] This crisis continued into the early 1980s.

In many respects, EAL responded effectively to the crises of the second half of the 1970s and most of the 1980s, demonstrating the corporate independence, self-reliance, ability to operate in an unconventional setting, and capacity to manage and survive setbacks it had acquired during the long partnership with TWA. Four concrete examples illustrate this.

First, under pressure from EAL management, Derg officials eventually agreed to appoint someone who understood the industry as CEO. Captain Mohammed, an aviation veteran, accepted the post in 1980 on condition that state intervention in internal matters would stop and that the airline would operate under international business practices rather than socialist doctrines.[29] The Derg accepted the conditions and the new CEO was able to turn around the nearly bankrupt EAL.

[27] EAL (1988).
[28] EAL (1988).
[29] See Oqubay (2019a; 2019b).

Second, the Derg had instructed EAL to cease purchasing US aircraft and to purchase them only from Russia.[30] This would mean a major policy shift for an airline that had built its capabilities and management style on the basis of partnership with a US airline (TWA) and a US aircraft supplier (Boeing). What happened next was clear testimony to EAL's maturity and emergence as an economically crucial industry. EAL management threatened collective resignation, forcing the government to reverse its decision. Subsequently, EAL introduced Boeing 767s, opening new opportunities for non-stop long-distance flights of up to thirteen hours across the Atlantic, and replaced its Boeing B720s with the new Boeing 737s. EAL expanded its technical services and training facilities accordingly.

Third, between 1975 and the fall of the Derg government in 1991, Ethiopia was engulfed in a civil war that drained resources and kept the economy stagnant. The decline in tourism caused shrinkage of domestic networks, currency overvaluation, and anti-export bias, constraining EAL's operations. In response, EAL prioritized its strategic routes and introduced measures to enhance effectiveness. As a result, EAL achieved modest growth in its fleet size and operations. It also made its first attempt to assemble an aircraft—the crop-spraying agro-aircraft, Eshet—under license in 1986.[31] Although this venture proved commercially unviable and was discontinued, it demonstrated EAL's catch-up aspirations. Throughout the 1980s, driven by its motto 'Bringing Africa Together', EAL vigorously expanded its routes to all African regions, a move that undoubtedly helped to save the aviation industry from the fate met by similar industries elsewhere in Africa.

Fourth, the collapse of the Derg regime in 1991 gave rise to a period of tension and uncertainty. The army of the Ethiopian Peoples' Revolutionary Democratic Front (EPRDF) approached the capital Addis Ababa, practically placing it under siege. EAL management decided at this critical juncture to protect and save the assets of the company from damage and destruction should the conflict spill over into the city itself.[32] The management unilaterally decided to move EAL's aircraft to Nairobi, negotiating with the Kenyan Aviation Authority to operate and service EAL's customers from Nairobi until the political tension in Ethiopia abated. This remarkable corporate independence, commitment, and responsibility was only possible because of the corporate culture developed in EAL and the training and commitment of its management.

An important lesson from EAL's experience is its ability to develop a corporate culture and a high level of commitment among top managers and other employees. Part of the explanation may lie in the management style introduced in EAL from its early days, whereby constant engagement by top management with all employees

[30] EAL (1988).

[31] EAL (1988).

[32] Interviews with former CEO Girma Wake and Group CEO Tewolde Gebremariam in 2018 (EAL, 2018b); minutes of the EAL management team.

and careful evaluation of staff welfare was a priority. From the early 1950s, several steps improved the well-being and working conditions of employees, including increased vacation time, recreational facilities for all staff, group accident insurance—the first of its kind in Ethiopia—and a collective bargaining system—also the first of its kind in Ethiopia. These and other measures, such a generous retirement plan introduced in 1969 and suggestion boxes to solicit the views of employees, created a sense of belonging and ownership among employees and a corporate culture that has lasted to this day (EAL 1958; 1959; 1964; 1967).

11.3.2 Transition, Lingering Crisis, and Modest Growth (1991–2000)

For nearly a decade following the fall of the Derg in 1991, Ethiopia was in transition from a closed and socialist-oriented economic system to an open and market-based one. The period was also occupied with recovery from nearly two decades of civil war, economic mismanagement, and neglect of infrastructure and institutions. The reconstruction efforts were both financially and organizationally demanding for the new government, which was simultaneously struggling to re-establish economic relations with traditional trading partners.

The impact of these developments on EAL was mixed. To EAL's benefit, the reconstruction program repaired and upgraded domestic airports, enabling the expansion of domestic routes and the recovery of tourism. The new government's devaluation of the local currency was also favourable for EAL. Reconstruction began to turn the economy from negative to positive growth, as evidenced by the modest 5 per cent annual growth rate achieved following the economic reforms. Economic recovery during the 1990s thus provided a welcome opportunity for EAL to revitalize itself and reinforce the technical and management capabilities it had built over the previous decades. The strategic importance of EAL was further magnified by the Ethio-Eritrean war of 1998–2000 and Eritrea's prior independence from Ethiopia in 1993, which had left Ethiopia landlocked.

But EAL's efforts to reignite growth and resume its expansion were impeded by the political uncertainties and its own changing management during the transition period. Even after 1991, EAL remained in crisis management mode as a result of government interference and the ambiguities of the political and economic environment, according to company insiders. For example, between 1991 and 2000, the board appointed three successive CEOs from within and outside the airline, creating uncertainty and disrupting EAL's longstanding coherent and stable corporate management structure and culture. It also fired thirty-seven senior staff—practically all the top management team—in disagreements over strategy and the future of the airline. A series of ill-advised reforms and policy experiments by the government damaged EAL's performance and undermined the morale of its management team and staff, leading many executive officers and technical personnel to resign. The 1990s were thus a period of transition, confusion, and policy experimentation, and the government's delay in resolving the situation caused unwarranted setbacks in EAL's recovery, growth, and expansion.

This episode shows that a firm's learning and catch-up can be hampered or accelerated by the type of governance and leadership provided. Internal and external crises can waste capabilities created over decades. But crisis in the political and economic environment can also present opportunities for learning by problem-solving and policy experimentation. At EAL, this happened in the 2000s when two EAL veterans, Girma Wake and Tewolde Gebremariam, returned—Wake from Gulf Air to become CEO and Gebremariam from New York to become deputy CEO.[33] The appointment of highly experienced insiders began to turn the fortunes of EAL from managing crises to pursuing growth and upgrading capabilities. The episode also reveals that managing vulnerability and crisis, given their potential to undermine capabilities and hamper catch-up, is as important managing growth.

11.4 Upgrading: High Growth and Catching up in the Twenty-First Century, 2001–18

11.4.1 A New Chapter in Twenty-first-century African Aviation

The 1990s and 2000s brought major changes to the global aviation industry. International competition intensified, spurred by advances in information and communications technology, both in general and in the aviation industry.[34] Mergers and acquisitions and alliances between airlines heightened competition. TWA, with about two hundred aircraft and considered one of the big four US airlines (along with American, United, and Eastern), ceased operating after seventy years and was acquired by American. Many flagship African carriers were also grounded. At the same time, globalization and the growing need for air connectivity increased opportunities for growth and expansion, including in developing countries exhibiting high levels of sustained growth and prosperity. These developments allowed EAL to realize its vision of becoming an industry leader in Africa and to strategize for the twenty-first century.

Economies of scale were essential to EAL's vision. Rapid growth and diversification required not only new aircraft but also technical excellence, new market capacity, organizational capabilities, continuous improvement, and a high level of absorptive capacity. With EAL's survival threatened by the increasingly competitive market environment, a new board and management team unanimously decided to

[33] Tewolde Gebremariam became CEO in early 2011.
[34] Belobaba (2016).

develop a fundamental new vision and long-term plan for rapid growth. Vision 2010 (a five-year plan for 2006–10) and Vision 2025 (a fifteen-year plan for 2011–25) laid out a fundamentally new trajectory for the company.

The new vision and the new management team created dynamism and optimism, and the airline surpassed its Vision 2010 targets with high financial performance and considerable market expansion. Within five years, EAL's fleet had increased by 60 per cent to forty-one commercial aircraft, its annual passenger capacity had doubled to 3.2 million passengers, and its cargo volume had tripled (EAL, 2004; Appendix)). The rapid growth inspired still greater confidence and commitment and more ambitious targets in Vision 2025.[35] Within five years, by 2015, EAL had become the largest African airline. In 2018, it transported more than 12 million passengers (a fourfold increase since 2010) and half a million tons of cargo, and had increased its fleet to more than one hundred new-generation aircraft (a threefold increase since 2010). Its network widened to 115 international destinations, including Los Angeles and Tokyo.[36] Its China–Africa routes alone are expected to carry 1 million passengers in 2018, making EAL the major airline linking Africa with China.[37] This rapid overall expansion has made EAL the most profitable aviation company in Africa, while other African airlines (including Egypt Air, Kenyan Airways, and South African Airways) have struggled to survive. Progress has been achieved in the face of intense competitive pressure from Gulf and Middle Eastern carriers, which enjoyed economies of scale and large direct and indirect subsidies. Competition from Middle Eastern state-supported airlines remains EAL's most formidable challenge. The intensity of international competition, with mergers and alliances, environmental protection requirements (for both air and ground pollution), and accelerated technology advances, make airline survival increasingly challenging. The aerospace manufacturing industry has consolidated, making Airbus and Boeing an oligopoly of commercial aircraft manufacturers.

In short, EAL's intensity of learning, and its determination to develop technological absorptive capabilities, enabled it to survive the crisis period, to reorganize itself for renewed growth and expansion, and to formulate an ambitious vision and a strategy for catch-up.

11.4.2 Modernizing the Fleet and Developing Technological Capability

The size and type of an airline's fleet shape its value to customers and its operational scope and scale. With advanced avionics and aerospace technology,

[35] EAL (2010).
[36] See EAL (2016, 1950–2018a, and 1950–2018b). See also Appendix for trends on growth and performance.
[37] Oqubay and Lin (forthcoming).

commercial aircraft have seen rapid technological progress. EAL was committed to expand and modernize its fleet as part of its upgrading and catch-up strategy by introducing the latest aircraft to secure first-comer advantages. EAL was the first airline in Africa to order the most modern aircraft—the Boeing Dreamliner B787—and the longest-range commercial aircraft—the Boeing B777-200 LR. After lengthy internal debate (and an intense bidding process) EAL decided to diversify its fleet with the Airbus A350, the latest and most environmentally sound aircraft. The technical and operational capabilities EAL accumulated over the years enabled it to acquire the advanced aircraft, which in turn have kept the airline at the frontier of aviation technology, with implications for forming skills, upgrading technology and infrastructure, and building organizational capability.

Although the A350 provided value for money, its acquisition affected EAL's inventory, maintenance facilities, and absorption capacity (in training pilots and technical personnel). All EAL's procurement arrangements include technical specifications and technological capacity development packages (such as training facilities and skill upgrading). EAL originally envisaged acquiring an additional 100 aircraft over fifteen years (to 2030), giving it the advantage of a bulk purchase. The initial aspiration of Vision 2025 was to increase the number of aircraft in the fleet to 120 by 2025 (a 20 per cent increase), subsequently to be revised to 200 (a 100 per cent increase) by 2025–30. Since EAL's annual absorption capacity of new fleet reached twelve aircraft in 2018, doubling the fleet within a decade seems entirely feasible (Appendix).

However, executing the high growth and expansion strategy was by no means smooth due to delays in new aircraft delivery (especially the Dreamliner) and common technical problems in their introduction. The greatest challenges to rapid technological upgrading are preparing sufficient pilots and technicians and managing rapid growth to avoid reducing service quality. Managing growth became a major pressure point, intensifying the need for learning by all staff from cabin crew, pilots, and technicians to the executive leadership. Another major challenge was inadequate physical infrastructure that required a new passenger terminal and cargo terminals. Such tensions are inevitable in a growing and upgrading firm that must improve continuously or risk being paralysed by crises. EAL's prior learning and capability building were key to resolving each problem and engaging in intense learning.

11.4.3 Improving Organizational Capability and Process

Building technological capability is often narrowly associated with acquiring hardware (machinery and equipment), and fostering innovation with dramatic new inventions. But an alternative view sees building technological capability as acquiring a range of abilities, including organizational capabilities and continuous process improvement. Schumpeter, for example, distinguishes categories of innovation, including new products, new production methods, new inputs, new markets, and new methods of business organization.[38] He distinguishes innovation as continuous improvement and incremental change from radical innovation and technological revolution.[39] Organizational capability and continuous process improvement have arguably been central to EAL's Vision 2025 because of the challenges arising from increasing size to seek economies of scale.

11.4.3.1 New Structure and Capability

A new organizational structure became necessary as EAL underwent a strategic shift from airline to a fully diversified aviation group (Ethiopian Aviation Group). Initially, the various services and operations were structured in seven autonomous strategic business units, each operating as an independent profit centre: international passenger service, domestic express service, cargo service, technical services (MRO—maintenance, repair, and overhaul), the aviation academy, ground services, and catering and hotel services.[40] With growing, upgrading capabilities, and diversifying into strategic services, EAL needed a more integrated structure that allowed strategic planning, coherence, performance monitoring, and accountability.

The new structure required a fundamental shift affecting all functions, including EAL's strategy for equity shareholding and in providing operational and management services to other African carriers. EAL acquired a 40 per cent equity share in ASKY (AfricaSKY Airline),[41] including management services, which allowed it to build a West African hub. Similarly, acquisition of a 49 per cent equity share in Air Malawi has enabled EAL to strengthen its southern African hub. Furthermore, in 2018, EAL's overseas operations expanded with the acquisition of equity shareholding in Guinea Airlines (49 per cent), Chad Airlines (49 per cent), Zambia Airways (45 per cent), and management contracts with CEIBA Intercontinental in Equatorial Guinea and Ethiopian Mozambique Airlines, a new domestic carrier in Mozambique.

EAL has also partnered with DHL Logistics (owning 51 per cent of the joint company), aiming to move beyond conventional passenger air services to become

[38] Schumpeter (1942).

[39] Fagerberg (2005); Fagerberg and Godinko (2005).

[40] EAL's MRO services were established in 1957 to provide MRO for aircraft, engines, and components of Ethiopian and third-party customers. At present, the MRO division employs over 1,800 qualified technical staff, and its facility is certified by international regulatory bodies. In addition to the maintenance base in Addis Ababa, the MRO division has some sixty senior and highly qualified maintenance personnel located at forty destinations in Africa, Europe, North America, South America, the Middle East, and the Far East. These technical staff provide line maintenance services to both Ethiopian and other carriers.

[41] ASKY is a private passenger airline, founded by West African governments to operate across several West and Central African countries, and based in Lomé, Togo. EAL is a major shareholder in ASKY and provides training, operational, marketing, and maintenance services under management contracts.

a leading logistics provider in Africa. EAL has initiated a new programme to develop and manage African airports, including air traffic control. The development of a more sophisticated organizational capability, building on knowledge acquired through learning by doing, has thus enabled EAL to spearhead a new strategic initiative, expand revenue streams, and reinforce its presence and competitive position in Africa.[42]

11.4.3.2 Continuous Process Improvement and Performance

Since mid-2000, EAL has developed several internal process improvement schemes, to which it has adhered consistently. Three are worth highlighting.

First, to achieve competitive excellence and enhance and maintain the airline's credibility and safety records, increase proficiency in engine maintenance, aircraft engineering, and planning capability; increase component maintenance, quality assurance, and environmental management system capability; implement the International Air Transport Association Operational Safety Audit programme; and adopt the International Civil Aviation Organization's Safety Management System. EAL also digitized its operations and became a paperless organization.

Second, to ensure continuous improvement, adopt a benchmarking approach that robustly links capability with performance. Although EAL had previously compared its performance with leading African airlines, its board and management decided to upgrade its benchmarking standards to compare its performance with leading global airlines—Singapore Airlines, United, Lufthansa, and Emirates. This has pushed performance closer to the industry's productivity frontier and has had a major impact on EAL's continuous performance improvement.

Third, to develop new market capabilities, build on EAL's core Vision 2025 motto, 'The New Spirit of Africa', as its prime marketing strategy.[43] In 2011, following almost two years of mentoring by Lufthansa that triggered improvements in service, processes, and safety standards, EAL became a member of Star Alliance, one of the largest and oldest global alliances. This consolidated EAL's access to wider global markets. New initiatives to upgrade its services such as Cloud 9 business class and Sheba Miles were introduced in the late 2000s.

11.4.4 Building Technical Capability and Skill Formation

With EAL's Vision 2025 goals, its focus on skill development, and its traditional technical excellence and self-sufficiency, EAL has developed new capabilities and

[42] See Arrow (1962); Cohen and Levinthal (1989).

[43] Over the years, EAL has adjusted its motto to align with its prevailing strategy. It started with 'To go to great length to please,' then 'Bringing Africa together and closer to the world' to reflect its dominance in the African market.

reinforced its absorptive capacity. For example, the aviation academy has invested in state-of-the-art facilities, including simulators that accommodate the latest aircraft, thus expanding its capacity and upgrading to the level of other leading global aviation academies. Similarly, the pilot school has opened centres in five cities and improved its intake and quality of pilot training. Both the EAL technical school and the cabin crew school have also expanded and upgraded. The technical school can now train more people than EAL can absorb, producing a surplus for the market.

But executive leadership development at different levels is a major limitation. With continued growth of the EAL Group, upgraded human resource management will be essential to motivate and retain the company's 15,000-strong workforce. Priorities include an employee housing project, performance-based payments, staff appraisal, and building a productive relationship between management and unions. Retention of core technical staff is critical to technological capability and organizational memory. To date, the turnover of pilots and technicians has been limited to 1 per cent a year, much lower than the industry norm.

Preparations for an aerospace manufacturing facility—part of the government's vision of Ethiopia as Africa's leading manufacturing hub—are complete. With system integrators such as Boeing and Airbus dominating aerospace manufacturing, the success of Ethiopia's initiative depends on EAL's ability to work closely with commercial aircraft manufacturers, component suppliers, and subcontractors. EAL signed a tripartite agreement with sub-manufacturers along with Boeing, Airbus, and other manufacturers in 2018 and has studied existing aerospace manufacturing hubs, such as those in Morocco and Singapore, to extract lessons and ensure the success of its new venture. This new frontier has great potential for technological spillovers and linkages to domestic manufacturing capability. A unique characteristic of EAL and a potential lesson for other late-latecomer firms has been its investment in institutions that enabled it to develop its absorptive capacity. It has invested US$500 million in upgrading its aviation academy and technical services infrastructure and another US $500 million in hubs infrastructure.[44]

11.5 Air Miles: Implications for Policy and Technological Capability and Lessons for Late-Latecomers

11.5.1 The Government and EAL's Catch-up

Technological learning and catch-up in Ethiopia's aviation industry would have been impossible without the government's strong commitment and support. EAL

[44] Terminal 2, which cost close to $400 million, was inaugurated on 27 January 2019. The new terminal increases passenger capacity from 12 million to 22 million. The first phase of its five-star hotel complex was also completed.

was established by the state at a time when no domestic private company had the required capacity, and it was nurtured by the state as a major industrial policy instrument for several decades. From the beginning, EAL was built into a national champion by the government, which maintained self-discipline in its relationship with the airline while playing a developmental role. Even during the 1975–2000 phase, when government interference posed major operational challenges, it was clear that ultimately the government of the day had no interest in jeopardizing the survival of EAL, which has always been regarded as a flagship state enterprise with unofficial corporate independence.

During the 2001–18 phase of EAL's development, the government used the airline as an instrument of industrial policy and offered it new growth opportunities by pushing it to serve the export sector.[45] The Ethiopian floriculture industry, whose development began in the early 2000s, would not have expanded without EAL investment and services. EAL also promotes tourism in all its destinations.

EAL itself has become the largest single generator of export earnings for Ethiopia, accounts for 4 per cent of GDP, and has directly or indirectly created employment for fifty thousand people. It has achieved a high level of domestic technological capability in a technology-intensive industry, and it serves as a role model for both state-owned and private African firms.

Government ownership has provided stability, growth opportunities, and the ability to pursue a long-term strategy rather than short-term profitability. The corporate culture and management capability developed during EAL's early evolution were clearly instrumental in generating a sense of independence and self-reliance. Equally important is the operational autonomy provided by EAL's corporate governance structure, notwithstanding isolated but damaging instances of interference. For example, it has been customary under successive regimes for the ministry of finance to pay for EAL services for the head of state or prime minister, and even in times of conflict, the government must compensate the airline for cargo transport services. The government's inability to subsidize EAL has clearly provided the discipline to EAL to ensure fiscal responsibility.

The case of EAL contradicts the myth that industrial policy should be limited to latent comparative advantage and new comparative advantage cannot be created in highly competitive industries. It also defies the notions that ownership determines performance and that public ownership is inferior to private, EAL having performed considerably better than many privately owned airlines. EAL has demonstrated the advantages of long-term strategic orientation rather than the short-term profit orientation dominant in the Anglo-Saxon corporate world. And it has shown that industrial policies are not limited to the manufacturing sector, but can encompass high-productivity service sectors.

[45] Oqubay (2019b). See also Cheru, Cramer, and Oqubay (2019).

11.5.2 The Dynamics of Technological Learning

EAL's story also demonstrates that technological learning does not occur in a vacuum, but is organically intertwined with a firm's struggle to survive and grow. Despite the inherent tensions, EAL had to develop its own absorptive capacity, which thrived with the company's growth and was shaped by its strategic vision and choices. This experience challenges the idea that prior knowledge and absorptive capacity are prerequisites for learning and technological capability building, especially for technological learning and catch-up by late-latecomers with underdeveloped domestic absorptive capacity. Rapid expansion and the gap in coping with growth pressured EAL's management and staff to focus on rapid development of technological capability. Reciprocally, however, EAL's accumulation of technological capabilities and growing confidence about its future, especially after 2000, shaped its vision and strategy. EAL's ability to exceed the goals of Vision 2010 encouraged it to adopt a new and more ambitious trajectory in Vision 2025, which in turn added impetus to revise the company's targets. While long-term strategy and vision were essential, building technological capability also required continuous assessment of the external and internal environment and the capacity to gauge and align the strategic drive. Vision and strategies are not static, and their interactions with technological capability go in both directions.

EAL's experience shows that technological capability is built at the firm level and that sectoral capability is expanded by the presence of competitive firms. So, firm dynamics are the most decisive factor. Technological capability development and intensity of learning become yet more critical due to the growth of the firm and, in the case of EAL, due to intensified international competition in the aviation industry in the early twenty-first century. Not only has learning become more intense, but its complexity has increased as new organizational capabilities are required to develop new markets, achieve continuous process improvements, develop sophisticated skills and facilities, establish a new structure and business model, and achieve new performance milestones. The EAL experience also shows that learning by doing is not limited to imitation, but also involves building capability through continuous process improvements. For EAL, learning by doing involved incremental innovations—suggesting the possibility of creating paths to developing entirely new industries.

Vital to EAL's catch-up was the passionate and concerted development of technological capability and dynamic learning by doing that blended incremental innovations in response to the challenges and opportunities the firm faced. Learning and catch-up are facilitated by the very newness of an industry such as aviation and thus critically benefit from an eye to the future and a long-term approach. The intensity of learning is promoted by aviation's very narrow latitude for poor performance, since high safety standards leave no room for failure.[46] The capital intensity of the industry makes operating at full capacity critical and sustaining creditworthiness a precondition for survival and growth. Intense international competition, which leaves no room for inefficiency, further increases pressure for learning.

11.6 A Safe Flight: Conclusions from the Journey of Ethiopian Airlines

The EAL experience presents a unique example of firm-level learning and catching up in an industry considered alien to a late-latecomer country struggling to reach middle-income level. The relevance of the Ethiopian experience to other twenty-first-century late-latecomers is less clear, depending on country specificity, government commitment, institutional development, and the internal and external policy environments.

Broadly, however, a review of the ups and downs in the transformation of EAL from a simple domestic airline into an internationally competitive aviation industry reveals five critical factors:

First, the more backward and late-starting a country is, the more intensive and assertive the state response needed for technological learning to influence capability building and catch-up. This is confirmed both by EAL's experience and by empirical research on the catch-up of East Asian economies.

Second, twentieth-century economic history clearly links learning to the rare instances of catching up. As Amsden highlighted, 'Diversity notwithstanding, all late industrializers have in common industrialization on the basis of learning, which has conditioned how they behaved.'[47] Learning by doing and emulation aimed at equalling or surpassing others is critical for late industrialization, especially in the early stages.[48] In EAL's experience, *intensity, pace,* and *direction* of learning are key determinants of technological learning, especially learning by doing.

Third, *path following* and, ultimately, *path creation* are required for catching up to leading firms or countries.[49] In this complex process, learning by doing and emulation must eventually combine with innovating.

Fourth, firms are the key drivers and the foundation of technological learning, although sectoral-level learning creates catch-up of the overall economy through the cumulative development of sectoral and national systems.[50] As EAL's experience shows, firm-level technological catch-up can be achieved while economic catch-up lags behind.

[46] Hirschman (1967).

[47] Amsden (1989: viii).

[48] While 'true innovation and learning by doing' are critical for overall productivity catch-up, learning by doing 'is arguably the most important source' in mature industries (Solow, 1997: 33).

[49] Lee (2013); Lee and Malerba (2018).

[50] Lee and Malerba (2018); Oqubay (2015).

Fifth, for late-latecomers, imported technologies and know-how are important sources of technological learning and capability building.[51] They may come through trade, turnkey projects, management contracts, technical cooperation, partnerships with leading global firms, and other ways. Just as technology transfer was an important source of learning and catch-up for nineteenth-century latecomers industrializing in continental Europe, so it is now for twenty-first-century late-latecomers. The main difference is that twenty-first-century latecomers have a wide choice of sources of new technologies—many emerging economies are in a position to supply them. However, the jury is still out on whether the diversity of sources has a qualitatively different impact on the pace and direction of late-latecomers learning and catching up.

In general, technological development paths are unique and country specific. Latecomers cannot simply copy or emulate them. Although the experiences of other firms or countries can provide valuable lessons, the most successful learning is based on adapting to local peculiarities and context: 'Catch up does not mean just cloning. What is actually achieved by successful catching up invariably diverges in certain ways from practices in the countries serving as benchmark models. In fact, this divergence reflects the fact that exact copying is almost impossible,' according to Lee and Malerba.[52]

This study has reviewed the path followed by EAL in transforming itself from a simple domestic airline into an internationally competitive and dynamic aviation industry. Three key points may serve as lessons for other late-latecomers:

First, TWA served as a role model and a source of inspiration and experience. The selection by the government of a reliable technological partner and teacher was a critical strategic choice that affected the intensity of learning and transfer of knowledge and know-how, as well as the pace and direction of catch-up.[53] Learning by doing played a dominant role in EAL's technological learning and catch-up. The investment in capability-enhancing facilities and infrastructure accentuated EAL's learning intensity and broadened its capacity to 'identify, assimilate, and exploit' knowledge from the environment.[54]

Second, the government's strong commitment to Ethiopianization—to building a national carrier entirely run by Ethiopians—shaped the learning process. From day one, the Ethiopian government was keen to make this strategy work. The supportive US political environment and the commitment to excellence of the foreign partner were also helpful. Ultimately, the commitment and readiness to learn and the process fostering this outcome primarily determined the intensity of learning.

[51] See Oqubay and Ohno (2019).

[52] Lee and Malerba (2018: 3).

[53] TWA's motivation was not simply money but also pride in helping establish a new and high-quality airline service in Africa that reflected the global standing of TWA itself.

[54] See Cohen and Levinthal (1989: 569).

Finally, crisis management was critical to increasing the intensity of learning. EAL had to survive and expand in difficult situations, and the intensity of airline industry competition with a narrow latitude for poor performance offered critical pull.

Acknowledgements

The authors thank Kenichi Ohno, Dirk Willem ti Veld, Christopher Cramer, Tewolde Gebremariam, and Fantu Cheru for useful comments. Special thanks go to Tewolde Gebremariam, the Group CEO of EAL, without whom this chapter could not have been written. We are grateful to Henok Teferra, Girma Shiferaw, Wogayehu Terefe, Aniley Eshetu, and Tigist Tassew of EAL; our research assistants Yohannes Gebru and Meron Tilahun for data collection; and to Deborah Mekonen and Binyam Arkebe for improvements to the draft study and for continued support.

Appendix: Growth and Performance Trends (1946–2018)

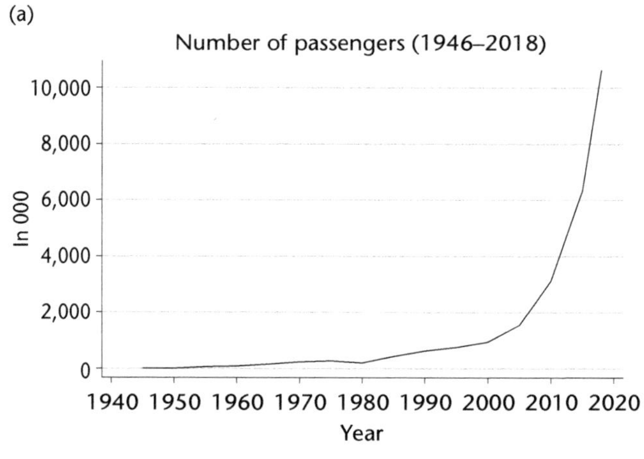

Figure 11A.1 EAL growth and performance trends (1946–2018)
Source: Ethiopian Airlines Annual Reports (1946–2018).

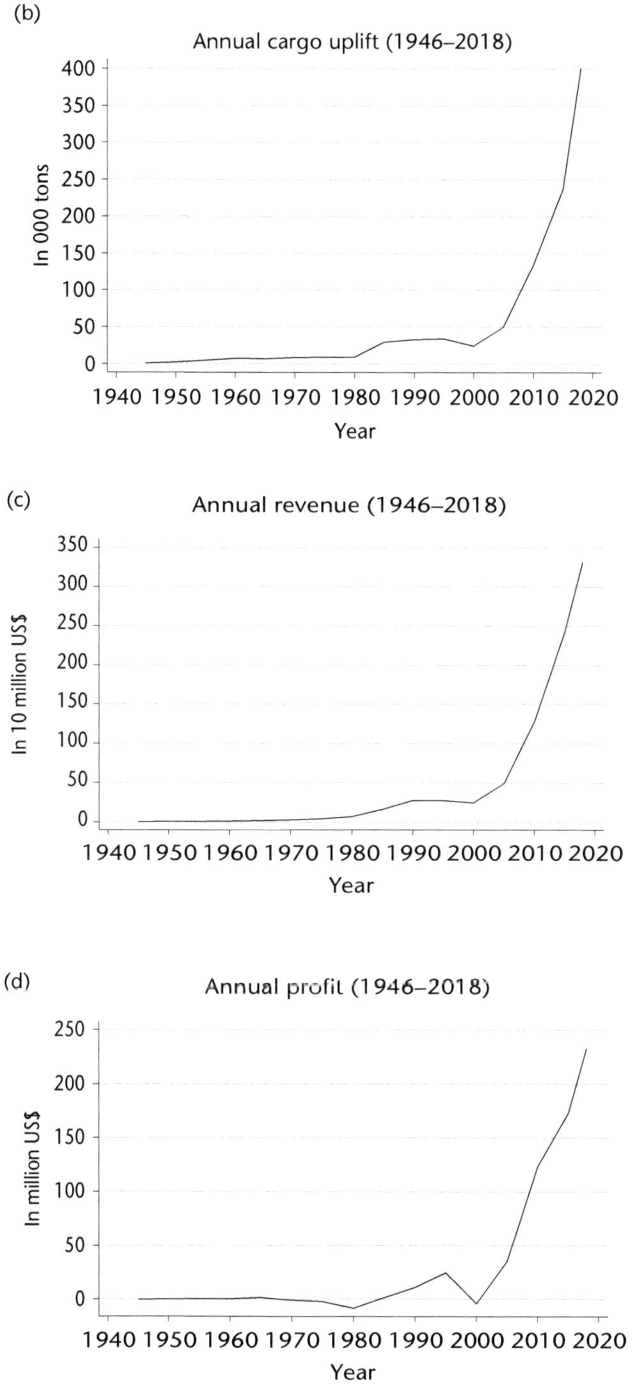

Figure 11A.1 Continued

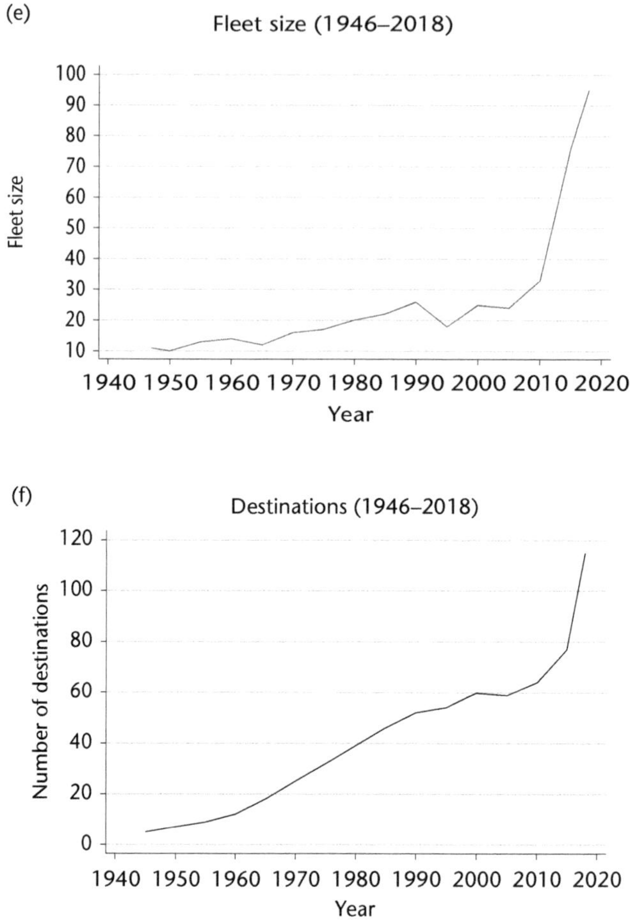

Figure 11A.1 Continued

References

Airline Weekly (2018) 'Independent Worldwide Coverage.' No. 678, 2 July.

Amsden, Alice (1989) *Asia's Next Giant: South Korea and Late Industrialization.* Oxford: Oxford University Press.

Amsden, Alice (2001) *The 'Rise of the Rest': Challenges to the West from the Late Industrializing Economies.* Oxford: Oxford University Press.

Arrow, Kenneth (1962) 'The Economic Implications of Learning by Doing', *Review of Economic Studies* 28: 155–73.

Bell, Martin (1984) '"Learning" and the Accumulation of Industrial Technological Capacity in Developing Countries', in M. Fransman and K. King (eds) *Technological Capability in the Third World.* London: Palgrave Macmillan, pp. 187–209.

Belobaba, Peter (2016) 'Introduction and Overview', in Peter Belobaba, Amedeo Odoni, and Cynthia Barnhart (eds) *A Global Airline Industry*, 2nd ed. West Sussex: Wiley, pp. 1–18.

Cheru, Fantu, Christopher Cramer, and Arkebe Oqubay (eds) (2019) *The Oxford Handbook of the Ethiopian Economy*. Oxford: Oxford University Press.

Christian Science Monitor (1988) 'West Africa Tries to Make its State-owned Airlines Fly Right: Managing a Capitalist Success in Marxist Ethiopia.' 22 November. Available at http://www.csmonitor.com/1988/1122/ffair.html.

Cohen, Wesley and Daniel Levinthal (1989) 'Innovation and Learning: The Two Faces of R&D', *Economic Journal* 99(September): 569–96.

Cohen, Wesley and Daniel Levinthal (1990) 'Absorptive Capacity: A New Perspective on Learning and Innovation', *Administrative Science Quarterly* 35(1), Special Issue: *Technology, Organizations, and Innovation*: 128–52.

Cohen, Stephen S. and J. Bradford DeLong (2016) *Concrete Economics: The Hamilton Approach to Economic Growth and Policy*. Boston, MA: Harvard Business Review Press.

Cramer, Christopher, Arkebe Oqubay, and John Sender (forthcoming) *African Economic Development: Evidence, Theory, and Policy*. Oxford: Oxford University Press.

EAL (1950–2018) Minutes of EAL Board of Directors. Addis Ababa, unpublished.

EAL (1958, 1959, 1964, 1967) Annual Report. Addis Ababa.

EAL (1971) Annual Report. Addis Ababa.

EAL (1988) 'Bringing Africa Together: The History of an Airline.' Addis Ababa.

EAL (2000–18) Annual performance reviews of EAL. Addis Ababa, unpublished.

EAL (2000–18) Minutes of EAL management team. Addis Ababa, unpublished.

EAL (2004) 'Vision 2010: ET's Growth Strategy.' Addis Ababa.

EAL (2010) 'Vision 2025 and Strategic Roadmap (Scaling up of ET's Growth Strategy).' Addis Ababa.

EAL (2016) Sixty years fleet data. Addis Ababa, Ethiopia, unpublished.

EAL (2018a) Factsheet. March, unpublished.

EAL (2018b) Interview with Ethiopian Aviation Group CEO Tewolde Gebremariam.

EAL (2018c) TWA–EAL agreements, unpublished.

Economist, The (1987) 'In Search of Excellence, the Hard Way', 31 December.

Economist, The (2018) 'Ethiopian Airlines Is Founding New African Flag Carriers'. Available at https://amp.economist.com/gulliver/2018/09/11/ethiopian-airlines-is-founding-new-african-flag-carriers.

Fagerberg, Jan (2005) 'Innovation: A Guide to the Literature', in Jan Fagerberg, David Mowery, and Richard Nelson (eds) *The Oxford Handbook of Innovation*. Oxford: Oxford University Press, pp. 1–26.

Fagerberg, Jan and Mauel Godinho (2005) 'Innovation and Catching-up', in Jan Fagerberg, David Mowery, and Richard Nelson (eds) *The Oxford Handbook of Innovation*. Oxford: Oxford University Press, pp. 514–42.

Freeman, Christopher (1987) *Technology Policy and Economic Performance: Lessons from Japan*. London: Pinter Publishers.

Gerschenkron, Alexander (1962) *Economic Backwardness in Historical Perspective*. Cambridge, MA: Harvard University Press.

Hirschman, Albert (1958) *Strategy of Economic Development*. New Haven, CT: Yale University Press.

Hirschman, Albert (1967) *Development Projects Observed*. Washington, DC: Brookings Institution.

Hobday, M. (2000) 'East versus Southeast Asian Innovation Systems: Comparing OEM and TNC-led Growth in Electronics', in Linsu Kim and Richard Nelson (eds) *Technology, Learning and Innovation*. Cambridge: Cambridge University Press, pp. 129–69.

Huo, Jingjing (2015) *How Nations Innovate: The Political Economy of Technological Innovation in Affluent Capitalist Economies*. Oxford: Oxford University Press.

Kim, Linsu (1997) *Imitation to Innovation: The Dynamics of Korea's Technological Learning*. Cambridge, MA: Harvard Business School Press.

Lall, Sanjaya (1992) 'Technological Capabilities and Industrialization', *World Development* 20(2): 165–86.

Lee, Keun (2013) *Schumpeterian Analysis of Economic Catch-up: Knowledge, Path-Creation and the Middle Income*. Cambridge: Cambridge University Press.

Lee, Keun and Franco Malerba (2018) 'Economic Catch-up by Latecomers as an Evolutionary Process', in Richard Nelson (ed.) *Modern Evolutionary Economics: An Overview*. Cambridge: Cambridge University Press.

List, Friedrich (1856) *National System of Political Economy*. 4 vols. Memphis, TN: Lippincott.

Lundvall, Bengt-Åke (1992) *National Systems of Innovation: Towards a Theory of Innovation and Interactive Learning*. London: Pinter.

Nelson, Richard (ed.) (1993) *National Innovation System: A Comparative Analysis*. Oxford: Oxford University Press.

Oqubay, Arkebe (2015) *Made in Africa: Industrial Policy in Ethiopia*. Oxford: Oxford University Press.

Oqubay, Arkebe (2019a) 'Ethiopia: Learning from an Experiment', in Célestin Monga and Justin Yifu Lin (eds) *Oxford Handbook of Structural Transformation*. Oxford: Oxford University Press.

Oqubay, Arkebe (2019b) 'Industrial Policy and Late Industrialization in Ethiopia', in Fantu Cheru, Christopher Cramer, and Arkebe Oqubay (eds) *Oxford Handbook of the Ethiopian Economy*. Oxford: Oxford University Press.

Oqubay, Arkebe and Justin Yifu Lin (2019) *China–Africa and an Economic Transformation*. Oxford: Oxford University Press.

Oqubay, Arkebe and Justin Yifu Lin (forthcoming) *The Oxford Handbook of Industrial Hubs and Economic Development*. Oxford: Oxford University Press.

Oqubay, Arkebe and Kenichi Ohno (2019) 'How Nations Learn: Technological Learning, Industrial Policy, and Catch-up', in Cheru Fantu, Christopher Cramer, and Arkebe Oqubay (eds) *Oxford Handbook of the Ethiopian Economy*. Oxford: Oxford University Press.

Schumpeter, Joseph (1942) *Capitalism, Socialism and Democracy*. New York: Harper.

Skytrax (2018) 'The Best Airlines in Africa 2018.' https://www.worldairlineawards.com/best-airlines-2018-by-region/.

Spencer, John (2006) *Ethiopia at Bay: A Personal Account of the Haile Selassie Years*. Hollywood, CA: Tsehai.

Solow, Robert (1997) *Learning from 'Learning by Doing': Lessons for Economic Growth*. Stanford, CA: Stanford University Press.

Wade, Robert (1990) *Governing the Market: Economic Theory and the Role of the Government in East Asian Industrialization*. Princeton, NJ: Princeton University Press.

12
Learning to Catch up in South East Asia

Khuong Vu and Kris Hartley

12.1 Introduction

A developing country encounters both opportunities and challenges when embarking on economic development. Gerschenkron (1962) argues that developing countries have the distinct advantage of backwardness, including the opportunity to acquire technologies and best practices already developed by more advanced countries. However, Abramovitz (1994) finds that this potential has not been fully realized across all developing countries, due in part to variations in technological congruence and social capabilities. Furthermore, Quah (1993, 1996) finds that cross-country distribution of per capita income is moving towards a twin-peaked profile, suggesting the presence of enduring structural hindrances to economic catch-up. In seeking to understand these structural determinants, many studies argue that total factor productivity (TFP) growth plays an essential role (Aghion and Howitt, 2007; Baumol, 1986; Dowrick and Nguyen, 1989; Easterly and Levine, 2001; Fagerberg, 1987; Klenow and Rodriguez, 1997; Lee, 2013; Solow, 1957). While this finding is significant, TFP driven by technological progress alone is not a sufficient basis for steering catch-up efforts, especially in developing countries. Indeed, Lin (2009, 2011) emphasizes the importance, in driving industrial upgrading and economic catch-up, of economic strategy that is focused on embracing comparative advantage and facilitating the change in endowment structure in favour of capital intensity.[1]

Understanding the policy frameworks and mechanisms that enable a developing country to achieve catch-up through a multi-pronged effort is not only theoretically meaningful but also practically useful. This chapter examines the catch-up performance of Asian countries between 1995 and 2015, with insights into underlying determinants and the contribution of learning efforts. The success of Asian countries relative to those in other parts of the world confirms that capital accumulation and TFP growth have been important drivers of catch-up,

[1] Ohno (2013) and Oqubay (2015), among others, provide valuable insights into the role of industrial policy in development success of a developing nation.

and that the absence of strategic efforts to exploit these drivers was a significant hindrance in some countries.

In problematizing this issue, this chapter introduces the concept of nation learning for catch-up, defined as consistent and strategic cross-sector efforts to identify pathways towards economic catch-up. Efforts to learn how high rates of capital accumulation and TFP growth can be sustained are, for the purpose of this study, paramount objectives in nation learning. As developing countries tend to have comparatively low levels of capital stock per capita, fostering catch-up by emphasizing capital accumulation is a defensible approach. One example is Vietnam, which is among the most successful Asian countries in parlaying capital accumulation into catch-up. Playing a crucial role in helping a government make sound strategic choices, nation learning can include a variety of approaches to rethinking the fundamental concepts of economic development, such as adopting a market economy, reorienting the private sector to embrace trends like globalization and the information and communication technology (ICT) revolution, and enhancing investment attractiveness through facilitative infrastructure, regulatory efficiency, and workforce up-skilling.

At the same time, lagging efforts to promote TFP growth are a hindrance for countries that have otherwise successfully boosted capital accumulation; examples are Vietnam, Indonesia, and Bangladesh. These countries shared two revealing features over the study period: contribution of TFP growth to catch-up performance was negative, and efforts to improve three conditions conducive to TFP growth (technology acquisition, innovation, and control of corruption) were insufficient. Nation learning with a focus on sustaining TFP growth alongside rapid capital accumulation requires vigorous efforts to build high-performing institutions and coordination capabilities.

The remainder of this chapter is structured as follows. The first section examines the global dynamics of economic catch up over the period 1995–2015, covering 167 countries. A catch-up performance index (CUPI) is introduced, and an analysis of sources of catch-up performance for Asian countries reveals insights into the importance of nation learning. Next is a deeper examination of the case of Vietnam and comparator countries in Asia, highlighting strategic approaches to boosting capital accumulation and factors underlying low TFP growth. The concept of nation learning for economic catch-up is introduced and a model for nation learning that emphasizes the role of government is presented. The final section summarizes the results and concludes with broader implications for research and practice.

12.2 Asian Countries and the Global Dynamics of Economic Catch-up

12.2.1 Catch-up Performance Index

To assess the catch-up performance of country i over T-year period $[0, T]$, we construct a catch-up performance index (CUPI) defined as follows:

$$CUPI_{0,T}^{i} = ln\left[\frac{rel\_y_{T}^{i}}{rel\_y_{0}^{i}}\right]/T \tag{12.1}$$

where $rel\_y_{t}^{i}$ is per capita income of country i in year t relative to the United States:[2]

$$rel\_y_{t}^{i} = \frac{y_{t}^{i}}{y_{t}^{US}} \tag{12.2}$$

Note that y_{t}^{i} and y_{t}^{US}, which are, respectively, the per capita income of country i and the United States in year t, are measured in purchasing power parity (PPP) dollars at constant prices.

By definition, $CUPI_{0,T}^{i}>0$ if country i is catching up $(rel\_y_{T}^{i}>rel\_y_{0}^{i})$, < 0 if it is falling behind $(rel\_y_{T}^{i}<rel\_y_{0}^{i})$, and $= 0$ if it is neither catching up nor falling behind $(rel\_y_{T}^{i} = rel\_y_{0}^{i})$.

12.2.2 Data and Results

We use the World Bank Development Indicators (WDI) dataset to compute the CUPI over a twenty-year period (1995–2015) for all countries with available data on per capita income (measured in PPP US$ at constant prices). The result shows that of the 167 countries in the dataset, 114 (68 per cent) were catching up and fifty-three (32 per cent) were falling behind (details on the CUPI for all 167 countries are provided in Appendix 12.1). Table 12.1 reports the result for nineteen Asian countries.

Three observations emerge from Table 12.1. First, nearly 90 per cent of Asian countries were in catch-up mode, compared to only 68 per cent across all 167 countries studied. In particular, China and India—the world's two most populous countries and together accounting for more than one-third of the world's population—were among the top five catch-up leaders. This is evidence of Asia's general rise in the global economy. Second, the coefficient of variation (CV) on per capita income for the nineteen Asian countries declined from 1.542 in 1995 to 1.156 in 2015. This is evidence of a convergence trend among Asian countries, although

[2] Woo (2011) calls this relative income level the 'Catch-up Index' (CUI).

Table 12.1 Catch-up performance of Asian countries, 1995–2015 (sorted by CUPI score in decreasing order)

Country	CUPI (1995–2015)	Relative income level (United States=100)	
		1995	2015
1. Myanmar	7.08	2.3	9.4
2. China	6.89	6.5	25.8
3. Cambodia	4.02	2.8	6.2
4. Laos	3.70	4.8	10.1
5. India	3.68	5.2	10.9
6. Vietnam	3.66	5.2	10.8
7. Sri Lanka	3.04	11.4	21.0
8. Bangladesh	2.44	3.7	6.0
9. South Korea	2.14	42.6	65.2
10. Singapore	1.46	113.6	152.2
11. Malaysia	1.36	36.6	48.0
12. Philippines	1.36	10.0	13.2
13. Indonesia	1.29	15.2	19.7
14. Nepal	1.24	3.4	4.4
15. Hong Kong	1.07	82.0	101.4
16. Thailand	1.00	23.9	29.1
17. Pakistan	0.23	8.5	8.9
18. Japan	-0.67	82.1	71.9
19. Brunei	-2.27	219.8	139.7
Mean (M)	*2.25*	*35.76*	*39.67*
Standard deviation (SD)	*2.30*	*55.17*	*45.88*
CV=SD/M	**1.02**	**1.54**	**1.16**

Source: Authors' calculation from WDI and APO datasets.

variations in absolute measures of per capita income remained large. Third, most Asian countries remained far below the United States on per capita income, ranging from a 2015 relative level of 4.4 (United States = 100) for Nepal to 152.2 for Singapore and including only modest levels for India (10.9) and China (25.8).

12.2.3 Sources of Economic Catch-up

Among the nineteen Asian countries examined in Table 12.1, seventeen have accessible data on growth-accounting decomposition as compiled by the Asian Productivity Organization (APO).[3] As presented in Appendix 12.2, the CUPI for each country can be decomposed into three sources: capital deepening, labour participation, and TFP growth. Each of these sources captures how well a given country performs compared to the United States over the period of examination.

[3] The APO dataset is available on line at http://www.apo-tokyo.org/wedo/measurement.

Table 12.2 Drivers of Asian countries' catch-up performance, 1995–2015 (sorted by CUPI score in decreasing order)

Country	CUPI	Contribution to CUPI by Component					
		Capital deepening	Labour participation	TFP growth	Capital deepening	Labour participation	TFP growth
		Value			*Share (total=100%)*		
China	*6.89*	*3.45*	*0.43*	*3.01*	50.1%	6.2%	43.7%
Cambodia	*4.02*	*1.60*	*1.38*	*1.04*	39.8%	34.3%	25.9%
Laos	*3.70*	*3.40*	*0.28*	*0.03*	91.7%	7.5%	0.8%
India	*3.68*	*1.37*	*0.07*	*2.24*	37.3%	1.8%	60.8%
Vietnam	*3.66*	*4.20*	*0.13*	*−0.66*	114.6%	3.5%	−18.1%
Sri Lanka	*3.04*	*1.20*	*0.69*	*1.15*	39.5%	22.7%	37.8%
Bangladesh	*2.44*	*2.80*	*0.47*	*−0.82*	114.5%	19.2%	−33.7%
South Korea	*2.14*	*1.55*	*0.05*	*0.53*	72.6%	2.5%	24.9%
Singapore	*1.46*	*0.92*	*0.54*	*0.00*	63.0%	36.7%	0.3%
Philippines	*1.36*	*0.32*	*0.27*	*0.77*	23.7%	19.8%	56.5%
Malaysia	*1.36*	*0.08*	*0.26*	*1.02*	6.1%	19.0%	74.9%
Indonesia	*1.29*	*1.62*	*0.49*	*−0.83*	125.9%	38.2%	−64.1%
Nepal	*1.24*	*0.54*	*0.62*	*0.08*	43.8%	49.7%	6.5%
Hong Kong	*1.07*	*0.68*	*0.35*	*0.04*	63.9%	32.6%	3.5%
Thailand	*1.00*	*0.56*	*−0.15*	*0.59*	56.3%	−15.5%	59.2%
Pakistan	*0.23*	*−0.53*	*0.31*	*0.45*	−225.4%	133.0%	192.4%
Japan	*−0.67*	*−0.68*	*−0.19*	*0.21*	102.4%	28.3%	−30.7%
Median	**1.46**	**1.20**	**0.31**	**0.45**	**56.3%**	**19.8%**	**24.9%**

Source: Authors' calculation from WDI and APO datasets.

Table 12.2 reports the sources of CUPI for the seventeen Asian countries over the period 1995–2015.

Several observations emerge from Table 12.2. First, for most countries, all three components—capital deepening, labour participation, and TFP growth—played a role in driving catch-up performance. This signals the importance of a comprehensive approach that fosters catch-up through multiple avenues. Second, capital deepening is the leading driver of catch-up performance for ten of the seventeen countries under consideration: Vietnam, China, Laos, Bangladesh, Indonesia, Cambodia, South Korea, Sri Lanka, Singapore, and Hong Kong. This implies that promoting capital deepening should be a top priority in developing a catch-up strategy. Third, the contribution of TFP growth was positive for fourteen of the seventeen countries but negative for only three: Vietnam, Bangladesh, and Indonesia, all of which showed high catch-up performance driven largely by capital deepening. The cases of Vietnam, Bangladesh, and Indonesia deserve more in-depth examination to understand obstacles to TFP growth and the risk of policy bias towards capital deepening.

The relationship between capital deepening and TFP growth (Figure 12.1) is negative but statistically insignificant, as captured by equation y = –0.0495x + 0.6131 ($R^2 0$). The three countries previously specified—Vietnam, Bangladesh, and Indonesia—lie notably below the trend line, indicating that their TFP growth or efficiency of using production inputs was much lower than expected levels. This suggests that the countries may have faced significant obstacles to TFP promotion efforts or that they overlooked this strategy due to a bias in favour of promoting capital deepening. Among these three countries, Vietnam stands out as the most notable case because it was also among the top five catch-up performers and recorded the highest

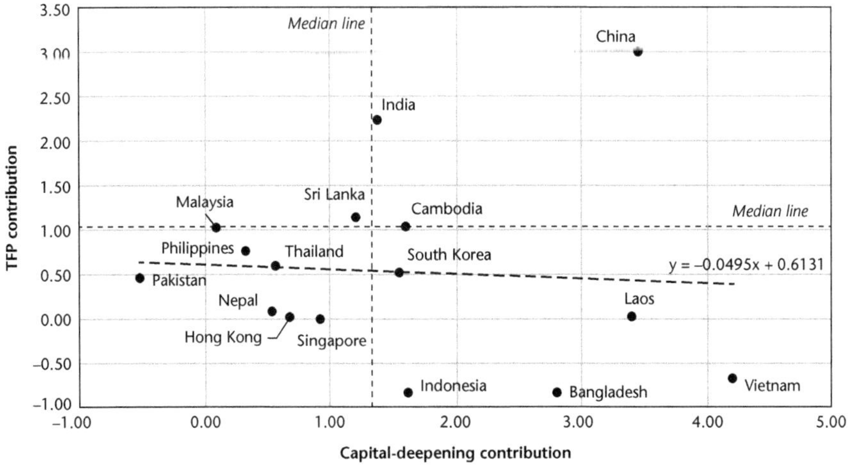

Figure 12.1 Contribution to catch-up performance: TFP growth vs. capital deepening

Source. Authors' calculation from APO data (http://www.apo-tokyo.org/wedo/measurement)

magnitude of capital deepening contribution among the seventeen countries considered. Below we consider the case of Vietnam in more detail in order to understand why the country successfully mobilized capital investment but failed to achieve meaningful TFP growth throughout its catch-up phase.

12.3 Vietnam's Nation Learning for Economic Catch-up

Over the past three decades, the economic reforms launched by Vietnam in December 1986 have produced considerable achievements in shifting the country from a Soviet-styled planned economy to a market-oriented and highly open system. The economic development process in Vietnam throughout this reform period was a hybrid approach drawing loosely from three development models: the China model, in which proactive reforms to modernize the economy were combined with adoption of market principles; the Africa model, in which aid donors had substantial influence on the country's reform agenda and sources of capital investment; and the Singapore model, in which the country attracted investment from multinational companies (MNCs) as a driver of economic development. Behind this profound economic transformation was a robust learning effort, especially in rethinking the fundamental concepts of economic development and making strategic choices. Specific initiatives included the following:

- Adopting market economy principles, enhancing the effectiveness of market forces, and legalizing and promoting the private sector;
- Opening up the economy and fostering global integration;
- Creating a favourable environment for business by stabilizing political and macroeconomic conditions;
- Giving priority to investments in key infrastructure projects;
- Embracing the ICT revolution and leveraging ICT to promote growth;
- Investing in human capital development.

In addition to these initiatives, Vietnam specifically emphasized benchmarking as a tool to foster nation learning. At the national level, the government has used yearly global rankings such as the Ease of Doing Business (EDB) index by the World Bank and the Global Competitiveness Report by the World Economic Forum to identify areas for improving the country's business environment. For example, the government promulgated a decree that outlines objectives and strategies to be a leader among ASEAN countries on the EDB ranking.[4] For

[4] The EDB ranking is based on a composite index constructed from ten sub-indices: Starting a Business; Dealing with Construction Permits; Getting Electricity; Registering Property; Getting Credit;

benchmarking that fosters learning at the provincial level, the government has also relied on the Provincial Competitiveness Index (PCI),[5] compiled annually since 2005 by the Vietnam Chamber of Commerce (VCCI) and USAID experts. The PCI report ranks Vietnam's provinces and province-level cities on economic competitiveness. This ranking has proved highly effective in encouraging provinces and cities, especially those with lower performance, to review their policy strategies and improve their business environments.

Vietnam's efforts to develop and implement sound strategic choices have produced measurable results. As shown in Table 12.3, Vietnam performs favourably among its Asian peers on factors influencing capital investment, including business environment (proxied by rankings on ease of doing business and political stability), infrastructure development (electricity consumption per capita and growth in electricity generation), embrace of the ICT revolution (Facebook penetration and speed of internet connectivity), and global integration (trade/GDP ratio, total export value, export value per capita, and FDI flow as a percentage of GDP). Notably, Vietnam outperformed most Asian peers on electricity consumption per capita and internet connectivity speed, although it lagged behind most countries on per capita income level. On human capital development, Vietnam was comparable to its peers on the education index in 2015 and strongest in improving this measure over the period 1990–2015.

Table 12.3 also provides information that helps explain Vietnam's poor performance on TFP growth. All three countries with negative TFP growth—Vietnam, Indonesia, and Bangladesh—shared three features: low or missing values on payment for technology acquisition, low performance on innovation, and low performance on control of corruption (in global rankings). Vietnam is the only country for which data on payment for technology acquisition are missing for every year, even though this information is available for countries with even lower per capita incomes such as Bangladesh and Cambodia. This suggests that Vietnam has not given strategic priority to monitoring technology acquisition efforts—an essential means of promoting catch-up by narrowing the knowledge gap with countries that are technology leaders.

Protecting Minority Investors; Paying Taxes; Trading across Borders; Enforcing Contracts; and Resolving Insolvency.

[5] The PCI is a composite index constructed from ten sub-indices: Entry Costs (Business Establishment Costs); Land Access and Security of Tenure; Transparency and Access to Information; Time Costs of Regulatory Compliance; Informal Charges; State-Sector Bias (Competition Environment); Proactivity of Provincial Leadership; Private-sector Development Services; Labour Training; and Legal Institutions.

Table 12.3 Selected factors influencing economic catch-up: Vietnam vs. Asian peers

	Vietnam	Indonesia	Malaysia	Philippines	Thailand	China	India	Bangladesh
A-Facilitators or favourable to capital deepening								
1. Business environment								
Ease of doing business (global rank), 2018	68	72	24	113	26	78	100	177
Political stability (% countries below), 2017	59.5	29.1	52.4	10.9	19.1	36.6	17.2	10.5
2. Infrastructure development								
Electricity consumption per capita (kwh), 2015	1,465	774	4,384	707	2,477	3,844	804	304
Electricity generation, 1995–2015 CAGR (%)	12.3	7.0	6.1	4.6	4.1	9.2	6.1	8.7
3. Embrace of the ICT revolution								
Internet users (% of population), 2016	46.5	25.4	78.8	55.5	47.5	53.2	29.5	18.2
Facebook penetration (% of population), 2016	41.9	33.4	61.0	52.0	60.0	0.1	11.7	12.7
Internet connectivity speed, 2017:								
Average (Mbps)	9.5	7.2	8.9	5.5	16.0	7.6	6.5	n/a
% exceeding 10 Mbps	37%	18%	32%	11%	72%	20%	19%	n/a
***4. Global integration*, 2017**								
Trade/GDP (%)	200.3	39.5	135.9	70.6	121.6	37.8	40.6	35.3
Exports in 2017 (US$ bn)	227.2	193.5	224.9	83.8	310.7	2,422.9	488.1	39.1
Export intensity (US$/Capita)	2,381	734	7,217	807	4,549	1,745	364	237
FDI flows/GDP (%)	6.3	2.7	3.1	3.0	1.7	1.13	1.5	0.8
5. Human capital development								
Education index, 2015	0.62	0.62	0.70	0.64	0.64	0.63	0.54	0.46
Health index improvement, 1990–2015 change	0.27	0.23	0.21	0.12	0.25	0.23	0.22	0.21
B-Inhibitors to TFP growth								
Payment for intellectual property (% of GDP), 2016	n/a	0.18	0.58	0.26	0.94	0.23	0.25	0.01
Innovation, global ranking (2018)	72	68	30	67	51	24	31	102
Control of corruption (% countries below), 2017	31.7	48.1	58.1	39.9	42.8	46.7	48.6	19.2

Sources: World Bank (World Development Indicators dataset; Ease of Doing Business 2018 report; World Governance Indicators); United Nations (UNDP 2015); Akamai Internet Connectivity Report 2017 (for internet connectivity speed); International Energy Agency (for electricity data); Global Competitiveness Report 2018 (for innovation).

12.4 Nation Learning to Catch up: A framework for Action

12.4.1 Strategic Focus

We have seen that catch-up performance is driven by the three factors: capital deepening, labour participation, and TFP growth. This sub-section focuses on capital deepening and TFP growth. Facilitating capital deepening should be the paramount objective in catch-up efforts for two reasons. First, capital deepening establishes a fundamental direction for the course of development through straightforward policy design and implementation efforts that can produce immediate and tangible results.[6] Second, most developing countries have a low level of capital stock per capita compared to the United States and their growth prospects are substantially hindered as a result; capital deepening focuses specifically on this problem.

Research shows that capital deepening has been a major source of economic growth and catch-up performance in developing countries (Jorgenson, 1995; Kumar and Russell, 2002; Vu, 2013a, 2013b). Sustaining high growth rates for capital deepening, however, requires robust TFP growth, especially when a country has reached a certain level of capital stock labour (Box 12.1). TFP growth has been found to play a dominant role in successfully driving long-term catch-up, especially in countries that are now developed. Nation learning to catch up should thus focus on both capital deepening and TFP growth. The following sub-sections highlight key features of a nation learning to catch up, with a focus on the strategic directions that enable a country to successfully promote capital deepening and TFP growth.

12.4.2 Three Main Actors

In nation learning for catch-up, particularly with respect to capital deepening and TFP growth, central and local governments, private firms, and workers are the three main actors. While they have differing underlying motivations for their respective learning efforts, their efforts are strategically inter-related. At the centre of the overall learning endeavour is the business sector. As a profit-seeking entity, each firm makes its own decisions about how much to invest, which technology to

[6] Hausmann, Pritchett, and Rodrik (2005), analysing the growth acceleration patterns of 110 countries over thirty-six years (1957–92), found that sustained acceleration in economic growth is stimulated by major reforms in economic policy. In addition, the authors also found that reforms focusing on macroeconomic stability and trade liberalization can stimulate growth and yield quick results.

Box 12.1: The importance of productivity growth in long-term economic performance

GDP generated by a country can be expressed in a Cobb–Douglas aggregate production function

$$Y = A.K^{\alpha}.(hL)^{1-\alpha} \tag{12.1}$$

where Y, as GDP, is a function of total factor productivity A, capital input K, number of workers L, and labour quality h. Parameter α, $(0<\alpha<1)$, is the income share of capital.

The marginal product of capital (*MPK*), therefore, can be expressed as:

$$MPK = \frac{\partial Y}{\partial K} = A.\alpha.K^{\alpha-1}.(hL)^{1-\alpha} = A.\alpha.\left(\frac{h}{K/L}\right)^{1-\alpha} \tag{12.2}$$

$$MPL = \frac{\partial Y}{\partial L} = A.\alpha.K^{\alpha}.(h)^{1-\alpha}(1-\alpha).L^{-\alpha} = A.\alpha.\left(h\cdot\frac{K}{L}\right)^{1-\alpha} \tag{12.3}$$

Under perfect competitive conditions, *MPK* is equal to the gross return rate of capital, while *MPL* represents the market rate for labour wages. Increasing *MPK* boosts investment while increasing *MPL* raises wages, ultimately boosting labour participation.

Equation (12.2) indicates that raising productivity A (through TFP growth) and human capital h are effective ways to increase *MPK*, thereby leading to further capital deepening. These strategies become more urgent as increasing K/L causes *MPK* to decline.

Equation (12.3) implies that raising productivity A (through TFP growth), human capital h, and capital deepening (K/L) are the main levers to increase *MPL*, ultimately boosting labour participation.

acquire, and how to innovate in order to enhance competitiveness. The main motivation driving workers to learn is to improve their individual quality of life. In an environment supportive of such learning, workers are keen to improve their skills in order to competitively position themselves in the labour market. These learning efforts not only augment their productivity and employability but also contribute to national absorptive capacity and nationwide efficiency improvements that ultimately boost TFP growth. Note that human capital development, as presented in Box 12.1, improves the marginal productivity of capital (*MPK*) and hence boosts capital deepening. Government is responsible not only for making public investments and executing certain R&D projects but also for playing a crucial role in fostering a facilitative environment and enabling efficient platforms for all actors and broader society to realize their full potential in contributing to catch-up. Next we consider the role of government in driving nation-learning efforts.

12.4.3 The Role of Government in Driving Nation Learning

Making investments, moving up the value chain, adopting a new technology, and taking risks in R&D projects are crucial decisions made by firms. Governments can nudge firms towards such activities by improving the cost–benefit structure and building expectations about the economy and economic system through robust analysis and data. In doing so, government should exhibit foresight and decisiveness in two areas: (i) strategic choices and (ii) building high-performing institutions and coordination capabilities.

12.4.3.1 Making Strategic Choices

The government's strategic choices are essential to nation learning because they establish the foundation on which all actors make decisions. Making strategic choices goes beyond a simple reasoning process; it includes robust rethinking of underlying assumptions about economic development, thoughtfully learning from experience, and vigorously embracing global trends. Examples of strategic choices are adopting market-oriented reforms, embracing global integration, investing in human capital development, creating a favourable business environment, prioritizing industrial and infrastructure upgrading, and seizing opportunities brought about by the digital revolution. The experience of Vietnam shows that making sound strategic choices can positively impact a country's development path and can substantially impact the process of capital deepening. At the same time, if a country makes poor strategic choices, unwanted effects are likely to follow. For example, Venezuela has adopted a particularly aggressive socialist model for the past two decades and is now suffering from a severe economic crisis.[7]

12.4.3.2 Building High-performing Institutions and Coordination Capabilities

Making sound strategic choices is fundamental for entering a growth trajectory complemented by robust capital investment and job creation—especially for countries with relatively low per capita income. However, achieving high-quality and sustainable economic growth requires learning efforts for building high-performing institutions and coordination capabilities. The negative TFP growth observed for Vietnam, Indonesia, and Bangladesh is suggestive of the challenges resulting from insufficient learning efforts.

Building high-performing institutions and coordination capabilities is not only supportive of a friendly business environment but also reduces market distortions and leads firms towards more productive choices such as value creation over rent

[7] Vu (2018) shows that Venezuela's global ranking on per capita income fell by thirty-three places over the period 1990–2017, from 42nd in 1990 to 75th in 2017.

seeking, collaboration over undercutting, and honesty over cheating. Building high-performing institutions and coordination capabilities is also essential for enhancing the quality of decision making and efficiency of resource allocation across sectors.

Singapore is an instructive example of how vigorous learning efforts can be applied to build high-performing institutions and coordination capabilities. In his memoir *From Third World to First: The Singapore story 1965–2000,* Lee Kuan Yew recalled:

> When we started in 1959 we knew little knowledge about how to govern, or how to solve economic and social problems... We learnt on the job and learnt quickly. If there was one formula for our success, it was that we were constantly studying how to make things work, or how to make them work better.
>
> ... I almost never made the same mistake twice, and I tried to learn from the mistakes others had made. I discovered early in office that there were few problems confronting me in government which other governments had not met and solved. So I made a practice of finding out who else had met the problem we faced, how they had tackled it and how successful they had been. Whenever it was to build a new airport or to change our teaching methods, I would send a team of officers to visit and study those countries that had done it well. I preferred to climb on the shoulders of others who had gone before us.[8]

Goh Keng Swee, credited with being the main architect of Singapore's economy, insisted that the ability to learn from others was a key factor in the country's success:

> There is nothing new under the sun—whether it is setting up an MRT system, a gifted education programme, an air force, a container port or whatever... We do not try to reinvent the wheel; we study how other people do it. We learn and adapt, not imitate without thinking.[9]

There are four channels for learning efforts in building high-performing institutions and coordination capabilities:[10] acquisition of competencies; benchmarking; experimentation; and continuous improvement. Examples of these efforts from Singapore include learning from the Shell Oil Company about criteria for recruiting government officials (acquisition of competencies); examining factors influencing the country's performance on global rankings (benchmarking), ranging from ease of doing business and global competitiveness to effectiveness and innovation in court; so-called sandbox programmes at the Monetary Authority of Singapore (MAS) focused on promoting the Fintech sector (experimentation);

[8] Lee (2000: 758–9).
[9] 'Dr. Goh's Recipe for our Success', *Strait Times*, 7 August 1984.
[10] Yeung et al. (1999) provide a rich discussion on learning capability.

and the application of performance-based management across government agencies and organizations (continuous improvement).

12.4.4 Nation-learning Capability

Cohen and Levinthal (1990: 128) introduce the concept of firm-level absorptive capacity, defining it as 'the ability of a firm to recognize the value of new, external information, assimilate it, and apply it to commercial ends'. This concept can be broadened to capture the learning capability of a nation in its efforts towards economic catch-up. Nation-learning capability (NLC) can be expressed in the following simple mathematical formula:

$$\mathrm{NLC} = \frac{\mathrm{P} * \mathrm{V} * \mathrm{A} * \mathrm{E}}{\mathrm{S} + \mathrm{C}} \tag{12.3}$$

where the components in the numerator are drivers and those in the denominator are obstacles. These are elaborated as follows:

- *P* is the pressure that forces a country to learn in pursuing economic catch-up. Underlying factors include security threats, lack of natural resources, and catch-up success in neighbouring or peer countries, among many others. These factors have been found to drive vigorous learning efforts in Japan, South Korea, Taiwan, and Singapore (Doner et al., 2005).
- *V* is leadership vision, which depends heavily on the quality of the country's top leaders. Lessons from historical failures can be a powerful force shaping the leadership's vision of the future. China and Vietnam have a vision that is arguably more receptive to market principles and global integration than that in similarly situated (previously closed authoritarian) countries; this may be due in part to the countries' costly experiences with a command economy and economic isolation.
- *A* is the aggregate absorptive capacity of government organizations and firms for adopting new strategies and reforms. Progress on the measurement of this component depends on not only the learning efforts of firms and individuals but also the government's effort to build high-performing institutions and coordination capabilities.[11]

[11] As an example, Singapore's Productivity Practices Sharing Platform created a platform to promote productivity by fostering the sharing of best business practices with SMEs. Business leaders were invited to partner with the National Productivity Board to develop curricular and training materials based on experiences and best practices in the three focus areas: customer service (Singapore Airlines); industrial engineering (Singapore Philips); and on-the-job training (OJT) programmes (Seiko Instruments).

- *E* represents the enabling conditions that facilitate nation learning. Underlying factors include globalization, the ICT revolution, strategic alliances, development assistance, and regional growth dynamics, among others. FDI is also a potentially powerful enabler, especially in efforts to reap benefits from spillover effects.
- *S* represents factors that maintain status quo bias in policymaking, including outdated regulations, ageing bureaucratic habits, and vested interests. Nation learning should seek to mitigate these factors as part of broader modernization reforms. For example, India's Make in India initiative has endeavoured to change bureaucratic culture, away from the ABCD approach (avoid, by-pass, confuse, and delay) and towards the ROAD approach (responsibility, ownership, accountability, and decisiveness).[12]
- *C* represents challenges related to the cost of nation learning, including pervasiveness of corruption, lack of transparency, and the absence of efficient mechanisms for knowledge diffusion.

Expression (12.3) suggests that a country can augment NLC through a comprehensive framework that focuses on specific factors. For example, a new leadership team that proposes a fresh vision of development with a commitment to pursuing catch-up should not only accelerate reforms (*V*) and establish a sense of urgency (*P*) but also reduce status-quo bias (*S*) and corruption practices (*C*).

12.5 Conclusion

The high performance of many Asian countries in pursuing economic catch-up presents an opportunity to examine strategic policy efforts and their impacts on traditional drivers of growth. Capital accumulation and TFP growth are shown in the literature to be contributing factors, but they fail to exhibit their full transformative potential in the absence of strategic policy visions. This chapter has argued that nation learning, i.e. the consistent and strategic effort among all sectors to identify pathways to economic catch-up, is a crucial undertaking for developing countries that lack the levels of capital stock per capita enjoyed by developing countries. In this chapter's examination of cases of lagging capital accumulation and TFP growth, nation learning was argued to be the missing link among otherwise aggressive policy efforts. Nation learning is a crucial step in helping governments to rethink their fundamental approach to economic development, including the adoption of market systems and facilitation of a vibrant private sector.

[12] Case study, *Make in India: The Operating and Marketing Challenge*, by Gaganpreet Sing and Simarpreet Singh, Ivey Publishing, 2014.

This chapter has argued that nation learning should draw from global case lessons and focus on generating sustainable performance in capital accumulation and TFP growth. Bias in favour of capital deepening while overlooking promotion of TFP growth is a common pitfall in economic catch-up efforts. Such efforts, including those systematized by an NLC-informed framework, should focus not only on capital investment but also on technology and other factors underlying TFP. The case of Vietnam provides a notable example. The country excelled among its Asian peers on the contribution of capital deepening to economic growth while being one of the three weakest on TFP growth.

Regarding concrete policy implications, the mathematical formula presented above for NLC offers specific guidance for pursuing catch-up, including which factors to emphasize (leadership vision, reform capacity, and conditions that facilitate nation learning) and which to minimize (status quo bias and costs associated with nation learning). More broadly, catch-up efforts must not be unduly concerned with performance targets on specific measures but must instead address reform and economic growth as a systemic process in which elements of the whole—institutions, private-sector behaviour, aid programmes, cross-sector collaborations, and others—are fundamentally interdependent and mutually reinforcing. This calls for a leadership approach that emphasizes rethinking and prioritizes unexploited pathways for economic growth.

A country's factor endowments and other endogenous economic fundamentals will determine whether it will be competitive in the global economy, but the degree to which the country is competitive depends on a variety of other factors including strategic policy vision, institutional performance, coordination capacity, and nation learning. There is considerable nuance in how these factors are measured and leveraged, and this chapter has sought to articulate that nuance in a way that generates actionable implications. As an illustration, the chapter presented Vietnam as a successful case of leveraging sound strategic choice into catch-up performance, including the adoption of market principles to promote a thriving private sector and investments in infrastructure and workforce development capacities. Countries such as Vietnam and others throughout Asia are instructive examples of the challenges and opportunities of development, and exhibit how nation learning is crucial for advancing broader development goals.

Appendix 12.1: Catch-up performance of 167 countries (sorted by CUPI score in decreasing order)

Country	CUPI (1995–2015)	Relative income level (United States=100)	
		1995	2015
1. Equatorial Guinea	13.48	4.9	72.6
2. Bosnia and Herzegovina	7.16	4.6	19.2
3. Myanmar	7.08	2.3	9.4
4. China	6.89	6.5	25.8
5. Azerbaijan	6.63	8.4	31.7
6. Georgia	5.39	5.8	17.1
7. Armenia	5.02	5.5	15.0
8. Turkmenistan	4.61	11.7	29.5
9. Liberia	4.34	0.6	1.5
10. Belarus	4.31	13.4	31.6
11. Mozambique	4.09	0.9	2.1
12. Cambodia	4.02	2.8	6.2
13. Lithuania	3.85	23.7	51.2
14. Kazakhstan	3.77	21.0	44.6
15. Laos	3.70	4.8	10.1
16. Latvia	3.69	21.0	43.8
17. India	3.68	5.2	10.9
18. Vietnam	3.66	5.2	10.8
19. Mongolia	3.53	10.8	21.8
20. Bhutan	3.49	7.4	14.9
21. Albania	3.46	10.5	20.9
22. Ethiopia	3.44	1.5	2.9
23. Uzbekistan	3.23	5.7	10.8
24. Cabo Verde	3.22	6.1	11.7
25. Rwanda	3.11	1.7	3.1
26. Sri Lanka	3.04	11.4	21.0
27. Trinidad and Tobago	3.03	32.4	59.4
28. Estonia	2.95	28.8	51.9
29. Cuba	2.68	23.3	39.9
30. Ireland	2.66	68.4	116.5
31. Panama	2.65	23.3	39.6
32. Poland	2.59	28.6	48.0
33. Iraq	2.51	16.6	27.4
34. Bangladesh	2.44	3.7	6.0
35. Dominican Republic	2.41	15.7	25.4
36. Sudan	2.37	4.9	7.8
37. Slovakia	2.37	33.4	53.6
38. Angola	2.35	8.2	13.2
39. Mauritius	2.34	22.4	35.8
40. Tajikistan	2.27	3.2	5.0
41. Nigeria	2.16	6.9	10.7
42. South Korea	2.14	42.6	65.2
43. Bulgaria	2.05	21.4	32.3
44. Chad	1.93	2.6	3.9

45. Romania	1.87	26.7	38.9
46. Ghana	1.80	5.2	7.5
47. Kyrgyzstan	1.77	4.3	6.1
48. Peru	1.74	15.8	22.3
49. Morocco	1.73	9.9	14.0
50. Russian Federation	1.72	32.5	45.8
51. Uganda	1.65	2.4	3.3
52. Tanzania	1.58	3.5	4.8
53. Moldova	1.55	6.6	9.0
54. Zambia	1.49	5.1	6.8
55. Serbia	1.48	18.7	25.2
56. Singapore	1.46	113.6	152.2
57. Burkina Faso	1.45	2.3	3.0
58. Tunisia	1.37	15.5	20.4
59. Malaysia	1.36	36.6	48.0
60. Philippines	1.36	10.0	13.2
61. Uruguay	1.31	29.2	37.9
62. Guyana	1.29	10.4	13.4
63. Indonesia	1.29	15.2	19.7
64. Nepal	1.24	3.4	4.4
65. Chile	1.24	32.9	42.1
66. Lesotho	1.22	4.1	5.3
67. Grenada	1.19	19.1	24.2
68. Seychelles	1.18	38.2	48.4
69. Botswana	1.14	22.5	28.2
70. Namibia	1.08	14.9	18.6
71. Hong Kong	1.07	82.0	101.4
72. Malta	1.06	50.2	62.1
73. Nicaragua	1.05	7.5	9.3
74. Turkey	1.04	30.0	36.9
75. Macedonia	1.03	19.7	24.2
76. Croatia	1.02	32.0	39.2
77. Costa Rica	1.01	22.7	27.8
78. Suriname	1.00	24.4	29.8
79. Thailand	1.00	23.9	29.1
80. Hungary	0.99	38.6	47.1
81. Egypt	0.89	16.3	19.4
82. Bolivia	0.88	10.4	12.4
83. Czech Republic	0.85	48.7	57.6
84. St. Vincent & Grenadines	0.85	16.8	19.9
85. Slovenia	0.84	46.7	55.2
86. Colombia	0.71	21.4	24.6
87. Iceland	0.65	71.2	81.0
88. Samoa	0.62	9.3	10.6
89. Luxembourg	0.62	157.4	178.2
90. Algeria	0.53	23.5	26.2
91. Ukraine	0.49	12.8	14.1
92. Sweden	0.46	78.7	86.3
93. Mali	0.45	3.3	3.6
94. Australia	0.37	76.9	82.8
95. Honduras	0.35	8.5	9.1
96. Saudi Arabia	0.32	89.5	95.4

(continued)

Continued

Country	CUPI (1995–2015)	Relative income level (United States=100)	
		1995	2015
97. Swaziland	0.29	14.6	15.4
98. Finland	0.28	69.9	74.0
99. Dominica	0.28	18.3	19.4
100. El Salvador	0.27	14.6	15.4
101. Israel	0.26	57.6	60.7
102. Jordan	0.25	18.5	19.4
103. Pakistan	0.23	8.5	8.9
104. Ecuador	0.22	19.6	20.4
105. Fiji	0.21	15.9	16.6
106. Djibouti	0.19	6.0	6.2
107. Sierra Leone	0.18	2.7	2.8
108. Argentina	0.15	35.2	36.2
109. Tuvalu	0.14	6.8	7.0
110. New Zealand	0.11	65.3	66.7
111. South Africa	0.06	23.2	23.5
112. United Kingdom	0.04	72.5	73.1
113. Malawi	0.03	2.1	2.1
114. Cameroon	0.01	5.5	5.6
115. Canada	0.00	81.6	81.6
116. Netherlands	−0.01	88.1	88.0
117. Kenya	−0.07	5.6	5.5
118. Brazil	−0.07	28.0	27.6
119. Mexico	−0.11	32.0	31.3
120. Austria	−0.11	85.4	83.6
121. Paraguay	−0.13	16.8	16.4
122. Germany	−0.13	85.2	83.1
123. Benin	−0.16	3.8	3.7
124. Guatemala	−0.17	14.3	13.8
125. Spain	−0.19	63.5	61.1
126. Senegal	−0.19	4.5	4.3
127. Belize	−0.20	15.7	15.1
128. Belgium	−0.21	82.8	79.4
129. Congo	−0.24	11.9	11.4
130. Norway	−0.25	126.8	120.8
131. Antigua and Barbuda	−0.28	43.5	41.1
132. Barbados	−0.37	31.5	29.2
133. Switzerland	−0.40	116.2	107.2
134. Denmark	−0.44	94.3	86.3
135. France	−0.45	78.4	71.7
136. Tonga	−0.46	10.8	9.9
137. Portugal	−0.47	55.4	50.4
138. Japan	−0.67	82.1	71.9
139. St. Lucia	−0.67	22.3	19.5
140. Cyprus	−0.75	67.0	57.6
141. Togo	−0.77	3.0	2.6
142. Greece	−0.82	53.8	45.7
143. Niger	−0.83	2.0	1.7

144. Côte d'Ivoire	-0.84	7.4	6.3
145. Guinea	-1.03	2.6	2.2
146. Vanuatu	-1.08	6.6	5.3
147. Marshall Islands	-1.18	8.8	7.0
148. Lebanon	-1.20	31.5	24.8
149. Italy	-1.29	84.0	64.9
150. Palau	-1.34	35.7	27.3
151. Bahrain	-1.35	108.7	83.0
152. Kiribati	-1.49	4.8	3.6
153. Madagascar	-1.54	3.6	2.6
154. Comoros	-1.56	3.6	2.6
155. Bahamas	-1.56	56.0	41.0
156. Oman	-1.58	97.6	71.2
157. Jamaica	-1.61	21.8	15.8
158. Gabon	-1.71	50.4	35.8
159. Solomon Islands	-1.94	5.8	3.9
160. Kuwait	-2.09	201.9	133.0
161. Guinea-Bissau	-2.15	4.0	2.6
162. Brunei Darussalam	-2.27	219.8	139.7
163. Burundi	-2.43	2.1	1.3
164. Yemen	-2.90	9.0	5.0
165. Zimbabwe	-3.25	6.1	3.2
166. Central African Republic	-3.42	2.2	1.1
167. United Arab Emirates	-3.85	269.2	124.7
Mean (M)	***1.03***	***31.24***	***33.71***
Standard deviation (SD)	***2.19***	***40.63***	***33.82***
CV=SD/M	***2.12***	***1.30***	***1.00***

Source: Authors' calculation from WDI and APO datasets.

Appendix 12.2: Sources of catch-up performance index (CUPI)

The CUPI, by definition, can be expressed as follows (see Vu (2018) for elaboration):

$$CUPI^i_{0,T} = ln\left[\frac{rel_{y^i_T}}{rel_{y^i_0}}\right]/T = ln\left[\frac{\frac{y^i_T}{y^{US}_T}}{\frac{y^i_0}{y^{US}_0}}\right]/T = \Delta lny^i_{0,T} - \Delta lny^{US}_{0,T} \qquad (A12.1)$$

Where $\Delta lny^i_{0,T}$ is the average annual per capita growth rate over period [0, *T*] of country *i*'s income.

Note that

$$\Delta lny^i_{0,T} = \Delta lnY^i_{0,T} - \Delta lnP^i_{0,T} \qquad (A12.2)$$

Where $\Delta lnY^i_{0,T}$ and $\Delta lnP^i_{0,T}$ are the average annual growth rate of country *i*'s GDP and population over the period [0, *T*].

At the same time, GDP growth can be decomposed into a contribution of capital, labour, and TFP as follows (see Jorgenson et al. (2002) for elaboration):

$$\Delta lnY^i_{0,T} = \bar{w}^i_{0,T}.\Delta lnK^i_{0,T} + (1 - \bar{w}^i_{0,T}).\Delta lnL^i_{0,T} + \Delta lnA^i_{0,T} \qquad (A12.3)$$

(continued)

Continued

where $\bar{w}^i_{0,T}$ is the average income share of the country i's capital service in period [0, T] while $\Delta lnK^i_{0,T}$, $\Delta lnL^i_{0,T}$, and $\Delta lnA^i_{0,T}$ are, respectively, its growth rates of capital services, employment, and total factor productivity over the period.

Combining (A12.2) and (A12.3) yields

$$\Delta lny^i_{0,T} = \bar{w}^i_{0,T}.\Delta\ln(K^i_{0,T}/P^i_{0,T}) + (1 - \bar{w}^i_{0,T}).\Delta\ln(L^i_{0,T}/P^i_{0,T}) + \Delta lnA^i_{0,T} \quad \text{(A12.4)}$$

Equation (A12.4) means that growth rate of a country's per capita income can be decomposed into three sources:

(i) the contribution of capital deepening in the population: $\bar{w}^i_{0,T}.\Delta\ln(K^i_{0,T}/P^i_{0,T})$,which is denoted as $kpopc^i_{0,T}$;

(ii) the contribution of labour participation expansion: $(1 - \bar{w}^i_{0,T}).\Delta\ln(L^i_{0,T}/P^i_{0,T})$, denoted as $lpopc^i_{0,T}$; and

(iii) TFP growth:$\Delta lnA^i_{0,T}$, denoted as $TFP^i_{0,T}$.

The CUPI in Equation (A12.1), therefore, can be expressed as

$$CUPI^i_{0,T} = (kpopc^i_{0,T} - kpopc^{US}_{0,T}) + (lpopc^i_{0,T} - lpopc^{US}_{0,T}) + (TFPG^i_{0,T} - TFPG^{US}_{0,T})$$

That is, the catch-up performance index (CUPI) for a country can be broken down into three constituent components capturing its performance relative to the United States on the three sources of per capita growth:

$(kpopc^i_{0,T} - kpopc^{US}_{0,T})$, which is the differential in capital deepening rate, which is referred to in the chapter as 'capital deepening';

$(lpopc^i_{0,T} - lpopc^{US}_{0,T})$, which is the differential in labour participation rate, which is referred to in the chapter as 'labour participation'; and

$(TFPG^i_{0,T} - TFPG^{US}_{0,T})$, which is the differential in TFP growth, which is referred to in the chapter as 'TFP growth'.

References

Abramovitz, M. (1994) 'Catch-up and Convergence in the Postwar Growth Boom and after', in W. Baumol, R. Nelsonand , E. Wolff (eds) *Convergence of Productivity: Cross-national Studies and Historical Evidence.* Oxford: Oxford University Press, pp. 86–125.

Aghion, P. and P. Howitt (2007) 'Capital, Innovation, and Growth Accounting', *Oxford Review of Economic Policy* 23(1): 79–93.

Baumol, W. J. (1986) 'Productivity Growth, Convergence, and Welfare: What the Long-run Data Show', *The American Economic Review* 76(5): 1072–85.

Cohen, W. M. and D. A. Levinthal (1990) 'Absorptive Capacity: A New Perspective on Learning and Innovation', *Administrative Science Quarterly* 35: 128–52.

Doner, R. F., B. K. Ritchie, and D. Slater (2005) 'Systemic Vulnerability and the Origins of Developmental States: Northeast and Southeast Asia in Comparative Perspective', *International Organization* 59(2): 327–61.

Dowrick, S. and D. T. Nguyen (1989) 'OECD Comparative Economic Growth 1950–85: Catch-up and Convergence', *The American Economic Review* 79(5): 1010–30.

Easterly, W. and R. Levine (2001) 'What Have We Learned from a Decade of Empirical Research on Growth? It's Not Factor Accumulation: Stylized Facts and Growth Models', *The World Bank Economic Review* 15(2): 177–219.

Fagerberg, J. (1987) 'A Technology Gap Approach to Why Growth Rates Differ', *Research Policy* 16(2–4): 87–99.

Gerschenkron, A. (1962) *Economic Backwardness in Historical Perspective: A Book of Essays*. Cambridge, MA: Belknap Press of Harvard University Press.

Hausmann, R., L. Pritchett, and D. Rodrik (2005) 'Growth Accelerations', *Journal of Economic Growth* 10(4): 303–29.

Jorgenson, D. W. (1995) *Productivity: International Comparisons of Economic Growth*, Vol. 2. Cambridge: MIT Press.

Jorgenson, D. W., M. S. Ho, and K. J. Stiroh (2002) 'Projecting Productivity Growth: Lessons from the US Growth Resurgence.' Resources for the Future Discussion Paper 02–42, Washington, DC.

Klenow, P. J. and A. Rodriguez-Clare (1997) 'The Neoclassical Revival in Growth Economics: Has It Gone too far?' *NBER Macroeconomics Annual* 12: 73–103.

Kumar, S. and R. R. Russell (2002) 'Technological Change, Technological Catch-up, and Capital Deepening: Relative Contributions to Growth and Convergence', *The American Economic Review* 92(3): 527–48.

Lee, K. Y. (2000) *From Third World to First: The Singapore Story 1965–2000: Memoirs of Lee Kuan Yew*. Singapore: Singapore Press Holdings.

Lee, Keun (2013) *Schumpeterian Analysis of Economic Catch-up: Knowledge, Path-creation, and Middle-Income Trap*. Cambridge: Cambridge University Press.

Lin, J. Y. (2009) *Economic Development and Transition: Thought, Strategy, and Viability*. Cambridge: Cambridge University Press.

Lin, J. Y. (2011) 'New Structural Economics: A Framework for Rethinking Development.' Policy Research Working Paper No. 5197, Washington DC, World Bank.

Ohno, Kenichi (2013) *Learning to Industrialize: From Given Growth to Policy-aided Value Creation*. New York: Routledge-GRIPS Publications Development Forum Studies.

Oqubay, Arkebe (2015) *Made in Africa: Industrial Policy in Ethiopia*. Oxford: Oxford University Press.

Quah, D. (1993) 'Galton's Fallacy and Tests of the Convergence Hypothesis', *The Scandinavian Journal of Economics* 95(4): 427–43.

Quah, D. T. (1996) 'Empirics for Economic Growth and Convergence', *European Economic Review* 40(6): 1353–75.

Solow, R. M. (1957) 'Technical Change and the Aggregate Production Function', *The Review of Economics and Statistics* 39(3): 312–20.

UNDP (2015) 'Human Development Data.' United Nations, Geneva.

Vu, K. M. (2013a) 'Information and Communication Technology and Singapore's Economic Growth', *Information Economics and Policy* 25(4): 284–300.

Vu, K. M. (2013b) *The Dynamics of Economic Growth: Policy Insights from Comparative Analyses in Asia*. Cheltenham: Edward Elgar Publishing.

Vu, K. M. (2018) 'The Global Dynamics of Economic Catchup: Patterns, Drivers, and Determinants.' LKYSPP Working Papers, Lee Kuan Yew School of Public Policy, Singapore.

Woo, W. T. (2011) 'Understanding the Middle-income Trap in Economic Development: The Case of Malaysia.' World Economy Lecture delivered at the University of Nottingham, Globalization and Economic Policy, pp. 17–34.

Yeung, A. K., D. O. Ulrich, S. Nason et al. (1999) *Organizational Learning Capability*. New York: Oxford University Press.

13

Learning to Catch up in Africa

Arkebe Oqubay and Taffere Tesfachew

13.1 Introduction to Learning and Catch-up

This chapter examines the dynamics of learning and catch-up in twenty-first-century Africa—a continent generally regarded as a laggard in technological learning and catch-up.[1] It argues that despite low levels of absorptive capacity and the increasingly restrictive and unbalanced world order created by the neo-liberalization wave, the dynamics of learning and catch-up in late-latecomer countries can be accelerated by proactive industrial policies, supported by strategic vision and the commitment to catch-up through intensive learning, including policy learning. To support this argument, the chapter presents industry-level case studies of learning and catch-up in Ethiopia, one of the fastest-growing economies in Africa.

In this chapter, catch-up is understood as a process of 'narrowing of a firm's or country's gap vis-à-vis a leading country or firm' (Lee and Malerba, 2018: 2; Lee 2013).[2] Economic catch-up is a rare phenomenon and only a handful of countries have succeeded in catching up and in sustaining the investment and technological capability required to maintain leadership at the frontiers of technology. This makes measuring progress in catching up difficult, especially when leading firms and countries are also moving forward by improving their capabilities, thereby widening the gap. This chapter proposes that for late-latecomers, a useful indicator of catching up is the ability of firms and industries to compete with those that have established a clear position of international excellence and leadership in the same products.

What are the main sources and drivers of successful technological learning and catch-up? Are the conditions required to spur technological learning and catch-up in the twenty-first century different from those applicable to latecomers in the past? Economic history and empirical evidence suggest that government support through proactive industrial policies, involving various forms of direct and indirect instruments to encourage intensive learning, has been an important characteristic of countries that have succeeded in catching up. This was the case both when

[1] See Cramer, Oqubay, and Sender (forthcoming) on historical and contemporary African economic development.

[2] See also Gerschenkron (1962) on the advantage of late development and innovative responses.

latecomers in continental Europe were industrializing in the nineteenth century and in the catch-up of the newly industrialized economies in East Asia in the twentieth century (Chang, 2003; Cohen and DeLong, 2016; Lee 2013). The role of industrial policy as a powerful tool to spur technological learning and catch-up is linked to two factors.[3]

First, industries or sectors vary significantly in their structures, their disposition to technological learning, and the conditions required for initiating the catch-up process. Setting aside the debate on whether industrial policies are the best instruments for picking winners (Wade, 2015), it is evident that they enable governments to target industries or sectors that are predisposed to technological learning and could, therefore, serve as role models in setting the process of learning and catching up in motion.

The second factor is the policy direction, particularly its export or inward orientation and its approach to foreign direct investment (FDI). This can have a profound influence on the pace and depth of technological learning and catch-up by local industries. The window of opportunity for learning tends to be greater in export-oriented industries, where interactions with buyers and competitors facilitate access to foreign knowledge spillovers, and there is greater pressure to improve efficiency and to meet international technical and quality standards. Targeted industrial policies can also influence the pace and direction of dynamic learning (both technological and policy), creating a sense of urgency and a collective mission and passion to promote learning. The 'learning intensity' these measures induce can be a powerful tool to fast-track dynamic learning.

The chapter is organized as follows. We first review the experiences of learning and catch-up in the export-oriented floriculture industry in Ethiopia and the impact of policy learning on the industry's accelerated development.[4] Next, we examine the rapid development of the cement industry in Ethiopia and its implications for learning and catch-up. Ethiopia's intensive efforts to build domestic absorptive capacity are considered, focusing on reforms in university-level, technical, and vocational education, and on the development of industrial hubs. The final section draws conclusions and highlights potential lessons for other late-latecomer countries.

13.2 Learning and Catch-Up In A New Export Industry

13.2.1 The Rise of a New Export Industry

Floriculture production and export in Ethiopia date back to the mid-2000s. As a relative newcomer to floriculture within East Africa, the country's rapid

[3] See Amsden (1989, 2001); and Amsden and Chu (2003). See also Oqubay, Cramer, Chang, and Kozul-Wright (forthcoming) on industrial policies. On learning by doing, so also Arrow (1962).

[4] See Ohno (2013).

development of export capacity is a remarkable achievement and a demonstration of successful learning and catch-up.[5] Since the mid-2000s, Ethiopia has emerged as one of the world's four largest cut flower exporters, generating more than US$2.5 billion between 2005 and 2018. Its exports are destined predominately for the highly competitive European market, where high standards and stringent regulations are strictly enforced. Ethiopia's floriculture exports originate from seventy firms, which have created more than 50,000 direct jobs in floriculture and 130,000 indirect jobs in the non-flower horticulture sector.

The floriculture industry emerged as the result of an active industrial policy implemented by a government willing to experiment with new policy approaches and to learn from policy mistakes. The first bold policy action was to invite Dutch flower growers who were already international market leaders to invest in Ethiopia. Measures taken to attract and support foreign investors included incentives such as duty-free machinery imports, tax breaks for exporters, and zero income tax for five years. New investors, both local and foreign, were also offered access to finance (from the Development Bank of Ethiopia) at subsidized interest rates, and land within a 160 km radius of Addis Ababa at affordable rents. Investment in the industry was further encouraged by general export incentives such as retention schemes and devaluation of the local currency. The Netherlands government also provided special financial support to Dutch firms.

At the time, Kenya was the leading flower producer and exporter in East Africa, with experience spanning more than five decades. The productivity gap between Ethiopian and Kenyan floriculture sectors soon narrowed, however, even though 30 per cent of the Ethiopian firms were newly established.

The key factors in the development of the industry were effective implementation of industrial policies and the intense and multi-dimensional learning process—which also applied to the government. FDI firms, with their long experience in floriculture (in some cases second generation), were also important partners in the intensive learning.

The government continued its engagement with foreign firms, providing facilitation services, and where appropriate financing, that encouraged foreign firms to support learning within the sector. Since the global hub of floriculture is located in the Dutch auction centres, the fact that most foreign firms were Dutch helped local firms to learn the flower business in a relatively short time. The export market was an important source of learning: exporting to Europe generated formidable pressure to improve performance on quality, timeliness of delivery, sustainability of production methods, and reliability.

[5] Floriculture is a high-productivity industry and exhibits many features of manufacturing.

13.2.2 Drivers of Learning and Catch-up

The similarity of floriculture, in some respects, to the manufacturing sector, also contributed to accelerated learning and catch-up.[6] The emergence of the industry prompted the introduction of high phyto-sanitary standards, skill-intensive production practices, and cool-chain logistics capacity from farms all the way to airports. Local and foreign firms established a dynamic industry association which conducted a regular dialogue with government and enabled all producers to be actively engaged in capacity building, market promotion, and advocacy. The skill-intensive nature of floriculture and its scientific production management requirements helped to develop a domestic workforce that was able to rapidly familiarize itself with modern manufacturing-type production. Indeed, the sector became a stepping-stone for workers to move to factories (especially in the apparel sector) and for workers seeking overseas employment opportunities in the Middle East.

The narrow latitude for failure and poor performance created significant pressure for managers, the workforce, and service providers, including air freight operators, to improve their learning intensity. While production and farm managers were initially mainly expatriates, most were soon replaced by Ethiopian professionals from colleges and university graduates specializing in horticulture, management, and engineering.

National learning systems and local absorptive capacity in general, therefore, played a critical role in the industry's development and catch-up. A government agency was established to support the horticulture industry and capacity-building programmes were implemented in cooperation with the industry association and with the support of Dutch partners. For instance, an MSc in horticulture introduced at Jimma University for eighty professionals working in the agency and in local firms helped upgrade and incentivize professional staff. The widespread use of English by Ethiopians, investors, and expatriates has been conducive to facilitating learning.

Government initiatives to promote linkages made a major contribution to learning new activities and the development of technological capabilities. Three typical examples of linkage dynamics generated as a result of learning and growth in the floriculture industry are those with Ethiopian Airlines (EAL), the corrugated packaging industry, and the cool-chain logistics industry. For many years, EAL's core business was passenger services, and air cargo emerged as a strategic business only in response to growing demand from the floriculture sector, which required a regular, reliable service and a modern terminal for perishable goods. The cargo business eventually became EAL's core business, with cargo capacity gradually expanding to one million tons. To date, EAL has airfreighted about

[6] See Kaldor (1967) on special properties of manufacturing and as a key driver of growth and structural change.

500,000 tons of cargo and full cool-chain storage facilities have been built at new airports. The corrugated packaging industry also developed from demand by the floriculture industry. More than a dozen corrugated packaging manufacturing firms were established after the introduction of additional support schemes, with a total capacity of 100,000 tons.

While the learning and catch-up in Ethiopia's floriculture industry has been exemplary, with potential lessons for other late-latecomers, the process is only at the initial stage and additional intensive learning efforts are required to advance further. There has been a lack of consistency in learning in key areas. For example, after the initial successes, the government failed to adopt appropriate policies and incentives to increase the capacity of domestic firms and their share in the industry. Despite locational advantage and the tremendous potential for export earnings and employment, it has been difficult to secure sufficient land and finance for expansion of production. The government has not supported the upgrading of growers to move into higher-value cut flowers and reduce their dependence on seeds subject to foreign royalties. Progress in diversification into and expansion of the non-flower horticulture sub-sectors has also been limited.

Market diversification and the development of new capabilities, such as product consolidation to facilitate economies of scale, similarly suggest that learning was partial and lacked vigour, contributing to slow growth of the sector after 2013. More importantly, policy lessons from floriculture were not systematically extracted and applied to other industrial sectors. The experience of the floriculture industry shows not only that learning is central to industrial policymaking, but also that continuous policy learning is essential to upgrading and ensuring continuous progress for targeted industries along the catch-up trajectory.

13.3 Learning in an Import-Substitution Industry

13.3.1 Slow Start but Rapid Growth and Learning

The cement industry, directly linked to construction and infrastructure development, has strategic significance for early industrialization. Despite its seventy-five-year history, Ethiopia's cement industry was slow to expand, especially during the Derg period when overall economic growth was sluggish. In 1990 cement was produced by a single state-owned enterprise, Mugher Cement Enterprise (MCE). Output was only 350,000 tons in 1991, doubling to 750,000 tons in the mid-1990s as a result of economic recovery, and the reconstruction programmes and private-sector investment associated with the shift towards a market-driven economy. Despite encouragement of both foreign and domestic private investment in the sector and the abundant availability of raw materials (including within a radius of 100 km of Addis Ababa, Dire Dawa, and Mekelle), there was no new investment for almost ten years. This was partly due to the industry's capital-intensive nature, requiring large investment outlays, and relatively complex technology, demanding effective project execution and operational management. However, demand for cement continued to grow in the 1990s, and a second factory was built in 2000, doubling production capacity to 1.6 million tons.

By 2003, both cement factories were operating at full capacity, although by 2005, cement shortage had become a binding constraint for a booming construction industry driven by rapid economic growth, increased per capita consumption, and massive public infrastructure projects (energy, roads, airports, public housing, schools, urban expansion, etc.) initiated by the government.[7] The construction industry had become a key driver of economic growth, with an annual growth rate of 11.1 per cent and 27.7 per cent during PASDEP (2005/6–2009/10) and GTP I (2010/11–2014/15) respectively, and doubling its share in GDP and employment (Oqubay 2019b: 632 and 641). The government became concerned with the lack of private investment and the possibility of cement supply shortages paralyzing public infrastructure programmes, resulting in cost overruns and delays. The import ban initially enjoyed by the industry was lifted, and the government started importing through private and government agencies.

The period prior to 2000 was highly lucrative for the existing cement factories, which enjoyed protection while demand was beginning to grow. After 2000, however, major changes in the industry were triggered by three factors: rapid growth of the construction sector and increased public investment in major infrastructure projects; the government's targeting of the cement industry as a strategic priority requiring intensive policy efforts; and the lifting of the import ban, signalling that the domestic demand for cement could not be met by the existing firms. The clear market signals produced heightened investment interest in the industry, disproving the previous assumption that only large companies with the appropriate capacity could manage investment projects in what was regarded as a highly capital- and technology-intensive sector.

Once investment started flowing into the cement industry, projects of all sizes were undertaken. Some investors, for example, chose to build small-scale cement plants using the vertical kiln system (primitive and small-scale technology) that required less finance and shorter gestation period. Others focused on building bigger-capacity equipment and technologies to benefit from economy of scale, moving from 1,000 to 5,000 tons per day clinker capacity. A total of sixteen firms invested in the cement sector, raising Ethiopia's total production capacity to 16 million tons (with four factories accounting for two-thirds of the output) and making Ethiopia among the top three cement-producing countries in sub-Saharan Africa. While in other African countries European MNCs dominate the industry, in Ethiopia domestic firms continue to dominate it. The growth of the cement

[7] For instance, the government's public housing programme required more than 1.5 million tons per annum in 2006–10.

industry has also encouraged new investment in the manufacture of other building materials, including reinforcing (rebar) steel.

As in floriculture, technological and policy learning was intense in the cement industry, especially after 2000. For the government, learning focused primarily on learning by doing, and trial and error. The cement industry is without doubt a successful story of learning driven by an activist industrial policy, encompassing learning from both positive experiences and mistakes.

13.3.2 Learning Framework in the Cement Industry

We have seen that the main sources or drivers of learning in the floriculture industry were FDI and exports, together with intensive policy efforts. What were the sources of learning in the cement industry?

First, new investment in the sector was induced by *demand formation,* stimulated by the public infrastructure and construction industry boom, and the government's significant commitment to importing cement. The resulting massive demand influenced the selection of technology towards larger economies of scale, with larger kiln capacity, and encouraged risk-taking. Cement was imported from Asian countries, and Pakistani cement suppliers reliably produced good quality cement at half the local price. This engagement with foreign suppliers was a valuable learning experience for both government and local firms, including in the use of coal for burning clinkers.

Second, learning was facilitated by the sole public enterprise in the sector. Former managers and technical heads organized themselves, conducted studies, and initiated the investment establishing Habesha Cement, mobilizing capital through local shareholding and forming a joint venture with a South African cement manufacturing group. The presence of the SOE encouraged participation in the industry by domestic firms such as Messebo and National Cement. A small privatized factory in Dire Dawa also became a vehicle for new investment by National Cement. Almost all new factories relied on the services and capacity of the SOE during the design and construction phase (laboratory facilities, information on mining areas, and staff training), and employed managers, professionals, and technicians previously trained by the SOE.

Third, most of the new cement projects were executed on a turnkey basis to reduce the risk of delays, cost escalation, and technical difficulties. Globally, the cement industry has been dominated by Chinese technology and equipment, and all new cement firms in Ethiopia used Chinese suppliers and contractors, who were cheaper and executed on time. Some also used non-Chinese consulting firms. Almost all new projects included training of engineers and technicians in Ethiopia and abroad. Learning took place during the design, execution, testing, commissioning, and trial stages, as well as during operations, with technical support from suppliers. The continuous production process required specialists and professionals, although in some cases, the smooth transfer of skills was hampered by language barriers.

Fourth, the government decided, having looked at other countries' experiences, to burn coal for energy, putting significant pressure on the manufacturers to shift from heavy fuel oil to the much cheaper coal. The introduction of coal was a major cost saving in the cement production process, saved considerable foreign exchange for the country, and enabled exploitation of local coal resources. The government arranged bulk purchase on a credit basis, which had advantages in terms of cost, cash flow, and logistics. The government also encouraged and favoured factories using large rotary kilns over the outdated vertical kiln system. These adaptations through learning contributed to cost competitiveness and enabled producers to maintain product quality. A short-term shortage of cement prompted initiatives to explore alternative building materials, though with only partial success. The supply of cement continued to grow as new factories began to compete and produce at full capacity, significantly reducing the price of cement.

Finally, further learning occurred as a result of changes in government policies towards consulting firms in the construction industry. University reform was already producing an important supply of highly skilled engineers for the industry. Relaxation of the requirements for engineers establishing consulting firms and construction companies now resulted in an explosion of the number of construction companies in the country. More than 150 consulting firms and 2,500 small contractors were established. They were given contracts to develop their capacity and participated in the construction of public housing, universities, health centres, and the telecoms network. New equipment was imported and loans were facilitated to strengthen capacity of these new construction companies.

The intense competition was also conducive to fast and intensive learning. As in the floriculture sector, the latitude for poor performance was limited by the political dimension of public infrastructure and housing supply, and by technological features of the industry.

13.3.3 The Role of Industrial Policy and Policy Learning

The cement industry is an example of successful transformation of a less significant inward-oriented industry into a strategic domestic industry. Proactive industrial policy and a number of measures taken by government induced intensive learning, including at policy level.

First, the government boosted investment in the industry through the SOE, and later became a source of technology and learning for the industry as a whole.

Second, the government subsidized interest rates and arranged various forms of financing, including through the Development Bank of Ethiopia (DBE), the Commercial Bank of Ethiopia (CBE), an industrial development fund, foreign financing, and concessional lending. The industry was also identified as a priority sector for foreign exchange allocation.

Third, the government provided mining concessions, made land available at nominal prices, and offered a five-year zero income-tax incentive and duty-free importation of machinery.

Fourth, the government permitted imports of cement during times of shortage, allowed the two manufacturers to enjoy super profits enabling them to invest in new expansion of their production capacity, and applied an import ban when there was oversupply. Investment restrictions on foreign companies in the cement industry were provisionally introduced to manage overcapacity. The development of freight capacity was also encouraged during the importing phase; spillover effects included fleet modernization and corporate reorganization for transporters.

However, policy learning was not automatic, and many mistakes were made. For example, the government lacked understanding of the industry's structure and a strategic approach to its development. Cement shortages led to unexpected political pressure. Inaccurate supply and demand forecasts, reflecting limited market research capability, led to errors in the first five-year Growth and Transformation Plan (GTP). There was no institute focused on the development of the cement industry and this institutional gap weakened the support scheme. Learning was limited by lack of sustained capacity building in the construction industry, and productivity was relatively low as rent-seeking behaviours dominated the sector.

13.4 Building Ethiopia's Absorptive Capacity

13.4.1 National Learning System

In the 1990s, Ethiopia focused on expanding education, particularly improving coverage and access.[8] In the 2000s, policymakers recognized the need for fundamental changes in education, as universities had very limited intake and were weak in technology and engineering, while high schools focused on mathematics and science, neglecting alternative skills. To achieve the goal of export-led manufacturing growth, in line with the government's industrialization strategy, would require a lasting solution to the chronic shortage of technically skilled

[8] For almost two decades about 7 per cent of GDP was spent on education; and public universities account for 32 per cent of the total education expenditure.

labour, including the trained engineers and applied scientists needed to accelerate technological learning and move the country up the development ladder.

In 2005, the Engineering Capacity Building Programme (ECBP) was established, to be spearheaded and implemented by the Ministry of Capacity Building in collaboration with the Ministry of Education. The key reforms included expansion and reform of universities, introduction of a technical and vocational education and training (TVET) system, and development of a national quality infrastructure. Alternative education systems compatible with Ethiopia's development objectives were explored, and the German education system, especially its apprenticeship scheme, was identified as a robust basis for the country's needs. Lessons were also drawn from South Korea, particularly its development of institutes to support sectors and its establishment of science and technology universities. The ECBP was financed by the Ethiopian government with technical support from the federal government of Germany.[9]

After almost fifteen years, this fundamental reform of Ethiopia's education system is recognized as the largest education transformation initiative in Africa (see Appendix for data on universities reform). The reform was fully backed politically, championed by the late Prime Minister Meles Zenawi, who also convinced the then Chancellor of Germany, Gerhard Schröder, to become a strategic partner in the endeavour. The three key components of the university reforms were a *rapid expansion of universities*, a shift from social science-oriented *to engineering-driven learning*, and the development of *linkages between universities and industries.*

13.4.1.1 The Expansion of Universities

The expansion of universities was challenging for reasons of capital resource and robust execution capability requirements. The construction of new universities was executed by a project team from the German development agency GTZ and the Ministry of Education, while in-house university project teams were responsible for expanding intake and developing new courses. GTZ provided technical support to develop economic designs and use low-cost technology. Construction of buildings (including dormitories for half a million students and residences for teachers) was relatively easy. However, equipping workshops and laboratories, and providing teaching staff and university leadership, was slower and more problematic. Although regional governments allocated the land needed for new universities and supported programme execution, the process was poorly coordinated, and courses had to commence before all facilities and equipment were available.

[9] See also MoE, ECB, MoCS, and MoCB (2016).

13.4.1.2 Reform of Engineering Education

Reforming the engineering education system was a complex process. More than forty-two undergraduate and thirty-five masters degree courses were introduced, and a number of students were sent to pursue PhDs through the German academic exchange service to meet the growing demand for teachers. A major new 'Ethio-German Homegrown PhD Programme' saw science and technology students spending a considerable amount of time in practice workshops and laboratories, and included a six-month mandatory internship during the fourth year. A total of 50,000 interns participated in this programme between 2010 and 2015.

13.4.1.3 New Structures and Institutions

A new three-model structure to support the new technology and engineering orientation was adopted, based on the most favourable international experiences. The first model was the establishment in 2009 of two independent *science and technology universities* (Adama Science and Technology University and Addis Ababa Science and Technology University), based on the South Korean model. The second model involved the establishment of autonomous *institutes of technology*; ten such institutes, each with its own specialization, were set up in ten different universities.[10] The third model involved the establishment of a *school of engineering* in all universities. Hundreds of expatriates from Germany, Austria, South Korea, and the United States were hired as university presidents, scientific directors, managing directors, school deans, and teaching professors. A Higher Education Relevance and Quality Agency (HERQA) was established in the mid-2000s. In 2018, an Ethiopian Institute of Higher Education (EIHE) was established, inspired by models from Germany and the Netherlands, with a mandate to develop management and leadership capacity in universities.

13.4.1.4 University–Industry Linkage and Research Capability

One of the central objectives of the reform programme has been to facilitate technology diffusion from universities to industry by strengthening university–industry linkages, which were previously almost non-existent. Universities appointed vice presidents to lead the development of linkages, and linkage offices were established in all ten technology institutes. Some universities also established technology and business incubation centres, although to date their impact remains limited. Guidelines on linkages were prepared jointly by relevant ministries, and

[10] The ten independent institutes are located where new industrial parks have been built. They include the Ethiopian Institute of Architecture, Building Construction and City Development (Addis Ababa University); Addis Ababa Institute of Technology (Addis Ababa University); the Ethiopian Institute of Technology (Mekelle University); the Ethiopian Textile and Fashion Technology Institute (Bahirdar University); the Jimma Institute of Technology (Jimma University); the Hawassa Institute of Technology (Hawassa University); Dire Dawa Institute of Technology (Dire Dawa University); and Kombolcha Institute of Technology (Dessie University).

annual conferences on university–industry linkages have been held since 2014. While these initiatives have increased awareness, their outcomes have been constrained by limited capacity in universities, as well as the low level of industrial development. Although the government has increased its budget for research, the resources allocated to academic research have been generally insignificant. On average, only 11.3 per cent of the academic staff in universities have a PhD-level qualification and most universities lack adequate research facilities (Nega and Kassaye, 2018).

The government has made concerted efforts to reform the national quality and standards infrastructure, and TVET systems. A new national quality infrastructure was implemented, product standards were introduced in most industries, and the former Ethiopian Quality and Standards Authority (EQSA) restructured into separate independent agencies (the Ethiopian Standards Agency, the Ethiopian Conformity Assessment Enterprises, the Ethiopian Metrology Institute, and the Ethiopian Accreditation Office under the newly established Ministry of Science and Technology) (ECBP, 2009). The new TVET structure includes a demand-driven skills production system, reflecting the requirements of the labour market and local industries; increased focus on practical training in firms; expansion of TVET centres and upgrading of existing facilities; new specialized teacher-training courses; and new competence assessment and accreditation systems (Ministry of Education, 2008, 2017). By 2018, TVET capacity had increased to nearly one million trainees (80 per cent of high school graduates) in about a thousand public technical schools and three hundred non-government technical schools. While the impact of the TVET system on catch-up cannot be assessed reliably, it has clearly contributed to skill formation and has helped to widen the entrepreneurial mindset, as reflected in the increasing numbers of micro and small firms in recent years.

13.4.1.5 The Remaining Challenges

The university reform programme goes to the heart of the challenges facing the Ethiopian national learning system, and addresses the key absorptive capacity constraints on accelerating technological learning and catch-up. In this respect, the government is moving in the right direction, and there are some signs that its efforts are bearing fruit. There are now many university graduates in engineering and technological fields easing the high-level technical skill shortages of the past. There are more than 500,000 students in higher education helping to boost economic dynamism.

On the negative side, however, the quality of university education has yet to reach the desired level, and there is a major gap between the supply of graduates, skills, and course content, and the demand from industry. Almost all engineering teachers lack practical industrial experience, and exposure of students to the reality of industry is limited. More importantly, the capacity of teachers has not kept pace with the expansion of universities. The inability of policymakers to resolve the inherent conflict between quality and quantity is exacerbated by poor leadership capacity in all universities (on boards and in executive management at university and department level), limiting their pursuit of excellence. Low-quality education in high schools and primary schools has contributed to worsening quality at university level. Universities are under-equipped in terms of facilities, including workshops, laboratories, and libraries.

Linkages with industry remain weak, with little guidance for higher education from industry (as evidenced in board composition, course design, and initiation of technology transfer linkages). This is a fundamental failure that may require significant changes to the current system. However, the evidence highlights the complexity of building a national innovation or national learning system and the difficulty of measuring its impact.[11]

In summary, university-level technical qualifications and skills are undoubtedly crucial to fostering technological learning and catch-up, which can be impeded by an underdeveloped 'national learning system' (including TVET). For late-latecomer countries with limited resources and budgets for education, one difficulty is striking the right balance between training highly skilled specialists (essential for technological catch-up), and training at primary and secondary levels (lack of which limits the economy's absorptive capacity and the development of dynamic SMEs).

13.4.2 Industrial Hubs as Instruments of Learning

The development of Ethiopia's industrial hubs illustrates the importance and dynamics of emulation, and the complex process of learning by doing and learning by experimenting. Ethiopia's strategic approach to industrial hubs has been based on three principal conceptual approaches.[12]

First is the relationship between policy learning and industrial policy. Ethiopia's approach to industrial park development is integral to its industrial policy of creating and developing new industries with new productive activities and technological capability at sector and firm level (Oqubay 2015, 2019a, 2019b).

Second, the industrial hub approach is associated with a learning framework, particularly the concept of absorptive capacity, which is directly relevant to learning at the firm and sectoral levels.

Third, the approach is also associated with agglomeration economies, focusing on the geographical concentration of economic activities and the interaction among related industries, which accelerate and shape learning and productivity catch-up.

[11] See Mowery and Sampat (2005) on universities as part of the national innovation system.
[12] See Oqubay and Lin (forthcoming) on industrial hubs and economic development.

Clustering of economic activities is an important feature of industrialization and urbanization (Jacobs, 1969; Marshall, 1920; Ohlin, 1933).[13]

13.4.2.1 Ethiopia's Learning Approach to Industrial Hubs

13.4.2.1.1 Emulation and New Learnings

Industrial hubs have played a broadly successful strategic role in East Asian newly industrializing economies. However, until 2010, industrial parks were not incorporated into Ethiopia's industrialization strategy, and references to economic agglomeration and industrial clustering were too general to serve as a policy guide. By 2013, there was only one industrial park in Ethiopia—the Eastern Industrial Zone, promoted by a Chinese developer from Jiangsu province. The developer faced many obstacles arising from the government's failure to put in place the required legislative, institutional, and policy framework. The first government-sponsored park was also subject to long delays, due to lack of strategic guidance and full understanding of industrial hubs as instruments of industrial policy. In 2013, acknowledging the need for in-depth research, the government launched an evidence-based study of a variety of successful and unsuccessful programmes to identify the most appropriate model for Ethiopia.

The countries considered were South Korea, Singapore, China, and Vietnam in East Asia, and Mauritius and Nigeria in Africa. East Asian economies pioneered industrial hubs within their industrial policies' framework and catch-up strategies (South Korea largely focusing on domestic firms for technological catch-up, while Singapore used FDI as the driver). These twentieth-century late-latecomers effectively integrated the development of industrial hubs within an industrial policy framework for late industrialization and technological upgrading.[14]

Other important sources of learning have been literature reviews and learning from industrial park specialists, facilitated through international partners such as the World Bank and UNIDO (on agro-industrial parks). Specialists and consultants hired through the World Bank included a Malaysian expert who supported the organizational structure of Industrial Park Development Corporation (IPDC) and the Ethiopian Investment Commission (EIC), and more than ten specialists brought in for a three-day consultation workshop. The legislative framework was prepared by a UK consultant; a Chinese consultancy, CADZ, conducted a study on the Dire Dawa special economic zone and strategic framework; and an additional adviser was hired to support the IPDC. Multiple studies were also

[13] See also Lazonick (2005: 35–6) who highlights that in the last half of the nineteenth century, when Britain became known as the 'workshop of the world', 'the localized, on-the-job character of skill formation was the major factory underlying the growth of industrial districts that made use of particular specialized craft skills'. He also notes that 'regional concentration encouraged vertical specialisation, which in turn eased firm entry into a particular specialty, thus resulting in high levels of horizontal competition'.

[14] See also Kuchiki and Tsugi (2008) on flowchart approach as a supplementary approach within industrial policy framework.

conducted on the Ethiopian Investment Commission. However, while these provided an important and diversified source of learning, they were not fit for purpose without an in-depth understanding of, and adaptation to, local conditions.

In September 2014 a White Paper was prepared and discussed at a meeting of almost a hundred policymakers at regional state and federal levels, chaired by the then prime minister, Hailemariam Desalegn. Among other outcomes, the importance of a strategic approach to high standards of environmental protection and sustainability was identified.

A second important lesson was that the government should focus on building specialized, sector-specific parks rather than generic or mixed parks to enhance learning, foster skills development, foster verticality, and accelerate education–industry linkages. Sector-specific infrastructure, international compliance standards, targeting of buyers and manufacturers, and exploitation of opportunities in global value chains would be applied. Industrial parks could also be located according to the requirements of each industry, for example, locating apparel parks in areas close both to ports and to the supply of trainable labour. The sector-based, specialized park approach to industrial policy and catch-up integrates incentive structures with policy learning according to the specific nature of each sector.

Third, the need for excellence in the study, design, construction, and operation phases was highlighted, and adopted as a working principle. The development of each park was to be supported by economic feasibility, environmental safeguards, social safeguards, and hydrology studies, and a master plan conducted by international consultants. It was also decided to shorten the development period to nine months, and procedures were established to select the best and most experienced designers and contractors.

Fourth, it was decided to focus on targeted investment promotion, identifying anchors and leading export-oriented manufacturers, as a means of accelerating learning by domestic firms and ensuring greater success in exporting to international markets.

Fifth, 'islands of excellence' with an enhanced business environment were created, and one-stop services were established in all industrial parks.

Finally, alternative methods were adopted for the development of industrial parks, including joint ventures by the government and private developers, together with a new approach to developing the existing infrastructure (especially railways and airports). These strategic approaches have been integrated into Vision 2025, which aims to establish Ethiopia as a leading manufacturing hub, and within the overall industrial policy framework.

13.4.2.1.2 Learning by Doing and Experiment

These new strategic directions were easier to establish than to put into effect, and it was important to maximize learning during the execution phase. First, it was necessary to design and introduce the strategic framework that included legislative, regulatory, institutional, and policy reforms. This included the preparation of a new proclamation on industrial parks, which facilitated execution and predictability for endorsement by Parliament (see FDRE, 2015). Related regulations and executive directives were approved by the Council of Ministers and the Ethiopian Investment Board respectively. The necessary policy decisions were taken and new incentive structures established.

The new strategic direction and policy required changes in organizational settings to establish the legislative, regulatory, policy, and institutional framework. The Ethiopian Investment Board (EIB), composed of high-level policy and regulatory bodies and chaired by the prime minister, focused primarily on industrial policy decisions. The Ethiopian Investment Commission (EIC) was restructured to serve as a regulatory body for industrial parks and to provide policy support for productive investment targets. The Industrial Parks Development Corporation (IPDC) was mandated to build and operate government-sponsored industrial parks, to serve as a land bank, to study the national master plan for industrial parks, and to facilitate off-site infrastructure facilities for investors.

A further challenge was to develop new industrial parks on the basis of this new concept. The government demonstrated its commitment to this strategic initiative by allocating sufficient resources, mostly from sales of government bonds (the Euro Bond). Other critical issues were selecting sites based on productive criteria but without neglecting political considerations, and maximizing agglomeration economies consistent with the concept of federalism. The government decided to develop a greenfield site in Hawassa, as a pilot specialized apparel and textile industrial park. Though complex and challenging, construction of the largest industrial park was completed within nine months, and to the highest international compliance standards. The 'plug-and-play' setting created favourable conditions, allowing production to commence in a few months. Within a year of becoming operational in July 2017, the park employed 20,000 workers.

Excellence in execution was critical, to win over sceptics among policymakers and to demonstrate to the public the opportunities presented by the strategy. This project was a learning ground for other parks, which were built on the basis of lessons from the Hawassa Industrial Park (HIP). It was also a showcase for Ethiopia's unique approach to industrialization, ultimately becoming a flagship and a model for other projects. PVH, the leading retailer and brand, served as an anchor investor, and about twenty leading manufacturers invested in this park. The investors' association established at HIP became an effective vehicle for a government–industry dialogue supported by a shared vision and strategy. The coordination of government agencies improved, led by the Office of the Prime Minister, although it fell short of the ideal level.

During the Growth and Transformation Plan II (GTPII, 2015–19), Ethiopia has developed a national network of industrial parks. The country's approach to learning, combining learning by doing with learning by experiment and emulation, has demonstrated policy learning and helped to create policy capability. This was a typical model of learning by experiment, aided by mutual learning in the partnership that has evolved between the government and investors. Many African policymakers and scholars have visited Ethiopia to learn from its experience.

13.4.2.2 Challenges of Absorptive Capacity and Emerging Issues

The new approach to industrial parks is a work in progress, based on industrial policies that foster technological learning, increase FDI inflows, facilitate domestic linkages and capabilities, and accelerate industrialization. Nevertheless, strategically significant constraints have emerged during this process.

The first strategic issue was the development of an industrial workforce and working culture for an industrial mode of production. While most firms have invested in skills formation, and despite abundant human resource and high levels of unemployment, absenteeism and high turnover have become apparent.

Second, the development of domestic productive capability has become a major challenge, as most firms have shown greater interest in the service sector than in manufacturing, particularly export-oriented manufacturing. New policy instruments and new learning are needed. An important related issue is the weakness of industry–higher education linkages.

Third, shortage of foreign exchange and balance of payment constraints have intensified in recent years, slowing economic growth. New learning and policy interventions are now required to build export logistics and trade facilitation capacity.

In summary, valuable as the lessons derived from other countries' experiences have been in developing Ethiopia's industrial hub programme, its implementation has itself been a learning experience, demonstrating the importance of learning in key policy areas for identifying and focusing on new policy constraints. This demands a policy learning approach based on comprehension of learning frameworks and of the catch-up process, in which targeted learning efforts help to identify new opportunities for learning, as well as contributing to successful catching up.

13.5 A Synthesis and Conclusions

This chapter presents evidence on an important issue that the literature on learning and catch-up has not yet addressed adequately, namely the dynamics of technological learning and catch-up in late-latecomers to industrialization in the twenty-first century. It is widely believed that globalization, internationalization of production systems, and rapid technological advances have made access to technologies easier. At the same time, however, the widening economic and technological gaps between countries resulting from globalization have made it increasingly difficult for late-latecomers with limited absorptive and learning capabilities—including most African countries—to catch up through dynamic technological and policy learning.

However, this chapter demonstrates that successful learning and catch-up can and does occur in late-latecomer countries. It presents sectoral case studies from Ethiopia, one of the fastest growing economies in Africa, to show how technological learning can be accelerated and sectors enabled to catch up with global leaders through effective application of industrial policy, active engagement by the government, and willingness to learn from policy errors and to promote intensive learning. Successful sectoral-level learning and catch-up in Ethiopia is largely a result of the relative success of its industrial policy, which predominantly reflects the country's indigenous approach to policymaking, based on policy learning, learning by doing, and policy independence. Ethiopia's industrial policymaking process has been marked by the selective adoption of policies that worked in latecomer countries and assimilation of other policies to local conditions through policy experimentation and active state involvement. The important lessons for other late-latecomers are that catch-up occurs largely within sectors, and that industrial policy is a key driver of learning, through its sectoral focus and creation of new industries. It also plays a role in setting strategic perspectives and establishing incentive structures to support institutions.

The Ethiopian experience also shows the unevenness of learning and policy outcomes across industries, reflecting variations in politics, industrial structures, policy direction, and specific features of each industry. This is clear from a comparison of the sources and drivers of learning and catch-up in the floriculture and cement industries. At the beginning of 2000, for example, floriculture was 'alien' to Ethiopia, which had neither produced nor exported floriculture products.[15] In less than a decade, however, Ethiopia ranked among the four largest flower exporters globally, supplying the competitive European market and narrowing the productivity gap with regional competitors that had started flower production and exports five decades earlier. A large part of the explanation for this rapid growth and learning lies in the industry's narrow latitude for failure and poor performance, because of its dependence on highly competitive and quality-sensitive export markets. This had a significant influence on the response of enterprises in the industry (both foreign and local) to technological learning and upgrading. In these conditions, survival depends on intensive learning and acquiring the technical and organizational capabilities required to meet the standards and logistical competency demanded by the international market.

[15] For an in-depth discussion on the genesis of the floriculture industry in Ethiopia and the policies and government actions that influence its development, see Oqubay (2015).

The pattern of development and export success of Ethiopia's floriculture sector were not only significant for the rapid learning that took place within the industry (Oqubay, 2015). Valuable lessons were learned by policymakers in a number of areas, including the targeted policies for export-oriented industries; investment promotion and development of facilitation skills through interactions with Dutch flower producers; export trade logistics and facilitation needs; the critical role of intermediary institutions in the development and technological learning of targeted sectors; and the importance of state–business interactions and dialogue (Oqubay, 2015; Ghebreyesus and Sonobe, 2012).

The experience of the floriculture industry in Ethiopia also suggests that with appropriate industrial policies, targeted investment promotion and facilitation schemes, and active government engagement, FDI can play an important role as a source of learning and transfer of know-how and as a channel for accessing international markets. This reconfirms the widely held view that, while the development impact of FDI is not automatic, its contributions to technology transfer and capability building though spillover effects can be enhanced through strategically targeted policies. As Akyüz (2017: 198) highlights, successful examples of FDI contributing to development in host countries are found 'not necessarily among countries that attracted more FDI, but among those which used it in the context of national industrial policy designed to shape the evolution of specific industries through interventions'.

The experienced and highly skilled foreigners who invested in the Ethiopian floriculture industry were attracted through a high-profile investment promotion campaign by the government, and clearly understood that they were investing in an industry identified by the government as a priority for exports. In addition to the usual investment incentives, the government was willing to advance finance to foreign investors and consult with them on logistical and other arrangements to ensure the development of the industry. This interactive approach induced the foreign investors to play their part in the successful development of the industry, actively participate in the floriculture industry association, share information on European markets with local firms, and exchange information with them about enhancing productivity.

As an import-substituting industry, cement production in Ethiopia did not face the same external market pressures as floriculture, and the role of FDI as source of learning was minimal. However, this chapter shows that a similar level of response and intensity of learning was generated by rapid increases in domestic demand accompanied by industrial policies aimed at prompting intensive learning through direct support, internal competition, and the use of imports as a policy option. In less than a decade, Ethiopia's cement production capacity increased from insignificance to one of the largest in Africa. Although the industry still needs to upgrade its technological capability and level of productivity to catch up with leading global producers such as China, the growth and learning achieved within a short period demonstrates the potential for achieving learning even in import-substituting industries. The important lesson and the overall message for late-latecomer countries is that even in inward-oriented industries, the opportunities for learning and capability upgrading can be considerable if governments take advantage of growing domestic demand to encourage competition, create an intensive learning environment, and engage actively in instigating learning through strategic policy intervention. As Lee and Malerba (2018: 13–14) highlight: 'The specificity of local demand with respect to global demand in terms of income per capita, consumer preferences, local industrial requirements, and public procurement, may provide a test bed for local firms and shelter them from international competition long enough to allow them to survive and then grow. When such demand is large, as was the case in China, India and Brazil, it also provides the economies of scale needed to set off virtuous cycles of learning, capability building and growth.'

In identifying the different sources and drivers of technological learning and catch-up, it is important to note that the pace and depth of their impact can vary between countries depending on the level of development of absorptive capacity, the intensity of policy efforts, and the capacity of governments to implement industrial policies effectively. Accumulating learning capability and developing the local knowledge base involves investment, policy effort, and building a wide range of technical skills and competencies necessary for intensive learning and catch-up. The key to building absorptive capacity that accelerates the pace of learning and catch-up is the development of high-level human capital. Countries that have successfully caught up in manufacturing and technological capability over the past half century show the importance of the education system or 'national learning system' in providing a supply of technicians, trained engineers, and scientists to help move their countries through the various stages of technological learning and catch-up (Ozturk, 2001).

In this respect, Ethiopia is heading in the right direction. Extensive university-level reforms and major expansion of technical and vocational training will develop domestic absorptive capacity, especially in the provision of technical and highly skilled professionals. While it is premature to evaluate the overall impact of these reforms, there are already clear signs that they are easing skill constraints in some industries and sectors.

The relationship between learning and catch-up is complex. Experiences observed elsewhere (Kim, 1998) suggest it is not learning per se that matters for dynamic learning and successful catch-up: more critical are the intensity of learning and the intensity of policy efforts. This highlights the importance of pace and direction of learning, and the cumulative and multifaceted nature of the learning process, which encompasses learning by doing, learning by experiment, emulation to match or excel, and the incremental changes required to sustain learning into more advanced stages of the catch-up process. In constructing industrial hubs that promote learning and capability building, Ethiopia has created an environment conducive to the diffusion of technology through linkages between local enterprises and foreign firms—a process which itself involved intense policy learning to ensure that, as policy instruments, industrial hubs were compatible with the country's development objectives.

Two factors in Ethiopia's successful learning and catch-up at sectoral level are particularly noteworthy as lessons for other late-latecomers. The first is the effective application of industrial policies targeting industries with a predisposition to instigate intensive learning and accumulation of technological capabilities through linkages and inter-firm interaction, including with foreign investors. The second is the government's development commitment and vision, and its willingness to apply intensive policy efforts and policy learning, including through emulation and learning by doing. Indeed, for the government, the selection of sectors and identification of the right and/or appropriate policies was itself a learning process, which was made possible by the government's choice to maintain 'policy independence' and the ability to experiment with policy options, free from pressures either from external forces or from domestic interest groups.

Appendix: Data on Universities Reform

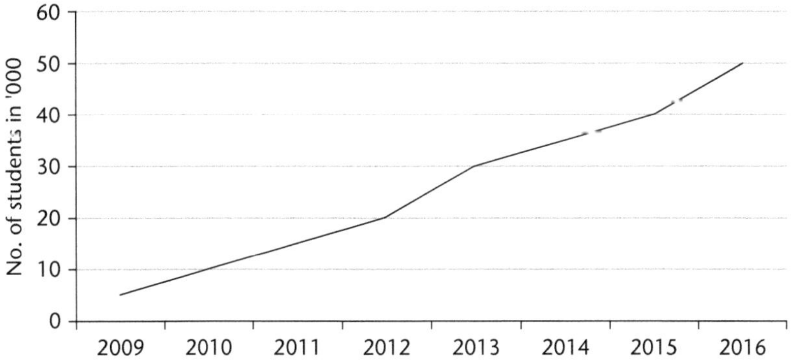

Figure 13.1 Number of fourth-year science and technology students on internship programme (Addis Ababa, 2009–16)

Note: Since 2009 more than 50,000 fourth-year science and technology students have gone through the qualified mandatory internship programme.

Source: MoE (2016a)

Table A13.1 Trends in undergraduate enrolment in all courses (regular, evening, summer, and distance) in government and non-government institutions, 2010–16

Courses	Gender	2010/11	2011/12	2012/13	2013/14	2014/15	2015/16
Total	Male	326,769	355,006	387,707	413,556	475,971	512,915
	Female	120,978	139,104	166,141	180,018	253,057	265,851
	Total	447,693	494,110	553,848	593,574	729,028	778,766

Source: ESSA (2017)

Table A13.2 Trends in postgraduate enrolment in government and non-government institutions, 2015–16

			2010/11	2011/12	2012/13	2013/14	2014/15	2015/16
Government	Masters	Male	15,996	18,169	20,060	20,871	23,129	34,398
		Female	2,490	4,635	5,043	5,246	7,337	9,706
		Total	18,486	22,804	25,103	26,117	30,466	44,104
	PhD	Male	690	1,530	2,809	2,922	2,755	2,444
		Female	99	319	356	370	380	281
		Total	789	1,849	3,165	3,292	3,135	2,725
Non-government	Masters	Male	682	779	2,339	2,433	4,820	2,779
		Female	193	228	697	725	1,866	1,913
		Total	875	1,007	3,036	3,158	6,686	4,692
Grand total		Male	17,368	20,478	25,208	26,226	30,704	39,621
		Female	2,782	5,182	6,096	6,341	9,583	11,900
		Total	20,150	25,660	31,304	32,567	40,287	51,521

Source: ESSA (2017)

Table A13.3 Trends in PhD enrolment, 2006–15

	2006	2007	2008	2009	2010	2011	2012	2013	2014	2015
Total enrolment	*64*	*122*	*258*	*325*	*791*	*789*	*1,849*	*3,165*	*3,292*	*3,135*
Female enrolments %	4.7	2.5	2.71	8	5.9	12.5	17.3	11.2	11.2	21.1
Total graduates	7	10	19	15	149	21	76	115	152	335
Female graduates %	0	0	5.71	0	12.1	4.8	9.2	6.1	8.6	6.3

Source: MoE (2016b)

Table A13.4 PhD graduates from public higher education institutions in Ethiopia, 2006–15

Institution	Status/type	2005–6	2014–15	%
Addis Ababa University	Comprehensive	7	221	66
Jimma University	Comprehensive	0	61	18.22
Haramaya University	Comprehensive	0	34	10.1
Ethiopian Civil Service University	Specialized (civil service)	0	16	48
Bahir Dar University	Comprehensive	0	2	06
Adama Science and Technology University	University of Technology	0	1	0.3
Ambo University	Comprehensive	0	0	0
Gondar University	Comprehensive	0	0	0
Hawassa University	Comprehensive	0	0	0
Mekelle University	Comprehensive	0	0	0
Total		7	335	100

Source: Ministry of Education (2016b)

References

Akyüz, Yilmaz (2017) *Playing with Fire: Deepened Financial Integration and Changing Vulnerabilities of the Global South.* Oxford: Oxford University Press.

Amsden, Alice (1989) *Asia's Next Giant: South Korea and Late Industrialization.* Oxford: Oxford University Press.

Amsden, Alice (2001) *The 'Rise of the Rest': Challenges to the West from Late-industrializing Economies.* Oxford: Oxford University Press.

Amsden, Alice and Wan-wen Chu (2003) *Beyond Late Development: Taiwan's Upgrading olicies.* Cambridge, MA: The MIT Press.

Arrow, Kenneth (1962) 'The Economic Implications of Learning by Doing', *Review of Economic Studies* 28: 155–73.

Chang, Ha-Joon (2003) *Kicking away the Ladder: Development Strategy in Historical Perspective.* London: Anthem Press.

Cohen, Stephen and Bradford DeLong (2016) *Concrete Economics: The Hamilton Approach to Economic Growth and Policy.* Cambridge, MA: Harvard Business Review Press.

Cramer, Christopher, Arkebe Oqubay, and John Sender (forthcoming) *African Economic Development: Evidence, Theory, and Policy.* Oxford: Oxford University Press.

ECBP (Engineering Capacity Building Program) (2009) 'Final Draft Strategy for the Implementation of National Quality Infrastructure (NQI) in Ethiopia.' Addis Ababa: Ministry of Science and Technology.

FDRE (2015) 'Proclamation on Industrial Parks.' House of Representatives: Addis Ababa.

Ghebreyesus, Mulu and Tetsushi Sonobe (2012) 'Global Value Chains and Market Formation Process in Emerging Export Activity: Evidence from Ethiopian Flower Industry', *Journal of Development Studies* 3: 335–48.

Gerschenkron, Alexander (1962) *Economic Backwardness in Historical Perspective.* Cambridge, MA: Harvard University Press.

Jacobs, Jane (1969) *The Economy of Cities.* New York: Random House.

Kaldor, Nicholas (1967) *Strategic Factors in Economic Development.* Ithaca, NY: Cornell University Press.

Kim, Linsu (1998) 'Crisis Construction and Organizational Learning: Capability Building in Catching up at Hyundai Motor', *Organization Science* 9(4): 506–21.

Kuchiki, Akifumi and Masatsugu Tsuji (2008) *The Flowchart Approach to Industrial Cluster Policy.* New York: Palgrave Macmillan.

Lazonick, William (2005) 'The Innovative Firm', in Jan Fagerberg, David Mowery, and Richard Nelson (eds) *The Oxford Handbook of Innovation.* Oxford: Oxford University Press, pp. 29–55.

Lee, Keun (2013) *Schumpeterian Analysis of Economic Catch-up: Knowledge, Path-Creation, and the Middle-Income Trap.* Cambridge: Cambridge University Press.

Lee, Keun and Franco Malerba (2018) 'Economic Catch-up by Latecomers as an Evolutionary Process', in R. Nelson (ed.) *Modern Evolutionary Economics.* Cambridge: Cambridge University Press.

Marshall, Alfred (1920) *Principles of Economics.* London: Macmillan.

Ministry of Education (2008) 'National Technical and Vocational Education and Training (TVET): Strategy.' Addis Ababa: Ministry of Education.

Ministry of Education (2017) 'Relevance of the Ethiopian TVET System towards Social and Economic Development: Historical Background, Current Reform Status and Future Investment.' Addis Ababa: Ministry of Education pia.

MoE, ECB, MoCS, and MoCB (2016) 'Engineering Capacity Building Program, Activities and Directions Set Going forward.' Addis Ababa.

Mowery, David and Bhaven Sampat (2005) 'Universities in National Innovation Systems', in Jan Fagerberg, David Mocery, and Richard Nelson (eds) *The Oxford Handbook of Innovation.* Oxford: Oxford University Press, pp. 209–39.

Nega, Mulu and M. Kassaye (2018) 'Research and PHD Capacities in Sub-Saharan Africa: Ethiopia Report.' British Council and German Academic Exchange Service (DAAD), Addis Ababa.

Ohlin, Bertil (1933) *Interregional and Internal Trade.* Cambridge, MA: Harvard University Press.

Ohno, Kenichi (2013) *Learning to Industrialize: From Given Growth to Policy-aided Value Creation*. New York: Routledge-GRIPS Publications Development Forum Studies.

Oqubay, Arkebe (2015) *Made in Africa: Industrial Policy in Ethiopia*. Oxford: Oxford University Press.

Oqubay, Arkebe (2019a) 'Industrial Policy and Late Industrialization in Ethiopia', in Fantu Cheru, Christopher Cramer, and Arkebe Oqubay (eds) *The Oxford Handbook of the Ethiopian Economy*. Oxford: Oxford University Press.

Oqubay, Arkebe (2019b) 'The Structure and Performance of the Ethiopian Manufacturing Sector', in Fantu Cheru, Christopher Cramer, and Arkebe Oqubay (eds) *The Oxford Handbook of the Ethiopian Economy*. Oxford: Oxford University Press.

Oqubay, Arkebe, Christopher Cramer, Ha-Joon Chang, and Richard Kozul-Wright (forthcoming) *The Oxford Handbook of Industrial Policy*. Oxford: Oxford University Press.

Oqubay, Arkebe and Justin Yifu Lin (forthcoming) *The Oxford Handbook of Industrial Hubs and Economic Development*. Oxford: Oxford University Press.

Ozturk, Ilhan (2001) 'The Role of Education in Economic Development: A Theoretical Perspective', *Journal of Rural Development and Administration* 33(1): 39–47.

Wade, Robert H. (2015) 'The Role of Industrial Policy in Developing Countries', in Alfredo Calcagno, Sebastian Dullien, Alejandro Márquez-Velázquez et al. (eds) *Rethinking Development Strategies after the Financial Crisis, Vol.I: Making the Case for Policy Space*. Geneva: UNCTAD, pp. 67–78.

14

How Nations Learn

Implications for Latecomers and Pathways to the Future

Arkebe Oqubay and Kenichi Ohno

The editors hope that, with its combination of diverse cases and country experiences, and the specialization and expertise of the authors, this volume will make a unique contribution to the ongoing debate on the dynamics of learning and catch-up. This final chapter focuses on two important areas: (a) our understanding of the notions and processes of learning and catch-up as discussed in existing literature; and (b) implications (and potential lessons) for countries still to go through technological learning and catch-up (i.e. late latecomers). The objective is not to present an exhaustive summary of the conclusions of various chapters but to highlight selected elements that have a direct bearing on late-latecomer countries' efforts to advance learning and catch-up.[1] The discussion is presented under four themes: the dynamics of technological learning; nature of catch-up, industrial policy and manufacturing as drivers of learning and catch-up; and finally, catch-up and the policy space in the twenty-first century.

14.1 The Dynamics of Technological Learning

As observed in the discussions in various chapters, technological learning has multiple features, as summarized below.

14.1.1 Dimensions of Dynamic Learning

14.1.1.1 Technological and Policy Learning: The Two Dimensions

Successful or 'dynamic' learning actually involves two dimensions: technological learning (private/firm level) and policy learning (by governments). How governments learn is as important as firm-level technological learning.[2] Firms and governments

[1] See also Gerschenkron (1962) on advantages of latecomers and responses.
[2] See Fagerberg, Mowery, and Nelson (2005), Kim (1998), Kim and Nelson (2000), and Lee (2013).

learn by doing, through policy experimentation, and from other countries' experience.[3] Most importantly, governments learn from their own mistakes and policy errors, and policy learning by governments should be regarded as an integral part of an industrialization and catch-up strategy.[4] This volume presents many examples of policy learning, including from early-stage catch-up countries such as Ethiopia and Vietnam, where learning by governments has been an important driver of successful industry- and sectoral-level learning and catch-up.

14.1.1.2 The Three Levels of Learning

Learning and catch-up generally take place at three levels: firm (micro), sector (mezzo), and national (macro). However, to be mutually productive, the different levels must interact and support each other. Not all firms or sectors develop at the same time and the same rate because the conditions required to kick-start successful learning and catch-up differ considerably between sectors or areas of economic activity. Catch-up may be attained in a specific industry/sector or by developing a specific 'niche' economic activity while the rest of the economy takes time to catch up or continues to lag behind. Furthermore, who leads and who follows among the three levels depends on the relative strength of each player in each society. In advanced societies, all players are likely to be equally strong and mutually supportive. In many of the less developed countries, the private sector is weak and the likelihood of private firms taking the lead is minimal. In this scenario, the state will guide and firms follow. In middle-income economies, private firms (including FDI) or business groups tend to be relatively stronger and often instruct policymakers what to do (for example, Thailand's automotive policy was developed by the association of private auto firms and submitted to the government for review and comment). However, not all interactions produce positive outcomes. Negative interactions and outcomes are also possible, for example, where the state dictates or leads without proper knowledge; businesses distrust government and politicians; and rent-seeking sector associations serve only a small segment of their members. Mapping the exact pattern of interactions in each economy and their effectiveness is a critical element in the catch-up strategy.

14.1.2 Capacities to Learn and Intensity of Learning

14.1.2.1 Capacity to Learn and Unlearn: Absorptive Capacity

In the literature, there is a tendency to assume technological learning as an automatic process that occurs when individuals and firms are exposed to

[3] See also Arrow (1962), Cohen and Levinthal (1989), Nayyar (2013).
[4] See Ohno (2013), Oqubay (2015).

technology and know-how. However, the case studies in this volume demonstrate that: first, an important precondition for successful technological learning is the development of domestic absorptive capacity—for example, the development of a local skills and knowledge base, and the building of the science and technology infrastructure and 'knowledge communities' in agriculture, manufacturing, and services that a nation needs to create a conducive learning environment.[5] This does not mean, however, that learning should wait or be postponed until all the necessary absorptive capacity preconditions are developed. Second, as Lee points out in Chapter 7, the acquisition of technology is a necessary but not sufficient condition for promoting successful technological learning. It is also necessary to acquire the tacit knowledge (or know-how) needed to understand how technologies operate. Equally important is the ability of firms and governments to 'unlearn' old habits or old ways of conducting business which could pose obstacles to learning new technologies.

14.1.2.2 Intensity of Learning and its Multiple Sources

A common thread among countries that have succeeded in promoting technological learning and catch-up is the intensity with which learning has occurred, including the intensity of policy learning and determination by government to push the catch-up agenda. This is similar to what Kim (1998) has termed 'intensity of efforts', referring to the amount of energy expended and the sense of urgency attached by firms and governments to speeding up technological learning or solving problems. The successful learning and catch-up experiences discussed in this volume are the results of intensive learning by both firms and governments.

Intensity of learning varies according to starting positions, availability of skills, and the level of absorptive capacity development. However, its main impact is to activate momentum for rapid technological learning and catch-up. In some cases, intensity of learning is built into the nature of products and technology that require continuous upgrading of capabilities and production techniques to keep up with quality standards or to retain parity with competitors. In other cases, particularly export-oriented activities, intensity of learning originates from narrow latitude for poor or sub-standard performance when competing in international markets. Intensity of learning could also derive from the need to manage crisis—at firm or national level—and find viable solutions. Another important driver of intensive learning has been the determination of leadership and governments to reduce the time it takes to develop technological capability.

[5] See also Cohen and Levinthal (1989: 569). They highlight the importance of how R&D 'enhances the firm's ability to assimilate and exploit existing information'.

14.2 Dimensions and Trajectories of Catch-up

14.2.1 The Balance between Common Factors and Local Uniqueness

The country experiences covered in this volume are highly diverse because countries differ in their starting positions, resource endowment, history, institutional capacities, culture, and so on. However, there are some features that are common to countries, sectors, and periods. These include the importance of: creating a competent and competitive industrial labour force; strengthening domestic firms; investing in the development of basic industrial infrastructure, especially power and transportation; supporting technological learning and policy learning for dynamic upgrading of capabilities and to cope with change; effective and constant engagement between the state and the private sector; creating a favourable business climate and a business-friendly government; and ensuring macroeconomic and social stability (as a background condition).[6]

Naturally, how these common features are achieved concretely and effectively differ between countries, and the period and context in which they are implemented. Nevertheless, it is important to distinguish specific experiences from those that are common to most countries and firms. Indeed, this pragmatic vision of balancing commonality and uniqueness should replace the futile debate between the 'one-size-fits-all' and 'everyone must follow this formula' crusade, and the 'anything goes and each country is different' view which resists systematic learning.

14.2.2 Strategic Divergences and Diversity of Projects Diversity

14.2.2.1 Diversity of Strategies

Strategies for achieving these goals differ between countries and depend on internal, external, and historical circumstances.[7] Policy goals are usually similar across countries but success patterns are many and varied. The key lesson is that there is usually more than one strategic option that any latecomer can adopt, although not all options may be open to it due to its unique initial conditions. For example, there are choices between state-led or private sector-led development, depending on the capacity of the state and the private sector, and the domestic and international political economy; and between gradual industrialization and leapfrogging, which depends partly on whether the industry is mature or emerging/frontline and partly on initial domestic capability. There are also many entry points to industrialization. For example, Taiwan's industrialization was initially driven by

[6] On the strategic role of the state in shaping strategic sectors, see Mazzucato (2011), Wade (1990).
[7] See Hirschman (1958), Chang (2003), Andersson and Axelsson (2016).

SMEs; South Korea's was propelled by *chaebŏls*; Singapore opted for attracting high-quality FDI in manufacturing, finance, and services; and Thailand created an automotive hub by attracting foreign car giants. Interestingly, despite the diversity of these strategies, they all succeeded in advancing technological learning and catch-up. This indicates quite clearly that there are many paths to catching up.

14.2.2.2 The Diversity of Project Design and Execution

Industry- and sectoral-level catch-up experiences show that countries carried out key industrial projects differently depending on initial conditions, resource endowment, and capabilities, and they all succeeded because efforts were made to fit the project design and implementation methods to the local context. There is no universal way to design and implement SME finance, export promotion, TVET–industry linkage, or industrial park development. For example, in implementing kaizen (factory process productivity improvements), the United States started with statistical analysis and top-down management in auto manufacturing (Fordist production system), while Japan (Toyota and others) converted the American system to a more incremental, bottom-up approach based on teamwork and expanded it to all manufacturing (and some service) activities.[8] India learned kaizen from Maruti-Suzuki (car maker) but Indian kaizen experts are more interactive and organized across firms with very little government assistance. Singapore learned how to engage in continuous improvement of productivity in manufacturing from Japan but applied it to all sectors including industry, service, and government.

14.2.3 The Time Element and Changing Context

One of the contributions of this volume is to underscore that although in principle the fundamental developmental requirements of countries are the same across time periods, the nineteenth, twentieth, and twenty-first centuries have offered radically different environments for catch-up. For example, as highlighted in Chapter 5, the Meiji restoration of late nineteenth-century Japan had to fight Western colonialism and the opportunity for foreign assistance was non-existent. Indeed, Japan also resisted foreign borrowing or FDI for fear of foreign dominance. Similarly, in the second half of the twentieth century, South Korea did not accept FDI but learned technology from foreign (mostly Japanese) automobile, steel, shipbuilding, and electronics firms.

Unlike Japan, South Korea also borrowed heavily from abroad. The developmental state pursued an active industrial policy and protected nascent domestic

[8] See Oqubay and Lin (forthcoming) on hubs as key facilitators of learning.

industries with a strong state–*chaebŏl*–bank developmental partnership. Replicating a similar policy approach and strategy would be increasingly difficult in the twenty-first century as developing countries and emerging economies face restrictions on copying technologies freely and introducing high protective tariffs under the rule-based and highly regulated global economic system.[9] They also face global and ICT pressure and must adopt environmental codes and labour rights from the beginning.

14.2.4 The Passion for Catch-up

Another important contribution of this volume is to demonstrate that while technological learning and accumulation of technical knowledge are absolutely necessary for successful catch-up, they are not, by themselves, sufficient. Virtually all great nations, sectors, and firms that have risen from technological backwardness to world prominence are driven by leaders and followers who are passionate about their work, determined to learn and catch up with the best, improve on their present lack of competitiveness, and take pride in others excelling. Financial rewards (salaries and bonuses), top-down orders, and assigned duties motivate average managers and workers, but the few who really transform the world are motivated, not by money or external instruction, but by the collective desire to see their society catch up, obsessed with their dreams, and willing to take huge risks for great achievement. They are not deterred by failures or setbacks.

As the experiences of Singapore, Taiwan, South Korea, and China discussed in this volume show, such Schumpeterian path-breaking innovators were the main drivers of the rapid technological learning and catch-up witnessed in East Asia in the second half of the twentieth century. Passion and a 'can-do' mindset are required not only in state leaders but at all levels, including CEOs, engineers, and workers.

14.3 Industrial Policy and Manufacturing as Prime Drivers of Learning and Catch-up

This volume underlines the critical role of industrial policy and 'policy learning' in creating a conducive environment for learning and catch-up. The experiences of countries that have successfully caught up with advanced economies and those that have made steady progress in advancing their technological learning show that industrial policies were the main instruments used to accelerate technological

[9] This is being challenged by the protectionist policies of the Trump administration in 2018 (UNCTAD, 2018).

learning, target industries and sectors as priority areas, and create the incentives, support institutions, and skills necessary to induce learning and set the catch-up process in motion. Many actions taken by governments to encourage learning at individual, firm, and sector level were actually industrial policies. Equally important, as demonstrated by the successful learning and catch-up experiences of Taiwan, Singapore, Vietnam, Ethiopia, and others, was governments' willingness to learn by doing, experimenting, and emulating, and from other countries' mistakes as well as their own. The ability and willingness to learn from role models along with the capacity to design industrial policies and implement them effectively, were singled out as key determinants of successful learning and catch-up.

It is evident from the experiences of these countries, particularly the East Asian economies, that the manufacturing sector, supported by a developmental state and proactive industrial policy, has been the main driving force of technological learning, structural transformation, and economic growth, and the engine that helped to accelerate productivity improvements and catch-up. Indeed, trends in structural transformation and rapid technological learning and catch-up across the East and South East Asian region since 1970 have been closely related to productive capacity building, industrial policies aimed at shifting resources from traditional to modern and higher-value activities, the application of increasingly sophisticated technologies and, above all, the development of a broad and robust manufacturing base.[10]

The latter was particularly critical, as manufacturing, by its nature, involves multifaceted activities that create inter-sectoral linkages, drive technological progress, and improve productivity—all essential for promoting technological learning and catch-up. Manufacturing exports are also crucial for upgrading technological capability, because they offer economies of scale as well as generating competitive pressure to learn and catch up.[11] While the relative importance of manufacturing diminishes as countries reach an advanced stage of industrialization, it is evident that the role of the manufacturing sector as a source of learning and industrial catch-up has been and will continue to be critical for late-latecomer industrializers in the twenty-first century.[12]

14.4 Catch-up and Policy Space in the Twenty-First Century

An interesting observation emerging from country experiences reviewed in this volume is that catch-up and learning occur and are facilitated or constrained by

[10] See Kaldor (1967) and Cramer, Oqubay, and Sender (forthcoming).
[11] See Amsden and Chu (2003).
[12] See Kaldor (1967), Passineti (1993), and Thirlwall (2013) on the spillover effect and the special properties of manufacturing and the strategic role of exports as sources of international learning.

power relations and the structure of power in global economic governance, which can have decisive influences on the pace and direction of learning, and the ability of newcomers to exercise policy independence in pursuing industrialization.

This has implications for countries that are still learning to build their technological capabilities and catch up.[13] The world economy has changed significantly since newcomers in continental Europe, North America, and Japan first industrialized in the nineteenth century, and since the East Asian economies accomplished their learning and catch-up miracles in the twentieth. At that time, the global economy was less open and countries had more policy space to protect their infant industries during the learning and catching-up phase of development. Intellectual property rights (IPR) regimes were less restrictive, and copying and imitation was the accepted form of learning and catching up.

The external environment faced by late latecomers in the twenty-first century is qualitatively different, with mixed impacts on learning and prospects for catch-up.[14] The global economy today is much more open, due largely to the numerous multi- and bilateral trade and investment agreements, including through WTO. It is also more crowded, with a multitude of countries simultaneously trying to realize the promise of export-led industrialization by exporting their manufactures. The world economy, highly globalized and dominated by global value chains, is much more competitive and the options for 'policy independence' (e.g. to impose local content requirements, violate patent rights, protect local industry by imposing higher tariff rates) are much more limited now than they were some seventy or a hundred years ago.[15]

However, advances in information and communication technologies and the rapidly developing transport network that links most countries and markets around the world have made it relatively easier and cheaper to manage far-flung production networks, giving late latecomers opportunities to become active players in the global economy. Foreign investments and international economic cooperation are now available on a larger scale, with arguably fewer direct imperialistic overtones than during the colonial era. Late latecomers do not have to devote a large amount of R&D resource to developing technology needed for production and communications and can instead leapfrog by acquiring the latest technologies.[16] From this perspective then, learning has become relatively easier.

[13] See Amsden (1989, 2001).

[14] See also Cramer, Oqubay, and Sender (forthcoming).

[15] In this connection, it is interesting to note the policy independence exercised by Ethiopia in pursuing its industrial strategy in the twenty-first century (see Chapter 13). The explanation may lie in Ethiopia's decision to rebalance the domestic power structure by opting for a 'developmental state' approach to economic management and resisting pressure from international institutions even at the cost of losing support.

[16] See UNCTAD (2018).

Acknowledgements

The authors are grateful to Taffere Tesfachew for his important inputs to this chapter and his exceptional and all-round support to this volume, James Mittleman for constructive suggestions, Deborah Mekonnen and Binyam Arkebe for their inputs to improve the draft and their continued support.

References

Amsden, Alice (1989) *Asia's Next Giant: South Korea and Late Industrialization*. Oxford: Oxford University Press.

Amsden, Alice (2001) *The 'Rise of the Rest': Challenges to the West from Late-industrializing Economies*. Oxford: Oxford University Press.

Amsden, Alice and Wan-wen Chu (2003) *Beyond ate evelopment: Taiwan's pgrading olicies*. MA: The MIT Press.

Andersson, Martin and Tobias Axelsson (eds) (2016) *Diverse Development Paths and Structural Transformation in the Escape from Poverty*. Oxford: Oxford University Press.

Arrow, Kenneth (1962) 'The Economic Implications of Learning by Doing', *Review of Economic Studies* 28: 155–73.

Chang, Ha-Joon (2003) *Kicking away the Ladder: Development Strategy in Historical Perspective*. London: Anthem Press.

Cohen, Wesley and Daniel Levinthal (1989) 'Innovation and Learning: The Two Faces of R&D', *The Economic Journal* 99 (397): 569–96.

Cramer, Christopher, Arkebe Oqubay, and John Sender (forthcoming) *African Economic Development: Evidence, Theory, and Policy*. Oxford: Oxford University Press.

Fagerberg, Jan, David Mowery, and Richard Nelson (eds) (2005) *The Oxford Handbook of Innovation*. Oxford: Oxford University Press.

Gerschenkron, Alexander (1962) *Economic Backwardness in Historical Perspective*. Cambridge, MA: Harvard University Press.

Hirschman, Albert (1958) *Strategy of Economic Development*. New Haven, CT: Yale University Press.

Kaldor, Nicholas (1967) *Causes of the Slow Rate of Economic Growth of the United Kingdom*. Cambridge: Cambridge University Press.

Kim, Linsu (1998) 'Crisis Construction and Organizational Learning: Capability Building in Catching-up at Hyundai Motors', *Organization Science* 9(4): 506–21.

Kim, Linsu and Richard Nelson (eds) (2000) *Technology, Learning, and Innovation*. Cambridge: Cambridge University Press.

Lee, Keun (2013) *Schumpeterian Analysis of Economic Catch-up: Knowledge, Path-Creation and the Middle-Income Trap*. Cambridge: Cambridge University Press.

Mazzucato, Mariana (2011) *The Entrepreneurial State: Debunking Public vs. Private Sector Myths*. London: Anthem Press.

Nayyar, Deepak (2013) *Catch Up: Developing Countries in the World Economy*. Oxford: Oxford University Press.

Ohno, Kenichi (2013) *Learning to Industrialize: From Given Growth to Policy-aided Value Creation*. New York: Routledge-GRIPS Publications Development Forum Studies.

Oqubay, Arkebe (2015) *Made in Africa: Industrial Policy in Ethiopia*. Oxford: Oxford University Press.

Oqubay, Arkebe and Justin Lin (forthcoming) *The Oxford Handbook of Industrial Hubs and Economic Development*. Oxford: Oxford University Press.

Passineti, Luigi (1993) *Structural Economic Dynamics: A Theory of the Economic Consequences of Human Learning*. Cambridge: Cambridge University Press.

Thirlwall, Anthony (2013) *Economic Growth in an Open Developing Economy: The Role of Structure and Demand*. New York: Edward Elgar.

UNCTAD (2018) 'Trade and Development Report 2018: Power, Platforms and the Free Trade Delusion.' Geneva: UNCTAD.

Wade, Robert (1990) *Governing the Market: Economic Theory and the Role of Government in East Asian Industrialization*. Princeton, NJ: Princeton University Press.

Name Index

Please note that page references to Footnotes will be followed by the letter 'n' and number of the note.

Subject Index

Please note that page references to Figures will be followed by the letter '*f*', to Tables by the letter '*t*', to Boxes by the letter '*b*', while references to Notes will contain the letter 'n' following the Note number